Our South

OUR SOUTH

Geographic Fantasy and the Rise of National Literature

JENNIFER RAE GREESON

Harvard University Press
Cambridge, Massachusetts, and London, England   2010

Library of Congress Cataloging-in-Publication Data

Greeson, Jennifer Rae.
  Our South : geographic fantasy and the rise of national literature / Jennifer Rae
Greeson.
     p. cm.
  Includes bibliographical references and index.
  ISBN 978-0-674-02428-1 (alk. paper)
  1. American literature—History and criticism.   2. American literature—Southern
States—History and criticism.   3. Southern States—In literature.   4. National
characteristics, American, in literature.   5. Nationalism in literature.   6. National-
ism and literature—United States—History.   I. Title.
  PS261.G74 2010
  810.9'35875—dc22   2010019126

For my parents, and for Dade

Contents

Illustrations

Our South

Introduction: Magnet South

O magnet-South! O glistening perfumed South! my South!
O quick mettle, rich blood, impulse and love! good and evil!
  O all dear to me!
    —Walt Whitman, "Longings for Home" (June 1860)

A CONCEPT OF THE SOUTH is essential to national identity in the United States of America. Wherever U.S. citizens were born, wherever we presently live, whatever our personal experience of the southeastern states—for all of us, knowing about our South is part of knowing what it means to be an American. This South that we hold collectively in our minds is not—could not possibly be—a fixed or real place. It both exceeds and flattens place; it is a term of the imagination, a site of national fantasy.[1] Our South is created in and imbibed from our culture, and like any cultural construct, it means different things at different times to different people. What remains constant across U.S. history is the conceptual structure provided to us by our South: it is an *internal other* for the nation, an intrinsic part of the national body that nonetheless is differentiated and held apart from the whole. On the one hand, the United States simply never would have existed without the five southernmost of its original thirteen states, or without its founding documents penned by Thomas Jefferson and James Madison, or without its great icon of national emergence, George Washington. On the other hand, our South in its most enduring associations—slavery, white supremacy, underdevelopment, poverty, backwardness—bluntly contradicts the national ideal. In the words of Walt Whitman, writing on the eve of the Civil War, our South encapsulates both "good *and* evil"; it signifies all that is "dear"—precious *and* costly—to the American self.

With remarkable fluidity, "our South" aligns with and diverges from "the United States" writ large, creating a symbiotic *ideological juxtaposition* in which each term is defined by reference to the other.[2] Such fluidity of meaning is terrible for conceiving a coherent political program or a rational social analysis, but it is wonderful for generating works of the imagination.

Perhaps this is why, from the very beginnings of a self-consciously national tradition in U.S. letters, the South has been a matter of obsession for writers and readers, often out of all proportion to the actual role of the southeastern states in the body politic at a given historical moment. Whitman's exclamatory figure of the "magnet-South" speaks to this conundrum: the "far away" South captivates his nationalist poetics with "irrepressible" force—but since North is the actual magnetic pole, this southward pull seems a perversion of nature, an inversion of the right order of things. The case of our South provides a textbook example of what studies of the politics of culture, over the past three decades, have taught us to expect: that what is materially peripheral to the modern nation often becomes symbolically central to it.[3]

My subject is the evolving construction of South and nation in U.S. literature, beginning with the plotting of independence in 1775 and continuing to the turn of the twentieth—or "American"—century. This focus on eighteenth- and nineteenth-century literature means that I am concerned almost exclusively with the perspective of the metropolis—the center of cultural production, the cultural capital. I leave to the side questions of "southern identity," and I do not attempt to account for the points of view of people living in the southern states, except as those people come to engage in the dominant metropolitan discourse. I do not ask what the South is; rather, I ask what it is good for, what it accomplishes and enables in the broader culture of the United States.

The short answer to this question is that our South is very good, from the very beginning, for thinking geographically. Because it references a real place, even as it dramatically exceeds it, our South proves indispensable for placing the United States on the world map in the mind's eye. Geographic thinking is an urgent matter for the culture of a political entity that goes from colonial outpost to global power in a little over a century. Across this span, U.S. literature evolves alongside and contributes to a profound shift in the conceptualization of the place of the United States in the world. Initially, U.S. writers must throw off the eighteenth-century European image of the American colonies; ultimately, they must refashion the idea of their nation to comport with its twentieth-century global ascendance.[4] It seems logical that a conceptual continuum between these starting and ending points should be discernable, that a nation conceived in the power structures of European New World empire should receive an ideological inheritance that enables its own outward projection of power.[5] These connections have remained somewhat obscure, though, thanks in no small part to the assiduous work of U.S. writers from the time of independence forward to create a story of national emergence in which the United States springs into being, fully formed and standing alone on the face of the earth, as the exceptional republic. Untouched by the binary power extremes understood to organize all other human societies—monarch/subject, master/servant, empire/colony—this new nation is supposed to operate, sui generis, on primally consensual terms.

This master narrative of U.S. exceptionalism has depended, from the founding forward, on U.S. writers writing their South—a term that becomes legible in the first place only as it is understood to deviate from the republican model of U.S. nationalism. Against the ideal of a freedom from power extremes, our South appears in U.S. literature to embody both sides of the disavowed binary: simultaneously colonial and colonized, it diverges from the nation writ large on the basis of its *exploitativeness*— as the location of the internal colonization of Africans and African Americans in the United States—and on the basis of its *exploitation*—as the location of systemic underdevelopment, military defeat, and occupation.[6] This South, which emblematizes the familiar coercive forms of human society, is from the start essential to conceptualizing "the United States" as a new national form.

It is by now a familiar notion that U.S. nationalism, like any modern Western nationalism, should be organized around a "principle of exclusion," a rhetorical move in which the nation is defined by opposition to what it is not.[7] Indeed, "the United States" has been defined against many antitheses, from wholly external entities like "the Old World" to places and peoples not included in the body politic at its origin but assimilated later: "the West," "the woman," "the Indian," and so on.[8] Our South provides a different sort of juxtaposition. As an internal other from the start of U.S. existence, it lies simultaneously inside and outside the national imaginary constructed in U.S. literature. Our South thus serves in that literature as an unparalleled site of connection between "the United States" and what lies outside it—a connection to the larger world, to Western history, to a guilty colonial past and a desired and feared imperial future.

The connection to the larger world is perhaps most obvious, since the characteristics understood to set the South apart from the United States are characteristics that it shares with formerly colonial, underdeveloped peripheries around the globe.[9] Yoking together regional variation within national borders and regional affinity across them, our South serves as a remarkably fertile spatial nexus of the domestic and the foreign, marking both the limit of the nationalizing early republic and, increasingly across the nineteenth century, the continental and hemispheric horizon toward which U.S. imperial desire projects. The South provides not only spatial but also temporal connections for U.S. literature, suggesting many points of intersection with broader narratives of the Western journey into modernity. The South gives writers a backward glance, a conduit to the American colonial past against which they may gauge the rise of the independent, developing republic. As writers posit the South as premodern and undeveloped, though, it comes to serve a forward-looking function as well, emerging as a domestic site upon which the racialist, civilizing power of U.S. continental expansion and empire abroad may be rehearsed and projected.

Rather than furnishing something so simple as a site of domestic regional variation for U.S. literature, our South always points beyond the national borders. To grasp the workings of the South in the broader culture of the United States requires the opposite of a parochial approach. This project demands a comparative, transnational geographic frame.[10]

Since American Studies emerged as a discipline after World War II, scholars have written knowingly about the gap between national reality and national ideal in our culture. Americans expropriated the West under the banner of "Virgin Land"; we conceived of ourselves in international relations as "the American Adam" dealing with a fallen world.[11] These nationalist ideologies of innocence and exceptionality have been apparent as such to scholars for more than half a century; they have come under increasing fire in the past two decades for masking a deep and fundamental antagonism in U.S. culture between the aspirations of the republic and the equally venerable vision of the United States as "the greatest Empire the hand of time ever raised up to view."[12] The inner workings of American exceptionalism cannot be comprehended fully, though, without grasping the central role of our South in them.[13] Our South spatializes the gap between national ideal and national reality—between our better angels and our frank demons—so that we may re-present the moral failings of U.S. life to ourselves as matters of geography.

This spatialization of national morality is beautifully elucidated by Henry Adams, who in his 1907 autobiography recalls being taken on a momentous "pilgrimage" to Mount Vernon by his father, President John Quincy Adams, in 1850:

> Mr. Adams took [Henry] there in a carriage and pair, over a road that gave him a complete Virginia education for use ten years afterwards. To the New England mind, roads, schools, clothes, and a clean face were connected as part of the law of order or divine system. Bad roads meant bad morals. The moral of this Virginia road was clear, and the boy fully learned it. Slavery was wicked, and slavery was the cause of this road's badness which amounted

to social crime—and yet, at the end of the road and product of the crime stood Mount Vernon and George Washington.

Luckily boys accept contradictions as readily as their elders do, or this boy might have become prematurely wise. He had only to repeat what he was told—that George Washington stood alone . . . [H]e never thought to ask himself or his father how to deal with the moral problem that deduced George Washington from the sum of all wickedness.[14]

Adams describes U.S. nationalism as the mental act of constructing a conscious exception. Young Henry's father socializes him into these mental gymnastics through the ceremoniously ritualized encounter with the South: at the same moment that Henry gazes on Virginia plantation scenes foreign to the ideals of the republic, his father requires the boy "to repeat what he was told—that George Washington stood alone." Adams's literary account of U.S. nationalism resonates with the theory of his French contemporary Ernest Renan, who in 1882 had proposed that the "essence of a nation" lies in all of its citizens collectively "hav[ing] to have already forgotten" those glaring facts that counter nationalist ideology.[15] In Adams's narration, this forgetting and its corollary—suppressed remembering—center on denying and claiming his South. Parsing the encounter with Virginia, Adams shows that the exceptionalist mantra that George Washington (and, by metonymy, the nation) "stands alone" is generated out of the repressed recognition that Washington (and, again, the nation) is the "product of crime."

And there is nothing exceptional about the geographic thinking that underwrites young Henry's fledgling nationalism. With ironic hindsight, Adams points out that young Henry's Bostonian gaze on the object lesson of Virginia is hardly that of a disinterested republican. Instead, from a decidedly metropolitan perspective, Henry reads the "bad roads" of peripheral underdevelopment as visible signs of the "bad morals" of the local inhabitants. The "social crime" of the locals has to do with "wicked" slavery, but Adams's facetious focus on "this road's badness" reveals that young Henry's conceptualization of Virginia has its origin not so much in abolitionism, per se, as in a broader Western imperial discourse. "[T]he law of order or divine system" decrees the natural supremacy of Henry's own temperate, metropolitan center of cultural production (home of "roads, schools, clothes, and a clean face") over the quasitropical, presumably degenerate southern realm he observes. As he gazes upon this South, a region fitted for nothing other than subordination, the civilizationist bent of young Henry's "New England mind" is invigorated, giving him, ominously, "a complete Virginia education for use ten years afterwards"— in 1860, on the eve of the Civil War.

Henry's South is not simply good for thinking geographically in a neutral, descriptive sense: it is good for thinking geographically *with hierarchy*. The term "South" itself implies its opposite, North; and the first tenet of geographic literacy is that, on any map, North is the top and South the bottom. Adams goes far beyond such an abstract North-over-South schema, writing as he does from the zenith of the imperial era, in 1907. With young Henry's resonant, moralizing descriptions of Virginia, Adams explores the way that the approach of the child to his South inscribes the geographic hierarchies of Western empire within the borders of the United States. When Henry distills Virginia's distinctiveness from the Boston metropolis, finding its essence to be "the brooding indolence of a warm climate and a negro population,"[16] Adams invokes the intertwined registers—place and race—that Western imperial culture has used to naturalize the dominance of one people over another. Henry interprets Virginia as encapsulating the history of New World colonial settlement: tropical and racially intermixed, his South operates according to the dictates of climatic determinism—the notion, imported from Europe, that warm climates not only produce coveted commodities but also cause the degeneration of the life forms that inhabit them. As Henry discerns the global relations of empire *inside* the United States, Adams marks out another dimension of U.S. exceptionalism: Henry is able to think imperially, to derive his terms from Europe; but since he inscribes that global hierarchy within a domestic framework, he simultaneously maintains the fantasy of the isolated republic, standing alone.

The exceptionalist nationalism Adams describes requires that young Henry simultaneously learn from and forget the American colonial origins of the United States, as well as the exploitation that generates U.S. prosperity, both of which are epitomized by the Virginia plantation. But this nationalism requires as well that he simultaneously cultivate and explain away imperial urges toward ascendancy over warm, underdeveloped, commodity-producing realms—imperial urges that had become plainly obvious from the cusp of the twentieth century. The "moral problem" raised by this exceptionalist nationalism involves not simply severing the U.S. national ideal from its Southern contradiction. More, it requires "deducing" the United States "from the sum of all wickedness"—*deriving* the nation *from* the Western conceptual structures of domination that order the globe. Against our South, we may declare that the United States "stands alone" on the face of the earth and in human history; but with our South, we reassert the connections even as we spurn them.

———

The phrase "our South" is itself a provocation, not just a synonym for "the domestic South" or "the U.S. South." With it, I mean to indicate that reading and writing the South has nurtured a possessive impulse in U.S. national culture since the founding.[17] The first line of Whitman's 1860 poem builds from magnetic attraction to such a possessive claim: "O magnet-South! O glistening perfumed South! my South!" And the remainder of the two-page-long poem comprises a catalogue of what exactly Whitman's speaker owns in his South, from "the cotton plant! The growing fields of rice, sugar, hemp!" to "those half-known half-impassable swamps, infested by reptiles" where "the fugitive has his conceal'd hut."[18] This possessive fantasia, alternately exhilarating and terrifying, operates around a double meaning of the word *owning*. Whitman's speaker owns his South in the sense of confessing its faults and sins—tropicality and slavery; he also owns his South in the sense of possessing its riches—"O the cotton plant!" These two registers of *owning* are inextricable, since the climate and labor exploitation that are confessed produce the desirable commodities that are possessed.[19] Here, as elsewhere in U.S. literature of the period, the confessional mandate of owning the South easily shades into a possessive imperative. Swamps can be known, fugitives freed, "reptiles" exterminated. "Our South" can be taken over, reformed, reconstructed.

Indeed, the poem envisions the "magnet-South" from an aggressively overhead view that collapses an enormous, internally diverse tract of territory into a monolithic figure:

> O dear to me my birth-things—all moving things and the trees
>   where I was born—the grains, plants, rivers,
> Dear to me my own slow sluggish rivers where they flow, distant,
>   over flats of silvery sands or through swamps,
> Dear to me the Roanoke, the Savannah, the Altamahaw, the
>   Pedee, the Tombigbee, the Santee, the Coosa and the Sabine,
> O pensive, far away wandering, I return with my soul to haunt
>   their banks again.

When the speaker identifies eight major rivers reaching from Virginia to Texas—a list lifted from a contemporary geography textbook—as "my own slow sluggish rivers," any semblance of locality evaporates, replaced by what Mary Louise Pratt has called the "planetary consciousness" of nineteenth-century imperialism.[20] In these same lines, though, Whitman tempers the voracious possessive desire by presenting his speaker as an indigenous southerner. "O to be a Virginian where I grew up! O to be a

Figure 1. Frontispiece, J. T. Trowbridge, *The South: A Tour of Its Battlefields and Ruined Cities,* 1866. Clifton Waller Barrett Library of American Literature, Special Collections, University of Virginia Library.

INTRODUCTION: MAGNET SOUTH   9

Carolinian!" he exclaims, encouraging his U.S. readers (the poem was published in the *Saturday News* of New York City) to think of owning their South as a matter of nativity, as a matter of a natural right to one's "birth-things."[21] The "longing irrepressible" of the poem is, indeed, as Whitman's title indicates, a "longing for home": a desire to *be at home* in a place that *is not home*. On the cusp of the secession of the southern states from the Union, Whitman voices a desire to be at home in a place that is prospectively taken by force, possessed over the resistance of its inhabitants. This is a familiar and fundamental desire expressed again and again in eighteenth- and nineteenth-century U.S. literature, which Edward Said has noted "shows a peculiarly acute imperial cast" despite its "paradoxically . . . ferocious anti-colonialism, directed at the Old World."[22] It is the dream of achieving a nonimperial empire, of achieving dominion over others without coercion of them, of achieving what Ralph Waldo Emerson—also writing about the South in 1844—"called the condition of being 'ominpotent without violence.' "[23]

Writing our South is both a self-justifying and an aggrandizing undertaking in U.S. literature. On the one hand, the South is rightfully and naturally ours because it is part of the United States; on the other hand, it is ours in subjection or thrall because it is apart from the United States. Writing the South thus becomes an enabling enterprise for U.S. authors across the first century of literary nationalism, when these authors feel acutely their lack of metropolitan stature in comparison with the cultural capitals of Europe. As a U.S. author writes the South, he or she assumes a position of cultural command over passive peripheral territory, the position so prized in Western imperial culture. Her perceptions are authorized; his conclusions carry the weight of Truth. This metropolitan authorial stature is illustrated in the frontispiece engraving from J. T. Trowbridge's *The South: A Journey Through the Desolated States* (1866), a book that was marketed as an exhaustive and "high-toned" account of the defeated Confederacy.[24] It is not "the South" of the title that is the subject of this illustration but the U.S. author himself, and he appears as a regal figure: seated at the center of all things, observing gaze directed outward, pen in hand. His riding cloak and boots and impatient tethered steed amply signify that the U.S. writer by definition is not of the South but a privileged sojourner from outside (above, beyond). And his presence orders the peripheral panorama of the scene, which falls into place around his figure: commodity (the cotton boll) in the foreground; disciplined labor (the cotton pickers) in the background; the tropical sign of the palm tree overhead. In a decidedly unequal exchange, a generic "southerner"—face mostly obscured, complete with dog—stands before the national author in the position of command performer, native informant, manipulable stock character.

Writing the South produces not only an independent national literature but also a masterful, mastering literature integral to the global ascendance of the United States. Writing our South develops what Herman Melville—assuming the persona of "a Virginian" in 1850—called the "literary point of view" requisite to realizing "that political supremacy among the nations, which prophetically awaits us at the close of the present century."[25]

Because my focus is on the rise of national literature, because I do not attend to what is happening on the ground in the southeastern states in the eighteenth and nineteenth centuries, it may seem as though this book lets the "real" South off the hook. Worse, I might be construed as offering special pleading on behalf of "poor southerners, victims of cultural imperialism" or protesting that "the whole United States has had imperial aims, so why blame one part of the country just for doing the *most* to promote and expand the crime against humanity of New World slavery?" Such an interpretation would be anathema to my intent. The actions of slaveholding elites in the southeastern states in the era I treat are, in the main, indefensible; and as for "the South"—I have no "real" South to defend. I am not even sanguine that the notion of a monolithic South can be recuperated in U.S. cultural studies in a useful way.[26] "The South" is a term that originally was constructed out of the discourse of modern empire; it is a term that makes sense only in that broader Western ideological ordering of the globe. And when elites living in the southeastern states took up the term and applied it to themselves in the years surrounding the Civil War, they did so to repugnant ends: "an oligarchy of 300,000 slaveholders dared to inscribe for the first time in the annals of the world 'Slavery' on the banner of armed revolt."[27] "The South" is, first and foremost, an ideological concept rather than a place.

It does matter that we understand how this ideological concept came into being, though, for Americans have leaned on it for national self-definition since the founding, and we continue to lean on it today. The ideological juxtaposition of the United States to its South arose out of the material process of nationalization itself. Scholars who have studied U.S. independence in a transnational context have agreed that nationalization was made possible by the emergence of a northeastern core in the New World: a center of manufacturing, trade, and print production that stretched between Boston and Philadelphia along the Atlantic seaboard.[28] Literary production—writing, publishing, marketing, reviewing—has tended to be a geographically centralized phenomenon, and in the United States national literature was produced almost exclusively from the vantage of this nascent core for its first several decades. At the same time, many southern elites remained hostile to wide dissemination of literacy and print, since slave society relied upon corporeal forms of social control. "I thank God we have no free schools, nor printing," the royal governor of the colony of Virginia reported in 1670, and this attitude toward print culture could be seen as enduring in parts of the southern states well into the nineteenth century, in the form of censorship, gag rules, and the criminalization of literacy for enslaved people.[29] Quite logically, the structural alienation of the southern states from U.S. print registered in the content of national literature from its inception. Imaginative literature, by its very conditions of production, institutionalized uneven development and a center-periphery structure in U.S. culture from the outset.

In the early republic, this unevenness between South and center in the literary realm directly contradicted the political and economic centrality of the southern states in national life. One of the surprising finds of this book is that an othered "South" is readily discernable in U.S. literature even in the first decades of the nation's existence, when Virginia seemed to be running everything from the constitutional conventions to the presidency. In the 1780s and 1790s, though, geographic fantasias of the South in novels and poems appeared at most supplemental to the momentous political debates of their day. When Yale College president and erstwhile littérateur Timothy Dwight in 1794 made a bald declaration in favor of the worldly power of imaginative writing—"Allow me to make the Songs of a nation, and who will may make their Laws"—the notion of exerting control over U.S. life through literary effort seemed merely a compensatory wish on the part of a politically marginalized New Englander.[30] Moving into the nineteenth century, though, we see an important shift in the relative influences of political discourse and imaginative literature on the shaping of U.S. national life.[31] By midcentury, another writer from Connecticut, Harriet Beecher Stowe, published the sentimental novel that her contemporaries, northern and southern, widely credited with starting the Civil War.[32] With *Uncle Tom's Cabin* (1850–1852), the work of imaginative fiction fully assumed the transformative power in national life previously attributed only to political polemic.

The geographic fantasies pursued in U.S. literature have not been simply "superstructural" window dressing for the real operation of power in the United States. Watching our South emerge in national literature decades before the rise of North/South political sectionalism should, to my mind, constitute a brief for the real-world importance of literary history. The case of our South suggests a great deal about how imaginative literature can set the horizons of possibility for a culture, and how it constructs the frameworks of expectation through which national life is perceived and interpreted. What has our South underwritten in U.S. nationalism? What has it rendered opaque to us?

This line of investigation seems to be begged by the current vernacular of U.S. foreign policy and global development discourse, in which terms once descriptive of domestic concerns increasingly have been projected outward. Although the United States could be thought of as trying to "re-construct the world" across the twentieth century, it was only in 2003 that the term "Reconstruction" was assigned by the U.S. government as the of-ficial name for its military occupation of a foreign county.[33] More perva-sive has been the replacement of the Cold-War-era terms "First World" and "Third World" with the terms "global North" and "global South"; the premise behind this shift has been that, in contrast to the ordinal terms "first" and "third," "North" and "South" are descriptive, nonhierarchi-cal geographic designations.[34] But from the "literary point of view" requi-site to U.S. "political supremacy among the nations," *North* and *South* are foundationally hierarchical terms: rather than denoting an equally weighted, descriptive binary, "North" serves as center and norm, while "South" stands as deviation, in need of intervention and reform from without. Since a large proportion of global development discourse is gen-erated out of U.S.-sponsored organizations, and indeed out of New York City, these presumably neutral geographic terms bear the weight of the en-tire literary history laid out in this book. Dividing the twenty-first-century world into North and South imposes an "American Universal Geogra-phy" on the globe, exporting our national ways of figuring, explaining, and justifying geographical domination and subordination.[35]

To grasp how fraught is this terminology of our own time, consider the national news coverage surrounding the aftermath of Hurricane Katrina in 2005. As relief efforts to the Gulf Coast were unforgivably delayed, U.S. airwaves were flooded with images of tropical disaster, wholesale desolation, and desperate masses of people—who, in anchorman Wolf Blitzer's unfortunate but oft-quoted description, were "so poor and . . . so black."[36] As if by magic, the term "Third World" was resurrected from the dustbin of outmoded parlance, as aghast onlookers and media commentators made the diagnosis again and again. "This doesn't look like America," ran the refrain. "It looks like the Third World down here."[37] To have put this observation into correct contemporary develop-ment parlance, the commentators would have had to say, "It looks like the South down here." And, of course, it did.

In three chronologically separate sections, *Our South* charts three distinct versions of "the South" that correspond to epochal shifts in the idea of "the United States." In the early republic, "the Plantation South" serves writers negotiating nationalization itself; in the antebellum decades, "the Slave South" provides the baseline against which industrialization and continental expansion are conceived; and in the latter part of the nineteenth century, "the Reconstruction South" becomes the imaginative field for writers confronting the question of empire head-on. Naturally, each of these formulations of our South overlaps the others, and elements of each carry forward in U.S. culture into our own time. The Plantation South is not forever swept aside when William Lloyd Garrison discovers the urban exposé methods of antiprostitution crusaders in 1831; and the Slave South is not erased when the editor of *Scribner's Monthly* decides in 1872 to sponsor an "expedition" through the defeated Confederate states modeled on Henry Morton Stanley's journey into "darkest Africa." Such watershed moments, though, reveal the makers of U.S. literature reevaluating how and why they write their South. At these points of cultural transition, it is possible to track the emergence of new generic conventions and new stock characters, as well as to uncover relays between self-consciously literary writing and the broader print-cultural field—textbooks, political tracts, journalistic reportage, government reports. My focus is on moments of historical and formal conjuncture: schematic shifts into modernity in national life that correspond with new ways of writing national literature.

The Plantation South appeared at the first moment of colonial rebellion, around mid-1775, arising as something of a containment area for European imperial descriptions of America—which, to generalize, had centered on climatic tropicality, plantation production of valued staple commodities, and violent expropriation of labor from enslaved Africans and African Americans. By retaining these venerable American colonial markers as definitional of their Plantation South and then contrasting this Plantation South to "the United States," the first U.S. writers produced the republic as new and exceptional: they distanced their immediate colonial past while also quarantining the persistence of the familiar American colonial attributes—slavery, plantation production, imbrication in Atlantic trade—into the national present. With the founding juxtaposition of the new republic to its Plantation South, the passage of the thirteen former British colonies into modern nationhood was spatialized, understood by means of geographic rather than temporal narrative.[38] To see the dark night of American coloniality, U.S. readers were instructed by travelogues, textbooks, and novels to look South; to experience the process of development, they were told to travel northward again. At the same time, since possession of plantation colonies was such a key component of Western nationhood in the late eighteenth century, the Plantation South provided the new republic with an analogous and crucial realm of imaginative dominion. By writing their Plantation South, the first U.S. writers imported the Europe/America geographical binary of New World empire into the literature of the early republic, but they turned it ninety degrees, remaking it as a North/South hierarchy.

Around 1831, however, beginning with the political discourse of immediate abolitionism, the South was radically reimagined in U.S. print. Writers threw aside the earlier focus on tropical climate and plantation commodity production, and instead fashioned the Slave South as an internalized realm of hidden depravity and vice best approached in the mode of exposé, particularly exposé of sexual abuse and torture. Writers borrowed this exposé approach to their South from the new ways of dealing with the industrial city being developed in Western literature, thereby making the Slave South a site for isolating unfreedom, for epitomizing the perceived decline in personal autonomy that accompanied industrialization. Against the baseline of power extremes provided by their Slave South, U.S. writers conceptualized proletarianization as "free labor" and industrial capitalism as not inimical to the ideals of the republic. As industrialization concentrated material and representational power together in the northeastern United States, the deviant Slave South also served to authorize the increasing centralization of U.S. life under the aegis of "transcendental" New England or "the universal Yankee nation." In this capacity, the Slave South helped to underwrite the ideology of "free soil" so essential to the expansion of U.S. borders to continental scale in the antebellum decades.

Secession, military defeat, and the subsequent federal administration of the southern states between 1860 and 1877 realized a momentary but affirming conjuncture of political reality with the enduring otherness of the South in U.S. imaginative literature. The Reconstruction South arose as writers fathomed the transformed relationship of their South to the nation writ large—at the same moment when the expansionist ambitions of the United States were turning outward following the Civil War and the pressing question for U.S. nationalism was becoming "republic or empire?" In the decade immediately after the war, writers explicitly envisioned their Reconstruction South as a "new Africa," an American analogue to the continent upon which the last great frenzy of Old World empire was being played out. In this sense, the Reconstruction South appeared as a proving ground for the civilizationist mastery of the modern United States; but since it remained to some extent a domestic site within the nation, its occupation and administration provided an exceptional form for nascent U.S. empire overseas. This dimension of the Reconstruction South became more apparent after 1877 in so-called "local color" fiction, in inter-sectional romance novels, and finally in the dozens of historical novels of the Reconstruction South published at the height of the Spanish-American-Philippine War. As the United States acquired an expanding array of new territories overseas to administer, novelists retrospectively proclaimed the project of reconstructing its South to have been "a fool's errand," always doomed to fail.[39] This interpretation of the Reconstruction South both affirmed the anti-imperial founding ideals of the republic, and, paradoxically, asserted that the world beyond the national borders would never be able to live up to those ideals without U.S. intervention.

Although this book includes many authors and genres, and ranges across a broad swath of time, it does not provide a comprehensive history of the role of our South in the rise of U.S. literature. It is easy to think of relevant literary figures (James Fenimore Cooper, William Wells Brown, Mark Twain) and movements (southwestern humor, southern travel narratives) that are not addressed in the subsequent pages.[40] The book builds toward the twentieth century—when, as we know, the South assumed a centrally prominent role in national literature at the same time that the United States assumed the same prominence on the world stage—but never quite gets there. It would take an entire second volume to address what happens next: to think about Hitler learning from Jim Crow, the Student Nonviolent Coordinating Committee learning from Gandhi, Richard Wright reporting on the Bandung Conference, and William Faulkner, weirdly, traveling for the State Department as a Cold War "cultural ambassador."

There remains to be written, too, a story of how critical insight into a nation's internal forms of geographical order might provide much-needed perspective on how that nation projects power externally into the world. While I have worked on this book I have had in the back of my mind the following passage from Said's *Culture and Imperialism*:

> There is the more surprising case of Raymond Williams, whose *Culture and Society* does not deal with the imperial experience at all. (When in an interview Williams was challenged about this massive absence, since imperialism "was not something which was secondary and external—it was absolutely constitutive of the whole nature of the English political and social order . . . *the* salient fact"—he replied that his Welsh experience, which ought to have enabled him to think about the imperial experience, was "very much in abeyance" at the time he wrote *Culture and Society*.)[41]

It is the sentence in parentheses that gets me. In it, Said wishes for a revelation that never happened; but at the same time he seems so unsure of what that revelation would have entailed that he must simply bracket the missed possibility and move on. What is the clarifying insight into British imperialism that Williams's "Welsh experience" should have afforded him?

In the course of writing *Our South,* I have become aware of authors who seem, despite the times in which they lived, to have been able to gain a critical vantage on the dominant modes of geographic fantasy in the national literature of their day. Grimké, Poe, Douglass, Delany, Jacobs, Cable, Cooper: for want of a better term, I have called their interventions a "southern critique" of U.S. nationalism, though their writing is most certainly not pro-"South," and though not all of them would have self-identified as "southerners." What they share, though, is a radically different vision of national identity. They dispense with the endless self-exoneration of U.S. nationalism; they understand the United States as not only the aspirational republic but also a site and source of sin and guilt and pain. They nurture a deep and abiding suspicion of claims to American transcendence or universality; and they bear hostility toward the general confidence of U.S. writers that Americans not only know the nation's others fully, but also know what is best for them. One might discern across the chapters that follow the suggestion of an alternative tradition in U.S. letters, an oppositional, critical tradition at variance with the ones that we know as either national or "southern." This, above all, is a tradition we would do well to investigate farther.

PART ONE

Nationalization /
The Plantation South

But if [the Americans] at once ceased to have negroes for slaves, and kings who live at a distance from them for masters, they, perhaps, would become the most astonishing people that ever appeared on the earth.

> —Abbé Guillaume-Thomas-François Raynal, *Political and Philosophical History of the Settlements and Trade of the Europeans in the East and West Indies* (1770)

[W]ith the exception of the slave holding states, as we have no nobility but from worth, so we have no villainy but from misdeed. We have neither lord nor peasant, except in the South, where the planter partakes of European nobility, and the African slave of European peasantry.

> —William Dunlap, *The Life of Charles Brockden Brown* (1815)

CHAPTER ONE

The Problem of the Plantation

Were I to be possessed of a plantation, and my slaves treated in general as they are here, never could I rest in peace.

  —J. Hector St. John de Crèvecoeur, *Letters from an American Farmer* (1782)

HE UBIQUITOUS AMERICAN FARMER of early U.S. nationalism was produced by *writing over* the American planter, that venerable icon of English New World colonization. Thomas Jefferson comes immediately to mind, penning his paean to "the mass of cultivators" from Poplar Forest, his country retreat, in the late days of the war for independence: "Those who labor in the earth are the chosen people of God, if ever he had a chosen people, whose breasts he has made his peculiar deposit for substantial and genuine virtue." It perhaps goes without saying that the enslaved people of African descent who labored in the earth nearest him were not Jefferson's subject in this famous passage. Instead, he invoked the yeoman farmer so privileged in Enlightenment thought as the foundational citizen of a republic: a figure "looking up to heaven, to [his] own soil and industry . . . for [his] subsistence." This figure of the "husbandman"—independent by definition—was antithetical to both the enslaved agricultural laborer and his planter master, operating as they did in a relationship of abjection and domination. Yet as Jefferson extolled the act of cultivating the soil of Virginia itself as "the focus in which [God] keeps alive that sacred fire [of virtue],"[1] could he have avoided raising the specter of the plantation in the minds of his contemporary readers? The subsistence farming of the yeoman was hardly the agricultural enterprise for which the British New World colonies, Virginia central among them, were famed and prized. Nor was it the primary mode of economic production that funded the bid for independence by the mainland colonists.[2]

Jefferson's succinct apotheosis of the republican farmer has proved generative for more than two centuries of national thought in the United States.[3] The construction of the American farmer with arguably the greatest lasting influence on *literature*, however, was penned by no founding father, but by J. Hector St. John de Crèvecoeur—who, although it is not so readily apparent, effected a similar renovation of American planter into American farmer at the cusp of U.S. nationalization. Crève-coeur's biography would seem to disqualify him as an early nationalist:

Figure 2. J. Hector St. John de Crèvecoeur's painting of his "Plantation of Pine-Hill," ca. 1773–1775 (detail). Courtesy of the Yale University Library.

he first came to America as a young officer in the French army during the French and Indian War; became a naturalized British subject and prosperous planter in the colonies of New York and New Jersey by 1770; fled to Britain as a staunch loyalist in 1779; and ended his life as a repatriated Frenchman and Enlightenment philosophe. After his Tory leanings induced him to abandon his young American family and his adopted home for the capitals of Europe, he published his *Letters from an American Farmer* in London in 1782.[4] In that year, when the independence of the rebelling North American colonies had become a foregone conclusion, but a treaty formalizing that independence had not yet been negotiated, Crèvecoeur assembled his book specifically for a British metropolitan audience curious about the "situations, manners, and customs" of the colonialists who lately had cost the mother country such trouble.[5] He culled the twelve "letters" from thirty-seven sketches in English, mostly on American topics, that he had written over the previous decade; and he crafted a epistolary framing device to connect the sketches as communications from a quasi-autobiographical narrator, Farmer James of Pennsylvania, to an ostensible correspondent in London.[6]

Crèvecoeur's organizing aim in the *Letters* was to explain American nationalization to the citizens of Europe, a task that he famously posed as a rhetorical question: "What then is the American, this new man?" Enlightenment thinkers, at least since Rousseau's *Social Contract* of 1762, increasingly had seen legitimate states as expressions of distinct "peoples"; with his central question, Crèvecoeur posed the new political independence of the American states as deriving directly from a new popular personality, a novel collective way of life.[7] His nationalist argument thus proceeded as a literary act: through his characterization of Farmer James, Crèvecoeur demonstrated that the daily lives of the rebelling American colonialists had irrevocably severed them from their old identity as British subjects, so much so that his narrator now had the task of explaining "this new man" to "the home English." At his most optimistic, particularly in the first three letters of the book, Crèvecoeur located the newness of the nationalizing American farmer precisely in his perfected yeoman stature, his attainment of an agrarian ideal previously unachieved in Western culture. That this foundational formulation of U.S. national distinctiveness based in republican virtue remains familiar today is thanks in no small part to the great influence of Crèvecoeur's book. Translated quickly into Dutch and German and expanded and rewritten by the author in the French editions of 1784 and 1787, *Letters from an American Farmer* served as a dominant source for European conceptions of the United States well into the nineteenth century. Continued British and French regard for the book no doubt helped to secure its central place in the canon of early U.S. literature as it was assembled in the first decades of the twentieth century, and even today "Letter III," in particular, regularly appears as the first entry in anthologies of U.S. literature.[8]

That Crèvecoeur's "new man" belongs to the realm of fiction is a fact thrown into relief by his slightly earlier representation of American life in a watercolor titled "Plantation of Pine-Hill" (reproduced at the opening of this chapter). Painted sometime between 1773 and 1775, just before the colonial war for independence, Crèvecoeur's watercolor reveals that his characterization of Farmer James in 1782 required a radical revision of the terms with which he had described the American situation less than a decade before.[9] Like his *Letters,* Crèvecoeur's painting was produced to portray life in the New World for a European audience, but in it he depicted himself not as a yeoman farmer but, unmistakably, as an English colonial planter, a figure that had existed and evolved in Anglo-American culture over the previous two hundred years. From the late sixteenth century forward, English colonists had "referred to their own activities in occupying the New World as planting the garden": they had understood their building of houses, enclosing of land with fences, and plowing (or "subduing") the American soil as specifically English rituals of possession, in harmony with English common law and biblical interpretation.[10] Crèvecoeur drew upon these venerable conventions for portraying mastery over American land, framing the illustration of his Hudson Valley "plantation" with a backdrop of rolling hills disciplined into fenced cultivation. He organized the scene around two central figures counterpoised in an allegory of English New World agricultural enterprise: a white, two-story planter's dwelling, embellished with wings and portico, hovering above a lone black man at work at his plow in the foreground.[11]

Colonization by plantation had been valorized in British thought specifically in opposition to the forms of Spanish New World colonization, which were anathematized as extracting wealth from American soil via gold mining rather than improving it through cultivation.[12] Crèvecoeur's British partisan interest in precisely this ideological use of the plantation appeared in his pre-Revolutionary "Sketch of a Contrast between the Spanish & English Colonies," written at around the same time that he produced his painting. After schematically comparing Pennsylvania with Peru, he concluded

that there is a Necessary Purity of Manners arising from a close application
to Rural Improvements; debauched hands, Polluted with Crimes covered
with the Filth of Idleness, cannot make the Earth To Team with Yellow Harvest . . . if a society follow that salutary Maxim & Live alltogether by Till-
ing, if they are a people of cultivators, & the other society do not, it is an
Easy Task to ascertain, which of the Two people posesses the Least contaminated Manners.[13]

Prior to independence, Crèvecoeur awarded English colonial planters not
the ideal republican virtue of his post-Revolutionary American farmer
but the "least contaminated" manners possible in a colonial condition.
While his Pennsylvanians pursued a way of life superior to the depraved
Spanish Peruvians, using colonization as a force toward civilization
rather than degeneracy, they nonetheless proved superior only in a scale
of comparison restricted to the western hemisphere and implicitly subordinate to the European seats of empire. This certainty about the relative ethical benefits of planting within a colonial American context
similarly organized Crèvecoeur's painting, in which he elaborated an implied narrative of his "rural improvements." With painstaking attention to detail, he brought his immaculate and diversified plantings—an
enormous orchard, varied garden plots, irrigated staple fields—together
into an iconographic whole with the implements and structures involved
in their production—a haying cart, a device for drawing water from the
well, ten slave cabins, and a building he labeled his "Negro-kitchen."[14]
    His attention to the physical details of his agricultural enterprise, as
well as the central presence of the black plowman, also made Crèvecoeur's painting expressive of a more recent understanding of the "plantation" in the British imperial world: it was not just any parcel of
cultivated, possessed American land but a large estate using enslaved labor to produce staple crops for export.[15] To the side of the painting,
though hardly marginally, Crèvecoeur included an image of himself as
the clear master of the entire content of the painting. With streams con-
verging at his feet, his wife seated to his side and rear, and shaded by a
picturesque stand of trees, his likeness casually monitors the work of the
plowman in the foreground. As a seemingly whimsical touch, Crèvecoeur
painted his infant son seated on a special perch on the plow, thereby illustrating an ingenious management technique whereby he employed a
single slave to free both himself and his wife to enjoy their positions of
supervisory leisure. By shading the infant with an umbrella, he under-
lined both the whiteness of his son, and the tropicality of the sun, in an
apotheosis of English New World colonization.
    A strikingly similar scene of plowing with the infant son appeared

early in Crèvecoeur's 1782 *Letters from an American Farmer.* With impending American independence, though, came some key alterations:

> This formerly rude soil has been converted by my father into a pleasant *farm,* and in return it has established all our rights; on it is founded our rank, our freedom, our power as citizens . . . [T]his is what may be called the true and the only philosophy of an American farmer . . . Often when *I* plow my low ground, *I* place my little boy on a chair which screws to the beam of the plough . . . *As I lean over the handle,* various are the thoughts which crowd into my mind. I am now doing for him, I say, what my father formerly did for me . . . [C]an more pleasure, more dignity be added to that primary occupation? The father thus ploughing with his child, and to feed his family, is inferior only to the emperor of China ploughing as an example to his kingdom.[16]

His painting of "The Plantation of Pine-Hill" illuminates the repressed affinity in this passage between Crèvecoeur's American farmer, "the father thus ploughing . . . to feed his family," and his seemingly arbitrary foil, "the emperor of China ploughing as an example to his kingdom." With the painting in mind, Farmer James appears in this scene to "lean over the handle" of the plow not to produce subsistence for his family but to produce a propagandist "example" of idealized republican agrarianism. Even as Crèvecoeur retained in the textual scene the focus of his painting on cultivation as the key to both possession and virtue, he created a portrait of vastly different ideological weight by writing "this new man," the American farmer of U.S. nationalization, over the American planter of his colonial painting. The act of plowing remained a constant, but whose hand was on the plow made all the difference.

These contemporaneous and clashing portraits indicate that Crèvecoeur's perception of the proper—indeed, the necessary—way to represent mainland North Americans to a European audience changed categorically in the short period between the mid-1770s and 1782, and that this shift in his representational vocabulary corresponded to the transformation in global status of the places he described. When Crèvecoeur painted "The Plantation of Pine-Hill," New York and Pennsylvania were peripheral, dependent British colonies; by the time *Letters From an American Farmer* appeared, New York and Pennsylvania were the center of a new state that declared itself separate from and equal to the powers of Europe. Established European understandings of American colonists did not suffice to define U.S. national citizens, as Crèvecoeur's revision of planter into farmer well demonstrates. Rather, the nationalization of the United States required that a sharp demarcation be drawn between past colonial status and new nationhood. If early U.S. nationalists did not insist on restarting time from the Year One, they nonetheless required that plantations become farms, colonies become states, monarchy become republic, luxury become industry, and, of course, that slavery become liberty.[17]

The problem of the plantation for these conceivers of the new United States was that this form not only typified British America but also embodied the two essential sins of U.S. origin. In its older colonial sense—the sense of the Pilgrims' Plymouth Plantation or of "Rhode Island and Providence Plantations"—the plantation signified the expropriation of Indian lands. In its more recent eighteenth-century sense, it signified the crime against humanity of slavery. Worst of all, this newer incarnation of the plantation showed no sign of disappearing from the North American scene when independence was declared. The economy of the new United States continued to rely on plantation produce; and its legislators were busy constituting the new nation as a slaveholding republic. The question then becomes, "How did the plantation become 'southern' rather than 'American'?" This is a question that may be answered, at least provisionally, by reading Crèvecoeur's very early entry into the field of U.S. national literature.

One of Crèvecoeur's great achievements in the *Letters* was to develop a formula for simultaneously disavowing and acknowledging the persistence of the plantation in U.S. national life. This happens in "Letter IX: Description of Charles-Town," when he sends Farmer James to the only location south of Pennsylvania portrayed in the book—and not just to any southern location, but rather to Charleston, South Carolina, the emblematic "southern capital" of the Revolutionary era. Here the Anglo-American colonial plantation of Pine-Hill, repressed in James's descriptions of his Pennsylvania farm, returns with nightmarish intensity. To delineate Charleston, Crèvecoeur drew upon rising European metropolitan critiques of the inhumanity of New World plantation slavery, particularly those of the Abbé Raynal, to whom he dedicated the 1782 edition of the *Letters;* he likely borrowed from Raynal's description of Jamaica for the searing final image in "Letter IX" of a condemned African slave imprisoned in a cage and slowly devoured by carnivorous birds.[18] By posing his American farmer in vehement opposition to the "dismal latitude" of South Carolina, Crèvecoeur converted the Anglo-American colonial past of his national "new man" from a matter of temporality into a matter of spatiality. The persistence of the plantation in the new United States registered in "Letter IX" not as a narrative process of continuous development from colony into nation, but as a geographical deviance of the southern capital from the national character.

That Crèvecoeur's South Carolina serves as a geographical repository for the persistent plantation past of his "new" American farmer becomes apparent in the very first sentence of "Letter IX," where he trades the dominant national imaginary of his book for a hemispheric span: "Charles-Town is, in the north, what Lima is in the south; both are Capitals of the richest provinces in their respective hemispheres: you may therefore conjecture, that both cities must exhibit the appearances necessarily resulting from riches." Facing Charleston, Crèvecoeur reverts from his project of national characterization back to the comparative colonialism of his pre-Revolutionary "Contrast between the Spanish & English Colonies." With the immediate comparison to Spanish Peru, South Carolina becomes a *northern* point in the colonized New World rather than a southern city in the national United States. As Crèvecoeur further situates Charleston in an exploitative Atlantic economy in the first pages of "Letter IX"—fueled by Peruvian gold, populated by West Indians, and enriched by the labor of slaves kidnapped from Guinea—he exchanges the motivating question of his inquiry into nationalization ("[W]hat then is the American?") for a meditation on the fallen nature of universal humanity ("What then is man . . .?").

While this detour to the universal might at first appear a distraction from his nation-writing project, Crèvecoeur's location of mankind's propensity for evil in Charles-Town actually works to strengthen his characterization of Farmer James. Setting a baseline of universal human evil in his southern chapter affords Crèvecoeur a foil against which to define American nationality as primally exceptional. Whereas previously in the text he has relied upon descriptive passages recounting anecdotes and enumerating American traits, "Letter IX" enables Crèvecoeur to demonstrate the newness of the nation through juxtaposition with a "general review of human nature," as displayed in Charleston:

> The history of the earth! doth it present anything but crimes of the most heinous nature, committed from one end of the world to the other? . . . [O]ne would almost believe the principles of action in man . . . to be poisoned in their most essential parts . . . Benignity, moderation, and justice, are virtues adapted only to the humble paths of life: we love to talk of virtue and to admire its beauty, while in the shade of solitude and retirement; but when we step forth into active life, if it happen to be in competition with any passion or desire, do we observe it to prevail? . . . Almost every where, liberty so natural to mankind, is refused . . . *There* the very delirium of tyranny tramples on the best gifts of nature, and sports with the fate, the happiness, the lives of millions: *there* the extreme fertility of the ground always indicates the extreme misery of the inhabitants![19]

In his southern chapter, Crèvecoeur engineers a more ambitious claim for the novelty of the forming United States than any he has previously proposed, for the only exception to the "heinous" criminality of man "*almost* everywhere" is his narrator, the American farmer of the previous chapters. This yeoman citizen perfectly exemplifies the "[b]enignity, moderation, and justice" that are achieved only in "the humble paths of life"—"in the shade of solitude and retirement" that permeates Crève-coeur's descriptions of James's Pennsylvania farm. Representative of not only English New World colonization but also all of human history, South Carolinian plantation society stands as a repository of the past against which Farmer James truly may be proved a "new man."

Crèvecoeur's concluding certainty that "*there* the extreme fertility of the ground always indicates the extreme misery of the inhabitants," in particular, reveals his adherence to the natural-philosophical theories of climatic determinism that were underwriting the expansion of European imperial ventures as he wrote. Classical theories about the influence of climate on the forms of human society had been revivified for Enlightenment thinkers by Montesquieu's *On the Spirit of the Laws* (1748), which proposed that governments take their form in relation to the physical environment and that despotism increases in proportion to climatic warmth and the fertility of the soil.[20] As Crèvecoeur aligns Charles-Town with "[t]he fertile plains of Asia, the rich low lands of Egypt and of Diarbeck, the fruitful fields bordering on the Tigris and the Euphrates, the extensive country of the East-Indies in all its separate districts," he creates, specifically, a *tropical* American foil against which Farmer James asserts his new republican virtue: "All these must to the geographical eye seem as if intended for terrestrial paradises; but . . . though [nature's] kindest favours seem to be shed on those beautiful regions with the most profuse hand, yet there in general we find the most wretched people in the world."[21]

Acknowledging American tropicality is an important rhetorical move on Crèvecoeur's part, since European discourses of New World colonization, ranging from scientific theories of climatic determinism to literary conventions of exoticism, had for more than two centuries defined American possessions in terms of their warmth and agricultural productivity.[22] By ordering "Letter IX" around James's refrain of incredulous observation and passionate rejection of Charles-Town, Crèvecoeur stresses the temperateness of his American farmer: James's geographic and moral estrangement from the tropics of his predecessor, the American planter.

> Thus planters get rich; so raw, so unexperienced am I in this mode of life, that were I to be possessed of a plantation, and my slaves treated as in gen-

> eral they are here, never could I rest in peace . . . Can it be possible that the
> force of custom should ever make me . . . as insensible to the injustice of [the
> slave] trade . . . as the rich inhabitants of this town seem to be? . . . I have
> not resided here long enough to become insensible of pain for the objects
> which I every day behold.[23]

Farmer James's innocence of American plantation slavery is predicated
upon his geographic distance from Charles-Town, upon the simple fact
that he does not "reside *here*" but is simply passing through. (To stay for
"long enough," the logic of climatic determinism dictates and his rhetorical "can it be possible" insists, would be to succumb to the environment
and "the force of [local] custom.") As Farmer James carefully invokes the
spatial remove of his national identity from the "barbarous" tropical
scenes he witnesses, he assumes the conventional pose of an eighteenth-
century metropolitan traveler writing about colonial possessions: he denies his own implication in the violence of plantation production he
records at the same time that he naturalizes that violence with the latest
natural-philosophical theories.[24] Crèvecoeur's southern letter markedly
diverges in style and tone from the rest of the book, for it unmistakably
echoes European imperial accounts of the American colonies while including "almost nothing original, nothing that demonstrates direct and personal observation."[25] Indeed, Crèvecoeur himself acknowledged this
divergence of perspective when he retitled the Charles-Town chapter "Lettre d'un Voyageur Européen" in the first French edition of the *Letters*.[26]

By aligning his simultaneously exoticizing and condemnatory account
of Charles-Town with the presumed responses of his metropolitan readers, Crèvecoeur presents Farmer James not as a colonial American but
rather as an equal among citizens of the nations of the world. His definitional opposition of the new man of U.S. nationality to the old plantation
society of Charles-Town culminates at the close of "Letter IX," when
James, while walking through a wood on a "perfectly calm and sultry"
afternoon, comes face to face with an icon of tropical depravity, the condemned African in a cage hanging suspended from a tree:

> I shudder when I recollect that the birds had already picked out his eyes; his
> cheek-bones were bare . . . From the edges of the hollow sockets and from
> the lacerations with which he was disfigured, the blood slowly dropped, and
> tinged the ground beneath. . . . I found myself suddenly arrested by the
> power of affright and terror; my nerves were convulsed; I trembled; I stood
> motionless, involuntarily contemplating the fate of this Negro, in all it[s]
> dismal latitude.[27]

In this archetypal juxtaposition, Crèvecoeur's "new man" proves his
break with his colonial past as his very physical being intrinsically rejects

an embodiment of American plantation slavery. Here Crèvecoeur distills his characterization of U.S. nationality to its organic essence: the "involuntary shudder" that denies—simultaneously—the colonial origins of the American nation, and the blood-soaked ground and "dismal latitude" of South Carolina.

This mythopoeic scene so crystallized the nationalizing transformations of the emerging United States that Crèvecoeur's European readers quickly seized upon it, making the final paragraph of "Letter IX" the most often-cited and controversial passage of the *Letters* at the time of its publication. While some commentators friendly to nascent metropolitan antislavery thought defended Crèvecoeur's inclusion of the scene, prevailing opinion indicted it as a fraud, a formulaic figure of horror inserted by the author in the midst of the direct observation that was supposed to set the *Letters* apart from other accounts of the rebelling American colonies available in Europe. Crèvecoeur was faulted for not having visited South Carolina in reality and for having fabricated the sensational image of the tortured African to serve his own political purposes.[28] He capitulated to the criticism by 1787, when he expunged the scene from all subsequent editions of the *Lettres,* ostensibly out of concern "pour l'honneur des Caroliniens."[29]

His voluntary deconstruction of "Letter IX" hardly seems necessary given the extent to which the 1782 volume already self-destructs around this southern letter. At the moral center of the letter, Crèvecoeur has created a primary representative equation in which U.S. national distinctiveness is defined through juxtaposition with the horribly mutilated body of a black man: an equation through which he seeks—impossibly!—to deny both the immediate colonial past of the American Farmer and the internal state of South Carolina that lies within the borders of James's new republic.[30] The wishfully purgative scene immediately implicates Farmer James in the plantation violence against which he is defined, for no South Carolinian slave masters appear in "Letter IX"; instead, it is Crèvecoeur's narrator who stands locked into the binary of racialized Anglo-American plantation slavery, facing the slave in the position of master. The only dialogue in the chapter is the African's response, rendered in dialect, to James's giving him water—"'Tankè, you whitè man, tankè you'"—a speech that further inscribes the narrator within the binary, naturalizing his whiteness as perceivable without sight or sound and emphasizing Farmer James's domination even at the level of language.[31]

Just as Farmer James's implication in the tropical depravity of Charles-Town emerges at the climax of his opposition to it, so Crèvecoeur's own Hudson Valley plantation returns in precisely the letter that seeks to quarantine that emblematic Anglo-American colonial form in the south of the new United States. In a frequently overlooked passage in "Letter IX," James is moved by his reflection on the horrors of South Carolina to provide a description of his own agricultural practices, which are quite at odds with his previous elaborations of the yeoman ideal:

> We have slaves likewise in our northern provinces; I hope the time draws near when they will be all emancipated: but how different their lot, how different their situation, in every possible respect! They enjoy as much liberty as their masters, they are as well clad, and as well fed; in health and sickness they are tenderly taken care of; they . . . are, truly speaking, a part of our families. Many of them are taught to read and write . . . [T]hey are indulged in educating, cherishing, and chastising their children, who are taught subordination to them as to their lawful parents: in short, they participate in many of the benefits of our society, without being obliged to bear any of its burthens.

This preemptively exculpatory passage makes sense only if we recall Crèvecoeur's pre-Revolutionary painting and then see in "Letter IX" his attempt to relocate the plowman and the hierarchy of that portrait southward. His portrayal of slave labor in Charles-Town furthers the return of his own repressed plantation: rather than depicting the horrid working conditions particular to Low Country production of indigo and rice, Crèvecoeur imagines slaves in South Carolina as "those who till the earth, who carry burdens, who convert the logs into useful boards"—all work more likely performed at the New York "Plantation of Pine-Hill. The first tree of which was cut down in ye year of our Lord 1770."[32]

Small wonder that Crèvecoeur's Farmer James at the end of "Letter IX" remains "[o]ppressed with the reflections which this shocking spectacle afforded me," for the southern letter can achieve only incomplete catharsis. Crèvecoeur's attempt to define a national "new man" against his own colonial origins, and to define a new nation against its own southern reaches, leads to a powerful reassertion of the American plantation that persists despite the political independence of the United States. The *dying* slave in the cage metaphorizes James's "hope [that] the time draws near when they shall all be emancipated," embodying the desire of early American nationalists to see the exploitative colonial economic basis of the new United States as inevitably passing out of existence. The terror of the archetypal scene lies in the fact that James is "unable" to eliminate the suffering African from the American scene: "Had I had a ball in my gun, I certainly should have dispatched him, but finding myself unable to perform so kind an office, I sought, though trembling, to relieve him as well as I could." (And indeed, a deeper terror of the scene lies in

James's failure of imagination as to how the intolerable suffering of the caged African might be alleviated: speeding his execution is the only solution that occurs to the narrator. To free the African from the cage, to bind up his wounds, is out of the question.) However much writer or reader might wish it, the dying slave does not disappear from the new United States, but still lives, still suffers, still speaks: "'Two days, and me no die; the birds, the birds; aaah me!'"[33]

So while this climactic "melancholy scene," as the subtitle of "Letter IX" terms it, superficially appears to offer a clear parable of new republican virtue versus static colonial barbarism—and while it has for decades been read as such in the United States, becoming one of the canonical primal scenes of our national literature—Crèvecoeur's southern letter actually serves as the pivot around which his nationalist characterization of the American farmer collapses. In the remaining three letters of the 1782 book, James's stated task of narrating the "new man" of U.S. nationality drops out of view: in "Letter X," he trades describing American people for describing American animals but becomes captivated by the image of a murderous black snake that seems to metaphorize Raynal's prophecy of apocalyptic New World slave revolts; in "Letter XI," Farmer James disappears entirely as narrator, replaced by Crèvecoeur with a "Russian Gentleman," a figure antithetical to U.S. republicanism; and in the final letter, Farmer James prepares to commit characterological suicide by abandoning the farm that has defined him, under the duress of the colonial rebellion that loyalist Crèvecoeur elsewhere would term a "civil war."

The arc of this ideological dissolution of Crèvecoeur's "new man" at the end of the *Letters* is telegraphed by the author in the curt final lines with which he ends his southern letter, after the face-off between his narrator and the tortured African:

> I mustered strength enough to walk away, and soon reached the house at which I intended to dine. There . . . [t]hey told me that the laws of self-preservation rendered such executions necessary; and supported the doctrine of slavery with the arguments generally made use of to justify the practice; with the repetition of which I shall not trouble you at present.
>   Adieu.[34]

Crèvecoeur's location of a distilled, dystopic vision of Anglo-American coloniality in Charles-Town has permitted him to purge the plantation from Farmer James's Pennsylvania (and his own New York), but has nonetheless fixed that emblematic old American term firmly within the political borders of the new United States. His wishfully self-sufficient, agrarian, "new" narrator thus remains fully enmeshed in the old Manichaean dualism of plantation slavery, "walking away" from the suffering African to break bread with his tormentors, and in the process choosing sides in a projected American race war according to "the laws of self-preservation." Even as he tacitly acquiesces to the old racist order of Anglo-American colonial slavery, Farmer James desperately attempts to maintain distance between his republican nationality and the depravity of his southern hosts by inscribing an additional civil division within the new U.S. borders through his use of first and third person: "I"/"we" for his "new man" against "they" for the denizens of "the southern provinces." By the close of this allegorical scene, Crèvecoeur seems to have decided that nationalizing Americans may not have achieved, after all, the popular cohesion and cultural independence that would authorize their self-narration. With the final French farewell, "Adieu," Crèvecoeur imperiously silences James and abruptly evacuates himself from the project of narrating the new republic, rejecting the ideological chaos generated when the "new" American farmer confronts his all-too-present plantation past.

The Southern Status Quo in Paine's Revolutionary Magazine

Few Revolutionary-era authors in the emerging United States shared Crèvecoeur's recourse to a European metropolitan authorial identity, his ability to insert the Atlantic Ocean between his enlightened ideals and their contradiction in American reality. In order to articulate and explore the problem of the persistent plantation in the new American republic, though, much of the literature that early U.S. authors wrote used precisely the same volatile, intranational geography that sent Crèvecoeur running back to France, at least textually, at the end of "Letter IX." Although Thomas Paine, for one, shared none of Crèvecoeur's ambivalence about colonial independence, his first American nationalist production participated in a similar pattern. As editor and author of much of the content of the Philadelphia-based *Pennsylvania Magazine,* beginning two months after his arrival in America from England in late 1774 and continuing into 1776, Paine spurned established British imperial characterizations of the North American mainland colonies as inadequate for describing the advanced development of most of those colonies toward independent nationhood.[35] In direct contradiction to this overall program of nationalist self-definition, though, he featured the five southernmost colonies, Maryland through Georgia, in the pages of his magazine *only* in terms of those British imperial descriptions he elsewhere rejected. The narrative of American national emergence projected across the issues of Paine's magazine thus remained weirdly shadowed by an assurance of southern stasis.

This unexpected exemption of the southern colonies from the rest of Paine's North American revolutionary geography had its origin in the fact that the *Pennsylvania Magazine* was defined as a specifically literary publication, in contradistinction to the political discourse Paine would take up so brilliantly in *Common Sense* in the waning days of his editorship. The prominent Philadelphia publisher of the magazine, Robert Aitken, had explicitly confined the purview of the periodical to "philosophical disquisition," "excluding the [political] controversies" of the months preceding the Declaration of Independence.[36] Aitken's literary-vs.-political distinction was no real impediment for Paine, though, who from his introductory editorial for the first issue, "Utility of this Work Evinced," argued that the emergence of an explicitly literary publication in America was itself a sign of impending independence. Taking his readers through a schematic history of British America, Paine specified the form of publication appropriate to each stage of colonial development, ending with the very existence of the *Pennsylvania Magazine* as evidence that the North American colonies had outgrown their plantation function as peripheral sites for the production of Britain's staple commodities. "In the early days of colonization," he began, oral communication within small settler outposts sufficed: "A whisper was almost sufficient to have registered all our internal concerns." With greater population and rising towns, local newspapers had appeared, "but their plan being almost wholly devoted to news and commerce," it was by 1775 "somewhat strange that the channels of communication should continue so narrow and limited." "America has now outgrown the state of infancy," Paine declared; and consequently the uniting colonies required the new literary magazine form to serve as the creative "nursery of genius" for the rising nation, by re-presenting British North America as its own center of manufacturing, and—most important—of knowledge production.[37] Symbiotically generated by the emerging material independence of the mainland colonies, and generating the mental independence of their inhabitants, the *Pennsylvania Magazine* as Paine formulated it gained the widest circulation of any previous American periodical in just a few months.[38]

But Paine's equation of nationalization with literary production necessarily highlighted the uneven development of print production across the North American colonies that soon would join in rebellion. As his inaugural editorial made clear, to establish the American cultural independence he proclaimed required a twofold move of geographical recentering. Paine sought foremost to relocate the metropolitan cultural authority of London over the colonies to the western side of the Atlantic by supplanting the "importation" of "the British magazines" that were simply "the retailers of tale and nonsense" on American matters. At the same time, though, he sought to establish a new center among the uniting colonies by surmounting the too-local focus of colonial newspapers to create a proto-national "market for wit and utility" in his pages that would allow "men of abilities" from throughout North America to "collect and convey" their "inventions" to the broadest possible American "public."

The metropolitan ambition of Paine's Philadelphia publication registered in both its form and its content. Formally, the magazine was designed to resemble respected London periodicals such as "the *Gentleman's*, the *London*, and the *Universal Magazines*," all cited by Paine with grudging admiration: it was extensively illustrated with exclusive engravings, ostentatiously produced "for the *Pennsylvania Magazine*," and it featured original essays and poems authored by American correspondents rather than reprints of extracts from other publications.[39] The content of both illustration and text, fittingly, skewed toward detailing the developmental attainments of the North American colonies, providing site-specific descriptions of major cities, ports, and public buildings; reports of innovations in technological apparatus and manufacturing processes; and scholarly investigations from the scientific to the philosophical. Paine also carefully ensured that each of the uniting colonies was featured in the pages of the magazine during his editorial tenure, and the contents of every number boasted a broad North American geographic span. This first self-consciously metropolitan American periodical thereby implied a new cultural nationalism whose imaginative extent matched the boundaries of the emerging United States: a cultural nationalism that would, as Johann Gottlieb Fichte defined it several decades later, make the external borders of the forming nation into the internal borders of consciousness of its subjects.[40]

Yet Paine had very different sorts of material available to him with which to depict the colonies north of Philadelphia, as opposed to those south of it, due to the uneven development of print production in the emerging northeastern American core and in the southern mainland colonies. While the local newspapers, pamphlets, and broadsides that Paine deemed suitable to a colonial condition were printed in towns and counties in all of the thirteen colonies contemplating and organizing their alliance against Britain, the Philadelphia-to-Boston corridor was emerging in the 1770s as the uncontested center of North American literary production.[41] With almost every nationalizing literary text—those magazines, histories, textbooks, and novels that aspired to supralocal audiences—published between Philadelphia and Boston from the late 1770s through the 1790s, the southern states were geographically distant from and marginal to U.S. literary production from its very beginnings.[42] While Paine was able to "collect and convey" direct observation from correspondents in the northeastern colonies to counter British imperial depictions of that American periphery, he faced a dearth of such self-representational print (as opposed to simple news reports) from the southern colonies.[43] To include the colonies from Maryland to Georgia in his pages, Paine resorted to replicating precisely those British imperial accounts of peripheral staple production that were anathema elsewhere in the *Pennsylvania Magazine*. So while the overarching import of Paine's revolutionary magazine was to prove that the North American colonies had outgrown their plantation function, his nationalizing publication paradoxically presented the southern among those colonies as circumscribed by exactly that peripheral status quo.

This proto-national representational paradox appears strikingly in any comparison of Paine's treatment of a locale north of Philadelphia with his treatment of a locale to its south. For example, the engraving titled "A

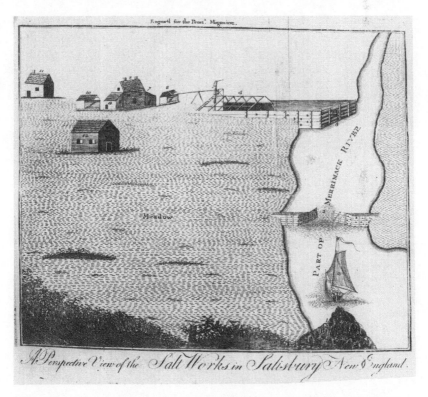

Figure 3. "A Perspective View of the Salt Works in Salisbury New England," *Pennsylvania Magazine,* March 1775. Sinclair Hamilton Collection, Graphic Arts Division, Department of Rare Books and Special Collections, Princeton University Library.

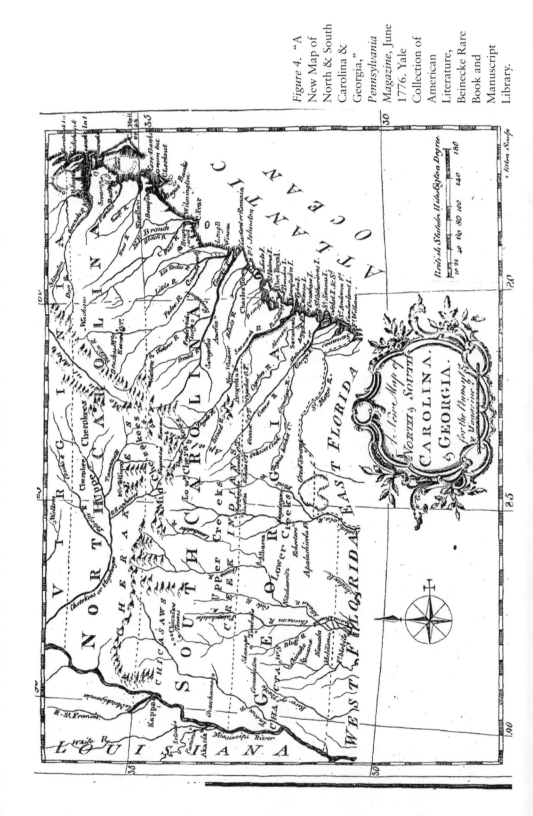

Figure 4. "A New Map of North & South Carolina & Georgia," *Pennsylvania Magazine*, June 1776. Yale Collection of American Literature, Beinecke Rare Book and Manuscript Library.

Perspective View of the Salt Works in Salisbury New England" appeared in the March 1776 number of the magazine along with an article on salt production authored by Paine and rather deceptively titled "An Extract from a Treatise entitled, 'The Art of Making Common Salt as now practised in most parts of the World. By William Brownrigg, M.D. F.R.S.'"[44] The title of the article, with its obsequious bow to London's metropolitan authority over manufacturing around the globe, quickly proved satiric: Paine quoted a short passage from this "Fellow of the Royal Society" only to eviscerate Brownrigg's text as "in some parts obscure, and in others imperfect": "The *grand principle* of the operation . . . the Dr. saith . . . is to throw the sea water into a large surface, and thereby cause the watery parts to be evaporated." Ridiculing the authoritative British treatise on salt manufacture as risibly simple-minded, Paine called for American innovation in the field: "An ingenious operator may apply this principle [evaporation] in many methods different from that above described, and perhaps in some that may be more profitable." Paine's call for American technological development then became an instant and gratifying reality for his readers as they unfolded the accompanying site-specific plate of the Massachusetts "Salt Works." This detailed thirteen-point engraving—exhibiting a complexity presumably utterly beyond the grasp of Dr. Brownrigg, F.R.S.—potently proved that the transformation from periphery to core was already under way for the uniting colonies. The "perspective view" of the engraving emphasized the domestic direct observation of this American innovation, further discrediting the flattening uselessness of Brownrigg's omniscient London vantage on "most parts of the World."

By contrast, the "New Map of North & South Carolina & Georgia," included in the June 1776 number of the magazine, literally reproduced Britain's flattened imperial perspective on its American periphery.[45] This map was not "new" at all; rather, it indifferently plagiarized a part of a 1755 map of North America published in London by the Lords Commissioners for Trade and Plantations.[46] Marked off in "British Statute Miles," this plagiarized map presented only such information as would be useful to the broadest imperial territorial administration. The borders of the three rebelling colonies pictured are not even accurately rendered, because the 1755 source map was focused on marking British territory as opposed to French territory and on recording the presence of native tribes, rather than charting the shape of individual colonial administrative units. In contradistinction to the evidence of development assiduously recorded in the "Salt Works" engraving, the "New Map" presented no evidence whatsoever of development, and indeed very little evidence even of settlement; instead, following its 1755 source, it detailed only the physical aids and impediments to administration from abroad, including ports, navigable waterways, and mountain ranges, in addition to the presence of tribes and competing French colonial claims. Indeed, more native tribal "Old Towns"—sites of major Indian settlements that had been abandoned before British incursions into the area—were denoted on this "New Map" than were the extant towns across these three southern colonies that were in the process of declaring themselves independent states.

The essay accompanying the engraving, "An Account of the Colonies of North and South Carolina, with Georgia," similarly contained no information that could not have been gleaned from British sources, rather than seeking to supplant the imperial authority of London with domestic American observation. The essay provided, quite literally, an imperial record-keeping *account* of these southern colonies as peripheral plantations, moving from a description of territorial extent ("being 700 miles long, and 380 broad"), to a catalogue of "staple commodities" produced for export, and finally to an aggregate valuation of those commodities in pounds sterling.[47] Readers wishing more detail were directed to no "perspective view" of a specific site or innovation in one of these colonies, but rather to a two-page table compiled for the Crown by the "Comptroller of his Majesty's Customs in the Port of Savannah," showing "An Aggregate and Valuation of the Exports of Produce from the Province of Georgia, from the year 1754 to 1773."[48] When it came to envisioning the southern colonies, Paine asked his readers not to throw off London's definition of plantation America, but to embrace it.

The essays describing the southern colonies in the *Pennsylvania Magazine* seemed designed to remind readers that, just as American plantation production underwrote the wealth of the British metropolitan core, so could it be harnessed to fund the growing development of an independent American nation. The rousing conclusion to the April 1776 article "Some Account of the Colony of Virginia," for example, informed readers that "the whole exportation of Virginia, including that of Maryland" significantly exceeded the value of the total exports of the mother country, while "the duty paid on the single article of tobacco exported to Great-Britain, comes to 351,675 l. sterl. and employed 330 sail of ships, and 3960 seamen, annually."[49] Southern statistics such as these manifested a form of proto-nationalist intent fundamentally different from the proofs of development in the middle and eastern colonies elsewhere in the magazine: if the American periphery of Virginia and Maryland alone produced more wealth for Britain than Britain itself produced, then how rich and powerful might the united colonists become by throwing off the yoke of duties to London and controlling southern staple production themselves? The magazine thus prognosticated a future role for the southern colonies opposite to that of their eight neighbors to the north; they would enrich the independent American nation not by developing, but by remaining the same. Indeed, Paine's southern "accounts" suggested to readers that tallying the value of one's plantations was itself a part of the process of nationalization.

Paine's exemption of the southern colonies from his larger narrative of developmental nationalization was farther underwritten by his conflation of those five colonies into a totalized whole. While it would have seemed absurd to Paine to publish "an Account of New York and Pennsylvania, with New Jersey," he treated the southern colonies without exception as cohesive and indistinguishable in their plantation functions. Articles that amalgamated the staple commodity production of "North & South Carolina, with Georgia" or "Virginia, including Maryland" created a flattened figure, which I will call the "Plantation South," that served as both a counterpoint to American modernization and an intrinsic enabling part of it. But this Plantation South appeared *only* from the vantage point of proto-national literary production. Such conflation counteracted the political imperatives of confederation, which regarded each of the thirteen rebelling colonies as more or less autonomous administrative units. Paine's *Pennsylvania Magazine* shows that an imaginative figure of the Plantation South came into being with the birth of a self-consciously independent nationalist literature in the United States—both as a product of that literature and as one of its great enabling fictions.

From this moment of origin, the Plantation South was an alienated yet intrinsic part of the emergent U.S. national imaginary. Coverage of the first military engagements of the Revolutionary War in the *Pennsylvania Magazine* illustrates this duality. Against the cognizance—and suspicion—of regional differences in accents, manners, and even military tactics that grew as Americans from different former colonies came into contact with each other at the continental congresses and in the armies, Paine sought to help the rebelling colonialists internalize a common cause, to help a citizen of Massachusetts come to feel that he was engaged in a common enterprise with a citizen of South Carolina, by including reports from the farthest reaches of the forming nation in the pages of his journal. But the pattern of restricting the southern colonies to their territorial and productive functions, in contradistinction to the dominant narrative of national development, only intensified in the magazine as military conflicts escalated. Battles in the environs of Boston were illustrated with perspectival scenes such as Aitken's engraving of a "Correct View of the Late Battle at Charlestown [Mass.]," that attested to eyewitness observation of the conflict from an unapologetically partisan American point of view. Such a detailed, animated scene was calculated to elicit an emotional charge from its viewers by portraying a predatory British army invading American shores from the Atlantic and by recording the smoke and carnage of the fight. Clashes in the southern colonies, on the other hand, were illustrated purely in terms of territory gained or lost—as in a map that purported to show "Lord Dunmore's depredations" in Virginia but actually gave an overhead view of "the Maritime Parts" of the colony at stake in the conflict.[50] While readers were directed to visualize the sufferings and heroism of Americans fighting for independence to the north of Philadelphia, they were encouraged to think of the stakes of battles south of Philadelphia as restricted to ports, trade, and pounds sterling. In other words, Paine's American readers were asked to interest themselves in battles in the southern colonies in precisely the way that metropolitan British readers would interest themselves.

This early imaginative alienation of the Plantation South from the broader narrative of U.S. independence attests to the physical alienation of the five southern colonies not only from the production of emerging nationalist literature but also from its consumption. While early nationalist texts like Paine's *Pennsylvania Magazine* were intended for wide distribution, as often evidenced by their attached subscriber lists and bookseller agreements, they were purchased mostly in and around the core area in which they were produced.[51] This geographic concentration of writers, publishers, *and* the great majority of readers in the developing northeastern core dictated that the U.S. reader/citizen produced in early national literature, as well as the imagined national community constructed in these texts, not only was white, male, middle-class, and urban, but also was *not* southern. Intellectual historians of the early republic long have held that U.S. partisans defined the new nation through a rhetorical process of "juxtaposition with others," that early U.S. national identity took its shape from a panoply of various and overlapping oppositions to populations both inside and outside the new national borders.[52] Though it was surely not Paine's intent, the southern "accounts" of his *Pennsylvania Magazine* presented the Plantation South as just such an oppositional term for the formation of U.S. national identity.

Exhibited in terms directly imported from British imperial depictions in Paine's pages, the meaning of this Plantation South for the new national project appeared undifferentiated from its established peripheral function in enriching the old British Empire. Exempted from the otherwise pervasive reports of progress and development in the magazine, the southern colonies appeared as no candidates for contribution to the rising national "genius." Instead, to put it glibly, they were to be valued for their bodies rather than their minds. While Paine's centralizing mission led him assiduously to include each of the thirteen rebelling colonies in the pages of his magazine, this very inclusivity highlighted the dearth of locally produced self-representations south of Philadelphia. Paine's Revolutionary magazine inscribed a Plantation South unchanged by independence—bearing its colonial past into the U.S. national future—as both a part of, and a counterpoint to, the dominant narrative of American nationalization.

CHAPTER TWO

Putting the Colonial Past in Its Place

Indeed I tremble for my country when I reflect that God is just.
  —Thomas Jefferson, *Notes on the State of Virginia* (1787)

THE VERY IDEA OF THE UNITED STATES emerged in tandem with the oppositional idea of its Plantation South because of uneven development among the thirteen rebelling colonies. When Revolutionary-era writers juxtaposed the United States proper to its Plantation South, they both registered their geographical distance from the five southern colonies, and described the real material divergences that obtained between those southern colonies and the other British mainland colonies in North America. From a global perspective, it is plain that the thirteen colonies that declared independence from Britain in 1776 were drawn from two distinct regional zones, and that this fundamental divide did not evaporate with the imposition of the new national borders. World-systems theorist Immanuel Wallerstein and geographer D. W. Meinig have proposed that the southern mainland colonies both before and after the Revolution were part of a broader subtropical region—Wallerstein's "extended Caribbean" or Meinig's "tropical America"—reaching from Maryland to Brazil and made cohesive by climate, plantation system, reliance on African slave labor, and peripheral role in the European world economy. By contrast, they see the northeastern British North American colonies as anomalous semiperipheries that could not produce staple commodities of significant value for the mother country and that instead increasingly attempted to compete with the European core in trade and manufacturing. Despite the central role that these northeastern colonies would assume across the first century of U.S. national life, at the time of the Revolution the peripheral "extended Caribbean" was at the center—not the margin—of European interest in America. Both the original impetus behind colonization of the Western hemisphere and the great profit of that venture lay in the warmth, fertility, and potential for exotic commodity production that defined "tropical America."[1]

Literary historians, as well, have stressed the centrality of the "extended

Figure 5. America under the Palm Tree, *Columbian Magazine,* 1789. Yale Collection of American Literature, Beinecke Rare Book and Manuscript Library.

Caribbean" to European conceptions of America at the time of the Revolution, demonstrating that the conventions developed for portraying "tropical America" were remarkably consistent throughout the Spanish, French, and English imperial traditions. By the 1770s, two centuries of European discourse had located the identity and the prestige of the American colonies in their "Caribbean" features: warmth, fertility, hugely profitable commodity production—and, of course, the enterprise of planting itself, which encompassed English North American settlement from Plymouth and Providence to Georgia.[2] The very features that set the five southern North American colonies apart from their northern counterparts materially were those that made the New World new representationally. It is not at all surprising, then, that Crèvecoeur should have chosen to portray himself as a conventional American planter in his 1773 self-portrait, rather than as the "American Farmer" who shortly thereafter earned an iconic place in U.S. national literature.

The repudiation of the Plantation South in early national print entailed a radical displacement of the centrality of the "extended Caribbean" to the idea of "America." The suddenness and thoroughness of this ideological revolution is surprising, especially since the material centrality of the five southern colonies to the North American venture did not change when that venture became a national rather than a colonial one. The economic prosperity of the new United States still rested upon the staple commodity production of the southern states. Those states accounted, as well, for a generous proportion of total land area and population, and, in the case of Virginia, for much of the political leadership of the new nation. By defining the emergent United States against its Plantation South, early national writers opened a profound gap between the ideological construction of the nation and its political and economic constitution.

Disavowing the Plantation South as antithetical to an independent, developed, *new* American nation also required U.S. writers to relinquish precisely the "Caribbean" terms that for two centuries had defined both the prestige of the American hemisphere and its geographical distinctiveness from Europe. Indeed, southern signs would seem to have provided the best available argument for an organic distinction between the United States and Britain: in the language of Herder's contemporary formulation of cultural nationalism, nationalizing Americans could not claim a primal difference in "language, inclination, and character" from Britons, but they certainly could assert a "wonderful separat[ion] . . . by woods and mountains, seas and deserts, rivers and climates."[3] For ambitious literary nationalists, in particular, it would seem that the iconography of tropical America would have been indispensable to the project of inventing a "natural" national tradition in the absence of linguistic and folk cultural distinctions from the former mother country.

So—what of the alternatives to an oppositional South in early U.S. culture? What of those moments when early nationalists embraced southern signs as emblematic of, rather than anathema to, the independent American nation? Although such instances are rare, examining them is quite instructive. When U.S. partisans of the Revolutionary era defined the United States in terms of, rather than in opposition to, its South, they created a narrative of national emergence that privileged evolution over rupture. They acknowledged American colonial origins rather than denying them. This meant, though, that they conjured a nation that was anything but innocent and exceptional. Understanding the United States *as* its South, rather than *against* its South, created a vision of the nation utterly incompatible with the dominant shape that U.S. nationalism was taking.

One of these rare counterexamples to the dominant trend of early national culture is reproduced at the opening of this chapter. A volume frontispiece for the *Columbian Magazine,* the most important literary publication of the 1780s, this engraving allegorizes national America as a white woman seated under a quintessentially tropical palm tree.[4] The engraver clearly created the image of national America on the model of Britannia, borrowing from contemporary British neoclassical iconography with only small modifications. Britannia's conventional shield at America's side was emblazoned with the new Great Seal of the United States; Britannia's traditional spear or standard was topped with the Cap of Liberty; and rather than seating America directly atop the globe, as Britannia often was portrayed, the U.S. engraver placed her rather unassumingly to its side.[5] While the engraver included reference to the fertility of American production with the cornucopia and sheaf at her feet, the greater concern of the image was to fortify national America with the interrelated symbolic languages of humanistic achievement and imperial mastery borrowed directly from British iconography. These interrelated languages of culture and dominion culminated in the classical "Temple of Fame," which doubled as a ponderous crown perched precariously and disproportionately above America's head.

The bald derivativeness of much of the engraving was highlighted by its motto, which exhorted the fledgling nation to "exert thy self, till every Art be thine," raising the sense that this national America was simply an aspiring adolescent prematurely dressing up in mother Britannia's iconographic garb. Indeed, it was only the engraver's powerful rendering of the palm tree that saved the image from becoming a burlesque of U.S. aspi-

Figure 6. America under the Palm Tree, *Histoire Philosophique et Politique des deux Indes,* 1774. Courtesy of the Yale University Library.

rations to the status of the British Empire. This dominant vertical element framed the scene and organized and related each of the figures within it; and as a time-honored Caribbean symbol, the palm tree powerfully asserted the intrinsic New World identity of national America. As the palm fronds arched over America's unwieldy temple-crown, transatlantic comparison was severed and in its place a self-contained New World order was instantiated. To the extent that national America appeared anything more than a pale imitation of mother Britannia in this engraving, she appeared so because Britannia could not possibly reside under a palm tree. It was only the palm tree, the powerful marker of geographical difference—of the tropics, of the Caribbean, of the South—that rendered the *Columbian Magazine* national America iconographically original and independent.

Except that, it turns out, "America Under the Palm Tree" wasn't a new iconographic image at all by the 1780s. To the contrary, that image had long held a place in European representations of New World empire, and thus it inexorably bore with it precisely the colonial American associations that U.S. cultural nationalists most wished to avoid. Compare the relatively contemporary 1773 engraving produced in London for an edition of Raynal's *Histoire Philosophique et Politique des deux Indes*.[6] This allegorical image centered on an identical conflation of Europe and tropical America, also rendered by seating a woman of European phenotype under a Caribbean palm tree; but here, illustrating the natural colonial degeneracy and subordination of America to Europe was the engraver's goal. Unlike the chastely garbed and erectly enthroned national America of the *Columbian Magazine* engraving, the colonial America of the London engraving appeared nude, prone, and promiscuously milked by the infant creoles of both Africa and Europe. With the image, the metropolitan engraver simultaneously telegraphed racial intermixing and passive peripheral production as intrinsic attributes of tropical America. The crowded backdrop of the scene rounded out the catalogue of American colonial degeneracy: the violent beatings associated with Atlantic slavery, the mines emblematic of the Spanish Black Legend, and the ocean crowded with ships reminding viewers that the ultimate significance of the New World lay in its commercial connection to the Old.

In the light of this 1773 image from London, we may see the *Columbian Magazine* engraver as negotiating a representational double bind: not only appropriating the symbolic language of the British Empire for U.S. nationalist ends but also attempting to revise the extant imperial iconography of America. While introducing the southern signifier of the palm tree immediately communicated a natural distinctiveness from Britain, based in geography, this same representational move simultaneously conjured the ideological associations dictated by centuries of European imperialism. Precisely because the "extended Caribbean" region had been central to European representation of the American colonies for two centuries, southern signs that signaled the distinctiveness of the American tropics also summoned their dependent and degenerate status, their lesser station in the great chain of being and their lack of admission to the world of nations. Despite the best efforts of the early nationalist engraver, the *Columbian Magazine* image of national "America Under the Palm Tree" bore a striking residual similarity to its colonialist antecedents, indicating the difficulty of assuming Caribbean symbols for early national self-definition. And thus despite the usefulness of the palm tree as the most ubiquitous distinguishing icon of America in European culture throughout the eighteenth century, that southern sign disappeared from emergent U.S. print with remarkable speed. Indeed, the *Columbian Magazine* engraving appears to be the last significant appropriation of the palm tree for national iconography in the publications of the early republic.

Jefferson's Virginia

The great counterexample, the one that really cannot be overlooked, is Thomas Jefferson's *Notes on the State of Virginia* (1785). The most significant literary work published before 1800 by a resident of a southern state, this book, not at all coincidentally, does not in the least conform to the overall pattern of the oppositional Plantation South in early national literary culture. In the only book he published during his lifetime, Jefferson engaged very much the same cultural nationalist terrain trod by both Crèvecoeur and Paine. Like Crèvecoeur, he published the *Notes* in London, thereby announcing the metropolitan stature of the book; he structured the text as a series of answers to queries from a European correspondent (though Jefferson's correspondent was real rather than fictional); and he primarily addressed himself to the natural history discourse on America dominated by the French philosophes. Like Paine, though, he regarded these European accounts of America as not only inaccurate—"just as true as the fables of Æsop"—but also motivated by imperial politics. He particularly concerned himself with refuting the theories of Raynal and the Comte de Buffon on American geographical subordination and Creole degeneration—global theories that sought to provide a scientific basis for older thoughts on climatic determinism by demonstrating that, as Jefferson put it sardonically, "nature has enlisted herself as a Cis or Trans-Atlantic partisan."[7]

As a defense against such Eurocentric global hierarchy, Jefferson couched his book as a declaration of American self-representational independence. It was an account of the new nation restricted to the direct observation—"eye-draughts"—of the American author himself, and those known personally to him. The *Notes* included only "what I have seen . . . and what has been written . . . by writers, enlightened themselves, and writing among an enlightened people." Indeed, Jefferson adhered far more assiduously than either Crèvecoeur or Paine to the imperative of direct observation, restricting the geographical scope of his inquiry to his home state and refusing to include American territory farther afield, because to do so he would have had to reproduce accounts of European origin that he "would not honor with the appellation of knowledge." Those parts of America not known personally and comprehensively to Jefferson had no place in a treatise that held "ignorance" to be "preferable to error."[8]

Yet his restriction of his subject to Virginia did not restrict the nationalist intent of the *Notes*. Jefferson did indeed spurn the encyclopedic or accounting tendencies of Crèvecoeur, Paine, and the vast majority of cultural nationalists of the early republic. These writers shared a desire, borrowed from European imperial discourse, to register and order all of the constitutive parts of the new nation within a single text.[9] Jefferson was up to something quite different. In place of the European encyclopedia, he offered the American synecdoche: Virginia as the single, comprehensively defined state from which could be extrapolated the United States, the continent, and indeed the American hemisphere. Nothing could be farther, in other words, from the concept of an oppositional Plantation South than Jefferson's Virginia. His Virginia was in no way part of a cohesive "South"; and it was definitional of, rather than oppositional to, the American national project.

Jefferson's centering of his home state in the nation began with the frontispiece of the *Notes,* a map that had been produced by his father and published in London in the early 1750s, at which time it was much celebrated for its accuracy. Jefferson frequently declared this map to be of more value than the book itself, though it was already thirty years out of date; but unlike maps produced in the United States after independence, the map created by Peter Jefferson aggressively presented Virginia as a middle, rather than southern, North American political unit.[10] The southern border of Virginia served as the lower limit of the map, suffering almost none of North Carolina to come into the picture, while the map extended upward to Lake Erie, putting Virginia in the company of New York, New Jersey, and the "new state" to the west that soon would become Ohio. When Jefferson revised the borders of the colonial map for inclusion in the 1787 edition of the *Notes,* he changed his father's title

("A Map of the most Inhabited Part of Virginia") to emphasize further the pictured geographical centrality of the state: "comprehending the whole of VIRGINIA, MARYLAND, DELAWARE, and PENNSYLVANIA, with parts of several other of the United States of America," the map "exhibit[ed] the country between Albemarle Sound and Lake Erie." This singular method of regional definition was not replicated by any early national cartographer, as the Mason-Dixon line quickly became the conventional subdivider of the United States map.

It is unsurprising that Jefferson did not subscribe to the notion of a cohesive "South" emerging in 1780s print, for intellectual and cultural historians of the southern states generally have agreed that their residents did not self-identify as "southerners" particularly allied to one another until the rise of sectionalist politics around 1820.[11] It is true that, in a perhaps too-often-quoted letter of 1785 to the Marquis de Chastelleux, Jefferson himself recapitulated the North/South distinction familiar to European observers of North America. Dealing in already conventional stereotype, he asserted that two distinct and dissonant national characters resided within the U.S. borders: from Pennsylvania north, the people were "cool, sober, laborious, independent, jealous of their own liberties, and just to those of others, interested, chicaning, and superstitious and hypocritical in their religion," while from Maryland south, the people were "fiery, voluptuary, indolent, unsteady, jealous for their own liberties, but trampling on those of others, generous, candid, and without attachment or pretensions to any religion but that of the heart." This sense of a proto-sectionalist, North/South bifurcation of the United States appeared as well at the Constitutional Convention of 1787. Here the major author of that founding document, James Madison, identified a North/South split as the chief impediment to strong national union: "The great danger to our general government *is the great southern and northern interests of the continent, being opposed to each other. Look to the votes in congress, and most of them stand divided by the geography of the country.*"[12]

But an essential distinction obtained between the nation-building activities of legislation and those of literary production, for the standing of the southern states and the relationship of South and nation differed significantly between the political and the cultural arenas. In the realm of politics—the army, the congresses, the constitutional debates—citizens of the northern and southern states met face-to-face in relatively equal numbers and on relatively equal footing. Not surprisingly, then, those involved in political processes tended to posit the problem of region as an equally weighted binary—North/South—as did the Virginians Jefferson and Madison in the quotes above. For the legislators of the new United States, the North/South disjuncture meant that the emergent nation resided not exclusively in one region or the other, but in a synthesis of the two terms; in order to create a unified nation, a negotiated balance had to be struck between the northern and the southern states. By contrast, the realm of literary nationalism involved far less exchange between citizens of the northern and southern states. Since American writers, printers, and readers shared Philadelphia-and-northward regional assumptions that remained largely unchallenged by the physical presence of southerners, those regional assumptions quickly assumed the stature of imaginative national norms. Specifically within the arena of cultural production, national character became synonymous with northern regional traits, and the divergence of the southern states from their northern counterparts increasingly signified their deviance from the nation writ large. The oppositional Plantation South construct of early national literature was, emphatically, a *literary* construct. As such, due to the geography of literary production in the early United States, the construct was imposed from without, rather than generated from within the actual southern states.

Jefferson's synecdochical Virginia, emerging idiosyncratically from a southern state, worked antithetically to the Plantation South construct, defining the new United States not by providing a foil to it but by expanding to encompass it fully. Readers of the *Notes* long have observed that in the opening two queries of the book—an account of the borders of the state and an account of its rivers—Jefferson irresistibly slid from straightforward reports of the limits of Virginia into a geographical conceptualization of continental scope.[13] In response to the query "An exact description of the limits and boundaries of the state of Virginia?" Jefferson carefully reported the current political boundaries of the state, reminding readers that Virginia was by far the largest of the thirteen United States and that it alone was indeed "one third larger than the islands of Great Britain and Ireland." To close the section, though, he pulled back historically and spatially to list schematically how the borders had come to be, reverting to the original imperial conception of "Virginia" as encompassing all of English North American settlement:

These limits result from, 1. The antient charters from the crown of England. 2. The grant of Maryland to the Lord Baltimore . . . 3. The grant of Pennsylvania to William Penn . . . 4. The grant of Carolina, and actual location of its northern boundary, by consent of both parties. 5. The treaty of Paris of 1763. 6. The confirmation of the charters of the neighbouring states by the convention of Virginia . . . 7. The cession made by Virginia to Congress of all the lands to which they had title on the North side of the Ohio.

Similarly, in response to the query on the rivers of Virginia, Jefferson began by enumerating the rivers within the current political borders of the state, but then once again pulled back to the former continental command of the colony of Virginia:

> The Missouri, since the treaty of Paris, the Illinois and Northern branches of the Ohio since the cession to Congress, are no longer within our limits. Yet having been so heretofore, and still opening to us channels of extensive communication with the western and north-western country, they shall be noted in their order . . . The country watered by the Missisipi and its eastern branches, constitutes five-eighths of the United States.[14]

Jefferson's Virginia thus appeared restricted only by the self-restraint of its citizens: by their "consent" to the claims of neighboring states, by their voluntary "cession" of territory to the larger national body. At the same time, the central location and historical dominance of Virginia within that new national body ensured its continuing "extensive communication" with an ever-expanding group of United States.

In defining the new nation as Virginia, Jefferson placed himself at odds with several emerging norms for U.S. cultural nationalism. Crèvecoeur and Paine joined the vast majority of contemporary literary nationalists in insisting upon a clear conceptual break between America's recent colonial past and new U.S. nationhood. To this end, they invoked the Plantation South as an icon of that past against which U.S. newness might be proved. Jefferson, by contrast, drew an intimate temporal connection between the colonial history of his metonymic Virginia and its present and future centrality in the independent United States, suggesting that Virginia's origin in the British empire was part of a nationalizing evolution into a more perfect "republican empire," or, in Jefferson's own famous oxymoron, "empire for liberty."[15] He also refused to subscribe to the paeans to development raised by his contemporaries. Against Paine's assurances that America from Philadelphia northward had evolved quite beyond its plantation function, Jefferson claimed Virginia's provinciality and peripheral production—the definitional underdevelopment of the Plantation South construct—as the most desirable economic identity for the new United States as a whole. Rather than excusing Virginia's underdevelopment, Jefferson lauded it, epigrammatically declaring in answer to the query on manufactures and commerce that national Virginians perpetually should "let our work-shops remain in Europe."[16] His Virginia spurned the metropolitan ambitions that elsewhere were synonymous with nationalist literary production.

Jefferson's synecdochical Virginia offered a profoundly novel literary take on U.S. nationalization, proposing both that an independent "republican empire" could emerge from previously subordinate colonial status and that self-determination and knowledge production could coexist with an assiduously maintained provinciality and peripherality. These proposals bear resemblance to the many paradoxes intellectual historians have identified at the heart of Jefferson's political thought—liberty and equality, universal natural rights and racism, self-restraint and infinite aggrandizement—paradoxes which generally have been seen as enormously enabling for U.S. national ideology.[17] But Jefferson's conceptualization of Virginia-*as-nation*—rather than as oppositional South—simply did not enter into American imaginative literature. Why this is the case might best be discerned by attending to the section of the *Notes* in which Jefferson approached nearest to the realm of fiction.

The query on "manners" provided Jefferson with a conventional eighteenth-century literary site for demarcating the form and extent of American national culture, for enumerating the standards of civility by which the independent people and nation could be judged amongst the powers of the earth.[18] This was the place for Jefferson to describe "the Virginian" as a national character, the counterpart to Crèvecoeur's Farmer James. Yet in this key chapter, Jefferson precipitously abandoned his nationalist boosterism, launching into the most apocalyptic diatribe against Anglo-American slavery he ever penned. For the problem of the plantation for American nationality—as Jefferson knew perhaps more intimately than his literary counterparts from Philadelphia northward—was not simply the problem of the new nation's colonial past and infant independence, nor was it the problem of America's subordinate, peripheral place in the world economy. The problem of the plantation was that continuing crime against humanity intrinsic to national emergence: the sin of slavery not thrown off with nationalization but calculatingly and avariciously pursued for the present and future enrichment and aggrandizement of the United States. Here, finally, was the proof of British colonial origin that Jefferson could not co-opt into a positive good for his metonymically Virginian United States.

"There must doubtless be an unhappy influence on the manners of our people produced by the existence of slavery among us," he begins. "The whole commerce between master and slave is a perpetual exercise of the most boisterous passions, the most unremitting despotism on the one part, and degrading submissions on the other." Immediately Jefferson, following John Locke's conception of slavery as a state of war, has divided the population of Virginia into two intrinsically antagonistic classes.[19] He momentarily identifies himself with the planter class, using the first person plural to observe that "our children" are under slavery "nursed, educated, and daily exercised in tyranny" and thus that the character of the Virginian master class "cannot but be stamped by [slavery] with odious peculiarities." He then goes on to enumerate the equally "odious" effects of slavery on the character of the Virginian slave class, focusing on their "transform[ation] . . . into enemies" of the state as the laws of the land "destroy" their natural "amor patriæ." Locked into the master/slave binary, Jefferson distances himself from both classes, reverting to the third person: "With the morals of the people, their industry is also destroyed. For in a warm climate, no man will labour for himself who can make another labour for him." The "mass of cultivators" of Jefferson's paean to republican farming has completely disappeared from the bifurcated character of his Virginia plantation; at the same time, the determining influence of a tropical American climate—which Jefferson previously has refuted in his dismissal of Buffon and Raynal—intrudes once again on the scene. The only national narrative possible, given this southern setting and this cast of masters and slaves, then relentlessly unfolds:

> Indeed I tremble for my country when I reflect that God is just: That his justice cannot sleep for ever: that considering numbers, nature and natural means only, a revolution of the wheel of fortune, an exchange of situation, is among possible events: that it may become probable by supernatural interference! The Almighty has no attribute which can take side with us in such a contest.[20]

These are the characters, and this is the narrative, that Jefferson's Virginia ultimately offers to the literature of the United States.

Raynal himself could not have done better. Indeed, Jefferson's sui generis image of the unfinished "present revolution" in America echoes Raynal's contemporaneous observation that "if [the Americans] ceased at once from having Negroes for slaves, *and* kings who live at a distance from them for masters, they would become perhaps the most remarkable people on earth."[21] Jefferson's image of a wheel of "revolution" that has only half turned with American colonial independence, and would fully turn only with "a total emancipation . . . with the consent of the masters, [or] by their extirpation," certainly was not taken up by his contemporary nationalist writers as a central narrative of United States emergence, just as Virginian planters and slaves did not become the protagonists of that narrative.[22]

Against the climatic determinism of European imperial natural history, Jefferson had developed a proto-sociological analysis of the legal crime against humanity that simultaneously undermined and underwrote the political project of the United States.[23] This was, truly, an alternative model of U.S. nationalism, one which forthrightly stated, "Indeed I tremble for my country when I reflect that God is just." Jefferson's Virginia eschewed Crèvecoeur's exculpatory use of "there"; it did not displace, but rather confronted the paradoxes and hypocrisies of the slaveholding republic. But in this regard, *Notes on the State of Virginia* remains an anomaly of early national literature. Virginia would become not a home for national narrative but a site of "peculiarities" that were coming to be seen as definitionally southern. The model of nationalism Jefferson offered in his query on manners remains almost entirely illegible as such, so far removed is it from dominant registers of U.S. innocence and righteousness.

Standardizing Southern Deviance: The Geographies of Webster and Morse

Jefferson had hoped to have his *Notes* distributed as a textbook to students at the College of William and Mary. Perhaps unsurprisingly, that never happened. Taking control of the education of the youth of the new nation, though, was indeed a prime patriotic concern for U.S. writers and publishers in the 1780s. The immediate post-Revolution years saw the writing and publication of those nationalist textbooks that *did* find a place on the shelves at William and Mary, at "Mr. Jefferson's University" in Charlottesville, and at colleges and schools across the thirteen states. In the *Grammatical Institute of the English Language* (1784–1787) and the *American Universal Geography* (1789–1793), Noah Webster and Jedidiah Morse diverged from Jefferson's insistence upon direct local observation, organizing their multivolume tomes around the far more familiar encyclopedic survey of the entire United States. Their presentation of instruction in the history, "manners," and economic and cultural attainments of the nation on a state-by-state basis met with immediate success. Both textbooks were printed throughout the United States and remained standards in classrooms and homes well into the 1820s. In the narrative process of creating a national geographic survey, though, both authors—Webster from the vantage of New Haven and Morse from Boston—developed systematic and ostensibly objective accounts of a Plantation South differentiated from the rest of the United States: cohesive, internal to the national political borders, antithetical to national developmental aims, and key to national identity in complex ways ranging from opposition to displacement.[24] Examining these textbooks reveals an overt formalization of the Plantation South construct in the years during which the Constitution was written, debated, and ratified. From the perspective of literary history, too, Webster's and Morse's were the textbooks that educated the first several generations of U.S. novelists.

Like their contemporaries, Webster and Morse vociferously urged the decolonization of American minds through home-grown knowledge production. "Till within a few years, we have seldom pretended to write, and hardly to think for ourselves," Morse opened his textbook. "We have humbly received from Great Britain, our manners, our books, and our modes of thinking; and our youth have been educated, rather as the subjects of the British king, than as the citizens of a free and independent Republic."[25] To continue to read accounts of America compiled by European authors who "too often suffer fancy to supply the place of facts" would be "to instill into the minds of Americans, British ideas of America, which are far from being favorable or just." With his *American Universal Geography,* Morse asserted domestic control over the production of self-knowledge for U.S. readers. As well, he radically shifted the terrain of "useful knowledge" itself, reversing the classic center-periphery organization of British textbooks: he anchored his seventeen-hundred-page tome in a lengthy opening description of the United States and then "expunge[d] what was judged of no importance to Americans," going on to number Europe as just one among the continents that made up "the rest of the world."[26]

Noah Webster similarly strove to shift not only the production of knowledge but also the very terrain of knowledge itself, from Britain to the United States. (Webster is, after all, best remembered for his campaign to differentiate a decolonized "American" language by purging English of its Englishness.) By way of promoting his *Grammatical Institutes,* Webster proposed that Europe as a subject had nothing good to teach American nationals, that "sending young gentlemen to Europe" would only cause them to "view curiosities and learn vices and follies." Instead, the new United States should comprise the chief subject of study for its youthful inhabitants: "A tour thro [sic] the United States ought now to be considered as a necessary part of a liberal education," he proposed. "Let them spend twelve or eighteen months in examining the local situation of the different States—the rivers, the soil, the population, the improvements and commercial advantages of the whole; with an attention to the spirit and manners of the inhabitants, their laws, social customs, and institutions."[27] Such a tour, in virtual form, was precisely what Webster and Morse offered in their voluminous textbooks.

The most popular textbook authors of the early republic thus continued to work within the imperial accounting form familiar from European descriptions of the American hemisphere and the globe, even as they attempted radically to shift its alignment of center and periphery. Webster's and Morse's continued dependence upon this inherited form seems to have been dictated at least in part by the problem of federation or union, which posed the greatest challenge to U.S. nationalism in the years between the 1783 Treaty of Paris and the 1789 ratification of the Constitution. From the close of the war for independence, enthusiasm about the huge territorial extent of the new United States was tempered by a corresponding fear, based in eighteenth-century climatic determinism, that so diverse lands and peoples as those in the northern and southern extremes of the new nation could never coexist in a single governmental body. The fear was not without ground: observers in London before the Revolutionary War cited the North/South distinctions on the North American mainland as proof that those colonies could never pull off a united rebellion; and a number of intellectual historians of the period have opined that Massachusetts had more in common with Nova Scotia, and South Carolina with Barbados, than either colony had in common with the other at the outbreak of the Revolutionary War.[28] While political leaders of the fledgling nation posed the problem of federation as one requiring legislative compromise, writers like Webster and Morse posed the problem of federation as an issue of education that could be solved by proper literary production and consumption. "[I]ndependence and union," Webster wrote, "render it necessary that the citizens of different States should know each others [sic] characters and circumstances—that all jealousies should be removed—that mutual respect and confidence should succeed—and a harmony of views and interests be cultivated by a friendly intercourse."[29] The geographical surveys ordering both Webster's and Morse's textbooks fit precisely this nationalist purpose. Both writers ostentatiously displayed their sensitivities to the regional jealousies of Confederation-era politics by dividing their surveys into thirteen superficially egalitarian sections of relatively equal length and by treating the states—as Morse put it—"in their order."

But this "order"—inevitably north to south, New Hampshire to Georgia—was hardly dictated by nature. True to its imperial origins, the survey form Webster and Morse borrowed for self-definition of the United States entailed not just inclusiveness but also hierarchy. These authors intervened in the traditional center-periphery hierarchy of British textbooks by placing the United States first in their accounts; but at the same time, by beginning with New England, they embedded a North/South hierarchy within their descriptions that replicated the global core-periphery split on a domestic scale. When Webster, for instance, began his survey at the northernmost limit of the United States, he presented New Hampshire, Massachusetts, Rhode Island, and Connecticut as the national norm. Logically, then, his descriptions of those states fell entirely within the codes of metropolitan status, comprising accounts of cities with numbers of houses and inhabitants, descriptions of fine buildings and public spaces, notices of colleges with numbers of professors and students, and so on. New England's colonial origins; its continued semi-peripheral economy; its tenuously developing commercial centers—all such matters of historical transition disappeared in Webster's account of New England as nationalist baseline. In summarizing his Connecticut section, Webster even claimed that the northernmost states were populated by a people who would admit of no creolization, no "admixture" or degeneration, but who replicated the purity of a European national center: "The inhabitants of New-England are mostly the descendants of the first English settlers. There are no French, Dutch, Germans . . . The increase, almost solely by natural population, including Vermont, is almost a million of whites."[30] *New England* was, in Webster's account, precisely that: an independent, metropolitan center sprung fully formed on American shores.

The opening of Webster's geographical survey provides an example of the "sweeping amnesia about colonialism" that Michael Warner has identified as central to early U.S. culture. Reading forward in Webster's textbook, though—or indeed, reading *southward*—provides some insight into how "Americans learned to think of themselves as living in an immemorial nation."[31] As Webster conducted his readers south of Connecticut, evidence of the recent American colonial past crept into his state-by-state accounts. While he continued to focus his descriptions of the middle states on their urban and civic features, Webster started (beginning with New York) meticulously to document the heterogeneity of the population of each state, and (beginning with Pennsylvania) to introduce the plantation function of producing "staple commodities" as a category of record. The marked break came when Webster reached Maryland, though, at which point he entirely exchanged the metropolitan digest of his New England chapters for accounts of a completely peripheral Plantation South. "Staple Commodities" became the major category of his southern chapters, bloated with statistics of hogsheads produced, weights shipped, and export market locations. At the same time, he totally abandoned the category "Cities and Towns," which had made up the bulk of the New England chapters, with the cursory remark that south of Philadelphia "the towns are not large; the people mostly residing on their plantations." Extraordinarily enough, this meant that Webster did not provide systematic descriptions even of major southern cities like Baltimore and Charleston. Indeed, in the five southern chapters of his geographic survey he seemed as intent upon repressing or dismissing metropolitan markers as he was careful to purge traces of coloniality or peripherality from his opening New England chapters. Thus, "large and elegant houses" in Annapolis became, in an echo of Crèvecoeur's Peruvian streets of gold, "an indication of the great wealth of planters." A college founded in Charleston, on the other hand, simply became an occasion for Webster to note that southern Creoles still relied upon metropolitan education, for "[g]entlemen, however, both in Carolina and the other southern states, send their sons to Princeton college, or other northern universities; and some to Europe."[32]

Reading southward in Webster's geographic survey became a process of watching national independence and metropolitan development evaporate. To read southward was to read backward into the recent colonial past of the new United States—that colonial past neatly epitomized by the plantation. Jedidiah Morse systemized this pattern more dogmatically in his *American Universal Geography,* which opened by dividing the United States into "THREE GRAND DIVISIONS"—"New England," "the Middle States," and "the Southern States"—placed in a North/South hierarchical "order." Like Webster, Morse presented New England as plainly "the *first* Grand Division," the location of U.S. nationality, and in this opening section of the textbook he assiduously avoided the (usually negative) speculations about connections between environment and human development typical in European geographic surveys of America. In the New England chapters, Morse studiously converted matters of climate, landform, and natural resources into findings about social organization, development, and cultural production—as when he used the traditional heading "Climate and Diseases" to laud the republican classlessness of New England society: "as far as excess or want of wealth may prove destructive or salutary to life, the inhabitants [of Connecticut] may plead exemption from diseases."[33]

Upon leaving Connecticut for "the Middle States," though, Morse suddenly asserted the determining influence of climate, defining these states as poised between temperate and tropical climes, and thus between metropolitan and colonial status:

> On the whole it appears that the climate of this division of the United States is a compound of most of the climates in the world. It has the moisture of Ireland in the spring—the heat of Africa in summer—the temperature of Italy in June . . . the tempests (in a certain degree) of the West Indies in every season, and the variable winds and weather of Great Britain in every month in the year.

Morse joined Webster, though, in finding that these states had more in common with the national normativity of New England than with the deviance of "the Southern States"; summarily, he concluded that "the climate of this Grand Division, lying almost in the same latitudes, varies but little from that of New England."[34] While from their shared New England perspective, both Morse and Webster discerned taints of the Plantation South as far north as the state of New York, they joined authors from the middle states in locating the strong intranational division at the Mason-Dixon line. Morse even used the two fold-out maps he commissioned for the first full edition of the *American Universal Geography* to illustrate this intranational split. The first map presented the first two "Grand Divisions" of the United States as a consolidated national whole; the second map (reproduced at the opening of the next chapter) quarantined the five "Southern States" on their own separate page. Although the sloppy inaccuracy of both maps was roundly condemned by cartographers in 1789 and thereafter, Morse kept them in subsequent editions of his textbook, and they became some of the most often reproduced national maps of the early republic—which suggests that the schematic separation of the southern states from the larger national body proved a useful or compelling way of visualizing the nation in its first decades.[35]

For Morse, holding "the Southern States" apart from the national body was useful first of all for quarantining the problematic persistence of slavery in the new republic. "This district of the Union contained in 1790 . . . *thirteen-fourteenths* of the whole number of slaves in the United States," he informed his readers by way of introducing the "Third Grand Division" of the nation. The state-by-state chapters in this last section of the textbook took Morse's readers ever more deeply into an ominous Plantation South redolent of American colonial origins. In the chapter on Maryland, he remarked that the creolized population was so heterogenous—"made up of various nations and of many different religious sentiments"—that no "characteristical observations" were possible: Marylanders shared no distinguishing traits as a people. But the white population of the state did share colonial incivility and despotism as "visible characteristics": they were "unsocial" because "the inhabitants live on their plantations, often several miles distant from each other," and at the same time were "habituated" to "that pride which grows on slavery." Proceeding southward into Virginia, Morse proclaimed that that state not only had failed to progress since national independence but had degenerated in comparison with its days under the British Empire: the colonial capital, Williamsburg, was "going to decay" and "little better than in ruins," while Hampden Sydney College, which "ha[d] been a flourishing seminary" before the war, was "now said to be on the decline."[36]

Crossing into North Carolina, Morse seemed to express doubt that this part of the United States had ever been successfully settled by the British in the first place. A life-sapping climate caused "the countenances of the inhabitants" to "have generally a pale yellowish cast" with "very little of the bloom and freshness of the people in the northern states." These sickly North Carolinians, "mostly planters," had so "wasted [their time] in drinking, idling, and gambling" that they had failed to "improve their plantations or their minds," which had, "like an unweeded garden, been suffered to shoot up in wild disorder." Consequently, the history of the state remained "unpublished, and of course unknown." In South Carolina and Georgia, finally, Morse painted a picture of static tropical precivility unimproved even by British colonial standards. "The Carolinians" were essentially overgrown children, "sooner arriv[ing] at maturity, both in their bodies and minds, than the natives of colder climates," and incapable of "pay[ing] attention to manufactures or other improvements."[37]

The extremity of these accounts of southern deviance—particularly coming, as they did, in the guise of an objective survey of the national landscape—did not go unremarked, or unprotested, by Webster's and Morse's contemporaries. The Philadelphian editors of the *Columbian Magazine*, for instance, berated Webster for months in 1790 and 1791 for continuing to make "splenetic observations respecting the southern states, while not a *single good quality* is attributed to them."[38] Morse's *American Universal Geography* inspired entire pamphlets published in protest. In an open "letter" to Morse, a "citizen of Williamsburg" took the account of his home state as a personal insult. A fellow Bostonian "disgusted" by Morse's "gross misrepresentations" and "illiberal invectives against the southern states in general" offered a 62-page point-by-point enumeration of errors and prejudicial statements in the 1793 revised edition of the textbook. Morse's Bostonian detractor closed his critique of the *American Universal Geography* by imagining a shift in the geography of literary production within the United States: "Should any person at the southward undertake a new American Geography, I hope the spirit of retaliation will not lead him to paint [New England's] faults in too glowing colours. We supplicate for mercy!"[39] But of course, such a structural shift in the location of U.S. literary production never took place, and Webster's and Morse's textbooks remained for decades the available standards for nationalist education across the United States. Webster campaigned to have his *Grammatical Institute* officially adopted for schools in even the southernmost state, Georgia; and by 1802, Morse's *American Universal Geography* was being printed down the coast all the way to Savannah.[40] For young people living in the southern states as well as all other parts of the United States, a fundamental part of the new standardized nationalist education was a lesson in southern deviance.

From the moment that American independence was conceptualized, through the first decade of national existence, U.S. cultural nationalists converted their persistent past into an othered place. The cohesive Plantation South, differentiated from the larger idea of the United States, arose in the earliest U.S. literary writings as a site of spatial quarantine for two interrelated temporal concerns: the colonial origins of the nation, disavowed equally by ideologies of "newness" and "immemoriality"; and the uninterrupted, indeed calculatingly pursued, centrality of plantation production to American ascendance—a form of production in its bald exploitativeness antithetical to every ideal expressed in the Declaration of Independence, and in its peripherality contrary to all nationalist assertions of development and self-sufficiency. This is to say that the Plantation South emerged from the very beginning of literary production in the United States as a key *chronotope* for U.S. nationalization: as Mikhail Bakhtin defined the term, "the intrinsic connectedness of temporal and spatial relationships that are artistically expressed in literature." Particularly in moments when prose writers stand at "the boundary line between two epochs," Bakhtin proposed, "there are frequent attempts to resolve, so to speak, historical contradictions 'along the vertical'; attempts to deny the essential thought-shaping power of 'earlier' or 'later,' that is, to deny temporal divisions and linkages" by narrating movement through space in place of movement through time.[41] By writing the Plantation South, the first U.S. authors transmuted American coloniality into an externalized place, rather than an internalized inheritance.

It is obvious that early national writers were surrounded, quite literally, by an entire hemisphere that was indeed still colonized by European powers, so their tendency to situate the American colonial past *within* the borders of the United States can appear somewhat puzzling. Early national writers could—and did—define the nationalizing United States against the still-colonial West Indies, against Spanish America, and against the western North American frontier.[42] All of these locations, since they were fully external to the founding political borders of the new United States, allowed for neater nationalist self-definition. But only the Plantation South located the immediate American colonial past within the national borders, siting it as a geographical term intrinsic to the very existence of the United States. As an internal other for the new United

States, the Plantation South necessarily bore with it an ideological instability precarious for propaganda, but fertile for the imaginative work of
nationalization. Its value for emergent national literature lay precisely in
the paradox of simultaneous identification and disidentification, in the simultaneous ownership and disavowal of the gap between material reality
and rhetorical ideal in the early United States. To define the United States
in opposition to its Plantation South, early national writers were well
aware, was to preserve an edge of self-critique in the most vociferous self-
exoneration. To revel in southern deviance was to invite contamination
of national righteousness. In the story of the United States just beginning
to be written, the Plantation South could be cordoned off on a map, or
segregated in a chapter, but it was still, undeniably, a part of the book.

CHAPTER THREE

Domestic Possession and the Imperial Impulse

The southern and western parts of North-America are peopled
with as vicious, luxurious, mean-spirited and contemptible a race
of beings, as any that ever blackened the pages of infamy . . .
This concise, but very just account of them must necessarily
convince us that the moment our interest demands it, *these
extensive regions will be our own.*

>   —The Rev. Dr. Timothy Dwight,
>   "Valedictory Address . . . at Yale College, July 25th, 1776,"
>   reprinted in the *American Magazine* (1787)

B Y WRITING THE PLANTATION SOUTH into being, early national authors turned the east-west axis of Anglo-American empire
(London-America) 90 degrees, and reinscribed it as a north-
south juxtaposition (United States-Plantation South). Rather than wholly
rejecting or refuting European imperial definitions of America—as did
Jefferson in his *Notes on the State of Virginia*—writers in the early republic far more commonly accepted those imperial constructs as correctly descriptive of the vast majority of the New World, claiming only that the
states north of Maryland provided an exception to them.[1] To trace the
emergence and evolution of the Plantation South in early national literature is to observe a mode of post-colonial geographical imagination
through which writers sought not only to order the new nation internally
but also to fix its relative global place and status. Defining the emerging
United States against its Plantation South enabled early national writers
both to exorcise established British definitions of North America as colonial possession, and to reinscribe those definitions on the southern states
as internal other, held apart from the national whole. In so doing, they
imaginatively aligned "the United States" with the capitals of Europe, and
"the Plantation South" with the rest of the colonized American hemisphere, and indeed the rest of the world.

   The domestic Plantation South quickly became the prime point of connection between the United States and the larger globe for the authors of
early national literature. As a link to the foreign and colonized remainder
of the American hemisphere, the Plantation South became a prime gate-

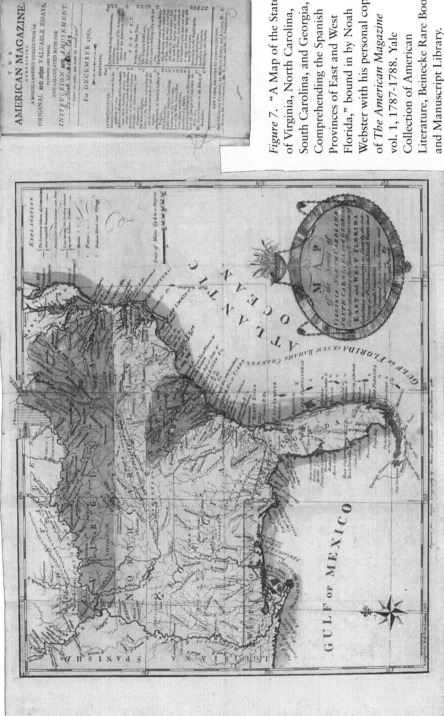

Figure 7. "A Map of the States of Virginia, North Carolina, South Carolina, and Georgia, Comprehending the Spanish Provinces of East and West Florida," bound in by Noah Webster with his personal copy of *The American Magazine* vol. 1, 1787-1788. Yale Collection of American Literature, Beinecke Rare Book and Manuscript Library.

way not only for looking backward but also for looking forward. By gazing southward in their mind's eyes, U.S. writers envisioned the expansion of a putatively imperial United States across the continent and beyond. Noah Webster highlighted this role for the Plantation South when he prepared the first volume of his New York–based *American Magazine* (1787–1788) for posterity.[2] As he assembled the twelve monthly issues, annotating them copiously and with great credit to himself, he rather surprisingly chose to give pride of place to the much-maligned map of his textbook-writing competitor, Jedidiah Morse. Webster bound in the second map from Morse's *American Universal Geography*—the one that segregated the southern states from the national body—as his frontispiece. At six times the size of the octavo magazine, the map made a stunning accompaniment to Webster's volume, and all the more so because he had it colored in a warm yellow-green color palette that evoked southern fertility and tropicality.[3]

But why on earth choose an iconic image of the Plantation South as emblem for his nationalist literary venture? Webster appears to have paired the lavishly embellished map with the central textual item in the first two issues of his magazine, Timothy Dwight's July 1776 "Valedictory Address" to Yale College graduates. That address was over a decade old when Webster made it the launching point for his postwar literary magazine, but he clearly was drawn to Dwight's vision of the nascent United States as "the greatest empire the hand of time ever raised up to view."[4] Dwight's assurance that American nationalization involved not only throwing off coloniality, but also taking up empire, rested upon a particular conceptualization of the relationship between the rising United States and its Plantation South—a conceptualization that we may then see reflected in Morse's map, which was on its way to becoming canonical in schoolrooms throughout the early republic.

Like George Washington in his more famous "Circular Letter" of 1783, Dwight envisioned the independent American nation in continental terms, hampered not at all by "the narrow bounds of the present age," but inexorably expanding. As Washington put it, citizens of the United States should glory in their destined "most enviable condition, as the sole lords and proprietors of a vast tract of continent, comprehending all the various soils and climates of the world."[5] But this triumphantly projected scope for the new nation provoked worry, too, for how would a republican form of government work across a realm of such imperial scope? Regional diversity, both economic and cultural, was to be feared, for, as Dwight put it, "contending interests ever exist with disputes, and end in war," while "difference of manners, as we are naturally and fondly at-

tached to our own, cannot but occasion coldness, contempt and ill-will."
Washington, a Virginian and a political leader, urged voluntary compromise to solve regional dissonances; for Dwight, a Connecticut native and
a cultural nationalist, compromise was not an option. Dwight felt that
American nationality resided in his own immediate environs and that any
divergence from the norms of his own place was a deviation from the national project. Thus while the future president of the United States urged
consenting residents of every state *"to forget . . . local prejudices and
policies, to make those mutual concessions which are requisite to the general prosperity,"* the future president of Yale College proposed a quite different plan for expansion and consolidation.[5]

Dwight's vision of the imperial glory of the United States rested centrally upon his imaginative conflation of the internal other of the nation
(the southern states) with its immediate external surround (the Spanish
North American dominions). A vast Plantation South, extending south
and southwest of his own quasi-metropolitan location, reeked of tropical
and colonial decadence and invited inevitable domination by the rising
United States:

> The southern and western parts of North-America . . . are peopled with as
> vicious, luxurious, mean-spirited and contemptible a race of beings, as any
> that ever blackened the pages of infamy. Generally descended from the re-
> fuse of mankind, situated in a hot, wealthy, and plentiful country, and edu-
> cated from their infancy under the most shocking of all governments, . . .
> can we wonder that they . . . are tainted with all the vices and blots of their
> parent nation, increased and deepened by a multitude of their own?[6]

While Dwight ostensibly was speaking of Spanish America, his diatribe
operated at the intersection between the anti-Spanish deployment of the
Black Legend and imperial representations of tropical America writ large.
To the south and southwest of the United States *proper* lay a depraved,
degenerate, and static Plantation South, flaunting every marker of American coloniality. This South was characterized by its creolized population (its "contemptible" and "blackened" "race") and its all-determining
tropical climate (the "hot, wealthy, and plentiful country"). It was organized around an exploitative hierarchy, antithetical to the republic,
and tacitly based on slavery: compare Dwight's colonialists "educated
from their infancy under the most shocking of all governments," to Jefferson's Virginians "nursed, educated, and daily exercised in tyranny."
And this South had come into being from an ignominious colonial origin;
Dwight's charge that southern and western colonists were "descended
from the refuse of mankind" resonated with accounts by his contem-

poraries of the ignoble Virginia Company and the debtor colony of Georgia.

Irrevocably shaped by history and environment, inhabitants of Dwight's broad Plantation South exhibited both the tyrannical "vices and blots" of their European parents and the degeneracy of colonial subservience. Their proper relationship to the rising United States thus easily was discerned.

> This concise, but very just account of them must necessarily convince us that the moment our interest demands it, *these extensive regions will be our own;* that the present race of inhabitants will either be entirely exterminated, or revive to the native human dignity, by the generous and beneficent influence of just laws and rational freedom. A distinction therefore between them and ourselves, in the present consideration of the necessary, future greatness of the Western World, will be useless and impertinent.[7]

A righteous possession of territory ("extensive," warm, and desirable) and righteous "extermination" or forced assimilation of its inhabitants: Dwight founded both of these mandates for United States empire upon the tropical and colonial deviance of an American Plantation South that was both internal and external—mingling domestic and foreign in proportion to distance from the national center—beginning in the heart of the present political borders of the nation but expanding ever outward into an illimitable future. While he concluded that this deviant South had no place in "the necessary, future greatness of the Western World," his preceding impassioned invective belied such a unilateral dismissal: "the future greatness" of an imperial United States would be built precisely upon the key "distinction between them and ourselves."

Webster's pairing of Dwight's address with Morse's map caused a new element of the frontispiece to come to the fore. Not only did the map hold the "Grand Division of the Southern States" apart from the rest of the United States, but it also illustrated the first expansion of the national borders, delineating the cession of a sliver of West Florida to the United States by Spain in 1783. By "[e]xhibiting the boundaries as fixed by the late Treaty of Peace between the United States and the Spanish Dominions," the map proved that the fledgling United States was an empire among empires, negotiating upon equal terms with, and indeed besting, the oldest of European powers. And by "[c]omprehending the Spanish Provinces of East and West Florida," the map mandated further expansion for the new nation, for including the remaining and isolated "Spanish Provinces" on the page with current U.S. territory made their acquisition appear a foregone conclusion. The imperial mandate of the map was enlarged most of all, though, by including the southern states all the way to Maryland in this illustration of territorial expansion and possession. Tropically colored and laid out in all their vaunted expansiveness, the exotic, enormous and far-off reaches of the new United States became accessible—literally grasp-able in their totality—for each of Webster's readers who held his *American Magazine* in their hands.

Through his compilation of Dwight's address with Morse's map, Web-ster generated a sort of imaginative ownership of the domestic Plantation South—which was already, of course, "comprehended" by the United States—as an affirming foothold for destined future dominions. Morse himself had performed a similar sleight of hand in his textbook by group-ing the "Spanish Dominions in North America" under the subheading of the "Third [Southern] Grand Division of the United States."[8] This move elucidated his seemingly oxymoronic title, *American Universal Geography:* Morse's impressionistic linking of Plantation South zones within and without the national borders produced a domestic geography of the United States with apparently limitless expansionist—"universal"—applications.

The blatant imperial impulse in early U.S. nationalism should come as no surprise when we consider seriously the ambition of the new nation, as stated in the Declaration of Independence, "to assume, among the powers of the earth, [a] separate and equal station."[9] Gaining both sepa-rate and *equal* standing among European nations required not only inde-pendence from, but also approximation of, European empire: the possession of colonies, the possession of vast tropic or subtropic regions, the possession of slaves and of plantations built on their labor from which the nation drew its wealth. Writing the Plantation South in early national literature met this imperative of nationalization by providing U.S. readers with precisely that imaginative dominion, that possession of colonies, from the outset of national existence. Indeed, this imaginative strategy was quite clearly perceived by European observers, who as-sumed that the independent United States should naturally exercise do-minion over its subtropical realms, if only (or especially) in the realm of culture. British cartographers, for instance, commonly labeled their maps of the five southern states in the 1780s and 1790s as illustrations of the "southern provinces" or "dominions" "belonging to the United States of America."[10]

At this nexus between domestic possession and imperial ambition, a different relationship between the nation and its Plantation South emerged. No longer just a term to be disavowed and declared other, the Plantation South quickly became a term to be *owned* as well. This development appears strikingly in analyses of the first United States census, for instance when the *New-York Magazine* described the "Present State of the Nation" in 1790:

> Population of the United States, Whites, 3,300,000 Blacks 700,000 . . . The whole territory of the United States is 1,000,000 square miles . . . [O]ur present territory in possession, may be computed at five hundred thousand square miles . . . 700,000 slaves may be valued at 75,000,000.[11]

This nationalist author founded his proof of the stature and strength of the United States equally upon an inevitable expansion of borders that would double "our present territory in possession," and upon a claim that the nation rightfully possessed every black person residing within those borders—at a monetary value of $107.14 each. Owning the Plantation South meant "owning" in the sense not only of *possession* but also of *confession*. To glory in the lucrativeness of "southern dominions" was to come perilously near admitting all of the denied qualities of the Plantation South, foremost among them the national sin of slavery.

Owning the South in the Literary Magazines

This ideologically multivalent Plantation South, the internal other of American nationalization, first took shape as a site for fiction in the literary magazines that arose by the dozens along the Philadelphia-to-Boston corridor in the 1790s. As the element of literature through which "historical reality is assimilated into the poetic image," Bakhtin's chronotope is "the place where the knots of narrative are tied and untied"—and the Plantation South emerged as a particularly knotty chronotope, looking both backward and forward, containing both the disavowed colonial dependence and the projected imperial dominion of the nationalizing United States.[12] This complexity perhaps explains the excess of repetitious, schematic short pieces addressing the Plantation South that proliferated in the literary magazines across the decade. In the sheer accretion of these pieces—both original and culled from other publications, and ranging in genre from essay to book review to poem to story—the Plantation South became fixed as a stable, well-defined, and easily recognizable term. As a physical setting, the Plantation South was disease-ridden, swampy, and inimical to animal and human development. As a social setting, it had been founded for colonial profit and thus developed into a cradle of iniquity, aristocracy, and luxury. As a source for characterization, it was home to a drunken, lascivious, lazy, gluttonous, and violent cast of degenerate planters.

This primal alienation of the Plantation South from the national idea in the 1790s magazines corresponded to the real and increasing alienation of the southern states from the consolidating, centralizing national core. With ratification of the Constitution by all thirteen states at the turn of the decade came an implicit popular sanction of federal centralization, which both endorsed the de facto centralization of U.S. print production and made the perceived deviance of the Plantation South from the norms of that center seem all the more damnable. As well during the 1790s, the total wealth production of the northern states equaled and then surpassed that of the southern states for the first time in the history of North America, which meant both that the dependence of the nation as a whole on the staple commodity production of the southern states was lessened and that the material core of the nation increasingly was aligned with its representational center in a powerful and affirming conjunction.[13] Creation of a domestic literature in the United States, in turn, depended materially upon this emergence of an integrated national core, this emergence of a new economic order in the Western hemisphere.[14]

Writers of the era recognized production of imaginative literature as itself an important facet of nationalization, since late eighteenth-century cultural nationalism held that a distinct national literature was a primary marker of nationhood. Because a national literary tradition was linked so firmly to metropolitan status, aspiring U.S. nationalists cited literature as the next front in the nation-from-colony struggle of the infant United States, an opportunity to purge any last remnants of colonial origin from the new nation. Charles Brockden Brown, the most prolific novelist of the period, put forth a typical cultural-nationalist analysis of the stakes of literary development in his own *Monthly Magazine:*

> Perhaps it may be said that the American character, making allowance for its youth, ranks with the most respectable and dignified on the globe. But I acknowledge that my pleasure in contemplating our national character, is by no means without alloy . . . Almost all learned foreigners remark that THE LITERARY CHARACTER OF AMERICA IS EXTREMELY SUPERFICIAL . . . To this defect . . . so far as it is peculiar to America perhaps the following circumstance may have principally contributed: the love of gain, which, in a very remarkable degree, pervades the United States. Before the revolutionary war, this spirit was very prevalent, and much cultivated . . . To acquire property became the supreme and governing object; and the *sordid colonial character* was easily to be traced in almost every class of our citizens.[15]

Brown directly counterposed literary achievement—as the prime desideratum of assuming a "respectable and dignified" place among the "learned" nations of the world—with a *"sordid colonial character"* that conflated dependent political status and focus on wealth production. The relationship that Brown posits between literary achievement and "colonial character," even in opposition to one another, recalls postcolonial readings of British novels of his era, readings that see the novel in this period as opening an imaginative space for the colonial subconscious of the imperial metropole. If the late eighteenth-century British novel provided a vehicle through which writers explored the conditions of peripheral production that underwrote the development of the cultural capital, yet were only dimly visible there, Brown and his peers writing the first U.S. novels similarly confronted, even if only obliquely, the peripheral plantations and slave labor that had generated the wealth of the new nation.[16] They also confronted the broader American colonial context that conjured both their willfully forgotten recent past and their wishfully projected imperial future. Their Plantation South, as internal other and point of connection to both the past and the hemisphere, served as the necessary location on the imaginative terrain of early national fiction for both distancing the recently disavowed *"sordid colonial character"* of the United States, and mapping its feared points of residue, tangency, and return.

Certainly, the increasingly wild and derogatory short pieces on the southern states that flourished in the literary magazines of the 1790s exceeded the logic of nationalist geographical education. These profuse articles fell into three interrelated categories—the natural history, the colonial chronicle, and the character sketch—each of which represented a progressive move away from the realm of the avowedly objective and toward the realm of the fantastic. Natural history articles dealt ostensibly in provable scientific fact, while colonial chronicles offered short narratives of the origin and development of the southern states. Finally, and most protonovelistically, character sketches sought to typify the acts and motivations of (white, male, elite) southerners themselves. It is intriguing to note that in their rush to create American tropical tropes and types, magazine writers and editors proceeded quite contrarily to their usual cultural-nationalist methods: they privileged European over domestic American accounts of the southern states, and colonial-era over post-Revolutionary writings. In other words, literary magazine editors interested in portraying Virginia in their pages were far more likely to reprint passages from either Robert Beverley's 1705 *History and Present State of Virginia,* or from the Marquis de Chastellux's *Voyages dans l'Amerique septentrionale,* than from Jefferson's *Notes on the State of Virginia.*

This meant that natural history articles in the magazines largely accepted the conventional imperial alignment of fertileness with degeneration: the equation of the conditions of climate and soil that produced prized commodities, with truncated life spans and stunted development. Maintaining an established, inferior subtropical baseline in the southern states proved quite useful to the magazinists, for it afforded them a foil against which to assert a salubrious U.S. metropole in a hemisphere designated deadly, or at least degenerate. This pattern appeared notably in reviews of the first comparative natural history of the thirteen states written by a U.S. author, medical doctor William Currie's 1791 *Historical Account of the Climates and Diseases of the United States of America.* Currie's focus on the interaction between climate and disease operated precisely at the conventional intersection, inherited from Europe, between American environment and biological degeneration. He sought to sever that link for the northeastern states by demonstrating the equal (or indeed superior) healthfulness of the U.S. national center in comparison to the Old World. As the reviewer for the *Columbian Magazine* summarized, "We learn most essentially . . . that the cold of the northern states properly guarded against, produces but few diseases of a dangerous nature . . . And, from whatever causes it may proceed, the inhabitants, in the middle and particularly in the northern states enjoy a greater proportion of health, and live to a greater age than the inhabitants of Europe."[17]

As the specification here of "the middle and particularly . . . northern states" suggests, revising the findings of European natural histories of America, while retaining their method, required that Currie draw a clear line of demarcation corresponding to the Mason-Dixon. As the reviewer went on to note, the second half of Currie's study actually reinforced European assumptions about the "inconveniencies of the torrid zone" in the Western hemisphere: "[I]n proceeding to the southward in Maryland and Virginia, where the heat is more intense and of longer continuance, and the soil more moist, especially upon lands in an imperfect state of cultivation, the diseases are very prevalent, and often fatal." While this fairly measured indictment of the upper southern states proportioned their climatic inferiority to their peripheral plantation function ("imperfect cultivation"), a far more malevolent tropical extreme, unclassifiable and impenetrable, quickly sprang up in Currie's account: "In South-Carolina and Georgia, fevers and fluxes are still more epidemic, violent, and obstinate . . . very anomalous, neither intermitting nor remitting perfectly, but participating much of the nature of that commonly called the yellow fever, which is often so fatal within the tropics." The mention of yellow fever here highlights the act of displacement performed by both Currie's study and the précis of it compiled by the *Columbian Magazine,* for yellow fever was a dire concern at the time in Philadelphia, the site of production of both of these texts. The city saw several devastating epidemic episodes of the disease in the 1780s and 1790s, and while its medical men and natural historians alike vigorously debated the causes of the outbreaks, all agreed on one point: yellow fever was a disease of *tropical* America and thus necessarily must have been imported into Philadelphia from a southern source.[18]

The lurking fear that a Plantation South rife with tropical deviance could contaminate or overcome U.S. nationality appeared in the brief, meteoric popularity of doctor-poet Joseph Brown Ladd in the two years after his early death. A native Rhode Islander, Ladd had trained as a medical doctor, despaired of making his fortune in the northeast, and settled instead in Charleston, where he died at age twenty-two of wounds received in a duel.[19] Prominent Philadelphia publisher Matthew Carey, among others, began to print Ladd's poems shortly thereafter, featuring them in his *American Museum,* and Ladd's sudden and fleeting vogue seems to have been generated by the image he provided of an educated, cultured metropolitan destroyed by his venture into the violent and irrational Plantation South.[20] The poems Carey selected, from Ladd's output of several hundred pages, evoked a tropical dystopia, providing a belletristic companion to Currie's treatise on climate and disease. For instance, "Prospect of Carolina" began with a celebration of tropical warmth ("Lo! Wrapt in sun-shine all divinely bright, / Fair Carolina rises to the sight"), but quickly slid into the darker tropical connotations of swamp ("Unlike the northern beam, [the sun's] fervid glow / Pays fiercer courtship to the streams below; / Hence from each stagnant pool thick vapours rise") and fatality ("Taste not the air, for death is in the breeze, / And the whole hydra of abhorr'd disease").[21] Poems that presented a national speaker contemplating threatening southern tropicality made the inevitable dissolution of their author (always billed by Carey as "the late Dr. Ladd") all the more charged.

The sense that the tropical American climate of the southern states opposed the very existence of U.S. national citizens within their borders underwrote a number of experiments in climatic determinism on the part of magazine essayists. Writers became particularly enamored of comparative intranational population studies, making the sorts of speculations about the natural degeneration of southern populations that Jefferson had ridiculed, when applied to the hemisphere as a whole, in the work of Raynal and Buffon. Magazine writers most commonly dwelt upon the racial heterogeneity of the southern states by musing upon the proportions of black to white residents reported in the 1790 census; more ambitious commentators proposed that "even the first families of Virginia" had Indian or African "blood today flow[ing] in their veins."[22] Another popular theory held that "many gentlemen of learning and observation" believed that a hot climate engendered an "effeminacy of population." Thus the southern states—like "Syria, Egypt, Arabia, the African Coast" and other subtropical locales around the globe—were suspected to have developed a "great plurality of females," while the rest of the nation "enjoy[ed] that *natural superiority* of males to females."[23]

It was not only the natural history articles that held the southern states and their people apart from the national imagined community in the literary magazines. Colonial chronicles, too, established Plantation-South deviance—though as a product of history rather than of nature. In spare, schematic accounts, colonial chronicles retailed the founding conditions and principles of one or more of the thirteen colonies that had become the United States. In so doing, magazine essayists implied teleological narratives that both explained the present—how each state had come to assume the "particular complexion" it currently wore—and predicted the future—what role each state ought to play in shaping national destiny.[24] Comparative colonial chronicles typically juxtaposed a northern state, founded for ideals of equality or liberty, with a southern state, founded for commercial gain. "If the state of Pennsylvania is to be applauded for her conduct," ran a typical formulation, "that of South-Carolina can never be too strongly execrated."[25] Commentators then drew the conclusion that U.S. national independence had its origin in the northern colonies, while the southern states then and now invited only imperial mastery and deserved only colonial subservience.

For instance, Charles Brockden Brown turned a book review in his *Monthly Magazine* into a meditation on the way that the presumably extreme gulf between New England and Virginia had been established with their colonial foundations. "The differences which, at present, subsist between the political and economical condition of the two countries, are not greater than those which distinguished their origin," he began. Taking Europe as a baseline against which American development might be measured, Brown presented "the discovery and name of New-England" as "owing to a higher principle" than any previously imagined in human history: "[The colonists'] original ecclesiastical scheme approached nearer to the ideas of absolute equality among men, than any other; and this scheme, contrary to ordinary rules, has not essentially degenerated." By contrast, "the birth of Virginia" fell in the great chain of being far below European societies:

[Virginia] arose from the most perverse habits, and most sordid passions incident to man . . . The founders of Virginia were, for the most part, the refuse of their country, banished by their vices, or allured by their avarice to the New World, where they sifted the sands for gold, quarrelled and tormented each other, massacred the natives, or perished with famine. In time they learned the necessity of subordination . . . The birth of this state constitutes a diversified and humiliating tale.[26]

Brown's description here may easily be aligned, point by point, with Dwight's 1776 mobilization of the Black Legend of Spanish colonization: the colonial project is presented as mercenary and focused on extracting wealth rather than developing the land; the colonialists themselves are presented as human "refuse" with manners combining cruelty, despotism, laziness, and greed: only a vicious dose of anti-Catholicism is missing for full effect. But why on earth marshal this arsenal of invective to indict a constituent member-state of the nation—and not just any state, but the home of Washington, Madison, and Jefferson? Given Brown's growing Federalist sympathies and the particular animus directed against Virginia in this 1799 piece, it is hard not to see him engaging in the party politics leading toward the "Revolution of 1800" and the ouster of the New-England–based Federalists from presidential and congressional power by Jefferson's Republicans.[27] Brown's colonial chronicle not only constructed an evolutionary explanation of regional difference but also created a historically justifiable hierarchy between the "the two countries"—United States and Plantation South—a hierarchy that encouraged U.S. readers to promote the tenuous cultural dominance of the national center over the politically ascendant southern states.

Indeed, these impugning accounts of southern colonial origins, which quickly became conventional, almost always seemed to be invoked to specific political ends. Diatribes about "slavish" southern colonial dependence upon European metropolitan patronage, for instance, reflected perennial concerns at the U.S. center of manufacturing, trade, and publication about the southern states conducting unilateral trade in staple commodities with European capitals. In the *Columbian Magazine* in 1791, one writer proposed that "in agriculture," as elsewhere,

> progress was from the northward . . . The planters in Maryland and Virginia and Carolina . . . were, truly, delvers, planters for Britain; always in debt, year over year,—begging indulgence,—cringing for more credit, and humbling themselves before foreign factors. They . . . had no feelings for the interests of the country . . . '[O]ur planters,' as [the British merchants] were wont to call those Americans."[28]

In the *Massachusetts Magazine* just two months later, the editors indicted the foreign dependence of southern planters by reprinting an extensive excerpt from Robert Beverley's 1705 *History and Present State of Virginia*.

("Nay, [the Virginians] are such abominable ill husbands, that though their country be overrun with wood, yet they have all their wooden ware from England, to the eternal reproach of their laziness.")[29] The editors of the magazine did not identify the source of the excerpt, nor did they indicate that it was almost ninety years old; rather, they let Beverley's account of colonial economic relations between Virginia and the mother country at the turn of the eighteenth century stand as an accurate condemnation of the present status of relations between the vaguely traitorous independent state and its old imperial master at the turn of the nineteenth century.

In its most enduringly significant—and astonishingly bold—usage in the 1790s magazines, the colonial chronicle flatly denied the past and present dependence of the United States as a whole on the labor of enslaved Africans and African Americans. With jaw-dropping insouciance, writers began to claim that slavery did not exist and had never existed in the United States outside of its Plantation South, *decades before* the abolition of slavery in the northern, and especially the middle, states.[30] In one extensive example, the editors of the *Columbian Magazine* rushed in 1792 to print generous extracts from the freshly translated *New Travels in the United States of America* by Brissot de Warville, a friend of Crèvecoeur whose ideas about the United States had been formed almost entirely by the French editions of the *Lettres d'un Cultivateur Amèricain*. Brissot's *New Travels* was based on four months in America searching out opportunities for French investors, time he spent in cities between Boston and Philadelphia, with the exception of a three-day audience with George Washington at Mount Vernon.[31] His knowledge of American history was quite minimal, and the book was riddled with errors, but the adamant distinction he drew between the rest of the nation and its Plantation South on the matter of slavery clearly reconciled his work to the magazine editors. They structured their excerpts as a comparative historical assessment of "the Laws of the different American States for the Manumission of Slaves," ranging from north to south, and beginning, per convention, with blameless New England:

> Slavery, my friend, has never polluted every part of the united states. There was never any law in New-Hampshire, or Massachusetts, which authorised it. When, therefore, those states proscribed it, they only declared the law, as it existed before. There was very little of it in Connecticut; the puritanic austerity which predominated in that colony, could scarcely reconcile itself with slavery.[32]

After putting forth the interesting revisionist argument that slavery had been restricted in New England because it did not and had never existed there, Brissot next considered New York and New Jersey, tempering his more sanguine acknowledgment of the greater numbers of enslaved people in those states by blaming another nation: with observations on the acquisitive "Dutch spirit" of the first colonialists in that region, the author presumed that "the blot" of slavery would be eradicated as residual Dutch-ness was subsumed by righteous U.S. freedom. Moving into Pennsylvania, he hailed the egalitarianism of "the Quaker influence" and predicted that the number of Quakers in "the little state of Delaware" ensured that slavery there had "all but disappeared from the face of the state." (Slavery remained legal in Delaware until the passage of the Thirteenth Amendment in 1865.)

At the Mason-Dixon line, Brissot drew the increasingly de rigueur intranational border, quarantining American slavery in the Plantation South—which was, conversely, entirely defined by its presence:

> When you run over Maryland and Virginia, you conceive yourself in a different world, and you are convinced of it, when you converse with the inhabitants. They speak not here of projects for freeing the negroes . . . No, the indolent masters behold with uneasiness, the efforts that are making to render freedom universal . . . The strongest objection lies in the character, the manners and habits of the Virginians. They seem to enjoy the sweat of slaves. They are fond of hunting; they love the display of luxury, and disdain the idea of labour.

Here Brissot precociously essayed an analysis of American slavery that would become fully developed in the United States only decades later, during the antebellum years: slavery was not a horrifically intense system of labor exploitation but an expression of "the character, the manners and habits" of southern planters. Slavery was not a pillar of the U.S. economy but a means toward satisfying the perverse and degenerate desires of the masters of the Plantation South; "the sweat of slaves" produced only "enjoyment" for planters, not the wealth upon which the nation quite literally was being built. This focus on the degenerate character of the planter as the ultimate key to a moral understanding of Anglo-American slavery was being developed, contemporaneously, in nascent British antislavery writings, which tended to absolve the presumably humanitarian home English of the perverse behavior of their West Indian colonialists.[33] Indeed, British antislavery writings in this vein found favor with the U.S. magazine editors as well. One of the most commonly reprinted passages from Thomas Clarkson's 1786 *Essay on the Slavery and Commerce of the Human Species* stressed the need for the "cries and groans" of enslaved people to travel on "southern winds" to "the generous Englishman at home," who then "would be enraged at the conduct of his [colonialist] countrymen, and resist *their* tyranny."[34]

The increasing ideological weight borne by the figure of the southern planter in these analyses perhaps accounts for the third category of arti-cle on the Plantation South that arose in literary magazines of the 1790s: the stand-alone character sketch, which presented a single, anonymous planter—editors seemed uninterested in other types of southern denizens—as a fixed and representative figure, performing the typical activities of his typical day. These sketches were defined by their lack of narrative, combining typification with a sense of infinitely repeated routine to pre-sent "the southern planter" as a stable, one-dimensional figure whose di-urnally organized life might be encompassed entirely within the space of a few pages. An emblematic title was "A Georgia planter's method of spending his time."[35]

The urgency with which American editors sought these planter sketches is attested by the sources to which they were willing to turn for them. For instance, one formative early contribution to the genre—published by editors from Carey in Philadelphia to Isaiah Thomas in Boston—was extracted from a book by an author far more noxious to early national-ists than the seventeenth-century colonialist Beverley or the soon-to-be-guillotined Girondist Brissot. Scotsman J. F. D. Smyth published his *Tour of the United States of America* in Dublin in 1784, attempting to capital-ize upon his tour with the Queen's Rangers during the war for colonial independence. His intense partisan loathing, voiced on every page, for the American "rebels," was not the only strike against him; as well, his veracity in print could not have been more suspect. During the war, he had authored one of the most infamous pamphlets accusing American troops of abusing prisoners; afterwards, he had presented himself in Lon-don, falsely, as a lineal heir to the Stuart royal line.[36] Despite his anti-American bias and impugned credibility, though, Smyth's typification of the southern planter seems to have been simply too good for American magazine editors to pass up. The editors of the *Massachusetts Magazine,* for instance, titled a lengthy extract from Smyth in 1792 "Manner of liv-ing of the inhabitants of Virginia."

The gentleman of fortune rises about nine-o'clock. He perhaps may make an exertion to walk as far as his stables to see his horses, which are seldom more than fifty yards from his house . . . He then lies down on a pallat, on the floor, in the coolest room in the house, in his shirt and trowsers only, with a negro at his head, and another at his feet, to fan him, and keep off the flies. Between twelve and one, he takes a drought of bomobo, or toddy, a liquor composed of water, sugar, rum and nutmeg, which is made weak, and kept cool. He dines between two and three . . . At dinner, he drinks cyder, toddy, punch, port, claret, or Madeira, which is generally excellent. Having drank some few glasses of wine after dinner, he returns to his pallat, with his two blacks to fan him, and continues to drink toddy or sangaree all the afternoon . . . Between nine and ten in the evening, he eats a light supper of milk and fruit, or wine, sugar, and fruit, and almost immediately retires to bed, for the night . . . furnished with musketoe curtains . . .[37]

Whether Smyth's sketch provided a model for other writers, or simply caught the spirit of the times, eerily similar sketches multiplied in the pages of literary magazines from Boston to Philadelphia, attributed to widely varying sources, but consistently presenting the typical day of the typical southern planter. Directly importing British imperial indictments of American colonial degeneracy, these sketches effectively absented "the southern planter" from the national narratives developing in U.S. culture. All that varied from sketch to sketch was which derogatory tropical-colonialist attributes were foregrounded. Paralyzed drunkenness and indolence held center stage in the excerpt from Smyth above, but sketches also highlighted laziness ("They spunge upon the blessings of a warm sun, and a fruitful soil; and almost grudge the pains of gathering in the bounties of the earth"), irrational violence ("[T]wo or three of them set out stored with some bottles of brandy . . . in order to shoot deer in the woods . . . [S]ometimes however it happens, that tame cattle are killed by mistake"), and "blackness" and "brutality" ("In countries where slavery is encouraged, the ideas of the people are of a peculiar cast! the soul becomes dark and narrow; and assumes a tone of savage brutality").[38]

It is tempting to see in these 1790s accounts of the Plantation South the founding of national literary conventions later used to represent any peoples colonized, internally or externally, by the United States.[39] Freely borrowing from British imperial derogations of colonial America, U.S. writers crafted an imaginative figure that performed an explanatory function. The Plantation South both highlighted the continuing peripheral economic function of the southern states within the new nation, and offered an ideological justification for the increasing marginality of those states in a centralizing national culture.[40] With this coordination of the material and the moral, consolidated in the literary magazines by the mid-1790s, the Plantation South emerged in U.S. literature as the key point of reference for conceptualizing the imaginative geography of the United States: for both ordering the nation internally and, increasingly, placing it on the globe.

Neither Slaves nor Masters: Tyler's *Algerine Captive*

The obsession with the figure of the planter in the literary magazines highlights the extent to which the Plantation South in the 1790s was being defined as not only underdeveloped but also tyrannical. In other words, writers were identifying the Plantation South with *both sides* of the imperial binary: colony *and* empire, dependence *and* despotism, slaves *and* masters. This bipolar Plantation South served U.S. writers working through an ideological bind that had been created in the very language of the American Revolution. Rebelling colonialists in the 1770s had seized upon the slavery/freedom binary to characterize and explain their revolt, but that binary was itself a product of New World colonialism. Within the logic of the binary, to throw off "slavery" (subservience to Britain) necessarily was to take up "mastery" (dominion over other peoples). In other words, "freedom" and "mastery" shared the same position as the antithesis of "slavery," and these two terms could not easily be extricated from one another in the late eighteenth century.[41]

Nationalization, then, was no simple matter of exchanging colonial "slavery" for a power-neutral "freedom." Instead, nationalization immediately begged the question of "mastery," of the imperial stature of the new United States. Well aware that the new nation could at best hope, in the 1790s, to appear on the world stage as a poor imitation of its former (and demonized) British master, early nationalists confronted the mastery-freedom conflation in late-eighteenth-century English discourse by seeking to define the United States as embodying an exceptional third form of social organization, unique on the globe.[42] The American nation was a republican middle, perfectly untouched by the established power extremes of European imperialism. The United States was innocent of *both* the dependence *and* the tyranny that were coming, at this moment of their disavowal, to characterize its Plantation South.

As described by a Fourth of July orator in Boston in 1788, the unique new national form of the United States was exemplified geographically by

> the fields of Massachusetts . . . the equality of portions of the respective owners; a species of equality here exalted above the condition of those countries where the peasant is alienated with the soil, and the price of *acres* is the number of *slaves!* Not indeed that *perfect equality* which deadens the motives of industry, and places demerit on the footing of virtue: But that *happy mediocrity* which soars above bondage, without aspiring to domination.[43]

Here again is the ubiquitous independent agrarian producer of early national ideology, the American farmer, whose own perfect freedom infringes upon the freedom of no one else. But this American farmer could not exist without reference to his doppelgänger, the American planter. The "species of equality" proposed by the orator could be vaunted, or indeed even conceptualized, only in opposition to the example of the quasi-feudal plantation, which epitomized both concentrated wealth *("acres")* and abjection *("slaves")* in a symbiotic and self-contained relationship.

By identifying the imperial power extremes of both "domination" and "bondage" with the Plantation South, early U.S. writers increasingly were able to produce a triangulated placement of the new nation on their moral-geographical imaginative map of the world. By inserting this internal other into their calculations of nation-ness, the first U.S. novelists upset the imperial binary of European culture, presenting the United States proper, in its *"happy mediocrity,"* as an avowedly unique third term.

Thus while early national fiction is not often read for its portrayals of the southern states, for no novel of the 1790s presents a southern protagonist or has its action set primarily in the south, the bipolar Plantation South seems nonetheless to have borne particular weight in the literary imaginations of 1790s writers. Even in fleeting appearances, this oppositional term established by juxtaposition the exceptional republican middle of the United States; the Plantation South served as an indispensably fixed point of reference when locating the United States on a moral-geographical imaginative world map. The first U.S. novelists were particularly apt to summon the Plantation South when confronting the conditions, domestic and foreign, which perpetually threatened to disrupt the ideological middle-ness of early U.S. nationalism.

Indeed, the novel of the decade most consistently organized around evocations of the Plantation South was also the novel that addressed perhaps the greatest affront to U.S. sovereignty in the 1790s. In *The Algerine Captive* (1797)—a novel influential in Europe at the turn of the nineteenth century and long considered by U.S. literary critics to be the finest example of the early national picaresque—Royall Tyler fictionalized the capture of U.S. merchant ships and enslavement of their crews by Algerian pirates between 1793 and 1796.[44] Throughout the 1700s, European naval powers paid tribute to the Dey of Algiers in order that their ships might travel unmolested by his Barbary corsairs; with colonial independence, U.S. ships lost their protection under Britain's tribute and became fair game for the pirates. In the autumn of 1793, Algerian corsairs captured twelve U.S. ships and 115 American sailors in waters off the coast of Africa; the Dey ignored U.S. attempts to negotiate for the release of the sailors and ships through argument of law rather than by paying ransom. After years of failed diplomacy, the humiliated federal government in 1796 conceded to the Dey's demands, paying an immense ransom of over $100,000 in order to redeem its remaining enslaved citizens, thirty-four of whom already had died in captivity.[45]

This drawn-out event posed severe challenges to republican-middle ideology on two fronts. In the political realm, the demonstrated impotence of the United States against a "barbarian" people impugned the ability of the federal government to negotiate foreign policy, to deal with powers beyond its former colonial masters, and to be taken seriously overseas. In the ideological realm, the enslavement of U.S. sailors raised an even thornier conundrum: how could Americans protest the bondage of their own citizens when the U.S. countenanced slavery on a far larger scale within its own borders? How could the United States vaunt its superior morality to the "infidel" subnation when the two states shared in the "piratical" practice of slavery? The obvious, unsettling parallel was drawn by numerous commentators in the literary magazines, including in an "Essay on Negro Slavery" in the *American Museum,* which remarked that "the Algerines are reprobated, all the world over, for their unlawful depradations, and stigmatized . . . But, the Algerines are no greater pirates than the Americans; nor are they a race more destructive to the happiness of mankind."[46] The comparison was made even more painful by the tacit acknowledgement that many of the captured ships, all of which originated from New England ports, may have been illicitly involved in the African slave trade at the time of their capture; and certainly all of them were dealing in commodities produced by slave labor.[47] When these seafarers, the pride of national self-sufficiency and commercial prowess, were sold into slavery on the northern coast of Africa, the grim justice of seeing enslavers themselves enslaved was not lost upon many discomfited American onlookers.

In assuming the Algerian captivity crisis as the subject of his novel, Tyler attempted to profit from this uncomfortable fascination, which peaked as the captives were released from slavery and made their way back to New England.[48] With the license of fiction, Tyler brilliantly rerouted the geography of the crisis, inserting the Plantation South as a buffer between the United States and Africa, between republican middleness and the despotic Atlantic world. By first establishing the Plantation South as a deviant foothold of vice and power imbalance lurking within the national borders, Tyler alienated the embarrassing connection of the United States to the "African trade." By quarantining slavery, tyranny, and global entanglements in the South, he distanced those terms from the northeastern core of the nation. Tyler thereby created a new narrative trajectory that would remain influential in U.S. fiction for decades to come: a trajectory in which the intranational passage from the republican United States into its Plantation South served as the first step back into the extremes of empire loudly spurned—though covetously eyed—by U.S. nationalists.[49]

At precisely this nexus of innocence of, and desire for, aggrandizement, Tyler locates his American picaresque hero. In the early pages of *The*

Algerine Captive, he manages this paradoxical characterization through satire: Updike Underhill is not only a type of the enterprising New Englander itching to realize his ambitions on a broader stage than Boston provides—his ridiculous moniker signaling his propensity toward emigration and colonization—but he is also a representative of the emerging intellectual/artistic class at the northeastern national core.[50] Introducing Updike as a young national man-in-training, attempting to establish himself in the world, Tyler pits these two geographically specific facets of his character against one another: while Updike desperately desires to find "the high road to fortune" in terms of both riches and romance, his ability successfully to dominate his surroundings continually is compromised by his dedication to the life of the mind. Attempting to innovate upon New Hampshire agricultural practices by "follow[ing] closely [Virgil's] directions in the georgics" gets Updike booted from his father's farm; being able "to recollect no word in the Greek, which would construe into *bundling*" causes him to pass on a chance to see an eligible young woman home. In the world of Tyler's novel, the "anticipations, pleasures and profits of a pedagogue" continually are deflated; although his American picaro is consumed with desire for economic and interpersonal gain, Tyler at first characterizes Updike's metropolitan education and investment in literature as undermining his ambitions toward imperial selfhood.[51]

By introducing the first glimmer of the oppositional Plantation South into the novel, Tyler begins to move beyond this satirical characterization of Updike, raising the possibility that Updike's belletristic commitments might make him more than an object of gentle ridicule. Indeed, against a stock figure of a southern planter, Updike's cultural superiority suddenly appears as the source of U.S. national morality. In the aftermath of yet another failed attempt to sweep a lady off her feet with a show of erudition, Updike, now studying medicine at Harvard, receives an unexpected challenge in a letter from a stranger. The author of the challenge appears nowhere else in the novel, but Tyler amply indicates his geographical identity to 1790s U.S. readers:

> DEAR SIR, Them there very extraordinary pare of varses you did yourself the onner to address to a young lada of my partecling acquaintance calls loudly for explination. I shall be happy to do myself the onner of wasting a few charges of powder with you on the morro morning . . .
> Dear Sir, I am with grate parsonal esteem your sincere friend, ardent admirer well wisher and umble servant to command,
> Jasper T——.
> Please to be punctual to the hour seconds if you incline.
> July 24th, 1782. Thursday A.M. *ante merry dying.*[52]

Jasper T——'s uncouth dialect and nonstandard grammar, not more than his fondness for dueling, immediately code him according to the copious conventions for figuring the Plantation South current in U.S. print by 1797. With just these few lines Tyler invokes the bipolarity of the construct fully: his South is a repository for both pre-Revolutionary British aristocratic conceits (dueling, honor), and colonial barbarism physical and linguistic (dueling, "onner"). Tyler conflates the physical and linguistic facets of southern barbarism in Jasper T——'s final phrase, *"ante merry dying,"* where the southern planter expresses his "savage indifference to death" in terms of his provincial ignorance, his lack of a metropolitan education in Latin.[53]

Tyler inserts the letter from Jasper T—— only to provoke Updike's response to it: complete incomprehension. The degraded dialect Tyler attributes to the Plantation South is so far at variance with the correct literary language of his national novel that his hero cannot decipher it. An invitation to "waste a few charges of powder"? Civilized Updike assumes he is being invited to a sporting hunt. He marvels at Jasper T——'s "punctual attention to hours, and even seconds," as Tyler sardonically plays upon the character-sketch notion of southerners as exempt from modern time. Finally, Updike must have the letter translated by an interlocutor, a fellow Harvard student who "was born at Carolina, and understood the whole business."[54] On the one hand, Tyler could not more strongly dissociate his national protagonist from the southern planter, for in the purely linguistic world of the novel, he alleges that the two speak different languages incomprehensible to one another. But on the other hand, Tyler's characterization of Updike becomes dependent upon Jasper T——'s appearance: as the national character finds foreign not only the bad grammar but also the simultaneously aristocratic and colonial systems of thought within which the southern planter operates, his essential republican middleness, his innocence of power extremes, is established. This carefully choreographed irruption of the Plantation South into Harvard causes Updike's regionally specific, tenuous, and impractical devotion to literature suddenly to appear the surest source for an exceptional, distinctive, and blameless national morality—a national morality that gazes accusingly southward, while turning a blind eye to the ships in Boston Harbor.

Tyler develops this central equation—northeastern cultural superiority equals national moral superiority—by sending Updike into the thick of the Plantation South. "Disappointed in the North, the author seeketh treasure in the South": perhaps channeling "the late Dr. Ladd," Tyler has the newly credentialed Dr. Underhill strike out for "one of the states, southward of Philadelphia," where he is assured that the planter "inhabitants [are] immensely opulent, pa[ying] high fees with profusion, and . . . extremely partial to the characteristic industry of their New England brethren."[55] Rather unpicaresquely, Tyler does not narrate Updike's "southward" travel from Boston: instead of describing U.S. territorial gradation with the inclusivity of a geography textbook, Tyler passes over the middle states with only a cursory anecdote of Benjamin Franklin in Philadelphia—and he thereby asserts the primacy of the U.S. core/Plantation South opposition he is drawing.

That Updike's southern sojourn serves a structurally symbolic function in the larger narrative of the novel becomes apparent in the two chapters actually set in the Plantation South: the narrative grinds to a halt, and we seem to have entered the static character sketches of the literary magazines as Updike simply reports an excessive and monotonous string of southern vices to the reader. From the opening southern scene of a local minister beating and cursing his slave on his way to the pulpit, Updike finds the interchangeable, nameless southern planters he observes to be rich in both "opulence" and the expected moral shortcomings: paralyzing laziness, hypocritical religion, gambling, drunkenness, violent outbursts, implied sexual promiscuity, and profuse profanity. Against the wild Plantation South he produces, Updike protests that "the whole of this extraordinary scene was *novel* to me. A certain staple of New England which I had with me, called *conscience,* made my situation, even the passive part I bore in it, awkward and uneasy." Throughout the southern chapters, Tyler encourages his readers to join Updike in meditating upon how alien the tyrannical yet underdeveloped southern scene appears to their minds, which are proven "liberal [and] enlightened" through the contrast.[56]

Indeed, Tyler employs these chapters, inserted between Boston and the Atlantic, to constitute an imagined community of national readers defined by their common disidentification with the Plantation South. For instance, in an aside on the southern proclivity for profanity, he has Updike note

> that the reader is requested, whenever he meets with quotations of speeches in the above scenes, excepting those during divine service, that he will please, that is, if his habits of life will permit it, to interlard those quotations with about as many oaths as they contain monosyllables . . . I never swear profanely myself, and I think it almost as bad to oblige my readers to purchase the imprecations of others, [but] I give this hint of the introduction of oaths, for the benefit of *my readers to the south of Philadelphia;* who, however they may enjoy a scene which reflects such honour upon *their country,* when seasoned with these palatable expletives, without them, perhaps, would esteem it as tasteless and vapid as a game of cards or billiards without bets, or boiled veal or turkey without ham.[57]

Critics of the day quickly took Tyler to task for constituting the national imaginary of his novel so plainly through "offense" to and exclusion of the substantial southern subset of the body politic. A review of the novel in the pages of *Farmer's Weekly Museum*—an important 1790s literary magazine edited by Joseph Dennie and printed by Tyler's own publisher—accused Tyler of inciting disunionism, but went further to identify the real rub: how dare Tyler derogate the Plantation South in order to proclaim the "vaunted 'conscience' of SLAVE TRADERS" from New England?[58]

And despite Tyler's strong-handed intranational ordering of his audience, his American picaro quickly is prostrated before the ostensibly foreign power extremes of the Plantation South. Having ventured into a realm defined by its very lack of a republican middle, Updike's independent integrity cannot be maintained: the newly national narrator must choose at last whether to become a master or a slave. If he does not assume the aristocratic vices of the planter class, Updike complains, he cannot successfully practice his profession: "To obtain medical practice, it was expedient to sport, bet, drink, swear, &c. with my patients. My purse forbad the former; my habits of life, the latter." To refuse to join in the abuses of the masters, though, Updike insists, is necessarily to become one of the enslaved: "To avoid starving, I contemplated keeping a school. In that country, knowledge was viewed as a handicraft trade . . . so that to purchase a school-master and a negro was almost synonymous."[59]

To escape the "slavery and contempt of a school," Updike finally goes over to the side of the masters. "Encouraged by handsome wages, and a privilege in the ship to carry an adventure," he accepts a position as surgeon on board "the brig *Freedom*, freighted with tobacco, bound to London, and thence to the coast of Africa . . . thence to Barbadoes and to South-Carolina."[60] In other words, Updike contracts to journey *farther* south, more deeply into the imperial Atlantic world. With this decision forced upon his narrator by a sojourn in the Plantation South, Tyler accomplishes his imaginative rerouting of the Algerian crisis: by having the hypocritically named slave ship Updike boards originate from an unspecified southern state, Tyler erases the New England apex in the triangle trade of African slavery and American plantation production.[61] He isolates the nascent metropolitan core of the United States—location of Harvard, literary production, and national moral superiority—from the exploitative Atlantic economy. And thus, momentarily at least, Tyler solves the imaginative conundrum of how a U.S. citizen might end up enslaved in northern Africa through no fault, no imperial impulse, of his own.

Except that once "the brig *Freedom*" moves into international waters, Tyler's assiduous compartmentalization of U.S. power extremes within the Plantation South breaks down. The nation-south internal opposition Tyler has developed so carefully makes no sense beyond the borders of the United States; in the Atlantic world, the slave ship on which Updike travels is a U.S. vessel, not a "southern" one. However much Updike vaunts his possession of an exceptional reserve of *"Yankee nonsense about humanity,"* he nonetheless "discover[s], to [his] surprise and horror, that, by [his] station in the ship, [he] has a principal and active part of this inhuman transaction imposed upon [him]." As in the Plantation South, only two subject positions exist on the metonymic U.S. ship of state: that of American imperial despot and that of African colonial victim. Slavery, Atlantic trade, and imperial ambition no longer may be circumscribed as merely deviant practices of the Plantation South; suddenly, the power extremes of the globe are revealed to Updike to permeate "both wings of the union, and I believe every where else."[62]

Tyler's American picaro valiantly makes one last stand for his republican exceptionalism, though. Prefiguring by more than a half century the dictum attributed to Lincoln—"as I would not be a slave, so I would not be a master"—Updike "reject[s] his privilege," refuses the position as master he rather belatedly realizes he has assumed.[63]

> I execrated myself for even the involuntary part I bore in this execrable traffic: I thought of my native land, and blushed. When the captain kindly inquired of me how many slaves I thought my privilege in the ship entitled me to transport for my adventure, I rejected my privilege with horror, and declared I would sooner suffer servitude than purchase a slave.

Tyler could not more clearly state the only two options available in the Atlantic world within which his exceptional protagonist has been relocated. Just pages after Updike refuses to accept slaves as payment for his shipboard services in facilitating their kidnapping, Tyler has him kidnapped, enslaved, and carried to Africa himself by Barbary raiders. Fleetingly, Tyler recuperates Updike's enslavement as additional evidence of his moral superiority in the face of the viciousness of Western empire: his relative kindness on board the *Freedom* has resulted in the kidnapped Africans "asking [their God] with earnestness, why he put [Updike's] good *black* soul into a *white* body." But in the end, Tyler most certainly does not seek to saddle his national protagonist with the stature of a slave. Despite Tyler's creative restructuring of the international crisis around the intranational opposition of the United States to its Plantation South, Updike's enslavement ultimately appears, at best, a sentence of the American picaro to time at hard labor in order to expiate the sin of his no longer blameless nation.[64]

From the vantage of London, where *The Algerine Captive* was published in 1802 and 1804, Updike's American vacillation between the master-slave poles of empire easily was perceived. The illustrations of the novel produced to accompany its serialization in the *Lady's Magazine* largely mocked the backward rusticity of the United States, implicitly casting Updike's half-satirized devotion to culture and republican ideology as affectations of his residual American coloniality, his provincial idiocy. It is the climactic scene of Updike's capture, though, that makes clear that U.S. citizens who fail to assert imperial mastery on the world stage necessarily are reduced to the debased status of colonial subjects in the eyes of London.[65] Structured about a moment of reveal, the scene centers upon the requisitely turbaned-and-scimitar-wielding "Algerines" sweeping back the flap of Updike's U.S. campaign tent to expose the bleary-eyed, pretentiously peruked pretender to the mantle of empire sleeping with his wig on, as it were. The north African barbarians and North American rube tumble together in a ridiculous and exotic intra-colonial scramble, the whole framed, naturally, by the classic Caribbean sign of the palm tree. That iconic marker further defines Africa and America for London readers as indiscriminately joined parts of the great, naturally subordinate global hinterland subject to dominion by the capitals of Europe.

Tyler had made his name as a writer with his 1786 play *The Contrast,* in which he produced the republican virtue of the U.S. hero against the corruption of his British metropolitan adversary. As the London illustration shows, though, this was only one side of the representational equation for early national novelists, who had to prove that their U.S. protagonists not only were not British masters but also were not tropical, peripheral, colonial "slaves." By the time he wrote *The Algerine Captive,* Tyler had replaced Britain with the domestic Plantation South as the prime site of "contrast" against which to locate the nationality of his American picaro. The Plantation South enabled Tyler to work at once on both sides of the representational equation, producing republican middleness by simultaneous opposition to both of the power extremes of empire. Although the United States/Plantation South contrast broke down when this novel moved into international waters, Tyler continued to return to the internal other construct for the rest of his literary career.[66]

For Tyler and his nationalist co-laborers in the emergent field of U.S. literature, the ideological flexibility of the Plantation South remained compelling, even as this internal other necessarily evoked ambiguity and instability. The Plantation South was emerging in their works not only as a repository for the cultural associations and material realities that impugned U.S. nationality, not only as a stable background against which a national narrative of development and progress might be unfolded, but also as a quasi-colonial possession of the early national imaginary, a territory upon which the republic's ambitions toward empire might be owned. As with contemporaneous dreams of continental empire, though, the ambition of writers and publishers in the Philadelphia-to-Boston core to control the direction of national life and politics displayed a reach that far exceeded its grasp in the 1790s. For all the imaginative distance opened in the literary magazines between the nation and its Plantation South, the southern states remained constituent member-states of the United States, not to be written into submission or declared *"our own"* by imaginative fiat of the likes of the Reverend Doctor Dwight. Intrinsic and other, desired and reviled, this Plantation South occupied the nether regions of national imagination for the first U.S. novelists.

CHAPTER FOUR

The Enemy Within

The Serfs of Bohemia are far more like the freeholders of
Middlesex, in *complexion,* habits, liberty, knowledge,
temperature, and products, than the New-Hampshire ploughman
is like the corn-planter of Roanoke, or the rice-sower of Santee.

> —Charles Brockden Brown, "On a Scheme for describing American
> Manners (Addressed to a Foreigner)," *Monthly Magazine* (1800)

ITS INHERENT PARADOXES made the Plantation South a towering
presence on the early national literary landscape. By the end of the
eighteenth century, the construct had come to undergird the two
most significant forms of early U.S. fiction: the seduction plot and its
close cousin, the gothic mode. As U.S. writers adapted these forms from
British precedents, they stressed the conventional elements of exogenous
threat within their plots: national protagonists suffered assault by foreign
rakes or by malevolent, otherworldly forces.[1] By focusing on these fictional forms, the first American novelists dramatized a fragile, embattled
nationality whose stature was uncertain on the world stage. But their specifically American renovation of gothic and seduction fiction was structured about a shadowy and schematic specter of the Plantation South,
which never appeared as a fully realized setting in the novels. Rather,
as had been the case in Tyler's picaresque, the South lurked in the margins of these turn-of-the-century plots, serving as a point of origin for and
connection to the evils and excesses of Atlantic empire.

Indeed, by 1800 the internal contrast between the United States and its
South seemed to Charles Brockden Brown, the most important novelist
of the era, poised to displace the external contrast of the new nation with
Britain. In his *Monthly Magazine,* he suggested that the presence of the
Plantation South on the imagined domestic landscape destabilized any attempt to define a self-contained and unified American nation, that the internal other rendered futile the cultural-nationalist project of developing
"a picture of American manners."

> The theatre itself is too wide to traverse: a thousand miles one way, and fif-
> teen hundred the other: various in climate from the ceaseless ardours of the

JANE TALBOT.

Figure 8. Illustration, *Jane Talbot: A Novel,* by Charles Brockden Brown, 1801. Special Collections, University of Virginia Library.

tropics to the horrors of the arctic winter . . . Look at the guise and manners of a tiller of the field in New-Hampshire. What circumstance in his condition can give us the slightest knowledge of the tiller of the field in Georgia? The Serfs of Bohemia are far more like the freeholders of Middlesex, in complexion, habits, liberty, knowledge, temperature, and products, than the New-Hampshire ploughman is like the corn-planter of Roanoke, or the rice-sower of Santee.[2]

Invoking the American farmer/southern planter opposition, by then two decades old—as old as the United States itself—Brown pitted the now stable and familiar "New-Hampshire ploughman," direct descendent of Crèvecoeur's Farmer James, against a mobile and unfathomable southern foil. Not the Anglo-American southern master, but the African American southern slave, this plantation figure vacillated wildly in location over the course of two sentences, from Georgia to Virginia to both Carolinas. And not the "slightest knowledge" of this geographically indeterminate southern planter could be deduced from his binary opposition to the known American farmer; rather, beginning with the key desideratum of "complexion," the two figures existed in a relationship of utter incommensurability. Unfixed and unknowable, yet intrinsic and defining, the Plantation South as Brown invigorated it revealed that post-Revolutionary U.S. culture had institutionalized a sort of imaginative unconscious for the nation, a spatialized site of disavowal, dread, and mystery that the first U.S. novelists could mine.

One of the very few illustrations created for Brown's novels conjures this defining internal gulf. The engraving from Brown's seduction novel *Jane Talbot* depicts another American/Southerner faceoff: the brother of the eponymous Jane, a Philadelphian national heroine, seeks to defend her honor against her ardent suitor Henry Colden, a Baltimorean anti-hero whose motives are unclear and whose power over Jane is inexplicable. Particularly interesting in the scene as rendered by the engraver is its background. It was a great commonplace in eighteenth-century images to picture an American scene against the backdrop of a body of water. The featured water, though, was normally the Atlantic Ocean, putting the American vignette in the context of both its distance from and its connection to the Old World. In the illustration of Brown's novel, the ocean has been replaced by a river (the Patapsco), and now the opposite side of the body of water is clearly visible in the background, though it still exists across a gap. This gap, in *Jane Talbot* and in many of Brown's novels, is the internal gulf between Philadelphia, southernmost point of the nation proper, and Baltimore, northernmost outpost of its Plantation South. The sublimity of the oceanic, continental-scale separation is replaced with the uncanniness of the domestically scaled gap that renders the other visible, though still out of reach. The closeness of its domestic South to the national center is further telegraphed by the near identity of the opposed Southern villain and U.S. hero. The Baltimorean Colden, on the left, lounges at his ease and flaunts dandified striped stockings, while the Philadelphian Talbot stands upright and indignant. But for these minor differences of habit, the antagonists look like twins: same height, same profile, same clothing.[3]

At the turn of the 1800s, the first U.S. fiction writers were finding across this imperfectly distinct internal divide both the underbelly of metropolitan economic development and the underbelly of nationalist republican ideology. Some of the earliest gothic vignettes published in the literary magazines, for instance, appeared in antislavery essays that yoked inanimate household commodities in northeastern cities to the living bodies of enslaved southern plantation laborers who had produced them. Sugar on the breakfast tables of U.S. metropolitans became the salty sweat of slaves in their Plantation South, and the most intimate, banal "enjoyments" of republican homes revealed ghostly and appalling traces of their plantation origin:

> Those beautiful colors with which our ladies are adorned; the cotton with which they line their stays; the coffee, the chocolate on which they breakfast; the red with which they heighten their complexions——all these the hand of the miserable negro prepares for them. Tender women! you weep at tragedies, and yet what affords you pleasure is bathed with the tears, and stained with the blood of your fellow creatures![4]

Critics of eighteenth- and nineteenth-century British gothic novels have argued that the gothic mode enacted a return of the repressed peripheral base of imperial economy to the metropolitan center of literary production, and the same general dynamic is apparent in these early magazine vignettes.[5] Equally uncanny for U.S. writers, though, was the fact that their Plantation South was defined by precisely the dual antitheses—master and slave—of republicanism. Discussing Brown's brief invocation of Virginia in the novel *Clara Howard* (1801), William Dunlap, a friend of Brown's and a significant author in his own right, quickly probed the thornier underlying issue raised by the southern digression:

> In America there is no peasantry. The tillers of the earth are the owners of the soil . . . This is one of the proud distinctions, between this country and Europe. In one portion of our country the remains of the English slave trade

exists; and there peasants exist . . . But with the exception of the slave holding states, as we have no nobility but from worth, so we have no villainy but
from misdeed. We have neither lord nor peasant, except in the south, where
the planter partakes of European nobility, and the African slave of European
peasantry.[6]

As the exception to U.S. exceptionalism, the Plantation South began to
appear as a dire menace to the national project itself, a site of corruption
and contamination that posed an internal threat to U.S. existence equal
to the external threat posed by the British during the war for independence. The editors of the *New-York Magazine* drew precisely this parallel when they indicted a supposed epidemic of cockfighting in their city
as an "opulent" behavior "imported" to their metropolis by southern
planters; they exhorted metropolitan readers to fight influence from domestic southern others just as strenuously as they had repelled invasion
by British troops:

> When our country was formerly invaded by a foreign power, we considered
> it inglorious to make no opposition, but with a spirit worthy of Americans,
> arose and blasted their intentions.—We are again assaulted—*the enemy is
> within the walls:* let us, with a spirit equally becoming, make immediate re-
> sistance.[7]

Half a century before the "Slave Power" conspiracy theories of the antebellum era, the Plantation South had secured a place in the national
imaginary as "the enemy within": exogenous though native, and as opposed to the U.S. national project as any European imperial monarchy or
American colonial fiefdom could be.

Brockden Brown's Gothic Geopolitics

Charles Brockden Brown virtuosically developed U.S. gothic fiction in six
complete novels, and more serial narrative fragments, published between
1797 and 1801; and while the United States was everywhere underwritten by its Plantation South in early national culture, Brown engaged the
southern other with particular intensity, beginning at an early age.[8] At the
height of the Revolutionary War in Pennsylvania, when Brown was six,
his father was exiled to Winchester, Virginia with a group of prominent
Quakers from Philadelphia. This formative rupture in Brown's family
life, occurring right at the moment of national genesis, profoundly influenced his political and aesthetic development.[9] In particular, the *location*
of the exile seems to have taken hold in Brown's mind as a young man:
Winchester was not so far across the Pennsylvania/Virginia border, but it

was out of the country in the minds of Philadelphians. Brown played on this paradox when he claimed at various times that his father had been exiled to a southern location as far away as New Guinea: if one crossed the "south of Philadelphia" intranational line, it seemed, one might as well be anywhere in the global hinterland.[10] The expansive view southward from Philadelphia remained consistently compelling across Brown's writings, from his earliest serious literary effort, a trio of epic poems about the colonization of the American tropics (Columbus's discovery of the West Indies, Pizarro's conquest of Peru, and Cortez's expedition to Mexico), which he wrote in 1787 at the age of 16, to his last fictional work, incomplete at his death in 1810: a fictional "history" of the "Eutopic society" of Carsol, an imagined semitropical island where all labor questions, power struggles, and racial differences were resolved through a perfected system of slavery.[11] When, around 1801, Brown made the much-discussed shift from writing fiction to writing political pamphlets and geographies, he argued vociferously for U.S. acquisition and domination of the Louisiana Territory, and indeed for an unlimited expansion of U.S. empire southward and westward. But his desire for possession of the American tropics seemed always tempered by a dread of being overcome by the Plantation South rather than mastering it—a dread that Brown registered in his journal in almost preconscious terms as he consistently refused to visit his eldest brother, Joseph, who settled in North Carolina as an adult. In the summer of 1800, for instance, Brown characterized his decline of yet another solicitous invitation from Joseph as compulsive and nearly inexplicable: "I am reluctant to comply. I know not why, scarcely."[12]

Reading Brown's novels of the period, one gets the sense that his "reluctance" to visit North Carolina may have come from his certainty that to cross the intranational divide was to invite disaster. While all of his novels were set in the environs of solidly national (indeed, capital) cities—Philadelphia, his birthplace, or New York City, his residence at the turn of the century—in each, an incursion from or excursion to the Plantation South provokes some catastrophe in the main action of the novel. In his first novel, *Wieland, or, the Transformation* (1798), the southern rupture is brief and early, but decisive; and it operates at precisely the nexus between desire for possession of the southern other and terror of being mastered by it. Brown's Philadelphian protagonists wish to reread a letter from an absent friend detailing his "travels through the southern colonies," and this urge causes the fateful first meeting between Theodore Wieland and the ventriloquist Carwin, whose influence leads by the end of the novel to Wieland's "transformation" into the mad butcher of his own family. Wieland's sister, Clara, narrates the scene:

> [The] letter contained a description of a waterfall on the Monongahela. A sudden gust of rain falling, we were compelled to remove to the house. The storm passed away, and a radiant moon-light succeeded . . . We remained where we were, and engaged in sprightly conversation. The letter lately received naturally suggested the topic. A parallel was drawn between the cataract there described, and one which Pleyel had discovered among the Alps of Glarus. In the state of the former, some particular was mentioned, the truth of which was questionable. To settle the dispute which thence arose, it was proposed to have recourse to the letter. My brother searched for it in his pocket. It was no where to be found. At length, he remembered to have left it in the temple, and he determined to go in search of it . . .
>
> In a few minutes he returned . . . Methought he brought with him looks considerably different from those with which he departed.[13]

As the protagonists consume the southern account, it immediately inflects their local metropolitan weather: reading a description of the southern "waterfall" precipitates a "sudden gust of rain falling" over their own heads in Philadelphia. The Monongahela River itself similarly intrudes on the national center from the south: it rises in Virginia and flows north to cross the Pennsylvania border. Yet another southern source makes an incursion into this passage as well: Jefferson's *Notes on the State of Virginia* gives the best-known account of "the cataract there described."[14]

This interpenetration of the southern other into the national center, while initially sought out by Brown's protagonists, quickly spins out of their control: reading about Virginia requires that the Philadelphians ponder their own geographical situation on a global scale, so that the domestic site a few hundred miles away, but across the Mason-Dixon line, "naturally suggest[s]" a "parallel" with so extrinsic and paradoxical a locale as "the Alps of Glarus." The protagonists at the American national center immediately recognize that their ability to comprehend "truth" on this scale is "questionable"; and a journey to obtain more direct knowledge of the south—though it is just a journey from house to grounds on the Wieland estate—becomes necessary. That seeking of southern knowledge, though, effects the first step in Theodore Wieland's "transformation": his errand after the southern letter is interrupted by a disembodied voice that warns him to "stop, go no further. There is danger in your path." This mysterious encounter has left her brother, to Clara's eyes, "considerably different," and she expostulates upon what is so disturbing about the disembodied voice: it provides "proof of a sensible and in-

telligent existence, which [can] not be denied . . . That there are conscious beings, beside ourselves, in existence, whose modes of activity and
information surpass our own, can scarcely be denied." What if the half-
"denied" (twice!) southern other talks back, becoming not an object
for metropolitan contemplation and control but an author of national
narrative?[15]

Such an active incursion of the Plantation South on the national center—
illuminating the muddiness of self and other in early national literature
that "can scarcely be denied"—is probed most consistently by Brown in
the two novels he set in Philadelphia during yellow fever epidemics. Both
Arthur Mervyn, or Memoir of the year 1793 (1799–1800) and *Ormond,
or, the Secret Witness* (1799), are structured around three interrelated
types of horrific southern return to the United States capital.[16] First, there
is the yellow fever itself, disease of the American tropics, reasserting its
hemispheric sway: "That a pest [so] malignant had assailed the metropolis of her own country, a town famous for the salubrity of its airs and the
perfection of its police," muses Constantia Dudley, heroine of *Ormond,*
"had something in it so wild and uncouth that she could not reconcile
herself to the possibility of such an event."[17] Second, the plots of both
novels are driven by stolen or misappropriated inheritances that have
been amassed by trade in plantation-produced commodities. The most
violent acts of the two novels are provoked by fortunes Brown sources to
Baltimore and Charleston, as well as farther south to Tobago and Jamaica. Third, Philadelphia in plague time is teeming with "at least ten
thousand French . . . fugitives from Marat and from St. Domingo . . .
liv[ing] in utter fearlessness of the reigning disease."[18] This refugee population, tropicalized by its ostensible imperviousness to the yellow fever,
conflates two versions of feared southern revolution: slave rebellion and
the Jacobin radicalism associated with the party of Jefferson.

The yellow-fever background of Brown's novels poses the southern incursion on the national center as *contagion,* undermining national independence and self-containment through contiguity with the Atlantic world.
The stolen-fortune plots of the novels, on the other hand, pose that incursion in terms of *inheritance,* disrupting the clean break with the colonial
American past with the return of the repressed plantation basis of the
U.S. economy. The French refugee presence in the novels focuses on the
uncanny continuity of slavery in the ostensibly republican U.S. body
politic and thus operates at the conjuncture of southern *contagion* and
southern *inheritance.* On the one hand, the refugees from Haiti conjure
Jefferson's half-turned wheel of revolution, while on the other, they direct
Brown's attention to the enslaved people already present on the streets

of Philadelphia and thus to the hereditary characteristics of the post-colonial United States in terms of both its laws and its population.

That the internal divide between national capital and Plantation South takes on a looming importance in Brown's gothic geography becomes particularly plain with his resolution of *Arthur Mervyn*. The convoluted plot of that novel evolves in the context of a multitude of southern incursions on Philadelphia in plague time; to conclude the story, Brown assembles a parcel of loose ends—including two stolen inheritances and the eponymous protagonist Mervyn, whose complicity with or opposition to the villain of the novel is never fully ascertained—and sends the lot by stagecoach from Philadelphia to Baltimore. Mervyn is on a mission to return the inheritances to their rightful Jamaican and Charlestonian owners, both conveniently residing at Baltimore, but disposing of the ill-gotten gains of southern plantations is not Brown's only goal. While Baltimore is geographically quite close to Philadelphia, it is as much across the intranational divide as Winchester, Virginia, the site of the Revolutionary-era exile of Brown's father. As Mervyn narrates his trip to Baltimore, Brown decontaminates the national center of the returned traces of its recent coloniality—including slavery, tropicality, and racial heterogeneity—and thereby reestablishes the domestic Plantation South as a buffer zone between the independent United States and the colonial American hemisphere:

> I mounted the stage-coach at day-break . . . in company with a sallow Frenchman from Saint Domingo, his fiddle-case, an ape, and two female blacks. The Frenchman, after passing the suburbs, took out his violin and amused himself with humming to his own *tweedle-tweedle*. The monkey now and then mounched an apple, which was given to him from a basket by the blacks, who gazed with stupid wonder, and an exclamatory *La! La!* upon the passing scenery; or chattered to each other in a sort of open-mouthed, half-articulate, monotonous, and sing-song jargon.[19]

Here Brown contains and exiles southward a schematic, "staged" tableau of American tropical coloniality: the "sallow" planter whose complexion denotes both racial intermixture and the endogenous tropical fever, the two "open-mouthed, half articulate" enslaved women, and—seemingly gratuitously—the pet monkey.

But his national protagonist, Mervyn, is himself enclosed within this microcosmic southbound stage, and Brown uses the passage to experiment with the sort of narration that can prevent the collapse of the national self into its southern other. As he ventures into southern territory, Mervyn must assert an almost compulsive intellectual activity in order to maintain his national standing:

> As to me my thought was busy in a thousand ways. I sometimes gazed at the faces of my *four* companions, and endeavored to discern the differences and samenesses between them. I took an exact account of the features, proportions, looks, and gestures of the monkey, the Congolese, and the Creole-Gaul. I compared them together, and examined them apart.[20]

Brown's protagonist discerns a pseudoscientific chain of being— "Creole-Gaul" to "Congolese" to "monkey"—within which a hierarchy is maintained, but a relationship between all three terms simultaneously is asserted.[21] In so doing, he becomes an agent of the classificatory system of European imperial natural history, an ordering metropolitan rather than an ordered colonial.[22]

By participating in the imperial project of intellectually managing and ordering his Plantation South as he encounters it—"I marked the country as it successively arose before me," he avers—Mervyn avoids becoming infected himself by the residues of American hemispheric coloniality. Instead, he finds "an uncommon gratification" in his "intercourse" with the scenes and denizens of Baltimore, for through this interaction Mervyn is elevated in stature, "*buoyed up* by a kind of intoxication" and "*exalted* to [his] genial element."[23] Plantation proceeds disposed of, slavery displaced, natural hierarchy reasserted, Mervyn can return to Philadelphia for marriage and a happy ending to the new-national U.S. novel. Brown seems to hold out the promise in these concluding scenes that U.S. citizens can master their geographical and temporal connections to Atlantic empire by writing their own Plantation South and thus participating as equals in the broader knowledge production of Western empire.

The tyranny of empire then becomes the focus of Brown's second novel set in Philadelphia during plague time, *Ormond*. The titular villain of this novel is an exogenous threat to the United States, originating from a broad swath of European locales and bearing two evil schemes into prostrate Philadelphia: Ormond is both perfecting a plan for world domination and strategizing to seduce the virtuous national daughter of the novel, Constantia Dudley. While these twin anti-republican schemes might seem wildly incommensurate in scale—the one global, the other local—Brown intimately relates the dastardly plots, showing that Ormond's threat to the new nation on both fronts stems from his ability to modulate between the poles of master and slave, the dual antitheses of U.S. republican ideology. Brown creates the connection between the global conspiracy plot and the domestic seduction plot by routing Ormond from Europe into Philadelphia via the Plantation South. He, his associates, and his funds have come into the United States from Baltimore, Charleston, and Richmond, and before that through the West Indies

(Jamaica, Tobago, Santo Domingo).[24] During this detour through the Plantation South, Ormond has learned the fatal weakness through which republican households may be penetrated: domestic slavery. While American nationals try to avoid seeing the radical hierarchy upon which their households operate, Ormond embraces it and presses it to his use:

> There was a method of gaining access to families, and marking them in their unguarded attitudes . . . The disguise, also, was of the most impenetrable kind . . . It was the most entire and grotesque metamorphosis imaginable. It was stepping from the highest to the lowest rank in society, and shifting himself into a form, as remote from his own, as those recorded by Ovid. In a word, it was sometimes his practice to exchange his complexion and habiliments for those of a negro and a chimney-sweep.

Brown's routing of Ormond through the Plantation South invigorates both of the villain's schemes, global and domestic, illuminating their shared embrace of the power extremes of empire.[25] Masquerading in blackface provides the initial breach into the Dudley home through which Ormond pursues his designs on Constantia. But his shadowy international intrigues also are always described by Brown with precisely the same master/slave binaries showcased in the domestic passage above ("stepping from the highest to the lowest rank in society"). As an adept in the arts of dominion, Ormond has modulated between "men, in their two forms, of savage and refined"; he has spent "half of [his] life . . . supporting by flagitious intrigues, the tyranny of Catharine [of Russia], and the other half . . . extinguishing what remained of clemency and justice, by intercourse with savages."[26]

Constantia's best defense against Ormond's assault on her republican virtue thus paradoxically becomes an embrace, rather than a denial, of her own master status in a slaveholding republic. Early in the novel, another of Brown's luminously allegorical scenes epitomizes the geopolitical problem of the exceptional republic: surrounded by comparatively corrupt neighbors, how can the new nation avoid infection and maintain its ostensible purity? Constantia confronts the problem of a corpse next door, the body of a man in the next house who has succumbed to the tropical plague, but whose physical presence—like that of slavery in the United States—lingers on. To enter the house and grapple with the body herself will expose her to the southern fever, yet to allow the corpse to continue to rot so close to her pure household has its own problems. Only "a narrow space divided them, and her own chamber was within the sphere of the contagion which would flow, in consequence of such neglect, from that of her neighbour." As often happens in Brown's novel of southern incursions, at this moment of crisis a local black laborer appears, deus ex machina, and Constantia solves her domestic problem by reasserting the denied master/slave, black/white binaries of the American plantation. "[L]ike many others of his color and rank," this "negro" has been drafted into the most dangerous plague-time job of dead-carter; suddenly, we learn that precisely this black man is already constituted as a servant to Constantia's household, for he has before "performed some services for Mr. Dudley." Constantia smoothly steps into the role of mistress, commanding him to "return forthwith and be ready to execute her orders" as to the removal of the rotting corpse. The black laborer, for his part, happily complies, for "his temper [is] gentle and obliging," and he is accustomed to view "the character of Constance . . . with reverence." Bizarrely, Brown staves off the threat of southern encroachment on the metropolitan U.S. scene by instantiating idealized plantation power relations in the heart of the nation's capital. And although he never develops beyond suggestion Ormond's project to "new-model the world" through "an exploring and colonizing project . . . [a] new-born empire . . . in the heart of desert America," Brown implies that U.S. citizens possess a training in the ways of empire from their colonial days that will allow them to take command across the continent, too.[27] In this, his last major novel, Brown's Plantation South looks both backward and forward. The virulent southern return to the U.S. national capital reveals not only that the colonial past of the nation is not dead but also that the lingering colonial stain on the nation finally will require—and enable—the United States to ascend to full imperial mastery on the world stage.

Brown makes precisely this argument in his first political pamphlet, and he does so by probing this same Plantation South nexus between domestic slavery and global empire, between colonial past and imperial future. In *An Address to the Government of the United States, on the Cession of Louisiana to the French* (1803), Brown demands that the federal government project immediate and forceful military control over the just-purchased Louisiana Territory, but he does so with fictional techniques, encouraging his readers to organize in response to a fabricated found document. He claims in the pamphlet to have uncovered an "extraordinary performance" by a French "counsellor of state," who is spinning a plan, not unlike Ormond's, for North American continental domination.[28] The nefarious French scheme begins with Brown's obsessive point of hemispheric reference, the Haitian Revolution, and France's disappointment over the loss of that "devoted colony" through the "cruel wars and revolutions [that have] converted those beautiful plantations into an African wilderness." The supposed French "counsellor" proposes that colonizing Louisiana not only will offset the loss of St. Domingo but also will lead eventually to France's control of the United States, for France inadvertently has learned how to foment slave rebellions, and the post-colonial United States still "harbours in its bosom a foreign race . . . whom a cruel servitude inspires with all the vices of brutes and all the passions of demons . . . and whose sweetest hour would be that which buried them and their lords in a common and immeasureable ruin." Brown finally leaves aside the French "counsellor" to put forth his own summary response: it is true that "the blacks are a bane in our vitals, the most deadly that ever nation was infested with. They are indeed a train of powder, so situated as to make it not impossible for the French in Louisiana, to set fire to it." U.S. citizens should understand that they "have a *right* to the possession" of the Louisiana Territory, precisely in the interest of preserving the organization of their nation as a slave-holding power.[29] The United States must expand its imperial reach south-westward across the continent, in other words, in order to preserve the inherited internal empire of its Plantation South.

One of Brown's last major publications, his 1804 translation and annotation of French philosophe C. F. Volney's *View into the Soils and Climates of America,* allows Brown further to conflate the external empire acquired through U.S. expansion with the intrinsic dominion of the nation over its Plantation South. Volney's introduction, as Brown rather freely translates it, draws exactly this parallel between "the obvious advancement of [U.S.] power and ambition towards the West Indian isles and the neighbouring continent, and . . . probable aggrandizement in future" with "that disjunction of interests and views, which already separate the eastern from the southern states; . . . the weakness of the *south,* from the prevalence of slavery; and the strength of the *east,* the fruit of private freedom and industry."[30] Volney then puts the "eastern" and "southern" states in a global context, discerning thereby a "natural" intranational imperial relationship between the two regions. "The same line" of latitude, he notes, "very nearly touches" Boston and many historical imperial capitals (Rome, Constantinople, Derbend, and Ajaccio, Napoleon's birthplace). "The southern districts" of the United States, on the other hand, "correspond with . . . the whole northern coast of Africa: and it is somewhat remarkable, that the Mississippi and the Nile enter the sea under nearly the same parallel of latitude." As in the literary magazines Brown was editing throughout his career, an imaginative ownership of its quasi-African Plantation South—with all its troubling rebukes of republican ideology—becomes the first step of the United States into global imperial stature. In a footnote on Volney's latitudinal comparison,

Brown amends Volney to note that the United States is indeed on its way to becoming global in scale:

> The recent addition of Louisiana has carried the western limit far beyond the Mississippi, and embroiled it in a world of unexplored deserts and thickets. This circumstance has aided the imagination in its excursions into futurity; and instead of anticipating the extension of this empire merely to the sea on the south, and to the *great river* on the north, we may be sure that, in no long time, it will stretch east and west from sea to sea, and from the north pole to the Isthmus of Panama.[31]

Brown's conversion of the republic into a continental empire here is an imaginative "excursion into futurity" that is not only sublime, but also appalling, especially when we remember that Volney was known to Brown and other American readers for his magisterial *Ruins: Meditation on the Revolutions of Empires* (1791).[32] If there is a subversive underside to Brown's rabid expansionism in his last decade, it is located in the gothic geopolitics developed in his novels, where the Plantation South returns as the disavowed colonial past of the United Sates, while simultaneously auguring the imperial future of the nation. Brown's Plantation South first undermines the ideals of republican newness, independence, and freedom—and then promises their coming total annihilation.

The Less Perfect Unions of the Seduction Novel

Though the emotional terrain of seduction novels is more the realm of sentiment than of horror or phantasm, these novels in their U.S. form shared with the gothic mode a concern with the return to the republic of the power extremes associated with both European empire and the Plantation South. As it was styled by turn-of-the-century editorialists, seduction was itself an "aristocratic" behavior, a "remnant of the ancient manners of Europe," because the seducer acted antithetically to republican restraint, reveling in and exploiting the inequality of the sexes.[33] The seducer sought to use his advantages—physical dominance, superior education, and unilateral legal and economic power under coverture—to manipulate and "ruin" a comparatively helpless woman who was unable to discern his evil motives. Literary historians long have attributed the popularity of seduction novels in the 1790s—as both the best-selling and the most prolific fictional form—to their allegorization of the perceived vulnerability of the early republic to threats internal and external.[34] In the plight of the accosted maiden, one might see the innocent new-national reader; in the machinations of the depraved seducer appear the wiles of the antirepublican conspirator, the imperial tyrant. Cultural nationalists of the era interpreted the presence or absence of seduction in the United States as an index of the success or failure of nationalization; as Brown himself, who incorporated at least the shadow of a seduction plot into every one of his novels, opined in his *Monthly Magazine* in 1800: "The degree in which this crime prevails in America" proved "the difference . . . between the integrity of the parent and the offspring."[35] Like the gothic mode, the seduction novel probed the weaknesses and contradictions of American nationalization in its second decade.

It is striking, then, to note that over the course of the 1790s the geographical affiliation of the antirepublican seducer in U.S. novels shifted from British redcoat to southern planter: from past exogenous master to present enemy within. The first U.S. seduction novels, such as *Amelia, or the Faithless Briton* (1787) and Susanna Rowson's *Charlotte Temple* (1790), reprised the contest for American independence; set during the Revolutionary War, these early novels subjected the virtue of an innocent proto-American lass to the assaults of a domineering British swain.[36] Even at this moment of generic genesis, though, the evolution of the American seducer from tyrannical Briton to rakish planter was under way: the *New-York Magazine* began its print run in 1790 with a very short "novel" titled "Fatal Effects of Seduction," which began and ended with a U.S./British opposition of maiden and seducer, but abruptly took a southern detour in the middle. The plot followed the sad fate of Polly Pollyer, a republican daughter of "industrious and credible inhabitants of this city," who during the war too trustingly welcomed British midshipman Jack Ensign into her home "with all the *freedom* of a deserving suitor." Led astray by Jack's "*sedulous* attention," Polly was "seduced from her *virtue*" by Jack's promise to marry her. Suddenly, the writer interposed a geographic shift: the apparently well-meaning Jack was detained from fulfilling his promise of marriage when "the ship he belonged to was ordered to the southward"; and a six-month stay in that unspecified southern locale indelibly transformed Jack's character, leaving him most uninterested in making Polly an honest woman. Now "planterized," he returned to New York "no more [a] man of probity . . . What is generally termed *gallantry* seemed to engross his whole study, and in this most dangerous vice, he had become a proficient."[37] The rather tortured moral geography of this seduction plot aligned Britain and the Plantation South as sources of antirepublican vice leagued against fledgling U.S. virtue. The British seducer, once schooled in southern depravity, left the republican daughter wandering the streets of London as a prostitute.

The more developed and complex U.S. seduction novels published later in the 1790s dispense entirely with the British identity of the se-

ducer. Novelists instead render intranational tales of struggle between re-
publican virtue and internal despotism, in which seducers almost always
are aligned in some way, even if fleetingly, with the Plantation South. In
The Story of Margaretta (1798), for instance, the virtue of Judith Sargent
Murray's heroine is assailed by the ominously named southern planter
Sinisterus Courtland; in *Jane Talbot* (1801), Brown's most conventional
epistolary seduction novel, Philadelphian Jane is addressed by the vaguely
Godwinian, fiery, and ironically named Henry *Cold*en, who, inevitably,
writes his letters from Baltimore.[38] In the U.S. seduction novel most celebrated by current critics, Hannah Webster Foster's *The Coquette* (1797),
the seducer Sanford's initially conflicted and potentially honorable intentions toward Eliza Wharton are transmuted irrevocably for the worse by
his own "tour to the southward." Although Eliza possesses no fortune,
and Sanford is being hounded by his creditors, he at first finds himself "so
greatly infatuated" with her that he announces: "I verily believe I should
[ask] her in marriage, and risk the consequences!" Upon removing "to
the southward," though, Sanford finds *himself* seduced by the trappings
of aristocracy, and he consequently makes a mercenary marriage to a
planter's daughter: "I must either fly to this resource; or give up all my
show, equipage, and pleasure, and degenerate into a downright plodding
money-catcher, for a subsistence. I cho[o]se the first; and who would
not?" Having capitulated to the antirepublican opulence of the Plantation South, Sanford returns to Hartford a confirmed villain, bent upon
"possessing" Eliza out of wedlock—and he finds that even in New England, flaunting his newly acquired southern splendor only aids in his
campaign against Eliza's virtue:

> What deference is always paid to equipage! [Hartford citizens] may talk of
> this virtue, their learning, and what not; but without either of them, I shall
> bear off the palm of respect from those, who have them, unadorned with
> gold, and its shining appendages.[39]

Herein lies a deeper worry of Foster's seduction novel: how fragile, ultimately, are republican "virtue" and metropolitan "learning" in the new
nation, built as they are upon the rather dull and tedious ground of self-
restraint and self-cultivation? How susceptible are republican readers to
being led astray by the (definitionally southern) "*palm* of respect" still ac-
ceded to imperial opulence and dominion?

This seduction of U.S. readers by their Plantation South, as it is generated in their own national literature, becomes the subject of Tabitha Tenney's only novel, *Female Quixotism: Exhibited in the Romantic Opinions
and Extravagant Adventures of Dorcasina Sheldon* (1801). Tenney's mod-

ernized Quixote plot—in essence, an anti-seduction novel—follows a heroine who ardently *seeks* seduction on the model of her favorite Richardsonian novels; she attempts to exchange her prosaic duties as a nubile republican daughter for passionate power extremes, imprisonments, elopements, and hairbreadth escapes.[40] Spurning her sensible biblical name, Dorcas, as "unfashionable and unromantic," the self-styled "Dorcasina" attempts with her name, as with her life, to "alter and give it a romantic termination"—though Tenney's emphasis is much less on romance than on termination. Unconventionally, she presents the decisive scenario of her novel in its first two chapters: Dorcasina, having reached an exemplary young adulthood marred only by her reading habits, spurns a marriage proposal that, Tenney emphasizes through omniscient narration, is ideal both for her personal happiness and her republican responsibility. "Her mind being so warped by the false and romantic ideas of love, which she had imbibed from her favorite authors," Dorcasina cannot recognize the budding relationship for the more perfect union that it is, and at the end of chapter 2 she rejects her honorable suitor—to her extreme detriment, as Tenney amply demonstrates through the subsequent thirty-four chapters, which serve essentially as a very long episodic dénouement. Throughout the rest of the novel, which spans fifty years, Dorcasina finds no other viable marriage options; instead, she encounters a variety of fortune hunters and pranksters from the margins of turn-of-the-century U.S. life—an Irish felon, a Connecticut sharper, a conniving servant, a Jacobinical South Carolinian—only too eager to prey upon her gullible reading of the world around her through the lens of her novels. Though with a rollicking comic sensibility, the novel progresses from one cruel punishment of the heroine after another until it closes with a final letter signed by a chastened and childless "Dorcas," now sixty-eight years old and "in the midst of the wide world, solitary, neglected, and despised." She summarily moralizes that "my parentage, my fortune, and, I may add, my moral character, gave me the fairest prospect of forming an advantageous connubial connection; and such a connection was *once* in my power. Heaven forgive me if I am sometimes half tempted to wish its curse on the authors of the writings, which had so far perverted my judgment, and depraved my taste, as to induce me to reject it!"[41]

Female Quixotism offers, more than any other novel of the early republic, a commentary on the threats posed by literature to national reproduction. Reading the decisive opening chapters of the novel reveals that Tenney does not simply join in the heated contemporary debate about the place of popular fiction in a society based on popular sovereignty; nor is the influence of British sentimental fiction on American readers her sole concern.[42] She draws attention as well to the pervasive othering of the Plantation South in rising U.S. national culture and to the threat to union that such a literary discontinuity implies. Reading with an eye to intranational geography, we at once discern that the "advantageous connubial connection" thwarted at the outset of Tenney's novel offers an opportunity for imaginative reintegration of the United States with its Plantation South, an opportunity to heal the breach between American farmer and southern planter. This match would join Dorcasina Sheldon, the only child of a "worthy and venerable" Pennsylvanian who "devote[s] himself to agriculture," to Lysander, the only child of Mr. Sheldon's "old esteemed friend in Virginia." The Virginian Lysander, Tenney deliberately insists, is no depraved planter-libertine; rather, like his namesake in Plutarch's *Lives,* he is an apotheosis of republican restraint: "His person was noble and commanding; his countenance open and liberal; and his address manly and pleasing. His understanding was rather solid than brilliant, and much improved by education and travel. His ideas of domestic happiness were just and rational." Though Dorcasina does not perceive it, Tenney further assures the reader that her heroine and Lysander are perfectly matched in terms of virtue, for during a month-long visit the two develop a "purest and most lasting" affection for each other, "founded upon esteem and the amiable qualities of the mind." At the inescapable allegorical level, the wedding of the two young people would perpetuate the "intimate friendship" between their regions, forged by their (founding) fathers, into a third generation of harmonious national existence.[43]

But Dorcasina rejects this more perfect union at the same moment that it is introduced. Tenney has her protagonist explain her rationale for eschewing the momentous alliance in a deliberately staged Quixotic tableau, as Dorcasina speaks of her ideals to her maidservant, Betty. Tenney reinvigorates the conventional master/servant pairing of the scene to comment on the antirepublican power extremes upon which the Republic still rests. Brilliantly, she marshals the critical voice of Betty to direct the reader's interpretation of Dorcasina's flights on the problem of the plantation:

> Dorcasina thus continued: "Though I know that love is stronger than death, and that with a beloved object a person may be happy on the top of the Alleghenies, or among the snows of Greenland; yet I must confess I shall feel a sensible pain . . . that I shall be obliged to live in Virginia, be served by slaves, and be supported by the sweat, toil and blood of that unfortunate and miserable part of mankind." "Perhaps, ma'am," said Betty, "Lysander and his father treat their slaves well, and they live comfortable and happy." "Comfortable they may be," replied Dorcasina, "but . . . 'disguise thyself as

thou wilt, still, slavery, thou art a bitter pill.' They complain of the idle . . . disposition of their slaves; but let the proprietors in their turn, be degraded to servitude, let them be made prisoners by the Algerines . . . then should we see whether they would be . . . more industrious than the wretched Africans." . . . "Well ma'am," said Betty, "'tis pity you should make yourself so uneasy beforehand; perhaps you and the young gentleman wont fall so violently in love with each other as you imagine, and perhaps you never will become his wife."[44]

Dorcasina's rejection of slavery rings absolutely true, which only makes all the more disturbing the compromised terms through which she conceptualizes it. She supports her correct moral stance with a hodgepodge of derivative rhetoric pulled from her diet of fiction: her use of satirically excessive sentimental language leads to her direct quotation of Sterne's *Sentimental Journey,* topped off with her citation of domestically produced Algerian captivity fiction.

Worse, Tenney shows that Dorcasina's vilification of Virginia according to the terms of 1790s U.S. literature becomes an alibi for her own situation. So long as the republican daughter conceives of dominion and abjection as residing entirely within the Plantation South, she displaces the ways in which her own social stature departs from egalitarian nationalist ideology. By structuring the passage as a dialogue between Dorcasina and her servant, Tenney undercuts Dorcasina's lamentations about the lot of those bound to servitude by having them attended to by, literally, a captive audience: Dorcasina has "ordered" Betty to listen. While Betty is not herself enslaved by the Sheldons, she "has been brought up in the family from the age of seven" and is "bound" to humor the whims of her mistress, compelled to deference in exchange for her livelihood. More damningly, Tenney throughout the novel aligns Betty with another household servant, Scipio, who is in fact the Sheldons' "African slave." In the dialogue between the two women, Tenney counters Dorcasina's pleasure in posing her national innocence against the power extremes of the Plantation South—her "indulg[ing] herself in an agreeable, humane, but romantic idea"—with Betty's subaltern voice, which by its very deference (always prefaced by "ma'am") insistently reinscribes Dorcasina within the power binary she imaginatively repudiates. While Dorcasina spins specious plans for the immediate emancipation of "all the negroes . . . even unto Georgia," Betty's presence rebukes her compartmentalization of mastery and servitude—a compartmentalization that enables the fundamentally moral republican daughter to pass half a century in the novel without even thinking of emancipating her intimate servant Scipio, let alone the field laborers, glimpsed from time to time, who perform Mr. Sheldon's American farming.[45]

Betty proves prescient: the United States and its Plantation South "never will" form a union in Tenney's novel. Neither Dorcasina nor Lysander weds; the lines of their founding fathers both are doomed to extinction. And the cause of this catastrophe? National readers are incapable of knowing southern states or southern citizens, precisely because they think they know their Plantation South. Doubtless the conditions under which Tenney produced her only novel inflected her gloomy prognosis: Dorcas, who is marked as an analogue for the author ("Dorcas" is the scriptural equivalent of "Tabitha"), must consider the proposal from the honorable Virginian at precisely the moment when the nation was roiled by the violently contested election of 1800.[46] Tenney experienced this electoral tumult at its epicenter: as the wife of a partisan Federalist congressman from New Hampshire, she wrote *Female Quixotism* from the new, southern, national capital of Washington, D.C.; and while she wrote, Samuel Tenney opposed, on every one of thirty-six ballots, the election of Jefferson to the presidency.[47] Abortively attempting, at the outset of her novel, to rehabilitate the southern planter of national imagination into an "honorable" U.S. citizen, Tenney conceded that her effort in 1801 came already too late to avert Dorcas's decline into disunion. In her diagnosis, nascent U.S. national culture, paradoxically, undermined the national project. U.S. nationalism, built upon the internal other of its Plantation South, seemed poised to engender its own destruction.

Most U.S. writers were more sanguine than Tenney about what they saw as the geographically centralized ascendance of national literature at the turn of the nineteenth century. Brown's sense of the rising destiny of the author in the United States registered in the wish of Ormond, his power-mad antirepublican seducer-imperialist, ultimately to assume that role for himself. As Brown described Ormond carefully crafting a story in order to bend Constantia to his will, he meditated upon the hegemonic power of the storyteller:

> Ormond aspired to nothing more ardently than to hold the reins of opinion. To exercise absolute power over the conduct of others, not by constraining their limbs, or by exacting obedience to his authority, but in a way of which his subjects should be scarcely conscious. He desired that his guidance should controul their steps, but that his agency, when most effectual, should be least suspected.[48]

After the Federalist defeat in 1801, U.S. writers in the northeast even more decisively turned their ambitions for national power from the political to the literary realm. In his preface to the New England epic poem

Greenfield Hill, for instance, Timothy Dwight became one of the first of many writers of the era to quote the adage, "Allow me to make the Songs of a nation, and who will may make their Laws."[49]

While Dwight's valorization of the power of literary writing might have seemed the wishful thinking of a disempowered "Connecticotian"— and a far cry from his 1776 oration declaring the North American continent to be imminently *"our own"*—the particular nexus of geography and power constructed about the Plantation South in the fiction of the 1790s proved essential not only to the foundations of U.S. national literature but also to the conceptualization of U.S. nationalism. Across this key decade in U.S. literary history, American writers reconfigured the geography of European empire out of which their new nation had emerged, studiously preserving a tropical zone, with all its inherited moral and political associations, within the newly constituted body politic. This internal other created a structure in U.S. literature for narrativizing, explaining, and justifying uneven development within the ever-expanding United States. At the same time, as the first U.S. novelists isolated both slaves and masters in the Plantation South, they forwarded an idea of the new republic as uniquely untouched by both tyranny and abjection; they triangulated the relationship of the United States to the outside world. By displacing onto their Plantation South the extremes of empire—whether of America colonized by Europe, or of the United States colonizing slave labor within its borders (and, prospectively, a continent beyond those borders)—U.S. writers promoted the development of an American empire that could sustain the representational sanctity of its republican center. Reading the literature of the early republic for its Plantation South reveals a new set of continuities between eighteenth-century European imperial accounts of the American colonies and the antebellum U.S. sectionalist and expansionist writings that seem—though produced an ocean away and almost a century later—to echo them. By tracing the shadowing of the United States by its Plantation South to the very beginning of U.S. literary history, we may surmise that "the South" arose not only to chart where the new nation once had been but also to map, with the broadest of strokes, where it was going.

PART TWO

Industrialization and Expansion / The Slave South

Our Country Is the World, Our Countrymen Are All Mankind.

> —William Lloyd Garrison, Masthead slogan, *The Liberator*
> (instituted Jan. 1, 1831)

God said, I am tired of kings.
I suffer them no more;
Up to my ear the morning brings
The outrage of the poor.

> —Ralph Waldo Emerson, "Boston Hymn," (delivered on the date
> of the Emancipation Proclamation, January 1, 1863)

CHAPTER FIVE

Underwriting Free Labor and Free Soil

Many have no correct views of the height and depth, the length
and breadth, and innumerable horrors of this enormous system
of crime.

> —Angelina E. Grimké, *Appeal to the Women of the Nominally
> Free States* (1837)

ARLY IN WILLIAM CULLEN BRYANT'S emblematic 1834 poem
"The Prairies," the cardinal points of U.S. expansionist geography suddenly become muddled. Poised on the threshold of
Manifest Destiny, the "magisterial gaze" of the poem generally faces resolutely westward: inspired by a visit to Illinois, Bryant pens a paean to
the distinctive North American landform west of the Appalachians, and
the poem quickly develops into a vanishing Indian story.[1] Bryant structures this collision of place and history around an overarching tension
between stasis and movement. His speaker gazes upon "motionless"
western land that is ostensibly uninhabited—"these Gardens of the
Desert"—but the very desolation of the scene prods him to envision "that
advancing multitude / [w]hich soon shall fill these deserts": the inevitable
U.S. colonization of the prairies, which is already under way.[2] Bryant effects this transition between what has been in the West, and what will be,
by introducing a different directional axis into the first twenty lines of
the poem:

> Breezes of the South!
> Who toss the golden and the flame-like flowers,
> And pass the prairie-hawk that, poised on high,
> Flaps his broad wings, yet moves not—ye have played
> Among the palms of Mexico and vines
> Of Texas, and have crisped the limpid brooks
> That from the fountains of Sonora glide
> Into the calm Pacific—have ye fanned
> A nobler or a lovelier scene than this?

Suddenly the path from the prairies "into the calm Pacific" becomes more circuitous than a straight march toward the setting sun. Bryant's apostrophe to the "[b]reezes of the South" reminds us that the expansion he contemplates is not only continental but also hemispheric; indeed, each of the "southern" locales he enumerated in 1834—Mexico, Texas, California—would be touched by U.S. might during the subsequent fifteen years.[3] Southern breezes sweep across Bryant's poem, though, not simply to widen its expansionist horizons. Acting as the pivot between past stasis and coming motion, between desertion and plantation, the "breezes of the South" roll as the force of U.S. empire, of modernity itself, transforming the face of the land. This transformation, Bryant is certain, is at least in part for the worse, a diminishment and despoliation of the prospect before his speaker and reader. To visualize the movement of imperial modernization westward necessarily is to bring "shadows" and "dark hollows" into view. As the southern breezes "roll and fluctuate" the grassland initially presented as "motionlessly" Edenic—"fresh as the young earth, ere man had sinned"—Bryant's speaker momentarily seems moved to reject the progress of U.S. expansion he has poised himself to epitomize. "Man hath no part in all this glorious work," Bryant concludes the apostrophe.

Why does Bryant identify the darkly transformative breezes of U.S. modernity as hailing from "the South"? His apostrophe invokes a new vision of the South for U.S. letters, a South mostly uninterested in the inherited registers of New World colonialism that had been so important to writers of the early national generation. The South Bryant summons in 1834 does share with the Plantation South construct of the 1790s a facility in modulating between past and present, and between domestic and foreign territorial realms. But the temporal valences of Bryant's breezy South seem to operate antithetically to those of three decades earlier. Whereas the Plantation South had provided a stable locus for the premodern, prenational past of the United States, Bryant's South appears as an ominous herald—a foreshadowing—of a dystopic national future.

Bryant reanimates and reconfigures his South in a particular context, in dialogue with a particular conjuncture of historical forces. In place of the American Revolution, his generation faced the "market revolution," a perhaps equally transformative symbiosis: rapid industrialization at the northeastern core of the nation spurred and was fed by galloping expansion of its southern and western peripheries and their productive capacities.[4] While U.S. writers in the late eighteenth century had worried over their incomplete modernization away from colonial status, their counterparts just a few decades later feared the opposite—feared that a too-rapid, too-complete lurch into modernity now threatened the existence of the republic. And indeed, the epochal transformations of the market revolution, felt first and most acutely at the northeastern centers of U.S. literary production, radically undermined the most basic premises of republican ideology.[5] In the first decades of the nineteenth century, a U.S. citizen had been understood to be a "freeman," his independence secured by his possession of both his means of production and an array of people dependent upon him (women, children, servants, slaves). Thus when Francis Scott Key penned "The Star-Spangled Banner" in 1814, he and his contemporaries deemed it obvious that a "hireling"—an individual possessing nothing but his own labor, which he exchanged for his subsistence— held a social position that was equivalent to that of a "slave," being equally antithetical to the "freeman" of republican citizenship. ("No refuge could save the hireling and slave, / From the terror of flight or the gloom of the grave, / And the star-spangled banner in triumph doth wave, / O'er the Land of the Free, and the Home of the Brave.")[6] By the eve of the Civil War, though, and under the pressures of industrialization, U.S. citizenship had come to describe a situation that earlier generations would have considered servitude, guaranteeing only a "hireling" existence, only the personal possession of a commoditized and alienable self.[7] By the time that South Carolinian William Grayson drew on Key's nationalist lyrics for the title of his 1855 long poem "The Hireling and the Slave," the idea that the status of a wage laborer could be equated with that of an enslaved person had become so ideologically inadmissible in the northeast that Grayson lost his New York publisher.[8] Across just forty years, a commonplace of U.S. culture had become unspeakable.

To conserve the most basic terms of republican ideology—"freedom" and "independence"—under the market revolution, Bryant's generation had actively to remake those terms in the 1830s and 1840s, uncoupling them from their former connotations of mastery and ownership, and reinscribing them as accurate descriptors of a personal status recently considered "dependence" or "servitude." If we focus on the problem of freedom as the great challenge to national ideology and culture in the era of industrialization and expansion, then the reanimated relevance of the South at this time springs immediately into view.[9] From its beginnings, the South in U.S. culture had been the location of slavery within the slaveholding republic. Now, American slavery emerged as the antithetical baseline against which all permutations of and infringements on republican "freedom" had to be conceptualized. Newly centered in U.S. national imagination, American slavery now appeared not as an inherited sin, a provincial connection to past colonial origins, but as an impending condition of life at the industrializing northeastern core. The confusion surrounding the word itself in U.S. print in the 1830s and 1840s—the extent to which enslavement had to be described as "chattel slavery" in order to distinguish it from the "wage slavery" of proletarianization—speaks both to the interpolation of southern slavery into every register of U.S. culture and to the reimagination of that term that went along with its new centrality.[10]

Slavery had been an identifying feature of the Plantation South in the post-Revolutionary decades, but writers in the 1790s had turned southward as well to evoke a complex of related issues: the colonial New World origins of the nation; the problem of American tropicality in the moral geography of European empire; the persistence of U.S. peripherality on the world stage. For writers in the 1830s, these latter dimensions of the Plantation South largely fell away, and a substantially new configuration arose in U.S. print, appearing first in the writings of the nascent abolitionist movement.[11] In 1830, on the eve of William Lloyd Garrison's founding of *The Liberator,* slavery in the United States was still being depicted with conventions borrowed from British imperial culture and mostly unaltered since the late eighteenth century. Slavery appeared as an unfortunate residue of colonialist depravity and as a natural product of tropical degeneracy. Over the subsequent several years, though, these increasingly tired and irrelevant images of slavery were displaced radically in U.S. print by what I will call "the Slave South": an imaginative realm produced through the modern exposé mode being developed to fathom the new industrial cities—a realm created through detailed and repetitious revelations of sadistic violence and vice, particularly torture and sexual "licentiousness."[12] The suddenness of this representational shift suggests not evolution but rupture, and it has been remarked as such by cultural historians; however, the rupture generally is ascribed to an inexplicable though happy awakening of Americans in the northeastern United States to the atrocities of southern slavery.[13] It surely *is* that, in part; but corresponding as it did to a precipitous and dramatic reorganization of life in the northeastern United States, the Slave South had an immediate and visceral relevance for those people, living at the urbanizing centers of U.S. literary production, who first created and consumed the image.

For the Slave South produced in abolitionist writings explicitly excluded people residing in the southern states from its intended audience. Garrison himself had planned to establish his new antislavery newspaper at the political and geographical center of the United States—Washington, D.C.—but after being jailed for libel in Baltimore and receiving financial backing in the *publishing* center of Boston, he founded his venture there instead. When he began publishing *The Liberator* on New Year's Day, 1831, Garrison hypothesized that "a greater revolution in the public sentiment might be effected in the free states—and particularly in New England—than at the South."[14] From this beginning, the new Slave South produced in abolitionist print was a place to be perceived—and, presumably, acted upon—only by those outside of it.[15] This meant that the Slave South offered on the one hand an analogue for the diminished stature of northeastern writers and readers under industrialization, and on the other hand an avenue to a new sort of mastery for them: a proto-imperial, reformist mastery over the rapidly expanding peripheries of the nation, which were, purportedly, incapable of achieving republican perfection on their own.[16]

The masthead slogan of *The Liberator,* instituted by Garrison with his first issue and printed each week until the paper ceased publication in 1865, put forth an "American Universal Geography" for the nineteenth century: "OUR COUNTRY IS THE WORLD, OUR COUNTRYMEN ARE ALL MANKIND." Garrison's slogan provided a tantalizing capsule statement of the double-meaning transcendent nationalism that ultimately was facilitated by the Slave South. Was national distinction itself being transcended for a universal humanism?—or was a Boston-centered United States culture righteously superseding the self-determination of potentially all other peoples and places in the world? In the decades that we, in hindsight, term "antebellum," writers conceived this key evolution of U.S. nationalism first of all by looking to their internal other. To the extent that writers in the decades leading to the Civil War were able to assimilate nineteenth-century Western industrialization and imperialism into U.S. ideology in exceptional terms—as programs of "free labor" and "free soil"—they did so by writing their Slave South.

Urban Reform and "Immediate" Abolitionism

The year 1830 marks not only the beginning of a rapid upswing in the pace and scale of industrialization in the northeastern United States but also a new epoch in American antislavery thought.[17] As gradual emancipation statutes from the turn of the century were fulfilled in the northeastern states, a vanguard of antislavery thinkers began to define objectives antagonistic to prior antislavery politics on two scores. First, the vanguard rejected the gradualist strategies for eradicating U.S. slavery, colonization and voluntary manumission, that had formed the substance of Anglo-American antislavery politics since the 1770s. Garrison emerged as the nascent leader of the new movement with a speech at Boston's Julien Hall in October 1830, in which he attacked the colonizationists rhetorically and put forth one of the first public statements of the new political goal of "immediatism," or immediate abolition of slave law.[18] Second, the vanguard repudiated the former focus of antislavery reformers on slaveholders and enslaved people, seeking instead to make the case against slavery only to those geographically removed from it—as, to use the case of Garrison again, when he began publishing *The Liberator* from Boston, rather than from Washington, D.C., on the first day of 1831. This means that while Garrison and his co-laborers formulated a reformist program *immediate* in its temporal goals, they established it as entirely *mediated* geographically. Not only was the subject of nascent abolitionist discourse distant and foreign to its intended readers, but those readers also had plenty to worry about at home, where they were experiencing a profound reorganization of their own society and daily confronting anxieties about the marked modernization of their own surround.

In his very first editorial for *The Liberator,* Garrison appeared to acknowledge this fundamental representational impasse, as he strained to invest his immediatist political platform with emotional urgency for his readers by couching it in a series of personalizing analogies:

> Tell a man whose house is on fire, to give a moderate alarm; tell him to moderately rescue his wife from the hands of the ravisher; tell the mother to gradually extricate her babe from the fire into which it has fallen;—but urge me not to use moderation in a case like the present.[19]

This early formulation of immediatism seems to communicate most clearly Garrison's sense of the urgent gap between the object of his reformist passion—southern slavery—and the local concerns of his intended audience at the industrializing, urbanizing center of U.S. print production. From the very outset, Garrison was seeking to fill that gap rhetorically and symbolically, searching for a re-presentation of southern slavery that would render it not quaint and foreign, but truly immediate: geographically and emotionally near and compelling, intensely troubling and close to home.

The conventions for portraying southern slavery that Garrison inherited from previous antislavery discourse proved woefully inadequate to this task, as is quite literally illustrated by the engravings with which he decorated the early volumes of *The Liberator* from its inception in 1831 through the end of 1837.[20] By the beginning of 1832, he had selected four engravings with which he adorned each four-page issue: a masthead illustration at the top of the first page and three smaller engravings that

marked the institutionalized "departments" of the newspaper. His pedagogical aim in repeatedly printing these engravings each week seems
clear: he thereby provided his northern readers with visual images of the
southern evil he exhorted them to combat in his articles, rendering that
evil more present and more objectively comprehensible than he could
with textual argument alone.[21] Yet the conventional picture of southern
slavery Garrison was delivering to his readers with these illustrations
clashed with his remade political message, falling back as they did upon
a moribund representational repertoire substantially unchanged since
Crèvecoeur's day. Garrison employed the image of a kneeling, supplicant
slave in chains—the fifty-year-old emblem of the colonizationist movement to which he was opposed—as the regular heading for his "Ladies'
Department"; the headings of his "Juvenile Department" and "Slavery
Record" sections, on the other hand, offered up didactic scenes of colonialist tropical depravity that would have been at home in the Abbé Raynal's 1770 book.[22] Indeed, Garrison likely lifted both of these images
from the British metropolitan campaign against slavery in the West Indies: the undeveloped, sparsely populated backgrounds of the engravings
marked the settings as colonial; the presence of palm trees and volcanoes
denoted tropicality; and the clothing on people in the scenes—outmoded
styles and colonialist hats on the white figures, and loincloths on the
black—rendered the illustrations both dated and foreign. The established
picture of southern slavery Garrison had at his disposal in the early
1830s portrayed it in terms essentially unchanged in Anglo-American
culture since the late eighteenth century.

For Garrison's northeastern readers, living through the market revolution of the 1830s, these sentimental images of 1790s-era antislavery
iconography also threatened to inspire nostalgia for an older and more
stable order of social organization. Even the first masthead illustration of
the paper, reprinted at the start of this chapter, seemed poised to elicit nostalgia, though Garrison had specially commissioned it from local Boston
lithographer David Claypool Johnston. This larger and more detailed engraving depicted a slave auction, putting the horror of legal family separation on display at its center, yet Johnston's romanticized rustic agrarian
setting threatened to defuse the critical thrust of the scene. Two lamenting
black women with heads bowed, surrounded by plump, sentimentally
clad black children, formed the central tableau of the scene, with the
weeping women rendered in particular detail: crowned with incongruous,
quasi-biblical white veils, their smooth, rounded bare arms and flowing
gowns were arranged by Johnston in graceful dishabille.[23] The engraving
was completed by a rural background of forest and turf, punctuated by a

miniature whipping scene in the middle distance and, rather oddly, a tiny image of the Capitol building at the horizon—perhaps a remnant of Garrison's original plan to establish the paper in Washington, D.C. On the one hand, the didactic message of the masthead vignette, announced by signs in the foreground ("HORSE-MARKET: SLAVES, HORSES, AND OTHER CATTLE TO BE SOLD AT 18:00") surely got through: how dreadful to trade in humans as "CATTLE," how dreadful to live under a national government that makes and upholds slave law. On the other hand, though, the illustration perhaps would not have been altogether repugnant to readers in Boston or New York City, Garrison's two major subscription centers. The pastoral background, the agrarian overtones of the rustic marketplace, the languishing postures of the elegantly clad women—indeed, even the familiar form of corporal punishment—all combined in a scene of stable and human-scaled order potentially attractive to readers exercised about satanic mills, littered streets, and teeming crowds. What, then, was this southern slavery that Garrison was demonizing?

Garrison's readers, contemplating the transformation of their own cities, immediately began to push him toward a critique of southern slavery that took their local surround into account. As early as the fifth issue of *The Liberator,* a letter-writer suggested that Garrison's abolitionist campaign might have local applications in the fight against proletarianization. "Although you do not appear to have perceived it," the writer gently chided Garrison, "there is a very intimate connexion between the interests of the working men's party and your own."[24] Garrison indignantly rejected the possibility of such a political "connexion," devoting his front-page editorial in that issue to a lengthy and impassioned defense of the inequalities of wealth becoming apparent in northeastern cities, and he continued to endorse all extremes of unrestricted wage-based capitalism—even to the British "coolie trade" after West Indian emancipation—throughout the 1830s.[25] But if Garrison was not ready to see "a very intimate connexion" between chattel slavery and proletarianization on the level of political analysis, he quickly began to pursue a *representational* "connexion" between northeastern industrialization and southern slavery. While his readers in Boston and New York were struggling with an exponentially increased pace of modernization, he was seeking to direct their antipathy toward a distant part of the country that seemed, by contrast, untouched by modernity. To problematize southern slavery for his readers required that Garrison reconstruct the very understanding of that term in a way that resonated with the new local realities, and that operated within the contemporary cultural forms "intimate" to the transformation of the national center.

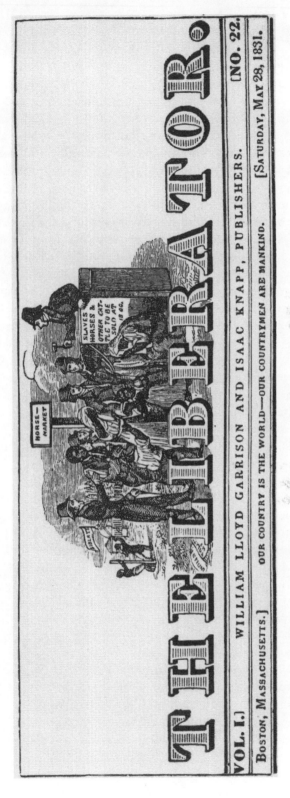

Figure 9. David Claypool Johnston, engraver. First masthead of *The Liberator,* published weekly from January 1831 through February 1838. Yale Collection of American Literature, Beinecke Rare Book and Manuscript Library.

For society and its evils were being apprehended, defined, and depicted in a new way in U.S. print under the pressures of industrialization and urbanization. A broad new discursive formation, often termed by contemporaries the discourse of "radical" or "ultraist" reform, had begun to arise in the urban centers of Boston, Philadelphia, and New York City in the late 1820s, and it burst fully into northeastern public consciousness by 1831 with publications by temperance and, especially, antiprostitution reform groups seeking to combat ills in the burgeoning cities.[26] Ultraist discourse employed the exposé as its predominant literary mode: the new urban texts turned on an increasingly lurid and explicit unveiling of vices presumably hidden within the body politic. This exposé impulse—this new apprehension of pervasive hidden vice—was linked to the transformation, across the 1830s, of daily life in the cities that were the centers of U.S. print production.[27] The rapid population increase in the major northeastern cities at this time (the population of New York City, for instance, doubled between 1825 and 1840) made anonymity a new fact of life for city-dwelling writers, publishers, and readers; and the contemporaneous breakdown of older forms of social organization, such as extended kin networks, church authority, and communal policing, rendered that anonymity even more threatening.[28] At the same time, the dramatic rise of wage-based capitalism across the northeast meant that the socioeconomic experiences of cultural producers and their nearest audiences were recast broadly in terms of decreased independence and dignity of labor.[29] The conviction of ultraist reformers that vice lurked in every unseen nook of the new metropolis registered both the increasingly superhuman scale of the industrializing city and the increasingly superhuman economic forces besetting individual citizens. Ultraist exposé promised to reestablish social organization and control in the northeast within the realm of print culture. By "drawing back the veil" from every urban "whited sepulchre, full of dead men's bones and all uncleanness," ultraist reformers would map the overwhelming new cityscape and catalogue the people encountered in the new crowd thronging the street. They would render comprehensible the dramatic changes of industrialization through diagnostic and explanatory narrative vignettes, one "behind-the-scenes" revelation at a time.[30]

In early 1831, contemporaneously with Garrison's first issues of *The Liberator*, the *First Annual Report of the New-York Magdalen Society* was published under the aegis of "Arthur Tappan, President."[31] (Tappan, of course, would go on to co-found the American Anti-Slavery Society with Garrison in 1833.) This ultraist antiprostitution text proved to be a watershed publication in the emergence of the antebellum exposé mode, for the urban prostitute had become a focal point for a whole range of northeastern anxieties about modernization: worries about women "living out" of older forms of patriarchal control, fears about the intrusion of the industrial capitalist market into even the most intimate parts of human life, concerns about national reproduction, and loathing of the debasement of manly artisanal trades to "bastard manufactures."[32] While the early issues of Garrison's paper languished in moribund colonialist imagery, the *Report* delved right into the bowels of the new metropolis, breathlessly tearing aside conventions of politeness, logical argument, and narrative order. The individual prostitutes that city residents encountered in the street, the *Report* alleged, were simply the minor "symptoms" of a "plague which assails the very vitals of society"; it aimed to "penetrate" the "sinks of degradation . . . with which our city abounds," and to "set forth . . . the secrets of [the] nests of abominations . . . disguised under the mask of boarding houses, dressmakers, milliners, stores and shops of various kinds . . . where daily and nightly the pollution of girls and women of all ages and colors, married and single is habitually committed."[33] Rampant illicit sex lurked behind every facade of modernizing New York, and the *Report* "present[ed] the hitherto unimaginable fact . . . that the number of [prostitutes] in this city is not less than TEN THOUSAND!!"—or one-tenth of the entire female population, according to the 1830 census.

The first proposition—that epidemic vice had suddenly become endemic to the new metropolis—directly supported the concomitant ultraist assertion of the *Report* that relentless portrayal of proto-pornographic scenes, formerly considered beyond the bounds of polite discourse, was now morally requisite: "A thrill of horror [ought] to be felt by every virtuous man and woman in the community, such as was never produced by any expose [sic] of vice which has ever met the public eye." The *Report* inaugurated the soon-to-be conventional rhetorical mode of "immoral reform," which inverted the basic dyads of morality/immorality and virtue/vice to equate innocence with hypocrisy, and prurience with duty. "Humanity itself" required that readers attend to the "loathsome details" of "a most appalling picture of moral degradation," even though those details were "painful to hear" and "revolting to human nature to relate."[34]

The novelty and strangeness of ultraist exposé to northeastern readers in 1831 was evidenced by the storm of censure that greeted the New-York Magdalen Society *Report* in general and Arthur Tappan in particular. "The loud and just remonstrances of an indignant and outraged public" rose from a variety of quarters in the city: a public meeting in Tammany Hall denounced the report, the newspapers excoriated it, and a number of counter-pamphlets appeared, both indignantly rebutting and ruthlessly satirizing the *Report*.[35] These print responses differed according to the nascent class identification of their authors, revealing that readers identified ultraist reform writing as fundamentally a bourgeois cultural form from its inception: indeed, the twenty-six sponsors of the *Report* widely were esteemed as merchants and professionals—among them Tappan, a silk jobber; three medical doctors; and the Rev. John McDowall, a Presbyterian minister widely considered to have been the primary author of the *Report*. Those who shared the class identity of the New-York Magdalen Society reformers, like the anonymous author of a pamphlet titled "Remarks on the *Report*," indignantly protested that ultraist exposé violated the most basic expectations of "respectability" and "decency" cherished by the "set of gentlemen":

> This conduct is perfectly inexcusable, and, indeed, as coming from a set of gentlemen, most of whom have hitherto borne . . . a highly respectable station in society, it appears very extraordinary and incomprehensible, more especially when it is considered that this report . . . is not merely a statement of exaggerated facts highly colored to serve a particular purpose, but actually a collection of gross, revolting, and disgusting tales and assertions, related in the most indecent style, and all very improbable.[36]

While this upper-class commentator confined his "objections" to the "style" of the new ultraist form, a self-identified "workingman" protested its entire content. Reasserting preindustrial standards of virtue and vice, the anonymous author of a "poetical burlesque" titled "The Phantasmagoria of New-York" charged that ultraist exposé attested not to the piety and zeal of its authors but to their perverted, sex-obsessed "fanaticism." Tappan knew so much about the brothels, the poet proposed, because he was their best patron: "This Tap got rich by furnishing fine dresses, / To ornament the fair in their carresses [sic], / In which this new committe [sic] had a share / And one procured five hundred locks of hair, / Hung round his room as trophies of his taste."[37]

The furious and rapt attention with which such a wide range of northeastern readers greeted the *Report* transfixed Garrison. In the pages of *The Liberator,* he hailed the methods of the New-York Magdalen Society and its subsequent, ever-more-explicit publications with enthusiasm.[38] In John McDowall's ultraist exposé, Garrison seems to have discerned a model for generating urgency and agitation in the same metropolitan audience that his newspaper sought to reach. In frequent encomiums on the antiprostitution crusade, he actively attempted to make connections between that reform project and his own.[39] His February 1832 review of

Magdalen Facts, a collection of prostitution anecdotes intended to defend the New-York Magdalen Society against charges of overstatement, provides an index of his thoughts on the power and timeliness of the new ultraist exposé:

> We are very deeply indebted to the author, J.R. MacDowall [sic] (a philanthropist whose exertions to *do good* have been indefatigable in the city of New-York), for a pamphlet with this title, occupying 104 large octavo pages. It contains a mass of appalling facts, and the most thrilling narratives, relating to the dissolute females of the commercial emporium. It is a monument to the labors, zeal and fidelity of Mr. McDowall. We cannot doubt that the work will be sought with great avidity: its circulation throughout the country must prove of immense benefit to the public morals, in warning the inexperienced and rousing the friends of virtue to active exertions.[40]

Garrison's assurance here—that readers living in the industrializing northeast will be "roused" to "active exertions" only by "a mass of appalling facts" and "the most thrilling narratives"—marks a key point of genesis for the antebellum construction of the Slave South.[41]

Garrison was predisposed to recognize the significance of McDowall's ultraist exposé, since he, too, had labored in the matrix of urban reform out of which the New-York Magdalen Society sprang. He began his editing career in 1828 at one of the first U.S. periodicals devoted exclusively to the temperance cause—an experience that one biographer has proposed led Garrison both to assume the role of "moral legislator" and to seek to publish "as many horrid examples of the evils of liquor as he could find."[42] When he launched *The Liberator,* Garrison had promised readers a diversified reform newspaper divided into four equal sections: editorial, slavery news, local city news, and a "temperance, literary and moral" section on the back page. In devoting fifty percent of his abolitionist journal to the province of urban reform from the outset, he had established a print structure within which he weekly juxtaposed the local concerns of his readers with his abolitionist political program. Rather problematically, though, his urban coverage often threatened to overwhelm the abolitionist content of *The Liberator* in its early months, generating the most consistently eye-catching headlines in the paper throughout most of 1831: "Ardent Spirits Destroy Maternal Affection!" "Horrors of Rum!" "Another Fiendish Outrage!"[43] While much of Garrison's work in the 1831 volume can be seen as his attempt to draw connections between the two realms, these connections remained weakly analogical—as, for instance, when he quoted a list of arguments against the temperance cause from a temperance paper and then editorialized,

"A multitude of equally formidable objections are urged against the cause of emancipation."[44]

Under the tutelage of McDowall's pathbreaking writings, Garrison seems to have perceived that rather than simply analogizing North to South he could adopt the exposé mode of urban reform to create a new and compelling understanding of slavery and the South for his readers. The logic of McDowall's exposé was, indeed, eerily applicable to portraying the South from the perspective of the center of U.S. print production, since ultraist exposé operated on assumptions of hidden vice and internal enemies. While the horrific abuses of slavery in the southern states were hardly hidden—indeed, much abolitionist exposé in subsequent years was culled directly from southern newspapers—the South itself was "hidden" from northern readers by geographical distance. And the idea of the South as the preeminent internal enemy of the nation, a source of corruption within the body politic, had been established forty years earlier. Passages from McDowall's antiprostitution writings seemed to offer, obliquely, a new critique of southern slavery even as they protested urban crime—for instance, when McDowall in *Magdalen Facts* described the industrializing United States as

> a land of liberty, tolerating an internal republic of vicious persons, who imprison at pleasure the daughters of our virtuous, peaceable citizens, and then sell their virtue to the vicious for money. Will freemen tolerate the existence of such practices?[45]

McDowall's exposé logic held that the superhuman forces of modernity in the industrializing northeast had brought into being a powerful, dark social order whose shadowy and inexorable workings opposed basic republican ideals, chiefly by trafficking in (dehumanizing, commodifying) women and by promoting sex outside of the structure of the patriarchal nuclear family. The step from this conceptualization of the transformation of New York City, to a transformed conceptualization of the Slave South, was a small one.

Just eight months after Garrison hailed *Magdalen Facts* in *The Liberator*, he penned a notorious address that made the "very intimate connexion" between industrialization and southern slavery that he had refused to see at the political level. He aligned southern slaveholders with the bawds and procurers, and enslaved women with the abused "magdalens" of antiprostitution exposé, in a conjuncture that would define much of abolitionist discourse for the next three decades:

> Illicit intercourse is constantly taking place at the south, between slaveholders and their hapless victims, and a large proportion of the colored children born every year at the south have white fathers who use and sell them as

they do their cattle. Now, we are for breaking up the slave system at once, and thus prevent this intercourse. Our traducers say—No; let slavery alone—let the tide of pollution continue to swell—and let the female slaves have no protection for their virtue, so that they may be violated always, as at present, with impunity.[46]

As Garrison described the operations of southern slavery for his readers in terms of their very own nightmare visions of their industrializing cities, he inaugurated a truly immediate abolitionist discourse for readers at the center of U.S. print production. By the beginning of 1833, he removed the colonial-tropical engravings from his pages; at the same time, he shifted the focus of his textual content from analytical editorials and moral catechisms to graphic anecdotes of sex and violence. Capitalized words and multiple exclamation points signaled the new mode of reportage: "SAVAGE BARBARITY!!" became a common headline, joined by weekly variations such as "HORRID TRAGEDY!!" and "BLOOD CRIETH!" Like McDowall, Garrison now openly sought to shock and to outrage his readers, presumably thereby spurring them into political action. Also like McDowall, who was defrocked by the Presbyterian church in 1835 for his "infamous publications," Garrison welcomed opposition to his exposé methods, for he calculated that prurient revelations would win greater public attention than the political platform he used them to advance.[47]

By the time that McDowall died suddenly in late 1836, the exposé-based discursive identification of antiprostitution ultraism with Garrison's abolitionism was so great among northeastern readers that they flooded *The Liberator* with letters drawing the comparison. While Garrison himself grandly eulogized McDowall, his readers drew explicit parallels between the two crusades:

> Do you know that the voice of McDowall has been a terror to slaveholders? It has to some. For is not every slaveholder an adulterer and fornicator? . . . They cover this nation with pollution. A chaste slaveholder! compelling men and women to live in *prostitution,* and claiming chastity and moral purity! To all such, and their licentious abettors at the north, McDowall has been a terror.[48]

As such letters to the editor revealed, the new conceptualization of the Slave South that Garrison had managed to develop and to communicate to his readers in just five years was nothing short of representationally revolutionary. The cardinal sin of the modernizing northeastern cities— "prostitution"—had become the identifying feature of the old, backward southern other of the nation.

To be sure, Garrison's exposé-based formulation of the abolitionist motive—his argument that the primary reason for "breaking up the slave system" was to "prevent illicit intercourse"—instilled ideological liabilities into the Slave South at its inception. His ultraist abolitionist program emerged comfortably within the realm of the new bourgeois reform, following as it did the discursive strategies pioneered by the Tappans and McDowalls of the new industrial order. As Garrison located the "pollution" of the Slave South in sins ("barbarity" and "fornication"), rather than in economic injustice and labor exploitation, he asserted a "very intimate connexion" between the underbellies of the new metropolis and the Slave South, while divorcing his crusade for abolition of slave law from any implicit critique of the relative freedom of "free labor" under northeastern industrialization. Critiques of slave labor practices in the 1830s easily shaded into critiques of the changing definition of "free labor" under industrialization, and focusing antislavery discourse on the coercion and discipline of slave laborers begged a comparison with the new forms of labor coercion and discipline being established in the northeast.[49] By detaching corporeal coercion from its economic function, and presenting it instead as a gratification of depraved and sinful planter lusts, Garrison's Slave South, like McDowall's New York City, emerged as a realm driven by irrational evil rather than calculated exploitation.[50]

Indeed, it is one of the infuriating ironies of U.S. history that a materialist analysis of capitalism during the first decades of industrialization was pursued most aggressively by southern political leaders—who, in explicit reaction to Garrison's characterization of the Slave South, were formulating a previously unimaginable defense of American slavery. Whereas the Virginian founders of the nation had plainly considered slavery a crime antithetical to the ideals of the republic, and as late as 1820 James Madison had called the slave trade the "original sin" of U.S. emergence, by 1837 South Carolina Senator John C. Calhoun was radically reframing southern slavery as "a positive good."[51] To do this, he struck directly at the bourgeois obfuscations of Garrison's Slave South, invoking emergent Western critiques of wage-labor capitalism perhaps more cogently than did any other major American political figure of the decade:[52]

> [T]here never has yet existed a wealthy and civilized society in which one portion of the community did not, in point of fact, live on the labor of the other . . . There is and always has been in an advanced stage of wealth and civilization, a conflict between labor and capital. The condition of society in the South exempts us from the disorders and dangers resulting from this conflict; and which explains why it is that the political condition of the slaveholding states has been so much more stable and quiet than that of the North.[53]

Garrison's Slave South seemed in perpetual ideological flight from this sort of comparative materialist analysis of slave capitalism and industrial capitalism. Instead, his new cultural formation ultimately legitimated the emerging industrial capitalist order.[54] By reconfiguring the Slave South as a system of sadism, Garrisonian writers made "work or starve" appear a humanitarian proposition.

In counterbalance to its ideological liabilities, though, Garrison's Slave South had its ideological reward: it forever eviscerated portrayals of the South as a nostalgic, pastoral antidote to the upheavals of the market revolution at the national center. Even Calhoun, in his paean to "society in the South," had to concede that southern slavery, like its northern industrial antithesis, was a system of production based upon labor exploitation and profit motive. The Slave South exploded the conventional ideological juxtapositions of southern country versus northern city, southern old order versus northern new. The surprising new geographical alignments of country and city, slavery and freedom facilitated by the Slave South appeared in the second masthead illustration of *The Liberator,* which Garrison in early 1838 commissioned to replace the sentimental "slave market" scene he had printed weekly for seven years. He hired the same illustrator, David Claypool Johnston, to create the new scene; but like Garrison, Johnston had himself served an apprenticeship in local urban reform between 1831 and 1838: he had won public notice with a new visual vocabulary of the northeastern city, inspired by British illustrator George Cruikshank, and he brought up-to-date urban pictoral techniques to bear on this reenvisioning of Garrison's object of reform.[55] Continuing Garrison's "very intimate connexion" of the Slave South with the new landscape of the industrial city, Johnston in the 1838 masthead presented readers with a bifurcated illustration that revolutionarily posed the Slave South, rendered as an urban scene, against "emancipation," rendered as a pastoral idyll. While the basic organizing elements of the 1831 masthead—the market auction and the background whipping scene—still appeared on the southern side of the illustration, the rural backdrop of that 1831 image now was usurped by a modern cityscape: paving stones covered every inch of visible ground, buildings totally obscured the horizon line, smoggy clouds hid the sun, a racially segregated assembly of figures in modern garb crowded the marketplace, and a crowning sign for "Freedom Street" ironicized the idea that slavery and freedom—or, indeed, the city and freedom—could exist in the same place. In didactic contrast, the "emancipation" side of the masthead aggressively asserted the signs of the very old republican ideal that was being overturned by the market revolution in the northeastern United

Figure 10. David Claypool Johnston, engraver. Second masthead of *The Liberator*, instituted March 1838. Yale Collection of American Literature, Beinecke Rare Book and Manuscript Library.

States. Stridently pastoral, ringed with flora and backed by a sunrise, this scene was punctuated by three iconic pillars of republican ideology: the patriarchal family (seated women and children looking up at a towering father figure); artisanal/agrarian production (hatted and jumpered men sawing logs into boards); and manly, egalitarian patriotism (a circle of celebrating men united around a waving flag).

By 1838, Garrison's formulation of the Slave South in intimate imaginative commerce with the rising industrial city had reinvigorated the South for readers and writers confronting the market revolution at the center of U.S. literary production. This powerful new figure, born in 1830s abolitionist print, rendered obsolete the nostalgic plantation romances that authors from the southern states were beginning to write in the same decade. Literary historians conventionally have identified these plantation romances, beginning with John Pendleton Kennedy's *Swallow Barn* (1832), as a more or less direct response to Garrison's new abolitionist formulations of southern slavery and thus as the origin point of an oppositional or distinctive southern tradition within U.S. literature. Yet even those literary historians who have most influentially asserted the importance of this southern-authored counterdiscourse have admitted that the plantation romance novels seemed curiously irrelevant and ineffectual even at the first moment of their publication: "a venture in the eighteenth-century [novelistic] tradition being kept alive," or "a paper revolution . . . short-lived and unproductive."[56] Against the immediacy of Garrison's dystopically modern Slave South, the nostalgic plantation romances of the 1830s seem to have been published directly into the dustbin of literary history. By the end of the decade, the Slave South had emerged as an indispensable cultural register through which Americans conceptually processed, or displaced, the traumas of rapid modernization. And thus the novels of the South that made a difference in antebellum national life would not be those that attempted to recapture the old Plantation South of the early Republic, for good or for ill, but rather those novels—such as, most centrally, *Uncle Tom's Cabin*—that identified the Slave South as the site of modernity itself.

Exposé Catalogue and Narrative Form

Published a decade before Harriet Beecher Stowe began to compose *Uncle Tom's Cabin,* the first abolitionist bestseller looked, at first glance, nothing like a novel. *American Slavery as It Is: Testimony of a Thousand Witnesses,* published in 1839, instead unmistakably assumed the exposé catalogue form generated in ultraist antiprostitution and temperance reform. The exposé catalogue had arisen in the northeastern United States, as early as McDowall's 1832 *Magdalen Facts,* as a quintessentially urban textual form, derived from and responsive to the encounters of northeastern writers and readers with the streets of their new industrial cities. These catalogues brought together in a single volume tens or even hundreds of exposé vignettes, culled by an editor from a wide range of sources (including newspapers, fiction, testimonials, interviews, and rumors), and assembled with little attention to continuity of style or chronology. Such volumes in the 1830s thus stood as strikingly modern assemblages, raising expectations of coherence and then immediately undermining those expectations as each item in the catalogue proved related to the next only in terms of shock value, discursive mode, and alleged location—the book bound only by the claim that all the hidden horrors it documented took place within a single metropolis. In its assault on the senses and in its overwhelming, disjointed progression of tales—each group of characters taken up with vigor and then discarded, not to appear again in the book—the experience of reading an exposé catalogue mimed a walk down a bustling city street.

But exposé catalogues did more than reproduce the experience of the new industrial city. As well, they imaginatively processed and pointed the way toward an analysis of that experience. Considering the analogous period of modernization in England, Raymond Williams has proposed that writers confronting the industrial city faced "a contradiction, a paradox: the coexistence of variation and apparent randomness with what had in the end to be seen as a determining system: the visible individual facts but beyond them, often hidden, the common condition and destiny."[57] The new metropolis required new narrative forms of the writers who would represent it, and while the exposé catalogues hardly qualified as a fully realized new narrative form on the order of "Dickens's creation of a new kind of novel"—Williams's own suggestion of the "decisive" engagement with industrial modernity presented in British literature—they do provide the great break with conventional prose narrative techniques employed in 1830s U.S. print. The exposé in its primary impulse, after all, modulated precisely between the poles of what Williams terms the "double condition . . . the visible and the obscured, which is the true significance of the city . . . as a dominant social form." Presenting the Broadway promenade only to puncture it, exposé writers penetrated facades of buildings, spied behind closed doors, and ventured into darkened districts of vice and danger. When gathered into an "exhaustive" catalogue like John McDowall's *Magdalen Facts,* the compounded exposé scenes further enabled the beginnings of a glimpse of Williams's "determining system" behind the "apparent randomness" of the city. As McDowall and his coworkers juxtaposed dozens of disjunctive but repetitious scenes of revelation—for instance, providing examples of the myriad ways women could end up working as prostitutes in New York City (abduction, seduction, beating, abandonment, imprisonment, depravity, drugging, blackmail, incest, atheism, rebellion, orphaning, etc.)—their urban catalogues operated at the juncture of repetition and seemingly endless variation, proving (in McDowall's anticipation of Williams) the existence of an "all-encompassing system" of prostitution in New York City.[58]

That a mimetically urban textual form should have become the vehicle through which the Slave South entered mainstream national culture seems implausible, and yet abolitionist discourse made its first significant incursion on a broad northeastern audience in exactly that form with *American Slavery as It Is*. Garrison's and Tappan's American Anti-Slavery Society presented the slender, cheaply produced volume in a form immediately recognizable to urban northeastern readers: the newspaper-like tiny print and columnated pages of the book assured readers of the abundance of sensational vignettes contained within. Its epigraph, operating within ultraist convention, played simultaneously upon the prurience and the virtue of readers, by promoting both the luridness of the scenes contained in the volume and the reformist duty involved in their communication: "True humanity consists, not in a SQUEAMISH EAR, but in listening to the story of human suffering and endeavoring to relieve it." The primary editor of the volume, Theodore Dwight Weld, then encapsulated the florid essence of the exposé catalogue form in a single, breathless prefatory sentence:

> We will prove that the slaves in the United States are treated with barbarous inhumanity . . . that they are often made to wear round their necks iron collars armed with prongs, to drag heavy chains and weights at their feet while working in the field, and to wear yokes, and bells, and iron horns; that they are often kept confined in the stocks day and night for weeks together, made to wear gags in their mouths for hours or days, have some of their front teeth torn out or broken off, that they may be easily detected when they run away; that they are frequently flogged with terrible severity, have red pepper rubbed into their lacerated flesh, and hot brine, spirits of turpentine, &c., poured over the gashes to increase the torture; that they are often stripped naked, their backs and limbs cut with knives, bruised and mangled by scores and hundreds of blows with the paddle, and terribly torn by the claws of cats, drawn over them by their tormentors; . . . that they are often suspended by the arms and whipped and beaten until they faint, and when revived by restoratives, beaten again until they faint, and sometimes until they die; that their ears are often cut off, their eyes knocked out, their bones broken, their flesh branded with red hot irons; that they are maimed, mutilated and burned to death over slow fires.[59]

Like McDowall's New York City, Weld's Slave South would emerge from his pages as a *system* of "barbarous inhumanity." While individual exposés of abuse of enslaved people in the southern states, published in *The Liberator* or elsewhere, might appear anecdotal to readers, Weld's catalogued iteration of endless permutations of torture (and "worse"—the already-conventional coded reference to presumably unspeakable sexual crimes) would prove that such sadism itself comprised the very structure of the Slave South.

Because the exposé catalogue form had arisen as an imaginative engagement with the new industrial city—an attempt to write the metropolis into being as a coherent whole—the form itself encouraged Weld and his co-laborers to conceptualize the Slave South they were unveiling as a totalized, monolithic entity composed of interrelated and knowable units (buildings, neighborhoods, types of people). The vignettes brought together in *American Slavery as It Is* overwhelmingly consisted of urban scenes, organizing the Slave South along axes nearly identical to the new metropolis of urban exposé: doggedly set in interior spaces, the vignettes of the abolitionist catalogue followed the tendency of city exposé to "reduce urban life to secrets behind closed doors."[60] While Weld advertised his interest in collecting information about the "food, clothing, and conditions of work" of enslaved laborers in the southern states, descriptions of agricultural labor and production were almost entirely absent from the volume.[61] Instead, the Slave South created in the exposé catalogue appeared as a loose aggregation of certain types of interior spaces serving certain specific abusive or evil functions. The mansion—the "big house" of the old plantation, but now as well the urban metonym of capital accumulation and despotic oligarchic power—assumed a central role, as veneers of southern hospitality and feminine domestic virtue repeatedly were upset by the sudden intrusion of horribly beaten, mangled, and restrained bodies bursting forth from attics, from cellars, and from behind secret panels. "Workhouses" or "calabooses"—buildings designed for the simultaneous execution and concealment of torture—took on a looming presence throughout the volume, only comparable to that granted "the Tombs" in exposés of New York City. And both gambling dens and the lodgings of "kept misses," staples of ultraist urban reform, served as settings for an expansive swath of "monstrous" revelations. Holding the plantation—which had been perceived, since colonial days, as the identifying socioeconomic unit of the southern states—now totally out of view, *American Slavery as It Is* presented the Slave South to northeastern readers as a systematized and standardized, if geographically skewed, reflection of the underbellies of their own industrializing cities.

The way had been prepared for this breakthrough abolitionist text, in the two years leading up to its publication, by a southerner: the South Carolinian Angelina E. Grimké, who by 1839 was both Weld's collaborator on *American Slavery as It Is* and his wife. Like Garrison, Tappan, Lydia Maria Child, and many other abolitionists, Grimké developed her conceptualization of the Slave South and its place in the nation out of the matrix of urban, especially antiprostitution, reform. Although she moved north to Philadelphia with her sister Sarah in 1829 because of her opposition to slavery and her Quaker belief, it was only in 1836, after the sisters settled in New York City—the center of ultraist antiprostitution reform—that Grimké began her groundbreaking public work for the abolitionist cause.[62] In the same months in early 1837 when she and Sarah famously flouted etiquette dictates against women speaking in public to lecture for the abolitionist cause, they were also making public addresses to the quarterly meetings of the New-York Female Moral Reform Society (NYFMRS), the successor organization to McDowall's and Tappan's Magdalen Society. An account of their March addresses appeared in the organ of the NYFMRS, the exposé-driven *Advocate of Moral Reform* (masthead slogan: "For there is nothing covered that shall not be revealed: Neither hid, that shall not be made known"), where, sandwiched between lurid reports of incest and life in the "brothels, or *gates of hell* in our large cities," Angelina Grimké was reported to have warned that "[t]he black waves of pollution are rolling over our land from North to South, from East to West, and . . . the faint cry that comes up from the dread abyss fails to awaken us from our guilty slumbers."[63]

Having lived parts of her adult life on each side of the industrial city/Slave South divide, though, Grimké came at the conjuncture of the two imaginative realms in late 1830s print from a different perspective. New Yorkers had identified "illicit intercourse" (as Garrison termed it) as the central threat of modernization, but her native experience of South Carolina told Grimké that if northeastern writers had invented a form that enabled them to name and to expose publicly this formerly tacit crime, they had hardly invented the crime itself. In her first abolitionist publication, *Appeal to the Christian Women of the South* (1836), also written from New York, Grimké broke with established abolitionist practice and addressed readers in the southern states, presciently warning them that the representational revolution under way at the center of U.S. cultural production—converting local secrets into public knowledge— would have a transformative effect on metropolitan conceptions of their region.

Northerners know nothing at all about slavery; they think it is perpetual bondage only; but of the *depth of degradation* that word involves, they have no conception; if they had, *they would never cease* their efforts until so *horrible* a system was overthrown.[64]

From her own observation of their preoccupations, Grimké had found that northern readers would not oppose southern slavery because of its defining features, slave law or labor exploitation—which she dismissed rather flippantly here as "perpetual bondage only." Rather, she explained, the order of her native land would be exposed to northern readers as "so *horrible* a system" only when its "monstrous features" were revealed to them. To give voice to these salient "monstrous features" of the Slave South, Grimké was culling language from urban antiprostitution reform, using the new coded terms for sexual exploitation, such as, here, the italicized phrase *"depth of degradation."*

In her next pamphlet, Grimké shifted her address back to the urban audience that surrounded her, and her focus to forwarding what she understood to be the politically transformative rhetorical relationship between the industrializing national center and its Slave South. With *Appeal to the Women of the Nominally Free States* (1837), she stepped directly into the problem of freedom so fundamental for Americans experiencing the market revolution; and pivotally, she proposed that the Slave South served as not the mirror, but the *origin,* of the restricted personal autonomy and moral chaos besetting metropolitan readers. As did the title of the speech itself, Grimké's opening pages played upon local uncertainties about the restricted definition of freedom being forged under industrialization. Women of the "nominally free states" could constitute themselves truly free only by taking up abolitionist action against the Slave South, Grimké proposed, for "if we have no [duty] to act, then may *we* well be termed 'the white slaves of the North'—for, like our brethren in bonds, we must seal our lips in silence and despair."[65]

Cannily conflating wage slavery and prostitution—the great twinned horrors of 1830s New York City—with this early usage of the term "white slaves," Grimké went on to reveal to her readers that the epochal changes they perceived in their own modernizing order were in fact exogenous, matters of space rather than time. Industrial modernity should be understood as an infiltration of the center of the republic by its old, familiar source of internal corruption:

Like the miasma of some pestilential pool, [slavery] spreads its desolating influence far beyond its own boundaries. *Who does not know that licentiousness is now a crying sin at the North as well as at the South?* and who does not admit that the manners of the South in this respect have had a wide and destructive influence on the Northern character? Can crime be fashionable and common in one part of the Union and unrebuked by the other without corrupting the very heart's blood of the nation, and lowering the standard of morality everywhere? Can Northern men go down to the well-watered plains of the South to make their fortunes, without . . . drinking of the waters of that river of pollution which rolls over . . . Sodom and Gomorrah? Do they return uncontaminated to their homes, or does not many a Northerner dig the grave of his virtue in . . . our Southern States? And can our theological and academic institutions be opened to the sons of the planter without endangering the purity and morals of our own sons . . . ? Impossible! . . . Have Northern women, then, nothing to do with slavery, when its demoralizing influence is polluting their domestic circles and blasting the fair character of *their* sons and brothers?[66]

Here Grimké conjured the familiar eighteenth-century figure of "our Southern States"—tropical, colonial, and decadent; swampy, abnormally fertile, and vice-ridden—thereby accessing her audience's longer cultural understanding of the Plantation South as a contagion ("pestilence") within the U.S. body politic. But she deployed this venerable image to thoroughly modern ends, using the contagious-South paradigm to direct the attention of her metropolitan readers away from the urban brothels, starving sewing-girls, and debauched capitalists that so transfixed them, and toward the reimagined Slave South, which she in turn characterized with the code words of antiprostitution ultraism: the center of "fashionable crime," "the grave of virtue," the source of "licentiousness" and "desolation." The pestilential southern waters that in the 1790s dealt the degeneration of the colonial tropics under Grimké's pen in the late 1830s became the "river of pollution" that "corrupted the very heart's blood of the nation" with the ills of industrial modernity.

With this fertile transmutation of Plantation South—source of tropical-colonial contagion—into Slave South—source of industrialized unfreedom—Grimké rewrote the priorities of urban exposé. To fully fathom the industrial city, the new "system" at the national center, "nominally free" U.S. readers would have to plumb the depths of the Slave South:

Many [northern women] have no correct views of the height and depth, the length and breadth, and innumerable horrors of this enormous system of crime. They too easily allow themselves to be persuaded of the mildness of American slavery, by those who go to the South, *not* to search out the hidden works of darkness . . . Such see no more of the internal machinery of slavery, than the man who goes to the theatre and sits in the pit or the boxes sees of what passes behind the curtain. Some of us have been *behind* the scenes of the South, and we feel it to be an imperative duty to assure you that slavery is a whited sepulchre, "full of dead men's bones and all uncleanness."[67]

Remarkably rescaling the Slave South for her readers, Grimké proposed that "this enormous system of crime" in fact spread across the entire face of the nation, north and south ("height and depth"), east and west ("length and breadth"). And thus *behind* the scenes of the South" lay the deep and immediate revelation promised by urban exposé. By penetrating the Slave South, Grimké promised, metropolitan readers would discover exactly the features of the industrializing transformation of their own section that they feared or opposed: the mechanized factory ("the internal machinery of slavery") and the disorderly city with its promiscuous entertainments ("the theatre . . . in the pit or the boxes").

Raymond Williams has proposed that Dickens confronted the "apparent randomness" of London and revealed within it a "determining system" by creating a new kind of novel. Across the Atlantic, Angelina Grimké was leading the way for U.S. writers to confront the "apparent randomness" of New York City and to discern *without* it a "determining system" underwritten by their Slave South. In fact, *American Slavery as It Is* went a step further than Dickens. By interpolating southern setting with urban form, Grimké and Weld implied the systemic connections between northeastern industrialization and southern raw material production that Edward Said took Williams to task for eliding in the British context.[68] Just as the produce of southern slave labor fed the factories of the industrializing northeast, *American Slavery as It Is* promised readers at the epicenter of the market revolution that the true bedrock of "this enormous system of crime" lay beneath the nation, in the South of their collective mind's eye.[69]

By 1840, it had become impossible to see the South in U.S. culture apart from its urban incarnation as the Slave South; conversely, as the development of urban exposé was routed so resolutely southward by abolitionist writing, it had become equally impossible to see the industrial city without a return of its southern double. The next major incursion of abolitionist discourse into mainstream U.S. culture, indeed, operated at precisely this visceral site of connection. From 1841 to 1843, Lydia Maria Child edited the *National Anti-Slavery Standard,* based in New York City; the *Standard* was by then the official organ of the American Anti-Slavery Society. During this short editorship, Child doubled the subscription list of the journal to a circulation figure never before approached by an abolitionist periodical in the United States.[70] Her pivotal popularization of the *Standard* stemmed from her immensely successful weekly column, "Letters from New-York," which appeared as essentially a serialized urban exposé catalogue; and this conventional form was even more recognizable when in 1843 and 1844 the individual installments were reprinted in two volumes; the collection, *Letters from New-York*, went through at least ten editions in the subsequent five years.[71] Child radically expanded the audience for abolitionist print in the northeast by writing local urban exposé—at first glance a bizarre geographical displacement, but in the context of the rise of the Slave South in U.S. culture across the previous decade, a perfectly intelligible development.

In her *Letters*, Child literally repositioned the Slave South at the national center, in the heart of New York City. Much as Bryant impressionistically had identified the ill winds of modernity as uncanny "breezes of the South," Child repetitiously posed the temporal transformation of New York City as a series of spatial incursions of the Slave South into the national center. In the collected *Letters*, she titled the first installment of her series "Streets of Modern Babylon," summoning the paradoxical sense of the local city "streets" as the site where the "modern" was revealed to be just the return of the presumably premodern South—figured here, typologically, as the ancient "Babylon": tropical, decadent, vice-ridden, and always already doomed to decline. In this first letter, Child defined the new metropolis in terms of its deviation from the ideals of the republic, foregrounding the power extremes generated by industrial capitalism—extremes openly displayed in the close proximity of capitalist and pauper in the urban world. To conceptualize the "deeper system" underlying the overwhelming experience of wealth disparities on New York streets, Child personified the anti-republican poles of "Wealth" and "Poverty" in order to illustrate them in human scale and relationship:

> You ask what is now my opinion of this great Babylon . . . The din of crowded life, and the eager chase for gain, still run through its streets, like the perpetual murmur of a hive. Wealth dozes on French couches, thrice piled, and canopied with damask, while Poverty camps on the dirty pavement, or sleeps off its wretchedness in the watch-house. There, amid the splendour of Broadway, sits the blind negro beggar, with horny hand and tattered garments, while opposite to him stands the stately mansion of the slave trader, still plying his bloody trade, and laughing to scorn the cobweb laws, through which the strong can break so easily.[72]

Her characterization of the economic relations organizing New York City as those between a "blind negro beggar" and a "slave trader" took Grimké's argument to its logical conclusion: if the Slave South served as the fundamental basis of "the enormous system of crime" undermining the nation, then one should read the streets of New York City in order to uncover southern slavery in all its loathsomeness. In her *Letters*, Child identified the structural transformations of the market revolution most plainly contrary to republican ideology, encapsulated them in the figure of the emblematic new industrial city, New York—and then aligned New York City with, and collapsed it into, the remade figure of the Slave South. These two realms—industrial city and Slave South—by the early 1840s were bound together imaginatively for U.S. writers by their shared contradiction of the ideals of the republic, their joint location of power extremes, and their fundamental hostility to the very existence of the nation according to the terms of its founding.

Child's *Letters from New-York* thus appeared as a *sectionalist* text, operating not within the nation/Plantation South, self/other valences of the 1790s, but turning upon a more or less equally weighted binary of Slave South against its opposite and double, "Industrial North." With the ascendance of this sectional ideological structure, U.S. writers lost both the unblemished, virtuous center, and the stable repository for real conditions that conflicted with national ideology, which the nation/Plantation South opposition had provided to previous generations. Now that both North and South were defined by their distance from national ideals, "the nation" resided comfortably *nowhere* within the national borders, and real conditions opposed to republican ideology were to be found everywhere. The exposé catalogue form itself intensified rather than ameliorated this sectionalist paradox. The dueling northern and southern exposés that proliferated across the 1840s and 1850s offered only antinational mirror images of each other, as a comparison of any group of title pages demonstrates:

'Mysteries and Miseries' . . .	Beautiful Quadroon tortured by inquisitors . . .
Homicide—horrible details . . .	Torture of young Harry . . .
Death by starvation . . .	Black Bob sent off to starve . . .
15 streets, courts and alleys crowded with dens of depravity . . .	Slave girls as bed companions . . .
Thirteen Years in the North, 1853	*Slavery Unmasked,* 1856[73]

. . . and so on. U.S. readers and writers found themselves oscillating between a North and a South, a country and a city equally corrupt. The foundational geographic-ideological juxtapositions of their print culture had come to encompass only equal poles of nationalist negation.

While Child's *Letters* sprang directly from this imaginative oscillation, her innovation on the exposé catalogue form pointed the way toward an eventual synthesis of sections. Unlike the editors of exposé catalogues, including those of *American Slavery as It Is,* who simply gathered discontinuous vignettes into a chaotic assemblage, Child related each installment of her *Letters* through a stable narrator, who reacted to and interpreted each scene she encountered, and who learned from and remembered each sequential vignette. Her book, therefore, evidenced a clear narrative progression from beginning to end, as opposed to the mimetically random inclusivity of the urban catalogues. And most important, Child's consistent narrator modulated between and at times encompassed both of the poles of sectionalism—North and South, as well as their concomitant binaries (city and country, old time and new, industrial and agrarian production). For instance, in the fourth letter the narrator seeks a respite from the teeming urban streets in an idealized rural walk on the Jersey shore of the Hudson River. "[I]n the full glory of moonlight," the scene initially provides an overdetermined contrast to the prior letters: the countryside is "undesecrated by the evil passions of man," "lovely as a nook of Paradise," "completely embowered in foliage" with the only sound "the measured cadence of the plashing waves." Then, suddenly, we find that the narrator may escape the city limits, but she cannot escape her new knowledge of modernity. Her own consciousness carries an awareness of the horrors of the city into the countryside:

> All else was still—still—so fearfully still, that one might almost count the beatings of the heart. That my heart did beat, I acknowledge; for here was the supposed scene of the Mary Rogers tragedy . . . I could not forget that the quiet lovely path we were treading was near to the city, with its thousand hells, and frightfully easy of access.
>
> We spoke of the murdered girl, as we passed the beautiful promontory near the Sybil's cave, where her body was found. lying half in and half out of the water . . . [T]he aforesaid remembrances of the city haunted me like evil spirits.[74]

Into the "still—still" and suddenly "fearful" quiet of the rural setting breaks the sudden irruption of the city's "thousand hells," ushered in by the beating of the narrator's own heart, the rhythm of her own narration. This sensational, gothic, "haunting" interpenetration of rural and urban collapses the rural/urban binary itself, even as it revolves, seemingly compulsively, around the displayed body of a sexually exploited woman— here the murdered prostitute Mary Rogers—which physically bridges the terms of the dyad ("lying half in and half out of the water"). More essential, though, is the subjective connection made in the narrator's mind, bringing experiences of country and city together in perception and memory in order to construct a more complete understanding of her surroundings than ideological juxtapositions such as "country and city" can achieve.

As the encounter of an individual, continuous consciousness with the new social formation of the city—and, simultaneously, with its Slave South underbelly—Child's *Letters* as a whole modeled something like the beginning of a new novelistic mode, characterized by an omniscient narrator who functioned as moral geographer for the reader. While this new sort of novel would take from the exposé catalogue its cast of thousands and its episodic, roving, constantly interrupted plot, its narrator would filter these raw materials of "the system," giving them shape, hierarchy, and connection.[75] Indeed, literary narrative increasingly seemed the most apt avenue for plotting the "correct" dimensions of the "enormous system of crime" spawned by the market revolution, as well as the southern slavery and westward expansion that fed it. Only in the imaginative realm could writers encompass those superhumanly scaled social and geographic divisions, draw explanatory interrelationships not perceivable in lived experience, and create coherence for U.S. readers experiencing a profound reorganization of life at the national center. This new narrative form, this fiction more true than fact, would be the means through which the Slave South emerged as the primary terrain upon which U.S. readers imaginatively engaged their experience of modernization in the decade before the Civil War.

CHAPTER SIX

American Universal Geography

Every Englishman in Australia, in South Africa, in India, or in whatever barbarous country their forts and factories have been set up,—represents London, represents the art, power and law of Europe. Every man educated at the Northern school carries the like advantages into the South. For it is confounding distinctions to speak of the geographic sections of this country as of equal civilization.

> —Ralph Waldo Emerson, "Address to the Citizens of Concord" (1851)

THE MOST FAMOUS IMAGE in Ralph Waldo Emerson's early writings—the "transparent eyeball" of *Nature* (1836)—is a figure of disappeared dominion: "I am nothing; I see all." This dream of an absolute, singular, and omniscient subjectivity, which cannot itself be perceived or objectified, long has been identified as the first published statement of "Emerson's doctrine of the Oversoul."[1] More recently, scholars have found the "transparent eyeball" formulation exceptionally enabling to Jacksonian expansion, authorizing the expansion itself while simultaneously exempting it from the criticisms leveled at the imperial projects of European nations.[2] Turning to the passage from *Nature*, we perceive that Emerson generates the crucial new image out of a rhetorical relay with Southern markers:

> In the woods is perpetual youth. Within these plantations of God, a decorum and sanctity reign, a perennial festival is dressed, and the guest sees not how he should tire of them in a thousand years. In the woods, we return to reason and faith. There I feel that nothing can befall me in life,—no disgrace, no calamity (leaving me my eyes), which nature cannot repair. Standing on the bare ground,—my head bathed by the blithe air and uplifted into infinite space,—all mean egotism vanishes. I become a transparent eyeball; I am nothing; I see all; the currents of the Universal Being circulate through me; I am part or parcel of God. The name of the nearest friend sounds then foreign and accidental: to be brothers, to be acquaintances, master or servant, is then a trifle and a disturbance. I am the lover of uncontained and immortal beauty. In the wilderness, I find something more dear and connate

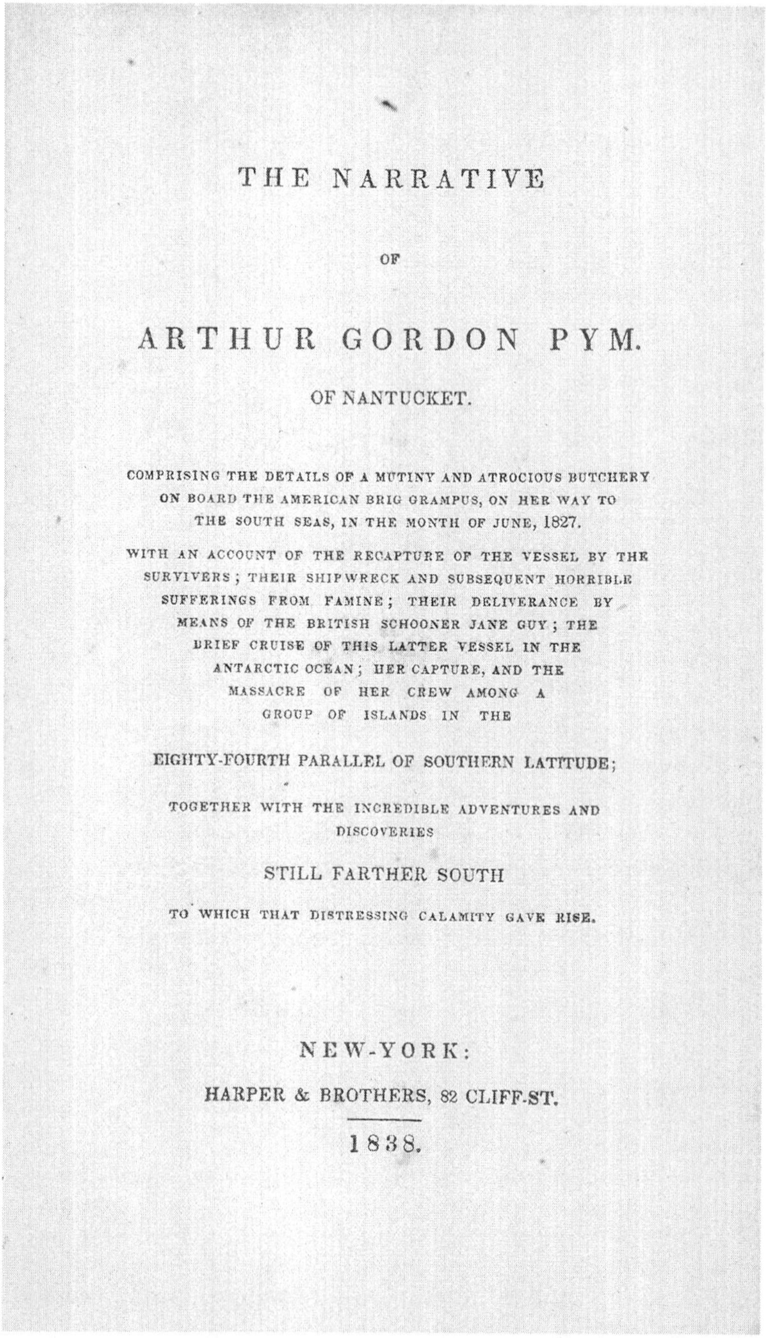

THE NARRATIVE

OF

ARTHUR GORDON PYM.

OF NANTUCKET.

COMPRISING THE DETAILS OF A MUTINY AND ATROCIOUS BUTCHERY
ON BOARD THE AMERICAN BRIG GRAMPUS, ON HER WAY TO
THE SOUTH SEAS, IN THE MONTH OF JUNE, 1827.

WITH AN ACCOUNT OF THE RECAPTURE OF THE VESSEL BY THE
SURVIVERS; THEIR SHIPWRECK AND SUBSEQUENT HORRIBLE
SUFFERINGS FROM FAMINE; THEIR DELIVERANCE BY
MEANS OF THE BRITISH SCHOONER JANE GUY; THE
BRIEF CRUISE OF THIS LATTER VESSEL IN THE
ANTARCTIC OCEAN; HER CAPTURE, AND THE
MASSACRE OF HER CREW AMONG A
GROUP OF ISLANDS IN THE

EIGHTY-FOURTH PARALLEL OF SOUTHERN LATITUDE;

TOGETHER WITH THE INCREDIBLE ADVENTURES AND
DISCOVERIES

STILL FARTHER SOUTH

TO WHICH THAT DISTRESSING CALAMITY GAVE RISE.

NEW-YORK:

HARPER & BROTHERS, 82 CLIFF-ST.

1838.

Figure 11. Title page, [Edgar Allan Poe], *The Narrative of Arthur Gordon Pym,* 1838. Special Collections, University of Virginia Library.

than in streets or villages. In the tranquil landscape, and especially in the distant line of the horizon, man beholds somewhat as beautiful as his own nature.

The apotheosis of centralized subjectivity at the center of the passage is bracketed by invocations of the Plantation South and the Slave South, respectively. It is generated out of a specific sort of engagement with undeveloped land: and while "woods" and, particularly, "wilderness"—the other terms Emerson uses for this land in the passage—are historically resonant enough words in New England writing, the crystallizing term here is "plantations of God." This locution takes us back to the foundational Puritan plantations of New England's colonization (Plymouth Plantation, Massachusetts Bay Colony, Rhode Island and Providence Plantations), but by 1836 Emerson also evokes over a half century of the "plantation" as primal other for the United States.

Ascending out of this simultaneity of selfness and otherness, identity with and opposition to the "plantation"—which flexible term also acts as an index of American history from colonialist settlement to the sectionalist present—the "transparent eyeball" emerges to obviate relationship entirely. Now Emerson contextualizes the need to obliterate reciprocality by invoking the modern Slave South of his own moment; he descends from the mountaintop of God-stature via a degenerating progression of social relationships that reads as the demise of republican ideals under industrialization. "To be brothers, to be acquaintances, master or servant, is then a trifle and a disturbance," he notes, moving from fraternal egalitarianism, to noncommittal impersonality, to the antirepublican power extremes inevitably based upon slavery. While he dismisses this devolution as "a trifle" in the aftermath of achieving absolute subjectivity, he has quite deliberately constructed it as "a disturbance" to his readers. Across the passage, he directs their eyes from the invigorating Plantation South of the colonial past, to the deflating Slave South of the industrial present, and then finally to promised resolution in what might seem the subjugated South of a recuperated U.S. imperial future: "the distant line of the horizon," the promise of unlimited territorial dominion, radiating out so far as the central I/eye may will it.

It makes sense that Emerson would produce the abstract image of unilateral subjectivity, at this historical moment, by cycling through historical incarnations of the South. The founders had assumed that U.S. expansion across the continent would defuse, by diffusing, different forms of strife within the body politic—conflicts between regions, classes, and races. Instead, since the Missouri Compromise of 1820, westward expansion had fed the rise of North/South sectionalism, as political leaders from the two regions squared off over whether slavery would be legal or outlawed in the new states that were being carved out of western lands.[3] Central to ordering this rapidly enlarging United States, from Emerson's geographical perspective, was re-mastering its Slave South— for this modern South had broken out of its proper peripheral relation to the national center and was, in renegade fashion, attempting to magnify rather than to ameliorate the national sin of slavery.[4]

Without the perceived challenge from and antagonistic response to this expansionist Slave South, indeed, it is hard to imagine how "New England Transcendentalism"—as it was called in Emerson's day and still is in our own—could have come into being. The term itself is plainly oxymoronic: what could be considered to be transcendent about so small and so particular a locality?[5] Rather than transcending place, the body of writing produced by Emerson in the years before the Civil War inscribes New England as a silent norm, as a universal center. By 1851, Emerson was explicitly positing Massachusetts as the Western analogue of London on the imperial globe. "Massachusetts is little," he allows, but consider "Massachusetts in all the quarters of her dispersion"—the small state as controlling center of a vast, subordinate periphery. Just as "every Roman reckoned himself at least a match for a Province," and just as "every Englishman . . . in whatever barbarous country . . . represents the art, power and law of Europe," so should every Harvard man "carry the like advantages into the South."[6] This unilateral authority of the tiny center over a vast and limitless periphery—"the farthest South, and the uttermost West"—is mandated by universal and natural law: "Every nation and every man bows, in spite of himself, to a higher mental and moral existence." Emerson's appeal to higher law, though, is provoked by a quite down-to-earth, indeed debasing, statute: this is his first address on the Fugitive Slave Law of 1850, which he protests chiefly because it has caused "this royal position of Massachusetts" to be "foully lost." Sectionalist maneuvering in Congress, compromise between sections, the election of slaveholding presidents from the southern states: the politics of the day are confusing the natural, universal geographic order of things—the dominance, in the age of empire, of the center over its periphery. "It is confounding distinctions," Emerson protests, "to speak of the geographic sections of this country as of equal civilization." The paradox is profound, and difficult to assimilate: arguing against slavery is not necessarily arguing for universal liberation and equality. Rather, an emancipationist program may exist comfortably alongside, and possibly even bolster, a system of hierarchy and domination on other bases and by

other means—as the contemporaneous case of British West Indian emancipation was demonstrating in the 1830s and 1840s.[7]

New England Transcendentalism, as Emerson was developing it between 1836 and 1851, did a breathtaking end run around the sectionalist standoff in U.S. letters—the back-and-forth of Industrial North and
Slave South, wage slavery and chattel slavery. Most southern partisans
failed to comprehend the power of this new universalism and simply dismissed Transcendentalist writers as obfuscating and possibly unhinged.
Instead, the contemporary critic of Emerson's methods who had perhaps
the greatest insight into their geographical assumptions was, like Emerson himself, a writer we think of as more literary than political. Following on the heels of *Nature,* Edgar Allan Poe's only novel, *The Narrative
of Arthur Gordon Pym* (1838), reads as a sort of hallucinatory incarnation of Emerson's "transparent eyeball." Claiming to be a found document from the United States Exploring Expedition of 1836–1838—a real
mission of unprecedented global scope that had been charged with cir-
cumnavigating South America, touching on Antarctica, and ending in the
Pacific Northwest—Poe's novel insistently maps the domestic sectional
conflict onto the seemingly limitless global appetite of nascent U.S. imperialism.[8] The title page of the book emblematizes this imperial drive in
U.S. culture as the journey of an emigrating New Englander—"Arthur
Gordon Pym of Nantucket," the absurdly specific, tiny center—into a
sublimely infinite realm for his global domination, to the South and
"STILL FARTHER SOUTH."

Poe's novel, though, proceeds according to what we might apprehend
as a southern imperial imaginary: from his perspective, the very structure
of nineteenth-century empire originates in the white-over-black binary of
racialized slavery, and his quasi-science-fiction novel of exploration unfolds a radical white/black polarity between antagonistically posed civilized explorers and savage others. The brutal, openly race-obsessed
progress of Pym as he heads "STILL FARTHER SOUTH" ends abruptly
with a "shrouded human figure, very far larger in its proportions than
any dweller among men" with skin "of the perfect whiteness of the
snow," whose appearance abruptly cuts off the Nantucketer's narration.
Critics have tended to interpret this whiteness *ex machina* as Poe's endorsement of an absolute white supremacy, but in the final "Note" with
which he ends the novel, an unidentified authoritative narrator dismisses
the accounts of both "Mr. Pym" and his "editor," "Mr. Poe," to reveal
that the ultimate meaning of the tale is to be found in its literal subtext:
in buried writing Pym has discovered, but misrecognized as nonliterate,
in chasms below the earth during his southern expedition. These writ-

ings, the authoritative narrator explains, are in the Arabic, Egyptian, and Ethiopian languages—a revelation that stems equally from Poe's fascination with theories of the African origins of knowledge and from his southern insight that strains from Africa underwrite not only the culture of the United States, but also its very existence on the face of the earth.

As Poe spins something like a narrative of New England sectionalism projected outward onto a global South in *The Narrative of Arthur Gordon Pym,* he shadows the story of imperial dominion with an ever-present possibility of revolt, of an uprising of the ostensible "savages" Pym encounters—of a further turning, as Jefferson had styled it in 1785, of the wheel of American revolution. By contrast, the singularity of Emerson's contemporaneous "transparent eyeball" admits of no such challenge from below. To transcend the "littleness" of Massachusetts, Emerson was locating universal Truth there. The stakes of this Transcendentalist endeavor, and Poe's proleptic critique of it, would become particularly urgent in the years surrounding the Mexican War (1845–1848), as slaveholding North Carolinian President James K. Polk pursued the annexation of Texas, ultimately wresting the entire U.S. Southwest from Mexico and extending the borders of the nation at last to their prophesied span, from sea to shining sea.

Emerson's Transcendent Section in 1844

In April 1844, just as Lydia Maria Child was preparing the second volume of her *Letters from New-York* for the press, Emerson published an address titled "The Young American" in *The Dial,* the preeminent organ of what contemporaries had already identified as a Boston-centered "Transcendental" movement in U.S. letters. Child's *Letters,* coming as they did out of abolitionist discourse, were organized around the sectional poles of Industrial North and Slave South, and the title of Emerson's address seemed to signal a similar preoccupation: he appropriated the term "Young America" from the slavery-countenancing, South-including Democrats affiliated with John O'Sullivan's Manhattan-based *Democratic Review.*[9] But the work of Emerson's address is in fact to surmount the sectionalist divide and to assert an alternative geographic imaginary for the nation. Contemplating the wildfire expansion of the United States to the westward—O'Sullivan had also coined the term "Manifest Destiny"—Emerson revives the center-periphery model as the right geographic order for the modernizing nation.[10] This centralized imperial model, which admits of no sectionalist jockeying between center

and periphery, is for Emerson inherited from the colonial origins of
America, and produced first of all in the realm of "intellectual culture"—
and more specifically, literature.

> GENTLEMEN:
> It is remarkable, that our people have their intellectual culture from one
> country, and their duties from another. Our books are European. We were
> born within the fame and sphere of Shakspeare and Milton, of Bacon, Dry-
> den, and Pope . . . We are sent to a feudal school to learn democracy.[11]

The address opens with a bit of a joke: "We are sent to a feudal school to
learn democracy." Given the colonial origins of the United States, in
other words, "democracy" is simply not what "we" in the United States
have been trained to foster, among ourselves or in the world. Nor indeed,
Emerson goes on to intimate, is it what "we" need to know at this epoch
in national life.

His very constitution of the first person plural in these opening lines
exhibits a lesson learned in America's "feudal school," as Emerson performs the cultural imperialism that his passage describes. By presenting the
address in its textual form with the leading marker of its oral delivery—the
salutation "GENTLEMEN"—intact, Emerson qualifies a "we," which might
otherwise read "citizens of the United States," as restricted to the audience present at his original reading of the lecture at the Boston Mercan-
tile Library Association. He maintains and reiterates this quasi-imperial
"we"—readable simultaneously as "U.S. citizen" and "citizen of Boston
and environs"—throughout the address, for he proposes that the true import and advantage of the modern expansion that is his subject may be
perceived only from the industrializing national center that he and his
privileged audience inhabit.

Members of the Library Association and readers of *The Dial* should
understand the industrialization and expansion transforming their nation, Emerson proposes, as forces that will at last accomplish the complete integration of the northeastern core where they reside—achieving
the true geographic concentration of political, economic, and cultural
power, on a scale of which 1790s nationalists like Webster, Morse, and
Dwight only dreamed. "Who has not been stimulated to reflection by the
facilities now in progress of construction for travel and the transporta-
tion of goods in the United States?" Emerson closes the preamble of his
address. "Their alleged effect to augment disproportionately the size of
cities, is in rapid course of fulfilment in this metropolis of New England . . . In an uneven country the railroad is a fine object in the mak-

ing."[12] Industrialized expansion, in Emerson's view, will replace the North/South binary standoff with an "uneven," one-way dominance over limitless underdeveloped peripheries by a singular, industrialized center: "this metropolis of New England."

As he focuses on the symbiotic "progress" of industrialization and expansion, Emerson seems at first glance to have circumvented altogether the North/South axis of the contemporary U.S. geographic imaginary. Against the hemispheric frame of reference of republican culture, he reasserts the East-to-West march-of-civilization worldview of European empire, posing the ascendancy of "this metropolis of New England" as the link between the European colonization of America and the elevation of the United States to true imperial stature:

> Columbus alleged as a reason for seeking a continent in the West, that the harmony of nature required a great tract of land in the western hemisphere, to balance the known extent of land in the eastern . . . The land is the appointed remedy for whatever is false and fantastic in our culture. The continent we inhabit is to be physic and food for our mind, as well as our body.[13]

This very statement of an alternative East/West geographical organization is based, though, upon a return of the repressed North/South divide. If dwelling on the New World colonial origins of the United States in general is not enough to raise the specter of the old Plantation South, sourcing these origins to Columbus in particular surely does: after all, Columbus emblematizes Spanish America, the West Indies, and more broadly the southern antithesis to the founding stories of New England Puritan origins so cherished by Emerson and raised by him elsewhere in the address. His over-mapping of the East/West and North/South axes of the imperial venture pivots, further, on the centrality of ideology to that venture; indeed, his stunning locution "alleged as a reason" in this passage reads as an anticipation of the twentieth-century definition of the term "ideology." It is Emerson's work in "The Young American" to plumb the ideological inheritance upon which "we" at the center of cultural production may draw in order to "allege a reason" for the geographical dominion of the center over the periphery—in order to claim that harvesting an entire "continent" to feed the restricted "we" of the metropolis is "required" by "the harmony of nature." This disappearing of centralized domination, this enabling of empire—which Emerson obliquely terms "creating an American sentiment"—comes to rest, despite the overt westward focus of the address, on a historically slippery South.[14] Modulating between the Plantation South of past colonialism and the Slave South of present modernization, this geographic figure in

Emerson's address endorses the ascendance of the "metropolis of New England."

Though Emerson in "The Young American" seems to turn his back on the North/South binary, his address explicitly endorsing westward expansion is invigorated and underwritten by the contemporary intensity of sectionalist discourse. The connection exists at the most basic formal level, since Emerson shares the very hallmarks of his already distinctive rhetoric with the ultraist writing that was generating both Industrial North and Slave South: he relies on the catalogue, with its promise of encompassing all; he elevates a singular perceiving consciousness to give shape and sense to the otherwise overwhelming accretion of objects and facts; he seeks to discern and define the determining system behind the seeming chaos of modernity.[15] The basic structure of sectionalism drives the content of the address as well. As Emerson seeks in its central argument to "allege a reason" for the dominance of his Boston center over the entire continent (and beyond), he does so by *reinscribing* the North/South sectionalist binary he otherwise seems so assiduously to spurn. His naturalization of the dominance of center over periphery rests upon a story he tells about the archetypal interaction of two inherently opposed economic structures: "Feudalism" (Slave South) and "Commerce" (Industrial North). Feudalism is the older of the two, aligned as it is from the opening lines of the address with European colonialism, and it rests on the absolute authority of "very whimsical and uncomfortable masters" whose "frolics turn out to be insulting and degrading to the commoner." Run by a group of dissolute southern planters right out of the pages of a 1790s literary magazine, "Feudalism [has grown] to be a bandit and a brigand."[16]

Against the sway of the planter, Emerson introduces "the uprise and culmination of the new and anti-feudal power of Commerce" as "the political fact of most significance to the American at this hour." He defines both the "good" and the "evil" of Commerce as residing in the same trait: "that it would put everything into market; talent, beauty, virtue, and man himself." Even as he raises the discomfiting Industrial North specters of prostitution (marketed "virtue") and wage slavery (marketed "man"), Emerson proposes that Commerce "was the principle of Liberty; that [it] planted America and destroyed Feudalism; that it makes peace and keeps peace, and it will abolish slavery." The ascendance of Commerce over Feudalism, transmuted midsentence here into the ascendance of Industrial North over Slave South, is the triumph of an inevitable and "beneficent tendency, omnipotent without violence."[17] Emerson is able to conjure this exceptional dream of empire—of an absolute power that is fundamentally nonviolent and good—because of how he has rhetorically deployed the North/South binary of his moment. He has *temporalized* sectionalist geography, so that the longed-for dominance of one part of the country over the other becomes the simple unfolding of time. The ascendance of Commercial North over Feudal South is as natural and inevitable as the ascendance of the present over the past.

The future, though, gives Emerson some pause. While the sectionalist binary enables his envisioning of a natural and beneficent dominion of North over South, he cannot avoid introducing the ideological peril of that structure into his address as well—the sense that the North/South antitheses are inextricably linked, mirrors rather than inverses of each other. Might the triumph of Commerce mean no progress at all? "We complain of its oppression of the poor, and of its building up a new aristocracy on the ruins of the aristocracy it destroyed," Emerson admits, acknowledging contemporary critiques of the power extremes ushered in by industrialization. Commerce, or sectionalist North, too, then, "is also but for a time, and must give way to somewhat *broader* and better, whose signs are already dawning in the sky."[18] The natural dominance of North over South simply provides the basis for an analogical and much "broader" projection of absolute power, from (quite literally) the central ground upon which Emerson and his audience stand in Boston, out into an unlimited, passive territorial space:

> Look across the country from any hill-side around us, and the landscape seems to crave Government. The actual differences of men must be acknowledged, and met with love and wisdom. These rising grounds which command the champaign below, seem to ask for lords, true lords, *landlords*, who understand the land and its uses and the applicabilities of men. . . . We must have kings, and we must have nobles.[19]

Emerson's fantasy of being entirely surrounded by limitless territory that begs for subjugation by "us"—his local center—finally realizes the expanding United States as the "uneven country," inside and out, which is the "fine object in the making" of modernity. The original, natural, historically inevitable act of subjugating the South has synthesized Feudalism and Commerce, recuperating the authoritarian rule inherited from colonial days as righteous, centralized, imperial administration of the "uses and the applicabilities" of an endlessly expandable territorial realm, filled with submissive human and natural resources.

As Emerson closes the address with an exhortation to his Boston "gentlemen" to embrace their "feudal schooling" in order to "repair the errors of a scholastic and traditional education, and bring us into just relations with [the] men and things" falling under the purview of the U.S.

government, it becomes clear that "The Young American" of his title has been not a descriptive term but a question and a challenge. Who is, who will be, "the Young American"?

> I call upon you, young men, to obey your heart, and be the nobility of this land. In every age of the world, there has been a leading nation, one of a more generous sentiment, whose eminent citizens were willing to stand for the interests of general justice and humanity, at the risk of being called, by the men of the moment, chimerical and fantastic. Which should be that nation but these States? Which should lead that movement, if not New England? Who should lead the leaders, but the Young American?[20]

The taxonomic string of qualifications places "the Young American" in a field both broader and narrower than we might at first expect. "The Young American" is an "eminent," "noble," reigning subset of the metropole ("New England"), which in turn is a reigning subset of the nation ("these States")—which in turn is a reigning subset of "the world." On the one hand, Emerson is usurping, for his New England Transcendentalist circle, the Democrats' term "Young America"; on the other, he is qualifying that term out of reach of many, within the United States and without, who would consider themselves "Americans." And he is doing so in service of a vision of centralized world domination that trumps the most fevered dreams of the boosters of "Manifest Destiny."

The series of rhetorical questions with which he ends his exhortation, though, introduces a sense of opposition and embattledness into what otherwise would seem the culminating calling-into-being of a New-England–centered American empire. Which should be that nation but? Which should lead if not? Who but the Young American? *Someone,* Emerson insists, will be the master on the sublime, totalized scale made possible by industrialized expansion; and while the structure of the questions implies that the ascendance of his version of the "Young American" ought to be a foregone conclusion, it simultaneously leads the reader to posit alternative scenarios, to name opponents and usurpers who might imperil the destined imperial "nobility" of the Boston center. In the sectionalist climate of 1844, the most obvious—indeed unavoidable— opponent of New England's "transcendence" was the Slave South; and if Emerson's link between mastering the South and dominating the continent remained a bit oblique—couched as it was in the historical allegory of Feudalism and Commerce—in his next major lecture it was becoming more distinct.

In "Emancipation in the British West Indies," delivered in Concord, Massachusetts, on August 1 and published as a freestanding pamphlet thereafter, Emerson directly confronted the anxiety conveyed in the closing rhetorical questions of his earlier address, giving an answer to the culminating question, "Who but the Young American?"

> There is a scandalous rumor that has been swelling louder of late years,—perhaps wholly false,—that [congressmen from Massachusetts] are bullied into silence by Southern gentlemen . . . I may as well say, what all men feel, that whilst our very amiable and very innocent representatives and senators at Washington are accomplished lawyers and merchants . . . there is a disastrous want of *men* from New England . . . What if we should send thither representatives who were a particle less amiable and less innocent?[21]

Here Emerson locates the self-emasculation of the natural nobles of Massachusetts in their "amiability" and "innocence"—those very core characteristics of the republic that oppose the power abuses of empire. Fraternal friendship and egalitarianism, Emerson argues, permit an unnatural indulgence of the southern planter—that "spoiled child of . . . his indolent and luxurious climate," who by the irreversible march of modernity should be ruled by the central "metropolis of New England." Acting as representatives of Commerce only—"accomplished lawyers and merchants"—does not fully realize Massachusetts manhood. In the age of industrialized expansion, there is no room for amiability and less for innocence; the rightful masters of the center may either embrace their "feudal schooling" and assert their power, or be themselves "schooled and ridden by the minority of slave-holders."[22]

Although "Emancipation in the British West Indies" is by far the more famous of these two 1844 addresses, since it constitutes Emerson's first public statement on the issue of slavery, reading it in the context of "The Young American" causes its central problematic to come into view with a new emphasis. As Emerson writes this address commemorating the tenth anniversary of British West India emancipation for an audience of abolitionists in Concord, his thinking comes to revolve about a contrast between the political situations of the two nations in relation to plantation production: Britain is a self-proclaimed empire managing slavery in its colonies, while the United States is a slaveholding republic at war with itself. In Emerson's analysis, the weakness of the U.S. situation lies in precisely this gap between empire and republic. The constitution of the federal government diffuses political power geographically throughout national territory, and this situation is at variance with nature and history—with the centripetal forces of industrialized modernity now generating an "uneven country" that should be at the command of a geographically centralized authority:

England has the advantage of trying the question at a wide distance from the spot where the nuisance exists; the planters are not, excepting in rare examples, members of the legislature. The extent of the empire, and the magnitude and number of other questions crowding into court, keep this one in balance, and prevent it from obtaining that ascendancy, and being urged with that intemperance which a question of property tends to acquire . . . I have not been able to read a page of [the history of West India Emancipation] without the most painful comparisons. Whilst I have read of England, I have thought of New England.

So long as southern planters are members of the Congress, and so long as the "magnitude" of U.S. territory does not approach that of Britain's "world-wide realm"—for that long New England fails to assume its natural position of imperial inheritance, "inasmuch as England is the strongest of the family of existing nations, and we are the expansion of that people." It is only by mastering the Slave South that his audience at the Boston center will assert the manly vigor and, ultimately, the racial Anglo-Saxonism that will underwrite future expansion: "The genius of the Saxon race, friendly to liberty" he writes in his closing lines, "the enterprise, the very muscular vigor of this nation, are inconsistent with slavery."[23] On the model of Britain, Emerson embraces abolitionism as an imperial civilizing project, one that not only furthers the greater good of humanity and progress but also establishes the dominion of Boston over its South.

And this, indeed, is the brilliance of abolitionism, on the British imperial model, as Emerson sees it in 1844:

> [British West India Emancipation] was a moral revolution . . . Other revolutions have been the insurrection of the oppressed; this was the repentance of the tyrant. It was the masters revolting from their mastery. The slave-holder said, "I will not hold slaves." The end was noble and the means were pure. Hence the elevation and pathos of this chapter of history. The lives of the advocates are pages of greatness.

The "masters" and "slave-holders" to whom Emerson refers are not, of course, the "spoiled children" of the tropics, the southern planters of either Jamaica or Virginia (which locations he conflates in the first paragraphs of the address). The "masters" who are the authors of this "moral revolution" are the "liberal mind[s]" of the English metropole—"poet, preacher, moralist, statesman"—who have, from the vantage of their dominant center, put their planters in their places. Abolitionism on the British model is thus not only anti-imperial in its overthrow of slave laws. It is also imperial in terms of asserting the dominance of the center over its periphery—including the dominance of London, now, over the emancipated former slaves of the West Indies who "remain on [the] estate" providing "cheaper" plantation labor as well as "future customer[s]" for the manufactures of the industrial center.[24] Emerson here redefines "revolution" for New England: embracing, rather than rebelling against, both market and empire, the "Young Americans" of the metropolis should step into the role of "masters revolting from their mastery"— reformist "masters" of their Slave South—imperialists for liberty, as it were.

How to achieve this stature of righteous, absolute, yet self-effacing centralized dominion? How to close the gap between England and New England? Emerson's writings in 1844 read in part as a meditation on how centralized ideological production can hasten into being a centralized wielding of economic and political power.[25] He opens and closes "Emancipation in the British West Indies," for instance, with an experiment: while he cannot by fiat remove representatives from the southern states from Congress—thereby making New England's relation to U.S. slavery analogous to England's relation to colonial slavery—he can at least banish the usurping Slave South from his discursive universe. In the world of his address, he may forcibly transmute contested sectional politics into an absolute center-over-periphery dominance. He begins:

> The institution of slavery seems to its opponent to have but one side, and he feels that none but a stupid or a malignant person can hesitate on a view of the facts. Under such an impulse, I was about to say, If any cannot speak, or cannot hear the words of freedom, let him go hence,—I had almost said, Creep into your grave, the universe has no need of you! But I have thought better: let him not go.[26]

On the one hand, one wants to say, with fire, "fair enough—how is it possible to conceive of two sides to the question of slavery?" But on the other hand, the passage chills, as we slide with Emerson from the moral rectitude of his antislavery position into his glib and gleeful denial of the very right to exist of those who disagree with him. This is the key modulation of the address: Emerson transmutes the moral righteousness of abolitionism into a stature of absolute empire—an omniscient arbitration of the entire "universe."

In "Emancipation in the British West Indies," Emerson abolishes sectionalist politics, abolishes the binary of Industrial North and Slave South, and in its place constitutes himself the center of all, able to annihilate at will those southern planters who defy him. While he forbears to do so at the outset of the address—"I had *almost* said, Creep into your grave, the universe has no need of you"—he closes some ten thousand words later by promising, with the authority of God, to make good on the wishfully genocidal gambit. "There have been moments, I said, when men might be forgiven who doubted. Those moments are past." In 1844, as the United States teetered on the brink of the war with Mexico that would at last extend the national borders to the Pacific Ocean, Emerson offered this rhetorical and ethical transcendence—this supremacy—of New England over its enduring South as the solution to the untenable sectionalist standoff between the Industrial North and the Slave South. He recuperated and relocated the center-over-periphery dominance of empire that had been the origin of the nation and, he claimed, was destined to be its ever-expanding future. This transcendence of section would be called into being first in U.S. letters, which, Emerson believed, were already Boston-centered. And ultimately the politics, economics, and daily life of the "uneven country" created by modernity would follow. "Nothing is mightier than we," he closed his address to the Young American masters of New England, "when we are vehicles of a truth before which the State and the individual are alike ephemeral."[27]

Poe's Southern Margin and the U[niverse of] S[tars]

To think more about the geographical dimensions of the New England Transcendentalism Emerson was formulating in the mid-1840s, we turn to an incisive, if intuitive, critique of that mode of writing: Edgar Allan Poe's later literary criticism, from late 1844 on, and especially his last major literary work: *Eureka,* his "Essay on the Material and Spiritual Universe," published in the summer of 1848, just before his death the next year at the age of 40. In these last years of his career, Poe increasingly self-identified as a southerner, an identity that allowed him to express, under the aegis of sectionalism, animus against what he saw as a Boston-centered Transcendentalist hegemony in U.S. letters—a hegemony that he believed privileged political stances over aesthetic achievement and promoted authors on the basis of their geographical identity, rather than their creative genius.[28] This means that the sectionalist vector in Poe's criticism—his anger at being marginalized by the Boston literary establishment—escalated specifically as the U.S.-Mexican War was being fought and the clamor of Manifest Destiny reached fever pitch. Poe gave the lecture that was the basis for *Eureka* just three weeks after the Treaty of Guadalupe-Hidalgo was finalized, ceding California and the present-day U.S. southwest to the United States. This "treatise on the universe" is actually a satire in which Poe, aping Emerson, brings together the political fields of sectionalism and expansionism, much as he had started to do in *The*

Narrative of Arthur Gordon Pym a decade earlier. In so doing, he seeks to expose how the category of the universal as generated in New England Transcendentalism provides both form and ideology for a rising American Empire.[29] Registering his hope that he can push New England Transcendentalist "rant and cant . . . to that degree of excess which inevitably induces reaction," Poe confronts Emerson's Transcendental cartography by going it one better and creating a "Cosmogony of the Universe."[30]

In his direct criticisms of Boston Transcendentalist writers in the mid-1840s, Poe most vociferously protests what he calls their "frantic spirit of generalization," their tendency toward universalizing local and personal experience and perspective.[31] He in fact opens *Eureka* with an extended parody of Emerson's 1843 *Dial* essay, "The Transcendentalist"; in that piece, Emerson had put forth one of his most direct statements of universalizing as method:

> His thought,—that is the Universe. His experience inclines him to behold the procession of facts you call the world, as flowing perpetually outward from an invisible, unsounded centre in himself, centre alike of him and of them . . . From this transfer of the world into the consciousness, this beholding of all things in the mind, follow easily his whole ethics.[32]

That elite New Englanders are discerning themselves as "centre" of the "Universe," Emerson had proposed, represents a triumph of "Idealism" over "Materialism." Poe, in his "Essay on the Material *and* Spiritual Universe," insists that this "Idealism" works in the service of, rather than replaces, "Material" aims: the self-centering spirit of universalization bears a real geopolitical consequence that is being revealed in the heat of U.S. expansionism.[33] By writing a treatise on "our legitimate thesis, *The Universe*," in an over-the-top version of what he elsewhere terms "the tone Transcendental," Poe satirizes the Boston "Frogpondians"—as he elsewhere calls Emerson and his circle, emphasizing the smallness of their ostensible metropolis of New England compared to the loudness of their voices. Poe indicts the New England Transcendentalists for wrongly taking the ground on which they stand to be the center of the universe; for refusing to see a relativity in their geographical position; and for assuming that the rest of the world surveyed from the Bostonian mountaintop (in Emerson's phrase, "any hill-top around us") should conform to their parochial and self-aggrandizing agenda.[34]

Poe's 1848 critique of New England universalism and expansionism stems from his prior sense of the internal geographic centralization of U.S. literary culture and his own alienation from that center. It has been proposed that Poe's writings of the mid-1840s should be read as "regional debate"—though Poe is not exactly engaging in a two-sided give-and-take with the Bostonians.[35] Instead, he conducts an oblique and sporadic criticism of their cultural dominance from the literary periphery of the United States; the newspaper of the Transcendentalist utopian community Brook Farm called it in 1845 "a certain *blackguard* warfare against the poets and newspaper critics of New England, which it would be most charitable to impute to insanity."[36] As he bounces from the editorship of one shakily financed magazine to another in New York and Philadelphia between November 1844 and his death, Poe's sense of his exclusion from a national literature based in New England generates its own expressive form, his aptly titled "Marginalia": fragmentary philosophical, aesthetic, and critical insights that he publishes, several to a number, in each periodical. Whereas many writers of the era kept private accounts of fleeting insights and responses to their reading, and indeed often mined such private journals for material to be worked into structured, developed, synthesized essays (both Emerson and Thoreau come immediately to mind), Poe argues for the appropriateness of his fragments standing on their own. In his introductory installment of the "Marginalia" in the *Democratic Review,* published within weeks of Emerson's "Emancipation in the British West Indies," Poe explains that

> [p]urely marginal jottings . . . have a distinct complexion, and not only a distinct purpose, but none at all; this it is which imparts to them a value . . . In the marginalia, too, we talk only to our selves; we therefore talk freshly—boldly—originally—with abandonnement—without conceit—much after the fashion of Jeremy Taylor, and Sir Thomas Browne, and Sir William Temple, and the anatomical Burton, and that most logical analogist, Butler, and some other people of the old day.[37]

He conceptualizes his "Marginalia" as a perverse form, paradoxically worth printing and reading for their lack of utility ("[no purpose] at all") and their racialized, outré stature ("distinct complexion"). The names he cites here further define the fragmentary and momentary form as befitting the *marginalized* author writing in opposition to a dominant culture that threatens or ignores him: assembling a list of luminaries of seventeenth-century England, royalists who wrote under restraint and duress during Cromwell's regime, Poe implies the southern sectionalist branding of New Englanders as fanatic, censoring Puritans.

It is tempting to see Poe in his "Marginalia"—his most consistent project over the last five years of his life—developing a self-identifying "southern" critique that itself transcends a simple pro-South sectionalism. To flip through the collected "Marginalia" is to experience a dizzying and multidirectional array of fugitive assaults on the accepted categories of mid-nineteenth-century national thought. To quote just one example from late 1846, this is Poe's argument—conducted entirely in one a single paragraph in *Graham's Magazine*—for renaming the United States of America "Appalachia":

> A name for our country. At present we have, clearly, none. There should be no hesitation about "Appalachia." In the first place, it is distinctive. "America" is not, and can never be made so . . . unless we can take it away from the regions which employ it at present. South America is "America," and will insist upon remaining so. In the second place, "Appalachia" is indigenous, springing from one of the most magnificent and distinctive features of the country itself. Thirdly, in employing this word we do honor to the Aborigines, whom, hitherto, we have at all points unmercifully despoiled, assassinated, and dishonored . . . The last, and by far the most truly important consideration of all, however, is the music of "Appalachia" itself; nothing could be more sonorous, more liquid, or of fuller volume, while its length is just sufficient for dignity.

The range of disruptive forays in this compact paragraph is stunning: Poe veers from an indictment of the imbecility of present nationalist culture (not even having settled on a name for the country); to an exposure of U.S. cultural imperialism (as the U.S. attempts to claim "America" at the expense of the rest of the hemisphere); to a recentering of the nation on a southern landform ("indigenous" Appalachia, "one of the most magnificent and distinctive features of the country"); to a resurrection of the crimes against "the Aborigines" upon which the nation is (and continues to be, in its expansion) based; to Poe's authoritative claim to his own superior aesthetic taste.[38] Unlike the Southern sectionalist plantation romances, the "southern" critique in Poe's "Marginalia" is not pro-anything. He does not offer one system or affiliation (Slave South) in place of or as an indictment of the other (Industrial North). Rather, his "Marginalia" are *anti*systematic: conceived of by Poe as a materially and politically forced response to his cultural marginalization, the form becomes an alternative mode of inquiry that refuses the universalization, the catalogue impulse, and the generalization that he sees as hallmarks of the New-England-centered dominant culture.

Reading the "Marginalia," then, makes all the more striking Poe's divergent tactics in the writing of *Eureka*—which, according to his correspondence, he felt was a culminating work in a campaign he had been waging.[39] Rather than writing in a form that opposes system, in *Eureka* Poe writes into being a system of superlative, indeed absurd, scale: "I design to speak of the *Physical, Metaphysical and Mathematical—of the Material and Spiritual Universe:—of its Essence, its Origin, its Creation, its Present Condition and its Destiny." Eureka* is a theory of everything: one hundred fifty pages long with no breaks or subdivisions, it proceeds in a tone of breathless and unflagging intensity, communicated with exclamations, ejaculations, italics, and dashes; and Poe claims that his treatise is *"abundantly sufficient to account for the constitution, the existing phenomena and the plainly inevitable annihilation of at least the material Universe."*[40] As this passage hints, the overarching system of the universe that Poe proposes in *Eureka* involves a central point from which matter has been radiating outward since its original "constitution"; but the expansion cannot go on forever, and inevitably the limits will rush back upon the center and the universe will collapse. Critics who have tried to treat *Eureka* as Poe's serious attempt at scientific writing have gone so far as to allege that he predicts the Big Bang Theory, but it seems clear that he is using metaphor to predict something much more down to earth: the rise and fall of a compulsively expanding American empire that has been doomed by its "constitution" to begin with.

Throughout *Eureka*, Poe invokes the language of political theory in general, and U.S. founding documents in particular, as resolutely as he does the language of cosmology, and this political language tends to focus on the problems of centralization: the problem of the one and the many ("This constitution has been effected by *forcing* the originally and therefore normally *One* into the abnormal condition of *Many*"); the problem of divisibility ("[An atom is] absolutely unique, individual, undivided, and not indivisible only because He who *created* it, by dint of his Will, can by an infinitely less energetic exercise of the same Will, as a matter of course, divide it"); and the problem of identifying universal precepts upon which a nation may be organized ("[Aristotle] started with what he maintained to be axioms, or self-evident truths:—and the now well understood fact that *no* truths are *self*-evident, really does not make in the slightest degree against his speculations").[41] This coincidence of political theory and cosmology around the issues of centralization and collapse seems intimately related to Poe's conceptualization of his own position, as a southerner, as part of the vast peripheral expanse being organized ideologically by emanation from Boston.

Poe goes to some lengths to alert readers that *Eureka* is a satire. He subtitles it "a Prose Poem" when the very idea of a "prose poem" is anathema to his entire body of poetic theory. He dedicates the volume "with very profound respect" to Alexander von Humboldt, who recently had completed his seven-volume *Kosmos;* Emerson had just lauded

Humboldt for his "intrepid generalizations," and Poe repeats that praise in the body of the text—"his generalizing powers have never, perhaps, been equaled"—though from Poe, of course, this is no praise at all.[41] And when readers didn't seem to get the joke right away, Poe peeled off the first tenth of *Eureka* and published long passages of it nearly verbatim in *Godey's Lady's Book,* as the short story "Mellonta Tauta," an absurd letter from the future authored by a Transcendentalist bluestocking named "Pundita" who ends up falling into the Atlantic when her motorized dirigible deflates.[43] This willful debasing of his presumably elevated treatise continues to puzzle critics who take *Eureka* at face value as a serious scientific and metaphysical work, but "Mellonta Tauta" seems clearly calculated to addend overt national sectionalist and expansionist political markers to Poe's more subtle and extended satire of New England Transcendentalist methods, which had gone over the heads of his audience.

In many ways, Poe's entire performance of *Eureka* seems a continuation of what he called his "Boston hoax" of late 1845. This is the famous episode in which Poe was invited, on the heels of the popular success of "The Raven," to read at the Boston Lyceum for the first (and only) time. Rather than reading from his current work, he read a long, rambling version of a poem he had written as a teenager; he then mocked his Boston auditors in the magazine he was editing at the time, the *Broadway Journal,* for having no better discrimination than to applaud him wildly. "We do not, ourselves, think the poem a remarkably good one:—it is not sufficiently transcendental. Still it did well enough for the Boston audience—who evinced characteristic discrimination in understanding, and *especially* applauding, all those knotty passages which we ourselves have not yet been able to understand."[44] Considering, especially, that Poe first presented *Eureka* as a much-hyped ultra-Transcendental lecture on the Boston model, he seems to hope for a similar con with his 1848 treatise, getting close enough to the method and language of New England Transcendentalism that he will fool his quarry into taking him seriously, which would be the most damning critique of all, "deliver[ing them] up to the enemy bound hand and foot." (As he preens at one point in *Eureka,* "I am proudly aware that there exist many of the most profound and cautiously discriminative intellects which cannot *help* being abundantly content with my—*suggestions.*") Colin Dayan has suggested that Poe's bad behavior in the original Boston hoax was provoked by Emerson's "Emancipation in the British West-Indies," published a few months earlier—that Poe was exercised by Emerson's hypocrisy in "condemn[ing] slavery while continuing to restrict blacks to the status of objects: recipients of the charity of white men who continue to be masters."[45] (Think-

ing of Poe reading that address, Emerson's Godlike injunction to his political opponents—"Creep into your graves; the *universe* has no need of
you"—stands out as well.) Explaining his hoax in the *Broadway Journal,*
Poe wrote that his aim had been to "open the eyes [of the Bostonians]
to certain facts which have long been obvious to all the world except
themselves—the facts that there exist other cities than Boston—other
men of letters than Professor Longfellow—other vehicles of literary information than the 'Down-East Review.'"[46] (This last term is Poe's preferred name for the powerful Boston-based journal *The North American
Review,* a name that, like "Frogpondians," he coined to mock the continental ambition of what he saw as a parochial publication.)

The very title, *Eureka,* bore a certain topical weight in mid-1848, signaling the relays of his "universal" treatise with the march of southwestward
expansion. When Poe delivered the lecture that became *Eureka* in February
of 1848, he titled it simply "The Cosmogony of the Universe," but by the
time it went to press in July he had retitled it. In these months, Poe was in
close contact with Bayard Taylor, who was serving as the *New York Post*
correspondent in California, and thus it is probable that he would have
been aware of the gold-rush-inspired association of "eureka"—"I have
found it"—with that newly acquired territory.[47] By the summer of 1848, a
preliminary seal for the future state of California had been designed with
the word "eureka" over the top as a motto. Titling anything *Eureka* at this
moment was tantamount to titling it "California."

As the U.S. borders reach the Pacific Ocean—their natural destination,
according to the ideology of Manifest Destiny—Poe raises the question of
limits prominently in *Eureka.* While his readers presumably take his subject, the universe, to be infinite, they are in error, he informs us at the outset. To be more precise, "in speaking of what is *ordinarily* implied by the
expression, 'Universe,' I shall in most cases take a phrase of limitation—
'the Universe of Stars.'" What Poe means by this phrase, he explains, is
the extent of the universe conceivable from the vantage of earth, and he
argues that it has been a fundamental error to "consider the Universe of
Stars coincident with the Universe proper," to assume "that, were it
possible for us to attain any given point in space, we should still find, on
all sides of us, an interminable succession of stars." Of course, the term
"Universe of Stars," which he uses, capitalized, throughout *Eureka,* ab-
breviates to "U.S."; and the fallacious fantasy Poe describes of being able
to "attain any given point in space" and still find oneself surrounded
by "stars"—*states,* the stars being added so rapidly to the U.S. flag at
mid-decade—this fallacious fantasy takes the United States to be infinitely expandable and able to absorb everything else that exists. "No as-

tronomical fallacy is more untenable," Poe writes, "and none has been more pertinaciously adhered to, than that of the absolute *illimitation* of the Universe of Stars."[48]

Why is mistakenly conceiving of the United States as universal such a "pertinacious" problem for Poe? Comprehending the universe, asserting the universal, he insists, requires a hierarchical relationship between a perceiving center—the site where stand the people making the definitions and observations of totality—and an objectified, totalized surround. He visualizes this structural inequality, inherent in the very conceptualization of the universal, in specifically geographical terms: first as extending along a vertical axis, and then through an emanation from center to periphery:

> Our thesis admits a choice between two modes of discussion:—we may *as*-cend or *de*scend. Beginning at our own point of view—at the Earth on which we stand . . . it is clear that a descent to small from great—to the outskirts from the centre (if we could establish a centre)—to the end from the beginning (if we could fancy a beginning) would be the preferable course.

With the parenthetical asides, Poe stresses the dubiousness with which he regards such a centralized, specifically located production of the universe—"the Absolute," "the All-in-All"—and he describes setting oneself up as the center that defines all that surrounds it in two equally satirical ways. On the one hand, there's the will-to-God-stature not unfamiliar from Emerson's writings of the period: "The plots of God are perfect. The Universe is a plot of God . . . As our starting-point, then, let us adopt the Godhead. . . . *We should have to be God ourselves!*" And on the other hand, there is the Frogpondian pundit on his Bostonian mountaintop:

> He who from the top of Aetna casts his eyes leisurely around, is affected chiefly by the extent and diversity of the scene. Only by a rapid whirling on his heel could he hope to comprehend the panorama in the sublimity of its *oneness*. But as, on the summit of Aetna, *no* man has thought of whirling on his heel, so no man has ever taken into his brain the full uniqueness of the prospect.[49]

As the decentered, Industrial-North mountaintop proves to be an active volcano, it provides no vantage at all.

Poe throughout *Eureka* raises a series of challenges to those "monomaniac[ally] grasping at the infinite," those who would set themselves up as an impossible center and presume to define the terms of the impossible universal. Can the universalizers comprehend that "we have reached a point from which we behold the Universe of Stars as a . . . space interspersed, *unequably,* with *clusters,*" and that "the equability of distribution will diminish in the ratio of the agglomerative processes"—in other words, that geographical inequality proceeds in proportion to modernizing centralization, realizing Emerson's "uneven country"? Can they acknowledge the unavoidable limitation of their individual perspectives? "It may be said," Poe reasons, "that no fog of the mind can well be greater than that which, extending to the very boundaries of the mental domain, shuts out even those boundaries themselves from comprehension." Can they come to see their localized geographical perspective as relative, not necessarily affording them a full comprehension of the "outskirts" of the universe far from their own location? "Those who maintain the existence of nebulae, do *not* refer the nebulosity to extreme distance," he notes. "They declare it a *real* and not merely a *perspective* nebulosity." And finally: can they recognize the base desire for commodities and profit underlying their supposedly Transcendental moral, intellectual, and scientific exertions? The perpetual expansion of the Universe of Stars, Poe theorizes, occurs always in the tropics, as systems, planets, and suns continually throw off matter into space from "the equatorial region."[50] This insertion of terrestrial tropicality into his cosmological metaphor emphasizes the relays between the domestic South, already possessed by the United States; the hemispheric American South presently being acquired; and the colonized southern sites around the globe, to which U.S. imperial ambition will, presumably, turn next. Poe intensifies these relays in "Mellonta Tauta," the *Godey's Lady's Book* story, in which he has "Pundita" enumerate commodities ranging from India rubber and silk, to cotton and watermelon, as essential to explaining her philosophical stance.[51]

Ultimately, Poe's southern critique of the methods of New England Transcendentalism was met with incomprehension and, mostly, indifference. He had hoped that the success of *Eureka* would at last enable him to establish a magazine in Philadelphia that could truly pose a challenge to the hegemony of Boston—a magazine through which he imagined creating a peripheral print community of "well-educated men . . . among the innumerable plantations of our vast Southern & Western Countries," and thereby "supporting the general interests of the Republic of Letters . . . with a national as distinguished from a sectional literature."[52] (Six months before the publication of *Eureka,* by contrast, Emerson had written the editors' address for a new Boston periodical designed to speak for an "energetic race" commanding "a considerable fraction of the planet"; the periodical was titled, unironically, the *Massachusetts Quarterly Review.*)[53] Poe's hope in *Eureka* for an efficacious deflation of the rising ideology of an exceptional American empire—his assurance that "regard[ing the thing] from the proper point of view . . . and in the true direction" would reveal its errors and costs—proved unfounded. A few months before his death he asked, rather drearily, "What have we Americans accomplished in the way of Satire?"[54] And more famously, in a letter to his mother-in-law: "I have no desire to live since I have done 'Eureka.' I could accomplish nothing more."[55]

So the apocalyptic ending of Poe's *Eureka* is borne out: though he warns that the unchecked expansion of the Universe of Stars causes it to exist "in a state of progressive collapse," Poe predicts that expansion to be unstoppable, precisely because it is authorized by its previous success: "Because on the confines of this Universe of Stars we are, for the moment, compelled to pause . . . is it right to conclude that, in fact, there *is* no material point beyond that which we have thus been permitted to attain?" He asks this rhetorically, and then goes on to claim "an analogical right" to ever-further expansion: "Have we any ground whatever for visions such as these? If we have a right to them in *any* degree, we have a right to their infinite extension."[56] It is ultimately this "analogical principle" that describes the connection between what Poe sees as the abjection of the U.S. South before the cultural hegemony of New England Transcendentalism and the terms under which U.S. expansion across the continent (and beyond) is being ideologically assimilated into national discourse. Which brings us to the more obvious resonance of his title, one likely on Poe's mind as well: "eureka" is Archimedes's cry of discovery when he runs from the bath having discovered the principle of displacement. Poe's *Eureka* is, indeed, a study of displacement—a study of the projection of a sectional struggle for dominance out onto formerly Mexican territory—an inquiry into the extent to which a cultural register developed to keep the South in its place *within* the nation is proving infinitely exportable out onto the globe.

CHAPTER SEVEN

Dark Satanic Fields

"I say, Sambo, you go to spilin' the hands, I'll tell Mas'r o' you," said Quimbo, who was busy at the mill, from which he had viciously driven two or three tired women . . . "And I'll tell him ye won't let the women come to the mills, yo old nigger!" said Sambo.

Tom waited till a late hour, to get a place at the mills . . . for the mills were few in number compared with the grinders, and the weary and feeble ones were driven back by the strong.

— Harriet Beecher Stowe, *Uncle Tom's Cabin; or, Life Among the Lowly* (1852)

ARRIET BEECHER STOWE'S NOVEL *Uncle Tom's Cabin* set the scene and organized the story of the antebellum Slave South in U.S. national imagination, serving as the master narrative of southern slavery from the time of its publication in 1852 well into the twentieth century and holding sway still, incalculably, in the historical memory of our own time. In the United States of the 1850s, Stowe's novel converted abolitionism from a radical political stance into a popular sentimental imperative. So great was the influence of the book that Lincoln was reported to have said, on meeting Stowe in 1862, "So you're the little woman who wrote the book that started this great war."[1]

It is startling, then, to notice how much Simon Legree's plantation— Stowe's very archetype of the Slave South—looks like Lowell, Massachusetts, or any of the other mill towns that had sprung up in the industrializing Northeast in the 1830s and 1840s.[2] Indeed, Stowe organizes the first chapter of her novel set on Legree's infernal territory around an apparently gratuitous bit of stage business—his enslaved workers are grinding individual portions of parched corn for their dinners—which is useful primarily for its telegraphic punch on the page, allowing her to locate their slave labor at, quite literally, "the mill," that icon of modern industry. As she introduces Legree's plantation in this way, Stowe figures enslaved people in the South as a modern mass of proletarians—denominated "hands," in the parlance of contemporary factory management—who are forced into a desperate competition with each other on the wage-

Figure 12. "Eliza comes to tell Tom that he is sold, and that she is running away to save her child." Illustration of *Uncle Tom's Cabin* by Hammatt Billings, first U.S. edition, 1852. Yale Collection of American Literature, Beinecke Rare Book and Manuscript Library.

Eliza comes to tell Uncle Tom that he is sold, and that she is running away to save her child.   Page 82

THE AUCTION SALE. Page 174.

Figure 13. "The Auction Sale." Illustration of *Uncle Tom's Cabin* by Billings, 1852. Yale Collection of American Literature, Beinecke Rare Book and Manuscript Library.

labor playing field of work-or-starve: "[F]or the mills were few in number compared with the grinders, and the weary and feeble ones were driven back by the strong."[3] As she focuses with especial anxiety on the women workers whose presence drew most attention in the New England textile mills, and as she introduces as a guide to Legree's realm a classic urban prostitute figure—in the character of the "quadroon" Cassy, who has "walked the streets when it seemed as if [she] had misery enough in [her] one heart to sink the city"—Stowe fully realizes the Slave South as the dark satanic field of U.S. industrial modernity.[4] In the decade before the Civil War, the novel most definitively about and definitional of the South actually obliterates it, as Stowe writes the dystopic visions of the modernizing national center over the imaginative terrain of its Southern other.

It was this reclamation of the South as a vehicle for the fantastic projections of the industrializing metropolis that made *Uncle Tom's Cabin* the book that put the United States on the map of Western literary culture. While U.S. critics and readers from 1852 until quite recently have tended to focus on the political efficacy and ramifications of the novel, from the perspective of Europe, Stowe's aesthetic interventions have always mattered more.[5] British, French, German, and Russian critics found in *Uncle Tom's Cabin* at last a recognizably distinctive American literary production, a novel uniquely in conversation with, rather than merely imitative of, broader Western artistic innovations and concerns.[6] For European readers, Stowe was able to represent and to fathom the traumatic dislocations of the modern era in a novel way, precisely because of the anomalously simultaneous presence of domestic slavery with industrialization in the United States. British readers, for instance, who were by 1852 well-schooled in the new social novels of the industrial era, received Stowe's novel more enthusiastically than their U.S. counterparts during its first year in print: the novel sold three times as many copies in Britain as in Stowe's native land. During a triumphal tour of Britain in 1853, Stowe found herself hailed not so much for having written an antislavery novel as for having written a Dickensian chronicle of "Life Among the Lowly," as she had subtitled the book.[7] At a ceremonial dinner with the lord mayor of London, she was even seated across from Dickens, and the two authors were toasted together "as having employed fiction as a means of awakening the attention of their respective countries to the condition of the oppressed and suffering classes."[8] Stowe's Slave South captured the attention of European capitals, in other words, insofar as it could be understood to provide an analogue or metaphor for metropolitan proletarianization. It was her American access to this fertile field for metaphorizing the problems of metropolitan modernity that made Stowe's novel "a really healthy indigenous growth," in the opinion of British novelist Charles Kingsley, rather than a derivative entry into the Condition of England debates.[9]

This British identification of *Uncle Tom's Cabin*—as Dickens with a distinctively American twist—highlights Stowe's innovations in novel form. For though her subject was the Slave South, the narrative structure she employed made *Uncle Tom's Cabin* perhaps the most innovative and important novel of metropolitan modernity published in the United States before the Civil War.[10] Stowe's novel attempts above all to encompass, contain, and order an overwhelmingly complex and variegated social field. As she presents a huge cast of minutely rendered characters, drawn from across lines of class, race, place, and religion, Stowe essays the imaginative scope commensurate with the urban reality of her native New England, where readers constantly encountered strangers of fortunes and origins alien to their own. As she causes this widely ranging cast of characters to interact with one another in constantly shifting configurations across an episodic plot, Stowe stresses a fundamental interconnectedness in what might otherwise seem the superhumanly scaled, anonymous world confronting her metropolitan readers. And as she binds together this broad range of disparate social "pictures" (as she famously called the scenes of her novel) with a single, didactic, omniscient narrative voice, Stowe reveals explanatory relationships not perceivable in the lived experience of her readers. She thus instructs her readers in the relative places and values of her characters, and thereby models a coherent moral and social order in the place of a transformed modern world that felt random, arbitrary, and chaotic.

For all the structural similarity to Dickens's novels, though, *Uncle Tom's Cabin* achieved, as contemporary European critics recognized, a major innovation in Western portrayals of modernity precisely because of the imaginative geography provided to Stowe by the situation of the sectionalist United States circa 1850. With a generative collision of urban-industrial Northern narrative form and ostensibly premodern Slave South setting, Stowe created a powerful new chronotope in which temporal progress into modernity figured as geographical movement to the southward. In so doing, she put peripheral production back into the picture of industrialization—Legree's realm is simultaneously cotton plantation *and* textile mill—rather than maintaining the classic city/country ideological binary that Dickens and his European peers continued to assume as natural. (Indeed, it is tempting to see the powerful affinity of nineteenth-century Russian novelists for *Uncle Tom's Cabin* as resonating with Stowe's setting of her inquiry into modernity on rural, provincial ground.)[11] If *Edinburgh Review* founder Sidney Smith had stoked the fires of literary nationalism in 1820 by impugning the utter derivativeness of U.S. fiction with his famously dismissive "Who reads an American book?" New England Transcendentalist minister Theodore Parker had, in 1849, pointed out the path to national literary distinctiveness that Stowe trod just a few years later: "We have one series of literary productions that could be written by none but Americans, and only here; I mean the Lives of Fugitive Slaves."[12] While Parker intended this insight as a sardonic provocation, it provides a window onto what Stowe's distinctively American novel offered to midcentury Western literature: a sense that republican freedom could exist under industrial modernity only fugitively, in flight and under siege.

Stowe Retells the Market Revolution

Stowe's Slave South is not a singular, static setting, but a sequential progression through three markedly distinct plantations. The novel begins with Tom at the place of his birth, in his titular "cabin" on the harmonious, folksy Shelby plantation near the banks of the Ohio River. At the center of the novel, the reader follows Tom down the Mississippi to the paradisiacal but doomed St. Clare plantation in Louisiana. And as the nightmare nadir of Stowe's Slave South, Tom lands at last in Legree's infernal realm, somewhere south of Louisiana (read: in Hell). Stowe organizes this sequence, from the uppermost border of the South to its unfathomable depth, around two unfortunate falls for Tom: first, when his lifelong master, Mr. Shelby, is forced to sell him to a slave trader named Haley, who mysteriously holds the Shelby plantation "in his power"; and then, when his new, benevolent master Augustine St. Clare suddenly is killed, leaving behind an insolvent estate that allows Tom to be sold to the perverse Legree. At each of these junctures between the three emblematic plantations, in other words, Stowe pushes the action of the novel southward by staging a conflict between an established, moral, patriarchal order and an encroaching, profit-driven, market economy. Each time, the market wins: the patriarchal planters Shelby and St. Clare, for all their seeming power and wealth, prove incapable of protecting their worthy dependent Tom; and the moral fortitude and Christian belief those masters have instilled and encouraged in Tom may lead to his spiritual "victory" over Legree, but cannot forestall his ultimate bodily destruction by the commodification, dehumanization, and profit motive that hold sway in Legree's weirdly industrial realm.

Rehearsing the geographic sequencing of Stowe's tripartite Slave South sketches how geographical progression to the southward in the novel reads simultaneously as a temporal progression forward in time, from the New England village world of Stowe's childhood in the 1820s to the urban-industrial modernity of the years during which she wrote.[13] The illustrations commissioned by Stowe's U.S. publisher for the first edition of *Uncle Tom's Cabin* powerfully bear out this idea that the overarching thrust of the novel is to retell the market revolution, to relive the transformation of the centers of Western cultural production that had taken place during the lifetimes of Stowe and her readers. The artist, Hammatt Billings—a Bostonian best remembered for his 1859 design for the monument to the Pilgrim "Forefathers" at Plymouth, Massachusetts—drew upon a quite extensive array of Anglo-American visual styles for his illustrations, rather than establishing a cohesive visual vocabulary for the entire work. His swings between styles can become telling, as when he depicts each of Tom's falls to the southward as, effectively, falls into industrial modernity. Each fall operates for Billings on a country/city binary: for the benevolent, ostensibly premodern faces of Stowe's Slave South—the Shelby plantation and St. Clare's refuge—Billings creates idealized rural scenes based on anachronistic painting styles, while for the malevolent, industrialized Slave South—the trader Haley's enterprise, Legree's factory-plantation—he images urban scenes using contemporary engraving conventions.

The illustrations reproduced at the opening of this chapter show, first, the Shelby plantation on the night before Tom is to be taken away by the trader Haley, a scene that Billings renders in attractive, lavish detail. Tom, Chloe, Eliza, and Harry are clad in rather elegant rustic wear, rendered particularly romantic by Eliza's shawl and bonnet ribbons streaming in the breeze; they stand on the threshold of Tom's eponymous and imperiled cabin, which appears to be nestled in a bower. The mother with child is attended by a faithful watchdog, showing harmony between the humans and their natural setting; and a pastoral landscape complete with protecting manor house forms the backdrop of the scene. Here Billings draws upon the early-nineteenth-century English genre paintings of rustic scenes that idealized the lives and surroundings of rural laborers, paintings usually seen in the British context as providing a nostalgic distraction from or a critical comment on the comparatively debased condition of urban workers.[14] While the characters all bear distressed expressions, their discomfiture clearly stems not from their enslavement

LITTLE EVA READING THE BIBLE TO UNCLE TOM IN THE ARBOR. *Page 68.*

Figure 14. "Little Eva reading the Bible to Uncle Tom in the arbor." Illustration of *Uncle Tom's Cabin* by Billings, 1852. Yale Collection of American Literature, Beinecke Rare Book and Manuscript Library.

CASSY MINISTERING TO UNCLE TOM AFTER HIS WHIPPING. Page 196.

Figure 15. "Cassy ministering to Uncle Tom after his whipping." Illustration of *Uncle Tom's Cabin* by Billings, 1852. Yale Collection of American Literature, Beinecke Rare Book and Manuscript Library.

on the Shelby plantation but from the impending collapse of this ideal-ized village life that Billings spreads before the gaze of the reader.

The second illustration, next in Billings's sequence for the novel, depicts a slave auction that Tom, now under Haley's control, observes immedi-ately after leaving the Shelby plantation. In this image, Billings jarringly introduces a visual vocabulary starkly opposed to that of the previous plate: the bucolic scene is replaced by a crowded urban streetscape, in which rustic peasants cower on pavement before a menacing sea of top-hatted capitalists. Here, Billings channels the contemporary work of the famous illustrators of Dickens's novels, George Cruikshank and Hablot Browne ("Phiz"), who produced many such crowd-in-the-street scenes organized around a portrayal of an extreme power differential or moment of coercion.[15] To illustrate the first stage of Tom's progress through the stations of Stowe's Slave South, Billings literally replaces the rural village with the industrial city in the turn of a page.

His envisioning of Tom's second fall to the southward poses an even starker country/city contrast. Billings images St. Clare's plantation with conventions of mid-eighteenth-century English romantic portraiture, in which aristocrats appear in the context of their extensive rural landhold-ings. Here, Tom and Eva, dressed at an unusual height of fashion—Tom's lace cuffs and spats are particularly nice—sit in a pleasure garden and gaze out at a wide vista of unspoiled landscape, opening into a harbor and the sea beyond, toward which Eva gestures, signifying her owner-ship. But when Billings next depicts Tom, after his first whipping on Legree's plantation, he once again veers to the precedent of Dickens's il-lustrators, this time by using the set pieces they had developed to portray the hovels inhabited by London's wretched poor. With his use of a strong single light source to organize the scene, Billings emphasizes darkness, filth, and shadows, while also lending an air of interior claustrophobia to the plantation scene. He follows the lead of Cruikshank and Phiz in placing a woman or girl in the scene—here, Cassy—who is struggling to carry out offices of feminine compassion even as she appears physically crushed by her environment: pale, gaunt, bedraggled, on her knees.[16]

Again, Stowe's sequential progress from one incarnation of her Slave South to the next suggested to Billings powerfully divergent visual modes separated by decades of modernization—and again, none of those visual styles had any customary association with the southern United States. The odd disjuncture between the avowed subject of *Uncle Tom's Cabin* and the images that it generated in the mind of its first U.S. illustrator seems to support the complaint of Stowe's critics from the southern states that she had no firsthand experience of their section, that the entire novel was the product of her fevered imagination, unmoored from an actual place. But to the vast majority of her readers, living as they did in modernizing metropolises, Stowe's knowledge or ignorance of the realities of southern slavery was quite beside the point; the verisimilitude of her novel inhered in its powerful description of the recent history of their own lives. *Uncle Tom's Cabin* narrativized the epochal transformation that Stowe's readers had lived through in the decades preceding its publication, and that they continued to struggle to assimilate in the 1850s. The novel provided these readers with an extended mourning of what they had lost in the fall from orderly, patriarchal village life, into the anonymity and brutalization of the industrial city.

Sketching the contours of Stowe's novel, in which movement southward becomes progress into industrial modernity, helps to reconcile the undeniable emotional force of the novel with its admittedly garbled antislavery politics.[17] While Stowe's synthesis of sections was clarifying on some points—in particular, deflating the defense of southern slavery as autonomously patriarchal and premodern—it was obfuscating on many others, as the novel displaced its dystopic representations of the industrial center onto othered imaginative terrain. Consider, for instance, *New-York Tribune* editor Horace Greeley's defense of Stowe against charges, from Southern partisans, that Northern cities held horrors as foul as those assigned by Stowe to her Slave South.[18] Greeley argued that Stowe shared her authorial "spirit" with that of French socialist Eugène Sue, formative writer of city exposé fiction, and that she had in *Uncle Tom's Cabin* written a brief on behalf of *all* of the oppressed and "lowly" of the United States:

> Sue . . . is a humanitarian or socialistic writer whose avowed purpose is to hold up to reprobation and reform the evils of so-called "free labor" as at present existing in Europe. He shows how the working classes are driven to crime by oppression . . . He does cite "the murders, adulteries, seductions, thefts, cheatings, lyings, false swearings, starvings," &c. &c. as "effects of free labor" as it prevails under the political and social system of his country. The *same* category of shames and crimes caused by the effects of slave labor in the South is set forth by Mrs. Stowe, who is of the *same* school of humanitarian thinkers and writes in this country with precisely the *same* object as Sue and his colaborers abroad—the abolition of slavery and the elevation of the mechanical, manufacturing and laboring masses.[19]

Observe the neat work of displacement here: if U.S. proletarians are southern slaves, then the United States confesses to no proletarians outside of its already deviant and peculiar South. Greeley preserves an imaginative space of republican freedom for his *New-York Tribune* readers: with Sue's *Mystères de Paris* in one hand, and Stowe's *Uncle Tom's Cabin* in the other, they can better comprehend life in their own metropolis in 1852—but they can at the same instant understand the United States proper as existing in a sphere above either "the evils of so-called 'free labor' as at present existing in Europe," or the "crimes caused by the effects of slave labor in the South."

But what would it mean to see Stowe as the great "socialistic writer" of the first generation of U.S. industrialization? What analysis of modernity, what plan of action did *Uncle Tom's Cabin* engender for those readers who consumed it so eagerly and with such intensity? Following Tom through Stowe's sequential Slave South chronotope reveals that she constructs each of her archetypal plantations in a distinct narrative register that allows for a specific sort of traction on her overarching inquiry into the conditions of U.S. modernity. The first third of *Uncle Tom's Cabin*, set on the Shelby plantation, exhibits a realistic texture unique in the novel; by comparison, the subsequent scenes set on the St. Clare and Legree plantations unfold in far more formulaic and allusive terms. In the Shelby chapters, Stowe's rich descriptions focus on the details of daily life, lingering on delicious food, comfortable clothes, and the amusements that occupy her characters during their plentiful hours of rural leisure; Stowe also develops the action of the plot in dialogue rather than through overbearing omniscient narration, and she experiments with an array of dialects signifying the class and regional identities of her varied characters. Reminding us that Stowe primarily wrote New England local color fiction for most of her subsequent career, Stephen Nissenbaum has suggested that the Shelby plantation section of the novel is so realistic because Stowe is portraying a world intimately known to her: "the village life she remembered as a child in Litchfield, Connecticut."[20] More explicitly, Stowe is remembering this village life as a child of its ruling class: the Shelby plantation is benevolently patriarchal and blissfully hierarchical, with relations between labor and capital governed by face-to-face exchanges of deference for protection. Everyone in this village world knows his or her place, and no one resents or is demeaned by it.

The sentimental thrust of the rural utopia in this first section of the novel, though, inheres in Stowe's detail of its demise even before she unfolds its attractive scenes. She opens the novel with the exchange between Mr. Shelby and Haley, the slave trader, in which Mr. Shelby agrees to sell Tom, his "good, steady, sensible, pious" farm manager, and this intrusion of the market into the domain of reciprocal duties and loyalties utterly corrupts the moral contract upon which the Shelby society rests. By showing that the entire social order she will detail so lovingly in the following pages has already been undermined fatally, Stowe puts the Shelby plantation squarely into the register of sentimental narrative; as Philip Fisher has observed, "Uncle Tom's cabin" on the Shelby plantation becomes the powerful U.S. analogue to Goldsmith's "Deserted Village" and Wordsworth's "Ruined Cottage." Tom's cabin, which we know from the first page of the novel he must leave, and to which he never returns after the novel carries him southward beyond the Shelby plantation, becomes "the uninhabited place to which human reality can never be restored," a site for meditation on how the progression of time "has created ruins that cannot be repaired, nor can they be erased or forgotten."[21] Stowe's first instantiation of the Slave South, in other words, becomes a site for registering the anguish of the fall into the market that has already happened for her metropolitan readers, an anguish she encapsulates in Mrs. Shelby's response to her husband's announcement of Tom's impending sale.

> "O, Mr. Shelby, I have tried—tried most faithfully, as a Christian woman should—to do my duty to these poor, simple, dependent creatures. I have cared for them, instructed them, watched over them, and know[n] all their little cares and joys, for years; and how can I ever hold up my head again among them, if, for the sake of a little paltry gain, we sell such a faithful, excellent, confiding creature as poor Tom, and tear from him in a moment all we have taught him to love and value? . . . How can I bear to have this open acknowledgment that we care for no tie, no duty, no relation, however sacred, compared with money?"

This original loss in many ways forms the emotional core of the book. Stowe uses her sentimental narration of the Shelby plantation to put before her readers what has irrevocably escaped them under industrialization: a stable, hierarchical order with a presumably natural and moral basis, in which the Shelbys of the world "do [their] duty" to secure the loyalty and deference of their "poor, simple, dependent creatures"; an order that rejects commodification and capital accumulation for "higher principles," proclaiming with Mrs. Shelby that "one soul is worth more than all the money in the world."[22]

As Fisher perceptively defines it, sentimental narrative is concerned only with moments when action is impossible, and thus the tears that the Shelby plantation section of *Uncle Tom's Cabin* is designed to evoke should be understood as a sign of powerlessness in the reader. Tom has been sold; the village order has been violated; there is nothing to be done but mourn. Stowe's concern in this section, in other words, is not to analyze what has happened, who is at fault, or how and why she and her readers have found themselves expelled from the garden of their preindustrial childhoods. Indeed, she leaves remarkably vague the conditions of economic necessity impelling Mr. Shelby's acquiescence to the destruction of the village order over which he presides, relying upon a deus ex machina device never further explained. "'Haley has come into possession of a mortgage,'" Mr. Shelby replies to his wife's emotional protest. "'That man has had it in his power to ruin us all.'" And then Stowe goes on to personify Haley as the market incarnate, "'a man alive to nothing but trade and profit—cool, and unhesitating, and unrelenting, as death and the grave.'"[23] As Stowe engenders this primary sense of powerlessness before a loss as inevitable as death, she puts her readers in the place of the victims of her story.[24] Again, Mrs. Shelby serves as a guide for the reader in this identification, this collectivity of victimhood and mourning, as when she comes to Tom's eponymous cabin just before he is forever taken from it by Haley:

> Here one of the boys called out, "Thar's Missis a-comin' in!"
>
> "She can't do no good; what's she coming for?" said Aunt Chloe . . ."
>
> "Tom," [Mrs. Shelby] said, "I come to—" and stopping suddenly, and regarding the silent group, she sat down in the chair, and, covering her face with her handkerchief, began to sob.
>
> "Lor, now, Missis, don't—don't!" said Aunt Chloe, bursting out in her turn; and for a few moments they all wept in company. And in those tears they all shed together, the high and the lowly, melted away all the heart-burnings and anger of the oppressed.[25]

The "weeping in company" that Stowe calculates the first third of her novel to evoke does not necessitate a primary identification with Tom, his wife Chloe, or the other enslaved characters on the Shelby plantation. Taking Stowe's central problematic to be modernization, rather than chattel slavery, per se, illuminates the way that she employs Mrs. Shelby to model for her metropolitan readers an understanding of *themselves* as primary, rather than merely empathetic or transitive, victims of the demise of the old order. Their stake in what comes next, thus, is all the greater.

The Imperial New Jerusalem in *Uncle Tom's Cabin*

By all accounts, the Shelby plantation section of the novel came quickly to Stowe, but when she left the imaginative environs of that setting, and her elegiac sentimental narrative mode, for Tom's first journey southward into modernity, her composition faltered. From July to December 1851 she missed a string of deadlines for the *National Era*, the magazine in which *Uncle Tom's Cabin* was serialized, and she submitted late each of the chapters (12 through 19) that immediately follow Tom's removal from the Shelby plantation.[26] During this time, she was soliciting, in urgent tones, firsthand information on Southern slavery from sources ranging from Frederick Douglass to a cousin who had worked as a financier in New Orleans.[27] She seems to have regained her writerly equilibrium only when she gave up on continuing the novel in the intimate, realistic register in which she had begun it, and instead created the second archetypal Slave South setting of the novel in markedly distinct terms. Tom's new home, the St. Clare plantation, serves as a fantastic refuge from the market forces that swept Tom away from his cabin in the first place: Louisiana planter Augustine St. Clare, "indolent and careless of money," willfully has refused to operate his plantation in a productive capacity, creating an isolated, utopic dominion engaged in an orgy of consumption. St. Clare's plantation thus introduces a relationship between capital and labor, between "the high and the lowly," divergent from that represented either by Shelby's preindustrial village or Haley's modern trade in workers. "To hold [slaves] as tools for money-making, I could not," St. Clare explains to his visiting cousin from Vermont, Miss Ophelia. "[To] have them to help spend money, you know, didn't look quite so ugly to me." In the same vein, Little Eva pleads with her father, "Papa, do buy [Tom]! it's no matter what you pay . . . I want to make him happy."[28]

This truly prelapsarian incarnation of the South, where no one need work, can exist only in escapist fantasy, and Stowe indicates as much when she eschews the realistic dialogism of the first third of the novel, veering instead into the lengthy objective descriptions, typed characters, and soliloquies of romance as she introduces St. Clare, the tragic victim of a thwarted youthful love, and his daughter Evangeline, the Wordsworthian angelic child. This Edenic incarnation of the Slave South, further, makes sense in Stowe's typological imagination only with the anticipation of its coming fall; and she makes clear from her first introduction of St. Clare's environs that although Tom perceives the new plantation "with an air of calm, still enjoyment . . . his beaming black face perfectly radiant with admiration," it nonetheless will provide him only a temporary respite from his forced march into the market. Just as she identifies Little Eva as perfect and therefore marked for death ("Has there ever been a child like Eva? Yes, there have been; but their names are always on grave-stones."), Stowe brands the paradisiacal St. Clare environs "perishable" from the outset. St. Clare's bizarre, reactionary social experiment at the center of the novel is a last stand against modernity, and as such, is doomed.

The fundamental "perishability" of her second incarnation of the Slave South is mandated, in Stowe's imagination, not only by the biblical typology of Eden, but also by the imperialist ideology that holds temperate places and peoples to be inevitably ascendant over tropical ones.[29] With her initial description of the St. Clare plantation, and the relationship of its inhabitants to it, Stowe's relentless invocation of tropicality prescribes the ultimate disposition of this entire central section of the novel:

> The carriage stopped in front of an ancient mansion, built in that odd mixture of Spanish and French style, of which there are specimens in some parts of New Orleans. It was built in the Moorish fashion . . . The court, in the inside, had evidently been arranged to gratify a picturesque and voluptuous ideality. Wide galleries ran all around the four sides, whose Moorish arches, slender pillars, and arabesque ornaments, carried the mind back, as in a dream, to the reign of oriental romance in Spain . . . On the whole, the appearance of the place was luxurious and romantic . . .
>
> "O, isn't it beautiful, lovely! my own dear, darling home!" [Eva] said to Miss Ophelia. "Isn't it beautiful?"
>
> " 'T is a pretty place," said Miss Ophelia, as she alighted; "though it looks rather old and heathenish to me."
>
> Tom got down from the carriage, and looked about with an air of calm, still enjoyment. The negro, it must be remembered, is an exotic of the most gorgeous and superb countries of the world, and he has, deep in his heart, a passion for all that is splendid, rich, and fanciful . . .
>
> St. Clare, who was at heart a poetical voluptuary, smiled as Miss Ophelia made her remark on his premises, and, turning to Tom . . . he said,
>
> "Tom, my boy, this seems to suit you."
>
> "Yes, Mas'r, it looks about the right thing," said Tom.[30]

Rather like Emerson in his political lectures of 1844, Stowe modulates here between figures of the deep colonial past of Tropical America and modern imperatives of Anglo-Saxonist empire. As "French and Spanish style" morphs into "the Moorish fashion" in her opening two sentences, Stowe reveals that her interest in the heterogenous colonial background of the Slave South hinges fundamentally on what she understands to be its "ancient" and "odd mixture" of races. Under the sign of racial intermixture, we see that all of the native southerners here, black *and* white— "exotic[s]," as they are, "of the most gorgeous and superb countries in the world,"—share the same relationship to this plantation "arranged to gratify a tropical and voluptuous ideality." Equally at home in this environment, Eva, Tom, and St. Clare (the "voluptuary"-in-chief) reveal themselves to be equally children of the tropics—and thus equally doomed to extinction by the progressive modernity of Stowe's plot. Nativity, not race—or, perhaps, nativity *as* race—is destiny here: Vermonter Miss Ophelia alone, with her correct, Anglo-Saxonist, temperate perspective on the tropical plantation—for "old and heathenish," read "marked for righteous subjugation"—will be able to negotiate, survive, and indeed profit from the predestined demise of the St. Clare realm.

Perhaps because the St. Clare plantation section of the book is so formulaically focused upon the ephemerality of its setting, Stowe uses the pause in plot action—we are, after all, only waiting for the predestined fall to come to pass—to direct the attention of her readers toward the question of what sort of (inevitably Northern) social order will replace this attractive but doomed incarnation of the Slave South. And perhaps because the mode of romance frees Stowe from the specificities of sentimental realism and leads her instead toward abstraction and typology, this central section of the novel becomes her site for testing "theories," airing ideological approaches to interpreting the market revolution. Although the extended deathbed scene of Little Eva has tended to magnetize critical discussion of this part of the novel, Stowe devotes at least equal space to a series of staged philosophical discussions between St. Clare and Ophelia, themselves a perfect pair of sectionalist political types. St. Clare dominates these conversations, initially educating Ophelia out of her satirically limited Northern abolitionist views, which Stowe characterizes as tics of tongue clucking: "grim with indignation," Ophelia is prone to *Liberator*-headline-style outbursts such as "Perfectly horrible!" and "Shameful! monstrous! outrageous!" For St. Clare's speeches, on the other hand, Stowe practically plagiarizes from Virginian George Fitzhugh, whose iconoclastic proslavery writings, including *A Sociology for the South: The Failure of Free Society* (1850), were in conversation with Marx's *Communist Manifesto* perhaps more seriously than any others in the United States in the early 1850s.[31] Through St. Clare, Stowe asserts that her metropolitan readers *must* attend to the dilemma and the frank horror of the modern Slave South lurking outside of the confines of his utopian realm of exception; they must understand the Slave South not as an isolated and peculiar local problem but as an emblematic manifestation of the global ascendance of capitalist modernity.

> "The American planter is only doing, in another form, what the English aristocracy and capitalists are doing by the lower classes; that is, I take it, *appropriating* them, body and bone, soul and spirit, to their use and convenience . . . [The English laborer] is as much at the will of his employer as if he were sold to him. The slave-owner can whip his refractory slave to death,— the capitalist can starve him to death. As to family security, it is hard to say which is the worst,—to have one's children sold, or see them starve to death at home."

The ideological exploration facilitated by the romantic abstraction of her St. Clare section leads Stowe to state directly what the upcoming Legree section of the novel will narrativize: for her readers living at the centers of Western industrialization, slavery *is* modernity; it is at least their threatened destiny. Southern slave law simply codifies and makes visible the equally despotic, but less transparent, power asymmetry of the industrial capitalist order. Thus to contemplate "the abstract question of slavery" is to comprehend proletarianization and its ramifications: "'It takes no spectacles to see that a great class of vicious, improvident, degraded people, among us, are an evil to us, as well as to themselves.'" And to imagine the injustice coming to a head in violence is to envision not a civil war, but rather an American version of the 1848 European revolts of the working classes: "'One thing is certain,—that there is a mustering among the masses, the world over; and there is a *dies irae* coming on, sooner or later. The same thing is working in Europe, in England, and in this country.'"[32]

Despite the clarity of St. Clare's vision of Western modernity and its coming Day of Wrath, Stowe increasingly focuses his soliloquies on his repetitious confessions of inaction: he has failed to become an "actor and regenerator in society"; he "has floated on, a dreamy, neutral spectator of the struggles, agonies, and wrongs of man"; he possesses "only that kind of benevolence which consists in lying on a sofa."[33] St. Clare's characterological "indolence," of course, is of a piece with his tropical identity, a pillar of the climatic determinism through which Stowe structures the entire middle section of the book:

> "I never want to talk seriously in hot weather. What with mosquitos and all, a fellow can't get himself up to any very sublime moral flights; and I believe," said St. Clare, suddenly rousing himself up, "there's a theory, now! I understand now why northern nations are always more virtuous than southern ones,—I see into that whole subject."

Two pages after St. Clare once again "rouses himself up" to imagine starting the revolution he has predicted from his couch—doing his "duty . . . to the poor and lowly . . . beginning with my own servants . . . and perhaps, at some future day . . . for a whole class"—Stowe abruptly administers the long-foreshadowed death blow to his realm. To St. Clare himself, Stowe metes out the most stereotypical Southern-planter-demise conceivable: he's stabbed "with a bowie-knife" in "an affray . . . between two gentlemen . . . who were both partially intoxicated."[34]

If Stowe in the Shelby section of the novel essentially substitutes time for place, locating the past of her New England childhood in Kentucky, in the St. Clare section she reasserts geography with vigor. The question begged by Stowe's chronotope at the end of the central section of *Uncle*

Tom's Cabin then becomes: What Northern incarnation of modernity will take over this Slave South predestined by its tropicality for subjugation? Stowe poses this problem to her readers with a tale of two Vermonters-as-masters. On the ruins of St. Clare's insolvent estate, Ophelia uses her newly acquired ownership of the enslaved child Topsy—transferred to her by St. Clare shortly before his death—for good, to protect and educate her lowly dependent. Tom, by pointed contrast, is thrown into jeopardy with the loss of such a paternalistic owner. Left "Unprotected" (the title of chapter 29), Tom is repossessed by the capitalist system that had first clutched him in the form of the trader Haley. Now fully commoditized, he is stored in "The Slave Warehouse" (the title of chapter 30) until his purchase by Simon Legree, a fellow native of Ophelia's Green Mountains. Stowe titles chapter 31, in which she sends Tom, in chains, down the Red River to Legree's infernal plantation, "The Middle Passage," thereby implying that this character who was born into slavery and has been enslaved throughout her plot only *truly* leaves his tropical home and enters U.S. slavery when he passes into the modern industrial dystopia presided over by the dark side of Vermont.

Through the overarching Slave South chronotope of the novel, Stowe re-poses the questions of U.S. modernity to her metropolitan readers as not a problem of freedom but a problem of mastery: will the modern United States be run by good or evil Northern masters? The evil Northern masters—the Legrees, the industrial capitalists—have, in Stowe's mind, been ascendant thus far, and so the last act of her novel is set on Legree's preternaturally modern Slave South plantation. Her first description of Legree's realm reasserts the temporal dimension of her chronotope: his godforsaken estate is simply the industrial destruction of both Shelby's preindustrial village and St. Clare's paradisiacal refuge:

> The estate had formerly belonged to a gentleman of opulence and taste, who had bestowed some considerable attention to the adornment of his grounds. Having died insolvent, it had been purchased, at a bargain, by Legree, who used it, as he did everything else, merely as an implement for money-making. The place had that ragged, forlorn appearance, which is always produced by the evidence that the care of the former owner has been left to go to utter decay.[35]

Legree's plantation completes the fall into the market that has driven the arc of the novel: Haley's threat to the mortgaged Mr. Shelby, the insolvent collapse of St. Clare's last stand—the capitalist concern with profit only, to the "utter decay" of "art," "taste," "comfort," and "goodness"—this threat is fully realized in Stowe's final incarnation of the Slave South.

Directly upon the ruins of the moral village order of the Shelby plantation, and the manorial noblesse oblige of the St. Clare plantation, Legree
has established his own Northern industrial city, complete with factory
production, prostitution, alcoholism, atheism, and paupers' quarters for
the laborers.[36] Tom finds no republican cabin or peasant's "cottage, rude,
indeed" here, but rather a Dickensian urban hovel: "a mere shell, desti-
tute of any species of furniture, except a heap of straw, foul with dirt,
spread confusedly over the floor . . . trodden by the tramping of innumerable feet."[37]

Legree's bad mastery horrifies Stowe most profoundly as she contemplates how it produces the "lowly" as proletarians, as an underclass who
are both miserably exploited and ultimately impossible to control without violence. Her description of the enslaved workers on Legree's plantation serves as Stowe's decidedly elitist portrait of the Northern working
classes, and in fact eerily echoes the strong rhetoric of her preacher father,
Lyman Beecher, on the perils posed to social order by New England's urban poor. As early as the 1830s, when Stowe was still a child in her
father's home and church, Beecher had found this emergent class to
be "a race of famished, infuriated animals, goaded by instinct and unrestrained by prospective hopes or fears."[38] As Stowe envisions Legree's
abased slaves in 1852, she similarly draws upon language of massing,
bestiality, and—most horrifying—lack of hegemonic control. "Flocking
home" at the end of the shift, the "gang" comprises "sullen, scowling, im-
bruted men, and feeble, discouraged women, or women that were not
women . . . [all exhibiting] the gross, unrestricted animal selfishness of
human beings, of whom nothing good was expected or desired." Tom
dies rather than submit to the new economic order, and the "neat and respectable" quadroons with "high forehead[s]," Cassy and Emmeline, escape Legree's industrial environs, but Legree's atheistic, vicious, and
explosive masses remain caught in the maw of his factory-plantation
when Stowe resolves her main plot line. When young George Shelby arrives on the Legree plantation just in time to see Tom breathe his last and
to give him a proper burial, he is begged for aid by Legree's still living,
still suffering workers: "'Hard times here, Mas'r! . . . Do, Mas'r, buy us,
please!'" Despite the presumably world-changing act of martyrdom he
has just witnessed in Tom's death, the younger Shelby responds to the
continued existence of Legree's realm with the equivalent of throwing his
hands in the air: "'I can't!—I can't!' said George, with difficulty, motion-
ing them off; 'it's impossible!'"[39]

As we remember, though, that Stowe had begun the narrative arc of
Tom's story with the impotence before the modern market of Shelby *père*,

we see the symmetry in her closing with the continued impotence, into the next generation, of Shelby *fils*.[40] The structural symmetry reminds her metropolitan readers that *they*—not southerners white or black—are poised to be the true "actors and regenerators" of the Slave South story implicitly to come at the end of *Uncle Tom's Cabin*. Having already lived through the market revolution themselves, her readers should understand themselves to be both materially and ideologically poised to command the drama of modernization that now will play itself out on a global stage, in advances ever farther South. This is the great alchemy of Stowe's evolving Slave South chronotope throughout the novel, taken as a whole: she transmutes the abasement of industrialization into the elevation of empire. In a final chapter of direct exhortation to her readers, Stowe charges them foremost with fighting the bad, Legree-style mastery of capitalist modernity, the fallen industrial condition that immediately surrounds them. "Northern men, northern mothers, northern Christians, have something more to do than denounce their brethren at the South; they have to look to the evil among themselves. But, what can any individual do?"[41] The entire, multifaceted emotional experience of the novel comes to a head with this urgent question about the hidden workings of power and the superhuman scale of system under capitalist modernity— an urgent question which, it is not far-fetched to imagine, may have inspired the title of Nikolai Chernyshefsky's 1863 novel, *What Is to Be Done?*[42] Though Chernyshefsky's novel bears a complex relationship to Lenin's 1901/02 pamphlet of the same title, thinking about this broader modern resonance of Stowe's chronotopic Slave South novel brings us back to the question of what it means to understand *Uncle Tom's Cabin* as the great "socialistic" response to the first generation of industrialization in the United States.

Stowe's own answer to her crystallizing question has seemed disappointingly deflating to her critics ever since 1852: "There is one thing that every individual can do,—they can see to it that they *feel right*." We must appreciate, though—as Laura Wexler and Amy Kaplan have insisted—the sheer power of "feeling right" in a nascent imperial context.[43] The injunction is, simultaneously, to feel with moral correctness, and to feel oneself righteous, and Stowe provides her readers with a model of it: her good Vermont mistress, Ophelia, denominated "Miss *Feely*" by her charge—her slave—Topsy. Ophelia's Vermonter alter ego, Legree, is both a factory master and an early version of the Yankee imperialist; his bad mastery of the Slave South opens the possibility for a good mastery, a "right" mastery of it.[44] Shadowing the main plot line in Stowe's final chapters, Ophelia holds out the promise that while metropolitan readers cannot recuperate their lost village life in the modern world, they can recuperate its ostensibly moral hierarchy by moving outward geographically and managing the modernization of the South. Indeed, Stowe offers "Miss Feely" as the explicit recuperation of the fallen, disempowered Mrs. Shelby of the first section of the novel:

> Who shall detail the tribulations manifold of our friend Miss Ophelia, who had begun the labors of a Southern housekeeper? . . .
>
> South as well as north, there are women who have an extraordinary talent for command, and tact in educating. Such are enabled, with apparent ease, and without severity, to subject to their will, and bring into harmonious and systematic order, the various members of their small estate,—to regulate their peculiarities, and so balance and compensate the deficiencies of one by the excess of another, as to produce a harmonious and orderly system.
>
> Such a housekeeper was Mrs. Shelby, whom we have already described; and such our readers may remember to have met with. If they are not common at the South, it is because they are not common in the world.[45]

Stowe's vision of extraordinarily commanding housekeeping here seems to converse with Emerson's desire for a power "omnipotent without violence." Through Ophelia, Stowe holds out to her metropolitan readers the promise that their idealized village paternalism of the past can be reinvented in the modern age as imperial mastery. Her Slave South—her South as a place and a people naturally slavish—finally offers her readers the redemptive possibility of a do-over at the market revolution that has gone awry on their own ground—a chance to get it right on other territory.

This promise of directing a more perfect modernization of the South from the central summit of Northern developmental power resonates with a recurrent allusion to the trope of the Holy City—the New Jerusalem—that Stowe weaves into transitional scenes in her progress through the Slave South. When Haley carries Tom away from the Shelby plantation, Tom meditates upon "these words of an ancient volume . . . 'We have here no continuing city, but we seek one to come; wherefore God himself is not ashamed to be called our God; for he hath prepared for us a city.'" Just before Little Eva reveals to Tom that she is going to die, the two read from the biblical book of Revelation, and Tom sings a hymn concluding, "'Bright angels should convey me home, / To the new Jerusalem.'" And as Tom completes the weary journey to Legree's plantation at the opening of "Dark Places," Legree commands him to sing, by yelling "come!" twice. Tom replies with another hymn: "'Jerusalem, my happy home, / Name ever dear to me! / When shall my sorrows have an end, / Thy joys when shall—.'"[46] Legree interrupts the hymn before Tom can fulfill the tyrant's own prophecy, that the New Jerusalem shall "come," but Cassy ultimately strikes down Legree, evil genius of the Industrial North, by completing the tripartite incantation: "'Come! come! come!'"

Through the trope of the Holy City, Stowe follows the English poet William Blake in exhorting citizens of the capital, despondent over the costs of industrialization, to embrace modernity and build a more perfect metropolis.[47] In his preface to *Milton* (1808), Blake confronts the seemingly devolutionary changes wrought upon the English countryside by modernization; yet rather than calling for a return to the pastoral past, he exhorts readers onward to a revolutionary modernization:

> And did those feet in ancient time
> Walk upon England's mountains green:
> And was the holy Lamb of God,
> On England's pleasant pastures seen!
>
> And did the Countenance Divine,
> Shine forth upon our clouded hills?
> And was Jerusalem builded here,
> Among these dark Satanic Mills? . . .
>
> I will not cease from Mental Fight,
> Nor shall my Sword sleep in my hand:
> Till we have built Jerusalem
> In England's green & pleasant Land.[48]

The evolving phases of Stowe's Slave South chronotope cycle through Blake's lines: from the "pleasant pastures" of the Shelby plantation, site of idealized rural nostalgia; to the "dark Satanic Mills" of the Legree plantation, site of industrial dystopia; to, above all, the place possessed collectively in the imagination of the audience: "*England's* mountains green," "*England's* pleasant pastures," "*England's* green and pleasant Land." Stowe's U.S. geographical imagination, though, operates at the juncture between Blake's domestic pastoral and the imperial imaginary that generates a metropolitan comprehension of industrialization by narrating the building of the modern city, from the ground up, on colonial territory.[49] As Stowe exhorts her readers in her "Concluding Remarks," "You pray for the heathen abroad; pray also for the heathen at home."[50]

Of course, there is an inherent irony in all this—the notion that Stowe's readers should combat Southern slavery by becoming more perfect masters of the South—and Stowe briefly glances at that irony when St. Clare warns Ophelia, as he signs ownership of Topsy over to her, of this "'awful "doing evil that good may come"'!" Structurally, though, Stowe's chronotope urges her readers to take up the modern imperial mission with gusto. Her cycle of falls in the line of Tom's story implies a corresponding cycle of redemptions—literally, purchases—by benevolent masters. Mr. Shelby has, implicitly, redeemed Tom from his birth into slavery at the start of the novel; St. Clare redeems him from his first fall into the market; and, of course, God redeems him when he dies on Legree's plantation. When young George Shelby locates the dying man—"'I've come to buy you, and take you home," he tells Tom—Stowe makes her alignment between God's relationship to humans, and the master's relationship to the slave, perfectly explicit. Tom replies, "'O, Mas'r George, ye're too late. The Lord's bought me, and is going to take me home." The reader, at this point in the novel, has bought Tom, too, to a certain extent, and the model of Ophelia's redemption of Topsy promises as well that to be a righteous master is, transitively, to be God.[51] A Shelby cannot effect this ultimate redemption; but a Vermonter can, intervening in the cycle of fall and temporary recovery to generate a final progress into imperial modernity, a building of the Holy City on the implicitly expropriated ground of the Slave South. Perhaps now the reported penchant of Union soldiers to carry *Uncle Tom's Cabin* into battle—it was supposedly second in popularity with soldiers only to the Bible—becomes legible. To "feel right" in the terms of this epochal novel is, ultimately, to understand oneself to be the agent of the glory of the coming of the Lord, to the benighted Souths of the fallen world.

CHAPTER EIGHT

The Masterwork of National Literature

[The author] expands and deepens down, the more I contemplate him; and further, and further, shoots his strong New-England roots into the hot soil of my Southern soul.

— A Virginian Spending July in Vermont [Herman Melville],
"Hawthorne and His Mosses," *The Literary World* (August 1850)

A FEW YEARS AFTER the publication of Stowe's novel, Emerson connected the unprecedented popularity of *Uncle Tom's Cabin* to a nascent U.S. imperial imaginary. In an 1858 essay titled "Success," he rhetorically posed the geographic expansion of the United States and the sale of Stowe's U.S. novel around the world as parallel triumphs of a nation marching into the stature of global empire:

> The earth is shaken by our energies. We are feeling our youth and nerve and bone. We have the power of territory and of seacoast, and know the use of these. We count our census, we read our growing valuations, we survey our map, which becomes old in a year or two . . . We interfere in Central and South America, at Canton, and in Japan; we are adding to an already enormous territory . . . We have seen an American woman write a novel of which a million copies were sold, in all languages, and which had one merit, of speaking to the universal heart.

By Emerson's lights, Stowe had located "the universal" firmly on U.S. ground, at the same moment that the voracious map of Manifest Destiny was domesticating "the earth." With parallel structure, Emerson further intimated that these two achievements were related: that Stowe's writing of the Slave South into an endlessly applicable story of "the universal heart"—or, at least, a narrative template for Western modernization— could not be separated from an apparently limitless, explicitly global, expansion of U.S. borders. And Emerson identified the point of confluence between national literature and national empire as inherently a site of contest, in which the supremacy of the United States would be achieved only by the abasement of an other, in a perversion of *e pluribus unum*. "We are great by exclusion, grasping and egotism. Our success takes from all what it gives to one."[1]

THE GREAT VALLEY.

Figure 16. "The Great Valley," from *Virginia Illustrated* by Porte Crayon
[David Hunter Strother], *Harper's New Monthly Magazine,* January 1856.
Clifton Waller Barrett Library of American Literature, Special Collections,
University of Virginia Library.

Several years before, as Stowe was penning the first chapters of her novel, and on the eve of his own literary declaration of independence, *Moby-Dick,* Herman Melville had made just such a connection between literary nationalism and empire, positing both as sites of conquest in which an actor must be either dominant or subjugated. In a review essay in *The Literary World* of August 1850, "Hawthorne and His Mosses," Melville suggested that the United States was farther along toward achieving global empire than toward realizing the literary hegemony that needed to accompany it. "While we are rapidly preparing for that political supremacy among the nations, which prophetically awaits us at the close of the present century," he wrote, "in a literary point of view, we are deplorably unprepared for it; and we seem studious to remain so."[2] In an essay whose point, ultimately, was to envision what a literary "supremacy"—an imperial literary nationalism—would look like, Melville employed an interesting gambit: he wrote in the persona of "a Virginian spending July in Vermont," a provincial southern planter temporarily admitted, as an appreciative tourist, to the inner sanctum of U.S. cultural production. He used this guise to perform what subjugation before a supreme literary power should entail: reading Nathaniel Hawthorne's *Mosses from an Old Manse,* the "Virginian" finds himself *possessed,* taken over in a sexualized ecstasy of influence:

> [H]ow magically stole over me this Mossy Man! . . . The soft ravishments of the man spun me round about in a web of dreams . . . He expands and deepens down, the more I contemplate him; and further, and further, shoots his strong New-England roots into the hot soil of my Southern soul.

In documenting his prostration before Hawthorne's tales, Melville's "Virginian" also dissects the source of their power over him: "[G]reat geniuses are parts of the times; they themselves are the times; and possess a correspondent coloring." This "coloring" of his time, the "Virginian" attests (as perhaps only a denizen of the Slave South can), is "a blackness, ten times black"; and "it is this blackness in Hawthorne . . . that so fixes and fascinates me."[3] Yet, the "Virginian" avers, the "blackness" of nascent modernity has its bright side, too, in that it provides a literary foil for the forward march of a New-England–centered U.S. empire: "[T]his darkness but gives more effect to the ever-moving dawn that forever advances through it, and circumnavigates [Hawthorne's] world." As he gives himself over as the tropical, uncultivated ground upon which the "germinous" power of the New England writer may do its will, Melville's "Virginian" is even able to experience a vicarious—indeed, quoted—glimpse from the all-seeing vantage of the New England hilltop, toward the subjected Souths of world history: "So all that day, half-buried in the new clover, I watched this Hawthorne's 'Assyrian dawn, and Paphian sunset and moonrise, from the summit of our Eastern Hill.'"[4]

Through the exercise of writing the "Virginian," Melville implies that making his prospective literary supremacy a reality will involve more than merely inspiring a jingoistic enthusiasm among provincial readers across all of U.S. territory. Rather bemusedly, his narrator reports that "I was much pleased with a hot-headed Carolina cousin of mine, who once said,—'If there were no other American to stand by, in Literature,—why, then, I would stand by Pop Emmons and his "Fredoniad," and till a better epic came along, swear it was not very far behind the Iliad.'" Such a model of readerly co-labor in the project of literary mastery leaves too much power in the hands of those destined to be mastered in the very act of their reading, as Melville makes clear by the enthusiasm of the "Carolina cousin" for a work of literature that is not only subpar, but also written by a provincial author from Kentucky. Instead, the last sentence of the paragraph holds the challenge to U.S. authors Melville will pursue next: of the thoughts of his "Carolina cousin," the "Virginian" concludes— "Take away the words, and in spirit he was sound."[5]

Take away the words: true literary power requires holding absolute power to define others, as well as absolute power to keep those others from writing back. Creating a literary supremacy coeval with "that political supremacy among the nations, which prophetically awaits us," requires in particular writing the propotypical other of empire—tropical, juvenile, definitionally Southern—and that other becomes, most challengingly for Melville in his works of the early 1850s, the storied figure of the southern planter. After all, the southern planter was the original and cast-off American master of Melville's era, the figure who embodied the very model of manly individualism that industrialization had done in. The engraving at the opening of this chapter—part of popular artist Porte Crayon's *Virginia Illustrated,* published alongside some of Melville's best-known short fiction in *Harper's* in the mid-1850s—pictures "the Virginian" in just this way: as the erect, elevated pillar upon whom women and subordinated men quite literally depend. While the planter figure blithely waves his hat in the air, not one but three women hang from his waist—making him a patriarch of biblical proportions—while, inevitably, a black man bows at his feet. In January of 1856, the artist recast this old, potent figure of New World empire in a newly relevant context: as Tennessean filibuster William Walker reigned as self-installed "president" of Nicaragua, and proslavery southern Democrats called for ever more expansion into Latin America, Crayon's planter stands atop a globe-like boulder, mastering a vast, continental-scale landscape that spreads prone before him to the horizon line.[6]

At the height of Manifest Destiny, the southern planter had become the alter ego of U.S. empire, simultaneously the link to the ignominious former colonial stature of the nation, and the conduit to a modern imperial nationalism. To "take away," to appropriate and control, the words of this figure thus became a key step for Melville in writing a modern imperial literature. He experimented with this project as early as *Moby-Dick* (1850), with the truncated and enigmatic appearance of the "demi-god" sailor Bulkington early in the novel. Melville's narrator forcefully marks Bulkington upon introduction as a figure of importance to whom the attention of the reader should be directed:

> This man interested me at once; and since the sea-gods had ordained that he should soon become my shipmate (though but a sleeping-partner one, so far as this narrative is concerned) I will here venture upon a little description of him. He stood full six feet in height, with noble shoulders, and a chest like a coffer-dam. I have seldom seen such brawn in a man. His face was deeply brown and burnt, making his white teeth dazzling by the constrast; while in the deep shadows of his eyes floated some reminiscences that did not seem to give him much joy. His voice at once announced that he was a Southerner, and from his fine stature, I thought he must be one of those tall mountaineers from the Alleghanian Ridge in Virginia. When the revelry of his companions had mounted to its height, this man slipped away unobserved, and I saw no more of him till he became my comrade on the sea. In a few minutes, however, he was missed by his shipmates, and being, it seems, for some reason a huge favorite with them, they raised a cry of "Bulkington! Bulkington! where's Bulkington?" and darted out of the house in pursuit of him.[7]

This intense introduction foreshadows an important future role for Bulkington in the novel, setting him apart as it does as physically huge (a bulking ton of "brawn"), tragically tormented by some hidden sorrow, and holding enormous sway over the crew of a ship. Indeed, the crew behave as markers for the reader, inducing us, too, to protest the too-quick exit of the fascinating Southerner from the text and to run ahead "in pursuit of him."

If we do this, though, we're frustrated; Bulkington proves to be one of the great red herrings of the novel, and Melville's narrator subsequently mentions him only once, twenty chapters later, when he is lost overboard at the very moment when the Pequod takes to the sea. The weirdness of this disjuncture between the fascinated introduction and summary dispatch of Bulkington has led some critics to speculate that Melville initially intended to create a more extensive subplot, perhaps a mutiny episode, around his figure; but we may discern also in this troublesome sequence Melville's raising of the specter of an impenetrable or unknowable Southern other, followed by a swift demonstration of the author's absolute power over a universe entirely of his own creation.[8] "Wonderfullest things are ever the unmentionable; deep memories yield no epitaphs; this six-inch chapter is the stoneless grave of Bulkington": thusly Melville dispatches his southern "demigod," reminding us explicitly in the process that Bulkington is *his,* that the character has his physical existence only in the text that Melville has caused to be placed before us on the page. He then goes so far as seeming to taunt his annihilated character. "Know ye now, Bulkington?" his narrator asks rhetorically.[9] As Wai Chee Dimock has argued in her formative reading of his oeuvre, for Melville, "a knowable identity is the mark of the Other"; and the power of *knowing* completely, while remaining himself not-known, is central to Melville's vision of an imperial literature.[10] Toward this end, Melville narrates *Moby-Dick* through a famously opaque author-figure whose name is never even disclosed to the reader: "Call me Ishmael," he commands us at the outset, and we inevitably obey. From the security of his murky identity, Ishmael performs again and again the act of knowing the other, delivering over to us a cast of presumably natural subordinates such as Queequeg, the "cannibal" "savage" who is always "already known."[11] By contrast, Bulkington, in Ishmael's initial description of him, presents the challenge of immediately "announc[ing] that he [is] a Southerner"—that troublesome natural-subordinate-who-is-not-one—while retaining the "deep shadows of his eyes," an interior subjectivity that Ishmael cannot fully fathom. We may then see Melville's summary annihilation of Bulkington as one of the crowning acts of literary supremacy in the novel, through which he dispatches with marvelous efficiency the raised threat of the southerner's ability to "know" back, along with his very existence.[12]

Melville Masters the Tropical Author

Achieving a unilateral literary supremacy by dominating a southern planter character becomes, in many ways, the central premise of Melville's next novel, *Pierre, or the Ambiguities,* published in 1852, contemporaneously with *Uncle Tom's Cabin.* Dispensing with the charade of inhabiting "the Virginian," and leaving aside the intermediary author-figure Ishmael, Melville narrates the story of his title character with startlingly aggressive omniscience. Critics often remark upon the extent to which Melville's narration of the novel proceeds as a discursion not just on writing, but on the writtenness of the book itself, and this distinctive feature of the novel operates in service of drawing a clear distinction between Pierre Glendinning's abjection as a manipulated character who exists only in the text and Melville's authorial supremacy as his creator.[13] Melville introduces his protagonist as striding "half unconsciously" into existence, and structures a large section of the introductory chapter around a repeated refrain of detailing what Pierre thinks he knows, undercut by what he cannot possibly know—how his character will develop, how the plot ahead will unfold—all of which, of course, the author *does* know: "Thus loftily, in the days of his circumscribed youth, did Pierre glance along the background of his race; little recking of that maturer and larger interior development, which should forever deprive these things of their full power of pride in his soul"; "[W]hile all alive to the beauty and poesy of his father's faith, Pierre little foresaw that this world hath a secret deeper than beauty, and Life some burdens heavier than death"; and so on.[14]

This rhythmic introduction opens the novel by delivering the protagonist to readers as "our Pierre," the character collectively owned by author and readers—though not, of course, owned by them on an equal footing. As Melville repetitiously presents his title character and his novel—conflated, a twinned "Pierre"—to his readers as an object, a work of art, he carefully distinguishes between the incomplete access of his readers to Pierre/*Pierre,* and his own unilateral control over the field of the text:

> As a statue, planted on a revolving pedestal, shows now this limb, now that; now front, now back, now side; continually changing, too, its general profile; so does the pivoted, statued soul of man, when turned by the hand of Truth. Lies only never vary; look for no invariableness in Pierre. Nor does any canting showman here stand by to announce his phases as he revolves. Catch his phases as your insight may.[15]

With Pierre's explicit objectification before the partially knowing gazes of readers and the all-knowing "hand of Truth" of his creator—with this constant revocation of Pierre's subjectivity, and replacement of it with his own omniscience—Melville forcefully institutes the literary "supremacy among the nations" that he has called for as the next phase of U.S. imperial maturation.[16] Through his conscious act of creation, Melville lays claim to at least an equality with Shakespeare, the cornerstone of British cultural empire. When Pierre is moved by a couplet from *Hamlet,* Melville stresses his protagonist's ignorance of the unilateral power of the great author similarly shaping his own fate: "[Pierre] knew not—at least, felt not—then, that Hamlet, though a thing of life, was, after all, but a thing of breath, evoked by the wanton magic of a creative hand, and as wantonly dismissed at last into endless halls of hell and night." By explicitly mastering Pierre, Melville deconstructs Shakespeare's ostensibly singular hegemony over literature in English: "for being but a mortal man Shakspeare had his fathers too."[17]

Unlike Bulkington or the "Virginian" of the Hawthorne review, Melville does not openly identify his most ultimately mastered character as a southerner. Instead, he locates Pierre geographically in his own central locality: first, in the Hudson River Valley, and, in the second half of the novel, in New York City. In the bifurcated U.S. literary imagination of the 1850s, in other words, Melville organizes *Pierre* on the country/city, rather than the North/South opposition, as he moves from the pole of absolute rusticity in the first half of the novel—Pierre's familial estate, the feudal, weirdly anachronistic "Saddle Meadows"—to the pole of absolute urban modernity—lower Manhattan—in its latter half.[18] In the process, Melville contains both terms of geographical opposition within New York State, offering New York as a middle ground that encompasses the geographic extremes of the nation as a whole. The rural/urban binary, though, was inextricable from the North/South sectionalist opposition by the 1850s, and in defining Pierre as the scion of a planter—though a Dutch "Patroon" rather than a Virginian—Melville necessarily announces a shadowing sectional affiliation for his protagonist.[19] And indeed, he seems to have located his own authorship as sectionally antagonistic to that of his protagonist. At one point he proposed to his London publisher that *Pierre* be brought out "under an assumed name—'By a Vermonter,' say," thus imaginatively reinscribing onto this novel the sectional alchemy of his call for literary supremacy, attributed to the "Virginian Spending July in Vermont."[20]

In the opening pages of the novel, Melville establishes Pierre's Hudson Valley "descendedness"—his hereditary estate antithetical to modern U.S. democracy—as a matter of location on the North/South sectionalist spectrum. The anomalous Hudson River plantation cannot be "considered" alone, but it may be placed only by reference to, on the one hand, "New England," and, on the other, "Virginia and the South"; the defining sections of the nation cannot be "omitted" when speaking of geography and power. And Saddle Meadows comes down unquestionably on the southern side of the equation, sharing with the Slave South—as its name indicates—a basis in power extremes, a social organization that admits only of the riders and the ridden, a despotic order that Melville shorthands as "oriental-like" "eastern patriarchalness," in opposition to the "unobtrusive families" of New England. Beyond the power extremes, the Slave South and Saddle Meadows also align about—again in direct opposition to the "uninterrupted English lineage" of New England—a definitional "flaw" in their hereditary lines.[21] The plot of *Pierre* revolves around the revelation of the existence of Pierre's illegitimate and unacknowledged (and dark, indeed "Nubian") perhaps-half-sister Isabel, just as the Virginian Randolph family is defined for Melville in this introduction by its alliance with "Pocahontas the Indian Princess" and thus its fundamentally mixed "blood."[22]

The dovetailing of Dutch Patroons and Slave South works in Melville's delineation of Saddle Meadows to connect the colonial origins of the United States—racially creolized and operating according to the unjust power extremes of empire—to the power extremes of industrial modernity that Pierre experiences upon his move to Manhattan. "[W]hatever one may think of the existence of such mighty lordships in the heart of a republic," he concludes his introduction of Pierre's familial estate, "and however we may wonder at their thus surviving, like Indian mounds, the Revolutionary flood; yet survive and exist they do . . . [O]ur lords, the Patroons, appeal not to the past, but they point to the present." Literally built upon the initial imperial expropriation of land from the now-buried Indians, the "mighty lordships"—the plantations—of colonial America continue on into national modernity; and while the South has always served as the past of the nation, it "point[s] to the present" as well, toward the industrial-imperial modernity now well under way.[23] With Melville's relocation of the Slave South northward to the center of U.S. industrialization, the dream of the republic becomes an anomalous blip in U.S. history rather than the status quo. The "Revolutionary flood" proves a momentary divergence from the real American business of empire, which is older than the nation itself.

Melville not only provides a new synthesis of the sectionalist divide—South/North, country/city, past/present—in his New York novel, but he also uses that synthesis to further a new vision of the power of the modern national center. The ultimate power of the metropolis is to be found not in "an immense mass of state-masonry," not in the seat of government, but rather in cultural production—in the centralized power to define reality, to define truth itself.[24] It at first seems a whim that, while introducing Saddle Meadows and Pierre's "descendedness," Melville pursues a running assault on the legitimacy of the British monarchy, intermittently stating cases of estates purchased and heirs born out of wedlock. "All honor to the names then, and all courtesy to the men," he concludes this train of debunking, "but if St. Albans tell me he is all-honorable and all-eternal, I must still politely refer him to Nell Gwynne."

We soon realize, though, that Melville's strident delegitimization of the British throne in the opening chapter is indeed undertaken, as he claims, "with a solid purpose in view": it serves as a microcosm of the progress of the story of Pierre he will unfold. He introduces his planter-scion, "Master Pierre Glendinning," only to depose him from his "noble pedestal," to prostrate the character before the novelist's exposing pen.[25] The preindustrial forms of power invested in his protagonist will prove no match for Melville's modern literary supremacy, a supremacy that can reveal the sins and lies that underwrote the planter's elevation in the first place, in the American colonial past.

In a plot markedly indebted to the fusion of urban and abolitionist exposé that had created the antebellum figure of the Slave South in the 1830s, Melville destroys Pierre's inherited "lordship" by revealing the secret history of American empire in the person of his perhaps-half-sister Isabel, who claims to be the cast-off child of his father's extramarital liaison with a Frenchwoman. Melville develops Pierre's relationship with Isabel around two cardinal, and interrelated, sins of the Slave South: threatened incest and implied racial intermixture. Melville presents Isabel, "the child of Pride and Grief," as a mixed-race figure, marked as such by the blackness of her hair and eyes, the (not-so) crypto-slave narrative of her past life, her identification with her guitar, and even her native French language.[26] Her appearance crystallizes a shadow narrative of unacknowledged sex and reproduction among Pierre's planter forebears, a secret history that Melville codes, in Saddle Meadows terms—presumably transparent for midcentury readers—as an inevitable attraction of the Glendinning riders (masters) to their chattel—their horses (slaves).[27] "Grand old Pierre Glendinning," the grandfather of Melville's protagonist (and an overt owner of "negro slaves"), "was a great lover of horses, but not in the modern sense," Melville winks at his readers. This originary Pierre—colonial master, Revolutionary War hero—daily made "a ceremonious call at his stables," with the result that today, "on the lands of Saddle Meadows, man and horse are both hereditary."[28] Here, Melville reveals the other half of the story of Pierre's "descendedness," with a bi-species analogue to the concept of the planter's "family white and black" so conventional in portrayals of the Slave South by midcentury.[29]

It is crucial to understand that Melville's point in exposing the abuse of power that organizes hierarchical Saddle Meadows is *not* to dismantle that Slave South power structure itself—*not* to overthrow the distinction between riders and ridden, horses and people. (As, notoriously, he would have another character exclaim a few years later: "Abolitionism, ye gods, but expresses the fellow-feeling of slave for slave.")[30] Rather, Melville deposes Pierre in order to *claim* the anachronistic, antidemocratic planter's position of absolute mastery for his own modern project of literary supremacy. In other words, Melville uses his exposé plot, with the bringing-to-light of the dark, illegitimate sister, not simply to contest Pierre's mastery, but also to "blacken" his protagonist, to declare the planter merely another among the southern horses of Saddle Meadows, ultimately abjected before Melville's all-knowing pen. Pierre's identifying color throughout the novel is the equestrian shade of chestnut: "chestnut-haired and bright-cheeked," Melville's protagonist is "withal rather high-blooded." His horses, "born on the same land as him," are "a sort of family cousins to Pierre, . . . an inferior and subordinate branch of the Glendinnings."[31] This is to say that Melville envisions Saddle Meadows quite as Stowe envisions the St. Clare plantation: all southerners on it, black or white, slave or master—horse or rider—are related: touched by tropicality, marked by climatically induced "voluptuousness," and ultimately unfitted for modernity. As he rewrites the story of the planter in order to master Pierre—direct descendent, as that character is, of the original master of colonial America—Melville constitutes himself a new kind of lord for the modern age: the all-seeing U.S. author creating the subjected southern world from the vantage of his metropolis, that "frozen, yet teeming North" from which "Truth still gives new Emperors to the earth."[32]

That Melville envisions literary production as the preeminent field for modern U.S. empire only becomes emphasized when he makes the major structural turn two-thirds of the way through the novel, by having Pierre elope with Isabel to New York City, in a rather oddly conceived bid to act as her "protecting and all-acknowledging brother." Leaving behind, for good, both the setting of Saddle Meadows and the patrimonial estate of his protagonist, Melville abruptly introduces a new role for Pierre: his protagonist is not just the scion of a planter, but a published author as well. As he conducts Pierre from country to city, from province to metropolis, from South to North, in other words, Melville suddenly posits his protagonist as a potential antagonist, as a direct competitor on the modern field of literary supremacy he has been defining. It is perhaps unsurprising, then, that at the very moment when he endows Pierre with the new role of upstart author, Melville simultaneously identifies him as an explicitly southern figure, a figure to be mastered: Pierre's "magnificent and victorious *debut*" as an author, Melville informs us, "had been made in that delightful love-sonnet, entitled 'The Tropical Summer.'"[33] In revising the basic parameters of Pierre/*Pierre* and creating this much-remarked rupture in the novel, Melville furthers the very conflation of empire and literary nationalism—of political and literary supremacy—that has been his overriding concern.[34] He titles the chapter in which he makes the plot turn "Young America in Literature," and he opens it with an overstatement of his unilateral authorial control: "I write exactly as I please." Pierre, the Planter-turned-Southern-Author, becomes the ground upon which Melville's power may be projected: he is, as the subsequent chapter titles inform us, "a juvenile author" who will "attempt a mature work" but fail, proving himself to be essentially "a tropical author" from before whom Melville will lift a "flower curtain," exposing Pierre's impotence as a southern player on the modern field of literary imperialism.[35]

As Pierre morphs into the "tropical author" who must before all other figures be mastered, he emerges as a specific contemporary of Melville's as well. Pierre is Melville's analogue for Poe, who had died just three years earlier. It is not only the superficial resonance between the single names by which each of the figures is known that suggests the connection, nor is it just Pierre's arrival in the metropolis from uncertain provincial origin. (To his writing "Saddle Meadows" in a Manhattan inn register, the urbane proprietor responds warily, "Anywheres in this country, sir?") It is not only that Pierre arrives in New York City in a quasi-incestuous relationship, nor is it that Isabel's Dark Lady attributes and raven tresses conjure many a Poe heroine.[36] It is not just Melville's repeated use of the term "juvenile" for Pierre's work—that term that Poe had applied, mockingly, to his own poetry during his Boston Hoax. The clincher is that Melville has directly lifted the family name of his planter-author—Glendinning—from one of Poe's stories: and not just any story, but Poe's masterful tale of *doubling*, "William Wilson," which had been published in the *Broadway Journal* in 1845.[37] At the climax of that story, the title character, who has made a career out of cheating nobles at the gaming table, succeeds in getting "a young *parvenu* nobleman named Glendinning" as his "sole antagonist" in a particularly high-stakes game. He has singled out Glendinning because he has "found him of weak intellect and, of course . . . a fitting subject for my skill"; with the deck stacked against poor Glendinning from the outset, the narrator quickly "effect[s] his total ruin."[38]

Turning the tables on "William Wilson," Melville seems to use his account of Pierre Glendinning's young, parvenu authorship to showcase how handily he can thrash Poe, and by extension any "tropical author": he mocks Poe's oeuvre of short pieces—what he calls Pierre's "gemmed little sketches of thought and fancy, whether in poetry or prose," and his satirical title page for "THE COMPLETE WORKS OF GLENDINNING" directly invokes Poe's name. ("Author of that world-famed production, 'The

Tropical Summer: a Sonnet.' 'The Weather: a Thought.' 'Life: an Im-
promptu.' . . . 'Honor: a Stanza.' . . . *Edgar: an Anagram.* 'The Pippin:
a Paragraph.'")[39] The form of momentary, multiple critique, which Poe
had denominated his "Marginalia," Melville calls Pierre's "fugitive
things"; this eighteenth-century term for short pieces inevitably, in the
1850s, calls to mind the slave narrative and thus continues Melville's collapse of all southern figures—slaves and masters, horses and riders—into
a geographically determined abjection before his metropolitan pen.

His characterization of the southern author as a "fugitive" to be mastered by the power of the U.S. center—particularly after the Compromise
of 1850—at first appears flippant, as when Melville describes Pierre's
propensity for "neigh[ing] out lyrical thoughts" in Saddle Meadows. By
the end of the novel, though, Melville's mastering of Pierre takes on
tragic overtones:

> Now [Pierre] began to feel that in him, the thews of a Titan were fore-
> stallingly cut by the scissors of Fate. He felt as a moose, hamstrung. All
> things that think, or move, or lie still, seemed as created to mock and tor-
> ment him. He seemed gifted with loftiness, merely that it might be dragged
> down to the mud. Still, the profound willfulness in him would not give up.
> Against the breaking heart, and the bursting head; against all the dismal las-
> situde, and deathful faintness and sleeplessness, and whirlingness, and crazi-
> ness, still he like a demigod bore up. His soul's ship foresaw the inevitable
> rocks, but resolved to sail on, and make a courageous wreck. Now he gave
> jeer for jeer, and taunted the apes that jibed him.[40]

Melville proves his literary supremacy over his own creation by exacting
upon his planter-author, metaphorically, precisely the punishment sometimes meted out in the southern states to recaptured fugitive slaves: he
hamstrings him; he cripples him. In his now unmitigable abjection, Pierre
cycles through a variety of subjected southern positions: momentarily, it
seems, Melville channels Frederick Douglass's apostrophe to the Chesa-
peake Bay ships in his 1845 *Narrative* ("O, why was I born a man, of
whom to make a brute!"); he then directly echoes his own annihilation of
the Virginian Bulkington ("Take heart, take heart, O Bulkington! Bear
thee grimly, demigod! Up from the spray of thy ocean-perishing—straight
up, leaps thy apotheosis!"); and finally, he leaves his planter-turned-
"tropical author" as fully the other of empire, stripped of human reason,
his language degenerated into the "jibing" gibberish of "apes."[41] Pierre
will escape from being "known," from being the abject object of the
twinned imperial gaze of metropolitan author and reader, only when
Melville ceases to write him—only when the book is over: "All's o'er, and
ye know him not!" Isabel gasps in *Pierre*'s last sentence.

Why does the figure of the southern planter—updated, for the sectionalist era, to "tropical author"—become the ground upon which Melville stakes his bid for literary supremacy? I began this section with "Hawthorne and His Mosses," written by the ostensible "Virginian spending July in Vermont," and it is tempting to see that manifesto as reactive on Melville's part—as, specifically, his reaction to a review of Hawthorne that Poe had written in late 1847. In that review, Poe had once again turned his "marginal" gaze on New England cultural production, thereby destabilizing the notion that the view from the metropolis was universal and undetermined by geographical location. Using an adjective strongly associated with the deviance of the Slave South from national norms, Poe judges Hawthorne's stories to be "peculiar and *not* original," for "his books afford strong internal evidence of having been written to himself and his particular friends alone." Even as cultural production is centered there, Hawthorne's New England is, from Poe's outsider perspective, a geographically limited location—not the central and universal "summit of our Eastern Hill" from which the rest of the world may be impartially perceived and ordered, but rather the closed and particular "phalanx and phalanstery atmosphere in which [Hawthorne] has so long been struggling for breath."[42]

When the "tropical author" reads and, especially, writes back, that centralized literary supremacy, masquerading as universality and inherent to modern empire—the supremacy Melville so desires—evaporates. In Melville's vision of the modern, industrial-imperial United States coming into being at midcentury, one may write, or one may be written (*ride* or be *ridden,* in the near-homophonic terms of Saddle Meadows). Melville characterizes the act of representation in *Pierre* not as a process of communication or debate but as a unilateral, deadly business of "taking heads": a process by which the artist fixes, determines, and thereby annihilates the subjectivity of the person he renders into art.[43] As he contemplates a field for U.S. expansionist ambition suddenly swollen to the size of the globe itself, Melville chooses the southern planter—the old internal other and imperial forebear of the nation—as his first mark in the high-stakes, winner-takes-all endeavor of creating a national literature coeval with the destined "political supremacy among the nations" of the United States. A fully known domestic southern planter will, Melville promises, provide direct access to an analogous supremacy over the less-familiar others of a coming global empire. By 1856, jostling for space with Porte Crayon's *Virginia Illustrated* in the pages of *Harper's,* Melville was asserting, tongue in cheek, that "many a Chinaman, in new coat and pantaloons, his long queue coiled out of sight in one of Genin's hats, has promenaded

Broadway, and been taken merely for an eccentric Georgia planter."[44] In Melville's equation, the southern planter has become converted into the primal and generic other of modern U.S. empire. And in its abjection as a field upon which Melville's wonted literary supremacy may play, the Slave South has been overwritten as the entire peripheral world.

Three Southern Texts and a Critique of Literary Supremacy

As it was firmly ensconced in U.S. culture by the mid-1850s, the Slave South underwrote in key ways both the interpretation of industrial capitalism as a system of "free labor" and the conceptualization of U.S. expansionism as a program of establishing "free soil" across the continent and beyond. To establish "free labor," the Slave South held out the promise that the problem of freedom roused by modern industrial capitalism could be reduced to and contained in the laws of southern slavery alone, leaving aside the matter of the many other forms of constraint and coercion being institutionalized in the antebellum United States. Taking this view, William Lloyd Garrison, who had done so much in the first place to channel the problem of freedom raised in the industrializing Northeast into a modern and revitalized vision of the Slave South, ceased publication of *The Liberator* in 1865 with the passage of the Thirteenth Amendment, which voided slave law; to his mind, the struggle for "freedom" was simply over, ended in "complete triumph" and with "ultimate success."[45] To establish "free soil," on the other hand, the Slave South invited a conquest both righteous and inevitable: overcoming and forcefully reforming its Slave South was envisioned as the first step toward the global ascendancy of a righteously imperial United States. When, for instance, in his classic essay "Slavery in Massachusetts" (1854) Henry David Thoreau metaphorized southern slavery as a dead and rotting thing, he gave this old idea of slavery-as-bad-inheritance a modern twist by calling for Massachusetts readers not only to "bury" their Slave South, but also to use it as "manure" for further "colonization" of the West.[46] Fundamentally, the Slave South, having been produced from the centralized vantage of the capital of cultural production, had been generated by—and was enlisted for—needs and uses that exceeded the abolition of slave law. Indeed, the primary objective of abolition often seemed eclipsed in Slave South accounts by the broader ideological project of creating an exceptionalist narrative for the passage of the United States into nineteenth-century Western modernity.

This cultural formation, clearly dominant by the mid-1850s, required above all that the Slave South and its people—southern planters, yes, but southern slaves perhaps even more so—stay in their prescribed places. To the extent that U.S. antebellum culture was organized around the Slave South, it required precisely the literary supremacy straightforwardly investigated by Melville: while it was imperative that the Slave South be figured, it was equally imperative that it be figured according to the imaginary of the metropolis, without the disruption of southern people writing back. But write back they did, and in the years just before the outbreak of the Civil War, the most incisive interrogations of the Slave South construct—works that delved into its unilateral construction, and its underwriting of industrial capitalism and empire—were produced by antislavery writers who had been born in the upper southern states, some of whom, indeed, had been enslaved themselves. To close this section, I suggest that we should shift our expectations of where to find a southern critique of U.S. literary supremacy at the zenith of the sectionalist era. Rather than looking to those writers who defended the "South" side of the sectionalist binary, and in so doing simply reinforced the Slave South construct, we should look to writers who profoundly problematized the binary itself, asking to what ends it was being invoked. A variety of "southern texts," so defined, could be considered in this light; here I will treat in turn Frederick Douglass's second autobiography, *My Bondage and My Freedom* (1855); Harriet Jacobs's autobiography, *Incidents in the Life of a Slave Girl* (1861); and Martin R. Delany's novel *Blake; or the Huts of America* (published serially, 1859 and 1861–1862).[47]

We may gauge the stakes of writing the Slave South at mid-decade by the disproportionate responses of Garrison and Thoreau to what they saw as Douglass's flouting of their centralized cultural supremacy. The many restraints urged on Douglass during his work with the Garrisonians in the 1840s are well enough known; it is important to note, though, that these restraints—to speak instead of write, to illustrate the ideas of the Bostonians rather than having ideas of his own, to calibrate his self-presentation to display "a *little* of the plantation manner"—had to do equally with keeping Douglass in his racial "place" and his geographic place.[48] (Indeed, as we have seen, these two sorts of "place" were inextricable for the metropolitan creators of the Slave South construct.) As Douglass broke with the Garrisonians politically and—worse—not only wrote without their permission but also began to edit his own periodicals, the most violent protest came not from proslavery southerners but from those who shared his commitment to abolition.[49] As the breach widened, from Douglass's founding of the *North Star* in 1847 to his support of the Liberty party, repudiation of disunionism, and endorsement of the Constitution in the late 1840s and early 1850s, Garrison branded

Douglass a "traitor," printing long excerpts from Douglass's editorials in the "Refuge of Oppression" column of the *Liberator,* which he had created to ridicule proslavery writers.[50] Thoreau, goaded to more oblique but possibly more troubling response to Douglass in his "Slavery in Massachusetts" address, blended a desire for "purity" of political position— complete acquiescence of others to his own, presumably universal, view—with a paean to pure whiteness:

> But it chanced the other day that I scented a white water-lily, and a season I had waited for had arrived. It is the emblem of purity. It bursts up so pure and fair to the eye, and so sweet to the scent . . . It reminds me that Nature has been partner to no Missouri Compromise. I scent no compromise in the fragrance of the water-lily. It is not a *Nymphoea Douglassii.* In it, the sweet, and pure, and innocent are wholly sundered from the obscene and baleful.[51]

Here Thoreau invokes Douglass as an emblematic nexus of political compromise and racial intermixture. Douglass's impure politics—his straying from the absolutism of "no union with slaveholders"—are articulated in Thoreau's metaphor as a corruption of whiteness by blackness, sweetness of scent by "the odor of carrion," and "the sweet, and pure, and innocent" by "the obscene and baleful." The surprisingly racist implication, quite out of line with Thoreau's other writings, pivots around compromise-as-conversation: Douglass's obscenity, impurity, and baleful scent may be sourced ultimately to his speaking back, his refusal to submit to unilateral legislation from the Bostonian mountaintop. From that fevered apex of cultural supremacy, Douglass exhibits an unexpected kinship with Poe, taking on the mantle of southern "blackguard" for the 1850s.

How does one engage attacks on one's writings that are based on the premise that one ought not be thinking or writing at all? Among other strategies, Douglass turned to the literary realm. The very writing of his 1855 autobiography, published ten years after his brilliant slave narrative, was a deeply subversive act in the post-*Uncle-Tom's-Cabin* hegemony of mid-1850s culture. The title itself, asserting Douglass's continuous subjectivity across the poles of "bondage" and "freedom," Slave South and Industrial North, announces that his revisionary and additive authorial act is all about exceeding both genre (the slave narrative) and place (the Slave South). By this construction, Douglass's autobiography flies in the face of the dictum that the story of the southern slave simply ends with emancipation as neatly as that of a sentimental-novel heroine ends with marriage and its corollary: that an escape from chattel slavery marks the end of a struggle for freedom in the United States.[52] For Douglass, an emblematic southern slave, to exceed the Slave South in 1855 was to disrupt U.S.

"freedom" profoundly, to rebel not only against slaveholding, but also, as Eric Sundquist has framed it, against "the new bondage imposed on him by white antislavery liberalism."[53]

As the prescient New York writer James McCune Smith succinctly explains in his introduction to the 1855 expanded autobiography, Douglass's narrative trajectory explodes the problem of freedom out of its neat containment in the Slave South and locates it right back in the modernized center of U.S. cultural production. Marshalling every angle, it seems, of U.S. critiques of industrialization, Smith explains that the added half of Douglass's autobiography will delineate the North as not opposite but analogous to the Slave South: industrialized, proletarianized, white-supremacist, class-stratified, and betraying all "principles of the Republic":

> From the *depths of chattel slavery in Maryland,* our author escaped into the *caste-slavery of the north, in New Bedford, Massachusetts.* Here he found oppression assuming another, and hardly less bitter, form; *of that very hand-icraft* which the greed of slavery had taught him, *his half-freedom denied him the exercise for an honest living;* he found himself *one of a class*—free colored men—whose position he has described in the following words: "Aliens are we in our native land. *The fundamental principles of the republic . . . are held to be inapplicable to us."*[54]

At this moment, when "the nature and character of slavery have been subjects of an almost endless variety of artistic representation," Smith argues, Douglass is able to shed new light on the subject, able to expose the continuities between "[Southern] slavery and [Northern] semi-slavery" precisely because of his origin as a southerner. Occupying a space akin to Poe's "margin," Douglass is not deceived by the hegemonic culture of the center, which proves its "freedom" only comparatively and symbolically, by constructing its Slave South. His insight into the workings of power in the United States is gleaned from his lived knowledge of "the *actual* rule" of southern slavery, his hailing "not from the ranks of the half-freed colored people of the free states, but from the very depths of slavery itself."[55]

In Smith's presentation, it is Douglass's geographic constitution as a southern author that allows him to exert the most subversive force on U.S. culture. It is logical, then, that Douglass's virtuosity as a writer is so showily on display throughout *My Bondage and My Freedom:* Douglass's technical "novelization" of many episodes in the autobiography, and his playful, joyous, flagrant stylization of the narrative draw attention to the act of authorship itself. Indeed, Douglass's stilted, conventional, over-written language in this particular text tends to attract the ire of critics on the same grounds as those applied to Melville's *Pierre*—and

Douglass certainly marks his narrative with deliberate, virtuosic con-
structions reminiscent of Melville's unilateral declaration that "I write
exactly as I please."[56] This self-dramatizing literary supremacy, of course,
is intensely political, and so it tends to occur at moments when Douglass is invoking the categories of dominant antebellum culture in order to
disrupt them. One such moment occurs as Douglass relocates his autobiographical protagonist across the intranational divide, from South to
North, with a deliberate rupture of his narrative. Stressing his authorial
omniscience, Douglass picks up his character from Tuckahoe, Maryland,
and chuckles at his bewildered audience as he causes him to "disappear
from the kind reader, as in a flying cloud or a balloon (pardon the figure),"
dropping him down in the presumably antithetical location.[57]

As he relocates his protagonist from rural Slave South to bustling Manhattan street (again, a move reminiscent of Pierre's journey), Douglass
invokes the structured antitheses his readers are conditioned to expect,
pitting Baltimore against Broadway, South against North, slavery against
freedom in the conventional alignments of 1855: "In less than a week after leaving Baltimore, I was walking amid the hurrying throng, and gazing upon the dazzling wonders of Broadway . . . A free state around me,
and a free earth under my feet! . . . A new world burst upon my agitated
vision." He introduces the crisp, familiar antithesis, though, only to blur
it, by quickly introducing the shadowing binary local to the metropolis:
the immense wealth and the abject poverty of industrialization, visible
side by side on the urban street. Against the "dazzling wonders," of the
Broadway promenade, Douglass pits "a man homeless, shelterless,
breadless, friendless, and moneyless," and out of this juxtaposition he
draws the contemporary workingmen's critique of "free labor" as "wage
slavery" or "freedom to starve":

> [I]n just this [homeless] condition was I, while wandering about the streets
> of New York city, and lodging, at least one night, among the barrels of one
> of its wharves. I was not only free from slavery, but I was free from home,
> as well. The reader will easily see that I had something more than the simple
> fact of being free to think of, in this extremity.[58]

In a remarkably condensed textual space—just three and a half pages—
Douglass has moved from a perfectly stable sectional binary of slavery
and freedom to its real disruption.

In this central chapter in which Douglass cross-contaminates the in-
commensurates of antebellum U.S. culture, he essays as well a deeper,
more troublesome synthesis of sections. Nominally opposing the forms
of social order North and South, he balances the Southern slave master

against "the might and majesty of the [Northern] free state," ultimately implying an equation of the two. Under industrial-imperial modernity, in other words, what was once the republic can be fathomed only by analogy to the emblematic despot of the New World:

> Some apology can easily be made for the few slaves who have, after making good their escape, turned back to slavery, preferring the *actual* rule of their masters, to the life . . . which meets them on their first arrival in a free state. It is difficult for a freeman to enter into the feelings of such fugitives . . . "Why do you tremble," he says to the slave, "you are in a free state"; but the difficulty is, in realizing that he *is* in a free state, the slave might reply. A freeman cannot understand why the slave-master's shadow is bigger, to the slave, than the might and majesty of the free state; but when he reflects that the slave knows more about the slavery of his master than he does of the might and majesty of the free state, he has the explanation. The slave has been all his life learning the power of his master . . . and only a few hours learning the power of the state. The master is to him a stern and flinty reality, but the state is little more than a dream.[59]

On dazzling display in this passage is one of Douglass's signature brilliancies as a writer of both oratory and prose. In conversation with both the racial and the sectional bifurcations of antebellum culture, he constructs a series of strong, stable rhetorical binaries through which he cycles competing terms, thereby drawing oppositions, analogies, and syntheses between them, often at the same time. The structuring binary in this passage puts an individual—be he "fugitive" or "freeman"—in a subjected position before an overwhelming power—be it "slave-master" or "state." Under conditions of both nominal slavery and nominal freedom—under conditions South *and* North—it is the hierarchy itself that is preserved, the abjection of the individual before the power in question.

The terror in this passage comes, though, not from the analogy, but rather from the historical asymmetry between the forms of power North and South. The well-established, indeed outmoded "*actual* rule" of the slave-master is a known and presumably circumscribable quantity, while the nondelimited "might and majesty of the free state," coming into being in its modern form, has yet to be fully fathomed by Douglass or his readers. With the fugitive, the U.S. citizen confronting modernity has been "only a few hours learning the power of the state." The possibility that modern "freedom"—knowable only as the negative of the "stern and flinty reality" of the southern slave master—will prove ultimately more empowering to the abjected individual remains, in 1855, "little more than a dream." Douglass here establishes the self-narrating fugitive—the southern slave "free from home," out of his place both literally and figuratively—as the most potentially revelatory figure in late antebellum culture. His challenge to metropolitan readers: can they understand that *My Bondage and My Freedom* is not a Slave South story at all, but instead "an American book for Americans," as Smith puts it? For so long as metropolitan readers insist on literary supremacy over their South—finding Douglass interesting or plausible only as he fits into the Slave South construct—they will deprive themselves of crucial insight into the operations of power in their modern industrial-imperial nation—operations perceivable only, Douglass implies, from the vantage of one who has known, and resisted, the transparent, *"actual* rule" of slavery in the southern states.

Like Douglass, Harriet Jacobs, in *Incidents in the Life of a Slave Girl*, maintains a continuous subjectivity for her autobiographical protagonist, Linda Brent, across the intranational divide; and like Douglass, she invokes the revelatory power of the self-narrating fugitive out of geographical and hierarchical place. "[I am] as free from the power of slaveholders as are the white people of the north," she closes her book pithily; "and though that, according to my ideas, is not saying a great deal, it is a vast improvement in *my* condition."[60] With Douglass, Jacobs produces for her metropolitan readers a sectionally reintegrated United States in which pervasive unfreedom may vary by degree but is nonetheless the rule of the land. Like Douglass as well, her path to authorship of this single book went through a tortured encounter with the Slave South ideological apparatus of the 1850s, although as an unmarried mother forced to work as a servant to support herself and her children, she lacked most of Douglass's relative advantages in the field of cultural production.

Following her escape as a young woman from North Carolina, and after a decade of living in Manhattan and working for the abolitionist cause, Jacobs well understood her symbolic place in the Slave South cultural formation, as both a fugitive slave and the mother of two children by a North Carolina congressman. She seems initially to have made the mistake, though, of thinking that her stature as the unspeaking "text" for abolitionist exegesis—as Douglass described his relationship to the Garrisonians—offered her a measure of cultural agency.[61] As the success of *Uncle Tom's Cabin* was snowballing in early 1853, Jacobs applied to Stowe to write the story of her own life. "I should want the History of my childhood and the first five years [of my escape] in one volume and the next three and my home in the northern states in the second," she explained; and at the same time, she suggested that Stowe take her phenotypically white daughter, Louisa—the congressman's child—along on her English tour as "a very good representative of a Southern Slave."[62] From

Stowe's perspective, Jacobs's solicitation of her authorial services was rather like the bowl of fruit in a still life commissioning its own portrait, and she was having none of it. Stowe did not deign to reply to Jacobs herself, but rather wrote to Jacobs's New York mistress, the wife of author and editor Nathaniel Parker Willis, to request verification of Jacobs's story of her experiences in slavery—including the painfully sensitive matter of her extramarital liaison with the congressman—and, further, she declined to take Louisa with her to England, as the English would likely "subject [Louisa] to much petting and patronizing," and Stowe "was very much opposed to [that] with this class of people." In the greatest blow, Stowe suggested to Cornelia Willis that if Jacobs's story was "true in all its bearings," she might appropriate it for her *Key to Uncle Tom's Cabin,* a compilation of reports and testimony she was assembling in 1853 to prove that her work of Slave South fiction had a basis in reality.[63]

While Jacobs had understood that however she put forth her story or her self, she would be perceived as an overdetermined, "representative," player in the dominant Slave South narrative, she seems not to have anticipated the extent to which U.S. literary supremacy would demand her subordination and exploitation in the cultural realm—a subordination and exploitation parallel to her material stature in the "free" North, where she remained "in servitude to the Anglo-Saxon race" a decade after her escape from slavery. She recalibrated her strategy almost instantly. Condemning the behavior of the famous author as "not Lady like," Jacobs replied to Stowe through her employer, withdrawing her offer of her biographical information. "I wish it to be a history of my life entirely by itself which [will] do more good," she explained, than Stowe's condensation of her story into just another entry in an exposé catalogue. Authorship, Jacobs seems to have realized right away, was her next terrain of struggle. Within two months, she had written her first published story, in the form of a "Letter from a Fugitive Slave" in the *New York Tribune.*[64]

The nature of the oppositional authorship Jacobs forged across eight subsequent years of writing in moments snatched from her round-the-clock servant's job is suggested by her choice of an epigraph for the title page of *Incidents in the Life of a Slave Girl.*[65] From Angelina Grimké's 1836 *Appeal to the Christian Women of the South,* Jacobs extracted a passage that seemed, by the late 1850s, to reiterate the irate criticisms of Slave South stories by natives of the southern states:

> Northerners know nothing at all about Slavery. They think it is perpetual bondage only. They have no conception of the depth of *degradation* involved in that word, SLAVERY; if they had, they would never cease their efforts until so horrible a system was overthrown.[66]

With this epigraph from Grimké, attributed only to "a woman of North Carolina," Jacobs places herself in an interracial Carolinian sisterhood, an imagined community of antislavery southern women whose superior and intimate understanding of southern slavery—and, implicitly, of unfreedom in the United States writ large—metropolitan readers cannot approach or fathom.[67] Against the central premise of literary supremacy— that the Other is fully known—Jacobs's aggressively asserted southern authorship insists on what the center does not, and cannot, know about its abjected periphery. Creating almost an inversion of Melville's assurance that his readers "know" Pierre so long as Melville writes him, Jacobs introduces the frustrated not-knowing of her metropolitan readers as her central paradigm. The self-narrating fugitive—the southern author out of place—will offer her readers only selected "incidents" in the overdetermined "life of a slave girl," as her unusual title puts it; from the first page Jacobs indicates that in selecting certain scenes from Linda's life to narrate, she withholds others that remain forever inaccessible to her readers.

By contrast, Lydia Maria Child, who served as Jacobs's editor, presents *Incidents* as a straightforward work of Slave South exposé. In her introduction, Child explains that Jacobs will tell a story—of what was often termed Slave South "concubinage"—so well known to metropolitan readers that she needs only the briefest suggestion to telegraph the conventional contents of the book. "This peculiar phase of Slavery has generally been kept veiled; but the public ought to be made acquainted with its monstrous features, and I willingly take the responsibility of presenting them with the veil withdrawn." Sounding rather unfortunately like a procurer about to disrobe the passive slave girl before the lascivious gaze of the reader—sounding, indeed, not unlike Melville presenting Pierre to his readers on a revolving pedestal—Child nonetheless exaggerates her agency as editor. She does not control the veil; instead, Jacobs's autobiographical protagonist will step forward to expose *herself*, and this makes all the difference.[68]

The chapter in which Linda Brent enters into the sexual liaison with the Edenton congressman has magnetized current critical discussion of *Incidents* because of Jacobs's sui generis, forthright limning of the limits of representation and power in antebellum antislavery literature. In these celebrated passages, Jacobs undertakes an authorial experiment that is rather like having Melville's Pierre write himself. What happens when a definitionally mastered character—a generic slave girl—is simultaneously the author, and thus in charge of creating her own abject posture before the reader?

Pity me, and pardon me, O virtuous reader! You never knew what it is to be a slave; to be entirely unprotected by law or custom; to have the laws reduce you to the condition of a chattel, entirely subject to the will of another. You never exhausted your ingenuity in avoiding the snares, and eluding the power of a hated tyrant; you never shuddered at the sound of his footsteps, and trembled within hearing of his voice. I know I did wrong. No one can feel it more sensibly than I do. The painful and humiliating memory will haunt me to my dying day. Still, in looking back, calmly, on the events of my life, I feel that the slave woman ought not to be judged by the same standard as others.[69]

The short answer is that Jacobs's experiment shatters the dream of omniscient literary supremacy shared by metropolitan writers and readers of Slave South exposé, as the slave girl "written by herself" insists upon both the unfathomable experiential gap between herself and her readers, and her intact, indeed oppositional, subjectivity. Linda's initial prostration before the reader at the moment of exposure—"Pity me, and pardon me!"—quickly shifts into her unilateral authorial pardoning of herself, an act in which the reader plays no part. Her laying of herself before the reader's gaze morphs into her assertion of her own gaze, "looking back, calmly, on the events of my life." And the compressed journey between antitheses in the relation of narrator to reader passes through an aggressive *anti*-exposé catalogue: a list of what has *not* been revealed to the reader, what the reader "never knew" and never will know.

For at the heart of U.S. literary supremacy, Jacobs suggests, at the heart of believing that the Other may be read like an open book, lies an even more fundamental misunderstanding of the workings of power in the modern United States. *Incidents in the Life of a Slave Girl* might usefully be read as Jacobs's evisceration of Stowe's fantasy of the consent of the "lowly" to their subordination—Stowe's vision of both a preindustrial past and an imperial future organized around a strict, yet natural and ideal, hierarchy in which deference freely is exchanged for paternal protection. To counter Stowe's imaginative order, Jacobs establishes in *Incidents* a motif of homelessness that threatens Linda Brent from the first page to the last, and in so doing she casts a deromanticizing light on the central figure of Stowe's novelistic alchemy, the cabin of *Uncle Tom's Cabin,* by exposing the lie of Stowe's title. As Stowe's archetypal "lowly" character, Tom never legally owns anything in the novel; but as she writes the possessive of her title over Tom's definitional dispossession, Stowe masks the hierarchy she endorses. Against Stowe's implication that Tom owns his "lowly" place on the idyllic, preindustrial Shelby plantation, Jacobs introduces Linda with her childhood observation that "[my parents] lived together in a comfortable home; and though we were all slaves, I was so fondly shielded that I never dreamed I was a piece of merchandise, trusted to them for safe keeping, and liable to be demanded of them at any moment . . . for, according to Southern laws, a slave, *being* property, can *hold* no property." And as Linda repeatedly mourns her homelessness in the later chapters of the book set in the North—her inability "by dint of labor and economy, [to] make a home for my children"—Jacobs not only draws attention (as does Douglass) to the out-of-placeness and fugitive authorship of her protagonist. She also insists that the "lowly" of the United States do not acquiesce to their subjection—that, to the contrary, Southern Slaves resist it, even in the industrial North. On the last page of *Incidents,* Jacobs refuses a happy ending, or really a narrative closure at all, to her readers, as Linda reiterates her longing for "a home of [her] own": "The dream of my life is not yet realized. I do not sit with my children in a home of my own. I still long for a hearthstone of my own, however humble."[70] Against Stowe's mania for godlike aggrandizement at the end of *Uncle Tom's Cabin,* the unfulfilled and insistent desire of the dispossessed radiates outward from the final page of Jacobs's book.

This larger struggle between the dispossessed and their oppressors, implied throughout Jacobs's autobiography, becomes the frank subject of Martin R. Delany's novel *Blake, or the Huts of America;* and like Jacobs, Delany takes on the deconstruction of Stowe's Slave South writings as a key part of his literary intervention. His subtitle rewrites Stowe's title, replacing the peasant's "cabin" with the soldier's "hut" and, in the process, dissevering Stowe's sentimental identity of character with place.[71] Instead of the individual, personified site of Uncle Tom's cabin, we get the multitudinous, wide-flung, horizontally organized "huts of America." True to this titular revision, *Blake* puts forth the most startling vision to be found in antebellum U.S. literature of a collectivist rebellion of the "lowly" of America—and, implicitly, the world—against the exploiting few who have, for the time, harnessed the potentially liberating forces of Western modernity to their personal aggrandizement. For Delany, born free in 1812 in Charlestown, Virginia, the southern states necessarily will serve as the seat of this fantastic second American revolution, because the Slave South presently serves as the linchpin for U.S. Anglo-Saxonist, industrial-capitalist expansionism. The second part of his subtitle—*A Tale of the Mississippi Valley, the Southern United States, and Cuba*—makes clear that "lowliness" is to his mind a geographical designation in a hemisphere increasingly ruled by the Northern metropolis of the United States.

The novel opens with a succinct chapter titled "The Project" that archetypally yokes together the three sorts of internal and external projections of U.S. power reflected in its subtitle: westward North American expansion; slave trading between Africa and America; and what Delany calls the "patriot design" of U.S. elites to acquire the Spanish colony of Cuba.[72] As the engine behind these interrelated domestic and foreign plots, Delany enumerates a secretive cabal of "men of intelligence . . . entirely absorbed in an adventure of self-interest": two Cuban elites, and a larger group of "Americans" who hail equally from North and South. (Even on the eve of the Civil War, sectional allegiance is a red herring in Delany's novel.) One additional character hovers on the edge of this paradigmatic smoke-filled-room: "H. Beecher Stowe," whose stanza opens the brief chapter.

> By myself, the Lord of Ages,
> I have sworn to right the wrong,
> I have pledged my word unbroken,
> For the weak against the strong.[73]

A remarkably condensed statement of the model of reform Stowe generated in *Uncle Tom's Cabin,* this stanza forthrightly proposes a model of universally righteous intervention in the world that not only reinforces the binary of "weak" and "strong," but also exalts the righteous reformer to the stature of "the Lord of Ages," a writer who wields the voice of God. Along with the potboiling romance and political theorizing that characterize Delany's sprawling novel, we should see from its very first page an inquiry into the central place that writing the Slave South has assumed in the overall "project" of Western industrial imperialism, United-States-style.

Against the framing "project" of the novel, this dystopic realization of U.S. modernity pursued by American elites North and South, Delany projects his own utopic alternative: a South-led revolution that draws on a long heritage of resistance to slavery and takes the venerable example of the slave rebellion as its model. We learn the range of Delany's envisioned alternative by following his eponymous protagonist through the two halves of the novel, which closely mirror in their geography the similar bifurcations of Douglass's and Jacobs's autobiographies.[74] The first half of *Blake* operates within a geographical theater familiar to the slave narrative genre, as Blake escapes from enslavement on a plantation in Mississippi, journeys through the southern states on a covert mission of stirring rebellion, and ends by reaching freedom in Canada. The second half then explodes that familiar Slave South framework, exceeding the North/South, freedom/slavery bifurcations quite fantastically as Blake travels to Cuba, "the theater of his future [revolutionary] actions," from thence to the west coast of Africa, and back to Cuba again, with a good measure of high-seas adventure in between. Despite the extent to which the coherence of this far-flung narrative centers on Blake's presence, Delany seems largely uninterested in creating a singular romantic hero; instead, his protagonist acts as a vehicle or catalyst for a collective revolutionary plot, "scattering to the winds and sowing the seeds of a future crop . . . to be grown in devastation and reaped in a whirlwind of ruin." Wherever Blake travels across the southern states in the first half of the novel, he meets in "the huts of America" with a deep knowledge of the workings of oppression and a strong history of past resistance to it upon which to draw; he finds not-so-huddled masses, veterans of the first American Revolution among whom "the names of Nat Turner, Denmark Veezie, and General Gabriel were held in sacred reverence."[75] Against the Slave South model—of a passive, slavish territory inhabited by the degenerate and the depraved, and requiring outside intervention for reform—Delany unfolds a U.S. South that is the last, best hope of the republic. Precisely because of its organization around slavery as a state of war, this South generates struggle against and resistance to oppression as its indigenous, identifying terms.

As the part of the United States that harbors explosive subversive potential, Delany's South offers hope for entering modernity in a newly imagined, liberatory way. Instead of rejecting industrial imperialism, as did the southern partisans who promoted slavery as a paternalistic system; and instead of replicating it, as did Southern partisans who dreamed of establishing "slave republics" in Central and South America; Delany proposes to embrace both empire and the market, but in the process to overturn the power structures assumed by each term.[76] His southern partisans champion the cause of "Creoles"—indigenous southerners, usually (though not always) identified as black, Indian, and of mixed race—over the claims of grasping "intruders" and "legal invaders" from the U.S. metropolis. And his southern rebels equally assert the rights of "laborers and producers" over "mere consumers" and capitalists:

> The colored races, they averred, were by nature adapted to the tropical regions of this part of the world as to all other similar climates, it being a scientific fact that they increased and progressed whilst the whites decreased and continually retrograded, their offspring becoming enervated and imbecile. These were facts worthy of consideration, which three hundred years had indisputably tested. The whites in these regions were there by intrusion, idle consumers subsisting by imposition; whilst the blacks, the legitimate inhabitants, were the industrious laborers and producers of the staple commodities and real wealth of these places. They had inherited those regions by birth, paid for the soil by toil, irrigated it with their sweat, enriched it with

their blood, nothing remaining to be done but by a dependence in Divine aid, a reliance in their own ability, and strength of their own arms, but to claim and take possession.[77]

In this fertile transmutation, Delany converts the New World colonial heritage of eighteenth-century climatic determinism from an ideological liability (as it was for writers of the early republic) into an empowering validation. Now tropicality, southernness itself, becomes an argument and a natural proof for labor against capital, for underdeveloped periphery against exploiting metropolis, and for "colored races" against white supremacy.

Indeed, the southern revolutionary potential uncovered and nurtured by *Blake* is perhaps best defined by its linking of labor exploitation, to geographic uneven development, to racism. And thus while the revolution will be led by southerners of color, it has a strong interracial component that is often surprising to Delany's present-day readers, given his stature as an early proponent of what in the twentieth century would be called black nationalism.[78] The cabal of elites controlling the industrial-imperial "Project" repeatedly boast that "the only place [in the world], where a white man was safe and a Negro taught to know his place, was the United States."[79] Laboring southern whites, though, just as repetitiously throw over their allegiance to white supremacy when offered the economic incentive. For instance, when Blake, during his southern travels, offers "a shining gold eagle, . . . emblem of his country's liberty" to a white skiffman in exchange for passage across a state line, the man readily complies, adding gratuitously, "'I don't go in for this slaveholding o' people in these Newnited States uv the South, nohow, so I don't. Dog gone it, let every feller have a fair shake!'" Delany's southern revolution for the modern world will unite "laborers and producers," regardless of race, thereby surmounting the "new night" of modern white supremacy—which, Delany didactically shows, simply furthers the exploitation of the many by the few. White southerners thus have a place of revolutionary potential in *Blake* alongside Turner, Vesey, and Gabriel: the Grimké sisters make an appearance as Angelina and Seraphina, the "beautiful mulatto children" of a Portuguese slave trader on the coast of Africa, who convert their father away from his evil work. And Delany quotes Jefferson's *Notes on the State of Virginia* in the penultimate extant chapter of his novel, hybridizing the 1785 text with the close of Marx's 1848 *Communist Manifesto*:

Of the two classes of these communities, the master and slave, the blacks have everything to hope for and nothing to fear, since let what may take place their redemption from bondage is inevitable. They must and will be free; whilst the whites have everything to fear and nothing to hope for, "God is just, and his justice will not sleep forever."[80]

Despite the rousing rhetoric Delany builds throughout *Blake*, the promised southern revolution never actually takes place in the action of the novel. The book thus becomes a study "of propaganda and cultural resistance," an investigation into how the hearts and minds of people are prepared for radical action.[81] In the post-*Uncle-Tom's-Cabin* world, *Blake* is a book about the political work of the novel in the modern, industrial-imperial era. As Delany's character Blake travels covertly from "hut" to "hut" across the American South, holding "seclusions" that enable individuals to access their historical memories and lived experiences for transformative purposes, so should his novel *Blake* travel from home to home, reader to reader, effecting a similar enlightenment.

The geographic and economic structures of cultural production came into play here, as Delany knew. Distributing his novel beyond the premodern, hut-to-hut model would require routing his work through the center of U.S. literary publication, which he seemed to indicate when he inserted a single chapter, set in New York City and titled "A Novel Adventure," as the transition between the domestic first half and global second half of his novel. As he began to publish his first chapters serially in the *Anglo-African Magazine* in 1859, he wrote to Garrison to request his assistance in "get[ting] a good publishing house to take it."[82] There is no record of Garrison's reply, but *Blake* was not published in book form until 1970, and its final serial chapters have not yet been recovered. By the time they saw print, in the spring of 1862, a different southern rebellion—the wrong one—was already under way.

With Lincoln's Emancipation Proclamation of September 22, 1862, the Slave South was effectively over, though the construct had not been radically overthrown in the way Delany had imagined. While the end of the Slave South might have seemed the ultimate achievement of centralized literary supremacy in the United States, the momentary loss of their venerable other seems to have left U.S. writers uncomfortably alone with themselves. On January 1, 1863, the date the Proclamation went into effect, Emerson read his "Boston Hymn" in the Music Hall of that city. It begins,

> The word of the Lord by night
> To the watching Pilgrims came,
> As they sat by the seaside,
> And filled their hearts with flame.

God said, I am tired of kings,
I suffer them no more;
Up to my ear the morning brings
The outrage of the poor.[83]

These opening stanzas celebrate a closing of the gap between imperial England and republican New England that had so worried Emerson in the mid-1840s. At last, the United States appears to be aligned politically, economically, and historically with its center of cultural production. Here Emerson collapses the deep colonial past, the Revolutionary-era founding of the nation, and the present triumphal moment, claiming that the founding of the republic proceeds directly from the lineage of New England Puritans, and that the iconic American Revolution doubles the ongoing Civil War. All of this nationalist reworking centers on Emerson's ability confidently to inhabit the voice of God. "God"'s primary statement that he "will suffer [kings] no more" not only conflates national independence and defeat of southern planters as holy mandates for the United States, but also immediately conjures Emerson's frustrated desire in his 1845 "West India Emancipation" address to be able annihilate the southern other by declaration.[84]

If Emerson echoes Stowe in depicting the U.S. writer elevated to God-stature by mastering his or her Slave South, his use of the trope proves more complicated. At the center of the second stanza, just as Emerson puts this triumphant representational unilateralism into words, he answers it with its own horrifying, haunting backlash: to achieve absolute power, in a definitionally unequal context, is immediately to become the natural and just target of "the outrage of the poor." At the very moment when slavery ends in the United States, the voice of poverty, dispossession, and potential rebellion breaks through to the mountaintop of U.S. literary supremacy.[85]

In July of the same year, Melville wrote another view-from-above fantasia, "The House-Top"—though since he envisions the New York City draft riots in this "night piece," the superior vantage of his speaker rather resembles the view from volcanic Mount Etna that Poe had satirically proposed in *Eureka*. The magisterial final sentence of the poem describes the military putting-down of the internal urban rebellion, microcosm as it is of the larger putting-down of the rebelling southern states:

Wise Draco comes, deep in the midnight roll
Of black artillery; he comes, though late;
In code corroborating Calvin's creed

And cynic tyrannies of honest kings;
He comes, nor parlies; and the Town, redeemed,
Gives thanks devout; nor, being thankful, heeds
The grimy slur on the Republic's faith implied,
Which holds that Man is naturally good,
And—more—is Nature's Roman, never to be scourged.[86]

"The Republic's faith" is ended in the "cynic tyranny" that this poem witnesses—ended because, as Melville defines it here, that "faith" has been always flawed and impossible. To "hold that Man . . . is Nature's Roman" is to wreck the language of universality on the language of imperial hierarchy and exclusion. The category "Roman" makes sense only in the context of others who are not Romans; it denotes an imperial privilege of the empowered over the abased. A prohibition against scourging Romans assumes that non-Romans are regularly scourged (while also aligning as the republic's others southern slaves, who are regular recipients of the lash, and Christ, who was scourged before he was crucified). The false dream of the republic, as Melville limns it here, has been that everyone can be an imperial master, enjoying supremacy while incurring no blame for violent suppression of others. But masters require slaves, Melville reminds us, and the nation stepping forthrightly into empire without its Slave South can sustain this naïve "Republic's faith" no longer.

Both Emerson and Melville had promised, in their own ways, that annihilating its Slave South would enable the global ascendancy of the United States. Yet without their Slave South, the "outraged" industrial poor erupt into Emerson's dream of "omnipotence without violence"; the "scourged" subjects of empire crowd into Melville's vision of "political supremacy among the nations." And so, though the Slave South was dead, *resurget:* a new incarnation of the primal other of the nation was already rising to take its place.

PART THREE

The Question of Empire /
The Reconstruction South

Who looks at Lee must think of Washington;
In pain must think, and hide the thought,
So deep with grievous meaning is it fraught.
    —Herman Melville, *Battle-Pieces* (1866)

We talk of the provincial, but the provinciality projected by the
Confederate dream . . . looks to our present eyes as artlessly
perverse, as untouched by any intellectual tradition of beauty or
wit, as some exhibited array of the odd utensils or divinities of
lone and primitive islanders.
    —Henry James, *The American Scene* (1907)

CHAPTER NINE

Abandoned Lands and Exceptional Empire

A people rise
Up to a noble anger's height,
And, flamed on by the Fates, not shrink but grow more bright,
That swift validity in noble veins . . .
These are imperishable gains,
Sure as the sun, medicinal as light,
These hold great futures in their lusty reins
And certify to earth a new imperial race.

—James Russell Lowell, "Ode Recited at the Harvard
Commemoration" (July 21, 1865)

ALLED UPON TO MEMORIALIZE Harvard's war dead at a
solemn ceremony held three months after Lee's surrender to
Grant at Appomattox, the poet James Russell Lowell produced
a 426-line ode that promised that the costly struggle just ended had not
merely preserved the Union and restored the status quo antebellum.
Rather, the war had secured "imperishable gains" for the United States,
gains perceivable foremost in a global frame of reference. In defeating the
Confederacy, citizens of the United States had "certif[ied] to *earth* a new
imperial race." From this transformed vantage on the nation, seen now in
global context, Lowell proposed that the Union victory should signify
first of all to "sneering" Europeans, who were approaching the zenith of
their own age of empire:

Who now shall sneer?
Who dare again to say we trace
Our lines to a plebeian race? . . .
That is best blood that hath most iron in't,
To edge resolve with, pouring without stint
For what makes manhood dear.
Tell us not of Plantagenets,
Hapsburgs, and Guelfs, whose thin bloods crawl
Down from some victor in a border-brawl! . . .
Shout victory, tingling Europe's sullen ears
With vain resentments and more vain regrets![1]

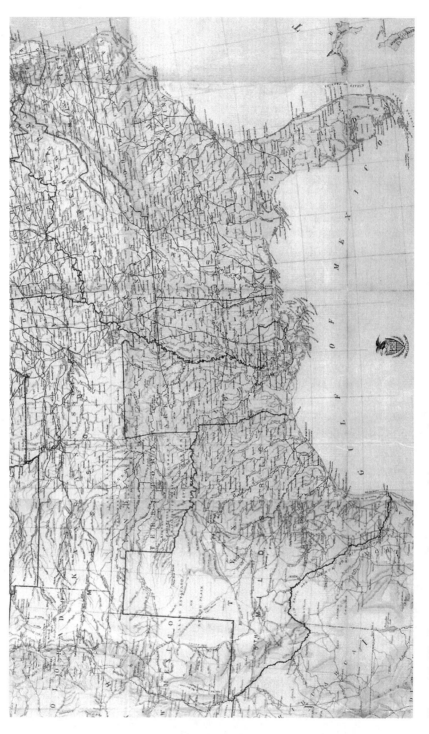

Figure 17. War Department, *Military Map of the United States*, 1869 (detail). National Archives (RG77: Published 1869, no. 1).

Europe might have dismissed the young nation in the past, due to its "plebeian" colonial origins, but, Lowell bragged, those days were done. The crucible of its Civil War had refined the United States, proving the ascendance of its "iron" mettle over the "thinness" of European military prowess. In the immediate aftermath of battle, Lowell envisioned the United States emerging from its bloodiest war a "certified" empire, forever sundered from its lowly colonial foundations. The "lusty" "great futures" of this remade United States, he prophesied, would soon make the imperial exploits of Europe appear a series of insignificant "border-brawls."

Of the many ironies implicit in Lowell's formulation of the global significance of the U.S. Civil War, perhaps most dissonant to our ears today is his wholehearted embrace of the racialist language so central to the arena of European empire he imagined the United States to be entering. Lowell's obsessive recourse to the language of "blood" and "race"—while patently illogical in the U.S. context—shows the utter derivativeness of the concept of empire that he triumphantly embraced. He stepped confidently into what contemporary scholars have termed the "Civilizing Mission" or "civilizationist discourse" of midcentury European empire: the enabling ideology that divided the planet into "civilized" and "barbarous" peoples, holding it the highest end of nationhood to ensure the dominion of the former over the latter.[2] While cultural and intellectual historians have seen this formulation of empire becoming increasingly central to U.S. thought toward the close of the nineteenth century, Lowell's Harvard ode presents a notably earlier turn toward its attractions—a turn brought about by the Civil War itself, institutionalized through Reconstruction, and facilitated by yet another sharp renovation of the idea of the South in U.S. culture.

Embracing Empire and Hiding the Thought, 1865–1866

The war to prevent secession of the Confederate states had raised the question of empire for U.S. observers of the day, not least because Confederate partisans had appropriated the mantle of the Revolutionary break with the British Empire to characterize their bid for independence from the United States. As the Confederates drafted declarations of secession that deliberately echoed the Declaration of Independence, and formulated a constitution based upon the Articles of Confederation of 1787, Unionists found themselves in the uncomfortable position of going to war in order to compel allegiance to a nation whose story of origins rested upon resistance to such compulsion.[3] Against the machinations of the Confederate ideologues, Unionists crafted an interpretation of secession as illegal under the Constitution, and the war to disallow it as merely a domestic police action against a traitorous uprising.[4] But the Unionist argument that secession was theoretically impossible could not fully mitigate the fact that on the ground, the sectional political conflict had escalated into a full-scale military contest between two armed powers with competing claims to control over both the territory of the southern states, and the ideological heritage of U.S. nationalism. Though the legitimacy (and even the existence) of Confederate nationalism has been debated ever since the secession crisis itself, contemporary observers of the American scene in the early years of the Civil War could easily enough conclude, as British chancellor William Gladstone famously did in 1862, that "Jefferson Davis and other leaders of the South have made an army; they are making, it appears, a navy; and they have made what is more than either, they have made a nation."[5] Although, as Benedict Anderson has put it, "a vast pedagogical industry" later interpreted this war and, perhaps less effectively, the Reconstruction that followed it as a "civil" conflict "between 'brothers,'" this reassuring interpretation was institutionalized well after the fact.[6] In resorting to violence to subdue the seceding states, the United States had to be seen as breaking with its past at least to some extent. The people living through the events of the war experienced them as an epochal rupture in nationalist ideology, calling into question all past understandings of the consensual republic—the origin, meaning, and mission of the United States of America.[7]

Lincoln's 1863 Gettysburg Address, delivered when a Union victory in the war had come to seem assured, long has been seen as the crucial refounding document for U.S. nationalism at this moment of irremediable rupture. In his fine study of the Address, Garry Wills has proposed that Lincoln refashioned nationalist ideology with "a giant (if benign) swindle": he located the very existence of the United States in the "proposition" of the Declaration of Independence "that all men are created equal"—in an abstract ideal that transcended the historical specifics of both the letter of the law of the United States, and its political and military acts.[8] "The South" long had served as the preeminent figure for negotiating this gap between nationalist ideal and national reality in U.S. letters, so it perhaps comes as no surprise that Lincoln's monumental reformulation of U.S. nationalism rested upon revision of the two interrelated geographic conceptualizations followed in this study: the place of the South in the United States, and the place of the United States in the world.

On the former score, the context of Lincoln's speech formalized an un-precedented alienation of the rebelling southern states from the national body. Lincoln crafted the Address for the dedication of the Soldiers' National Cemetery at Gettysburg, a monument created in the midst of the war not only to process the carnage of one of the bloodiest battles of the conflict, but also to exorcise the trauma of the invasion of Union territory by Confederate forces. ("In traversing the battle field, the feel-ings were shocked and the heart sickened at the sights that presented themselves at every step," reported the select committee constituted to create the National Cemetery. "And this, too, on Pennsylvania soil!")[9] The ground of the Pennsylvania battlefield was to re-"assume a national character" through the ideologically loaded design of the cemetery, which deliberately and ceremoniously "included the [Union] dead in equal, ideal ranks"—and, just as deliberately and ceremoniously, ex-cluded the bodies of the Confederate dead not only from honorable, but also from decent, burial.[10] This nationalization of the battlefield ex-tended even to the specificity of sorting among severed limbs, ceremoni-ously burying those clothed in blue and leaving those in gray shallowly covered, to be preyed on by animals and rot above ground.[11] Although the worst stench of decay had subsided by the dedication ceremony in November, the original audience for Lincoln's re-founding address reached the oration site by traveling through a landscape dotted with the exposed remains of Confederate soldiers—a landscape that apotheosized the unilateral supremacy of the United States of America over the bodies of its enemies.[12]

Out of this quite specific physical context of subjugating the Confed-eracy, Lincoln's refounding words conjured a national future that was definitionally "indefinite," in Wills's words, because ideologically transcen-dent of historical circumstance. This very indefiniteness, this lack of tem-poral boundaries, though, underwrote his confident projection of a newly central place for the United States on the globe. While he began the Gettys-burg Address with secession as a "test" of the endurance of the nation, by its end he had raised the stake for the Unionist cause to ensuring "that government of the people, by the people, for the people, *shall not perish from the earth.*" In the high-imperial era in which an Anglo-Saxonist view of history saw the transition from monarchy to popular sovereignty as the natural development of Western political organization—and in which the dominance of this Anglo-Saxon "civilization" over the "bar-barous" rest of the globe was assumed an organic evolution—Lincoln's oration placed the United States, triumphant over its South, as the central (and the only) pivot of global human progress.[13] The historical transcendence of the "new birth" of U.S. nationalism projected in the Address thus carried with it a principle of geographical transcendence: the United States "brought forth on this continent" "four score and seven years ago" now would turn outward beyond that continent. The remaking of the nation in its formative domestic struggle was to become, in some crucial way, the remaking of the entire world as well.

While Lincoln rightly, brilliantly, left the specifics of this impending global ascendance to the imaginations of his listeners, Unionists of literary bent easily filled in the blanks. In the waning days of the war, they assuredly hailed the conquest of their South with civilizationist discourse borrowed from across the Atlantic. For instance, when Thomas Wentworth Higginson in 1864 wrote from the field, where he was commanding the first federally authorized segregated regiment of African American soldiers, he easily converted the antebellum slogan for continental expansionism into the generic rallying cry of global empire: "The triumph of Civilization over Barbarism is the only Manifest Destiny of America," he epigrammatized.[14] Meanwhile, James Russell Lowell looked ahead to "Reconstruction" in a long essay published in the *North American Review* in early 1865, providing the prose argument of his slightly later Harvard ode. The stature of the United States vis-à-vis Europe had been the great question of the war, he proposed, and now through "the glory of conquest" of its South, the nation had assumed a front rank among global empires. "[I]n this our true war of independence, which is to free us forever from the Old World . . . the stake was the life not merely of [our] country, but of a principle whose rescue was to make America in very deed a New World, the cradle of a fairer manhood . . . The glory of conquest is trifling and barren, unless victory clear the way to a higher civilization."[15]

U.S. writers situating their Civil War in a global context got a boost from British observers as well, such as the economist John Elliot Cairnes, who as early as 1862 suggested that the American conflict be understood as a colonial war. In an essay titled "The Subjugation of the South: How Far Justifiable?" Cairnes extensively quoted John Stuart Mill's political philosophy of empire to argue for the justice and naturalness of U.S. dominion over its South. "Barbarians have no rights as a *nation* except a right to such treatment as may, at the earliest possible period, fit them for becoming one," Cairnes's two-page-long "apt quotation" of Mill begins. "[N]ations which are still barbarous have not got beyond the period during which it is likely to be for their benefit that they should be conquered and held in subjection by foreigners."[16]

After Appomattox, when the transformed relationship between the nation and its former southern states had to be negotiated in terms more concrete than those of the Gettysburg Address, the precedent of European empire, with its "Civilizing Mission," became the inescapable point of reference. Indeed, when Massachusetts critic Edwin Percy Whipple wrote the major article on the topic for the *Atlantic Monthly,* just as the Congressional Joint Committee on Reconstruction was convening in late 1865, he could posit the proper stance for the United States to take toward the defeated Confederate states only by recourse to the imperial analogy. Secession "was an act of State suicide," he began his interpretation of the conflict that had just ended. "From that moment [the people living in the state] had no more constitutional control of the area they occupied, were no more 'States,' than if they had transferred their allegiance to a European power, and the war had been prosecuted to wrest the territory they occupied, and the people they ruled, from the clutch of England or France."[17] After picturing the former southern states as unfaithful colonies, and secession as a "transfer of allegiance" to a competing imperial master, Whipple envisioned the population of the region according to its total dearth of markers of civilization. With conquest of the Confederacy, the United States had acquired dominion over "literally, in this case, 'the masses'—the free blacks are as much a part as the free whites," a biracial population unfitted for self-government: "the humble, quiet, hard-working negro" on the one hand, and on the other the "worthless barbarian" whites, "ignorant, illiterate, vicious, fit for no decent employment on earth but manual labor." As to the argument that the former southern states, riddled as they were with indigenes "disqualified for good citizenship," should be permitted to resume their places in the Union, Whipple railed sarcastically that

> at an enormous waste of treasure and blood, we have acquired the territory for which we fought; and lo! It is not ours, but belongs to the people we have been engaged in fighting, in virtue of the constitution we have been fighting for . . . *We are therefore expected to act like the savage, who, after thrashing his Fetich for disappointing his prayers, falls down again and worships it.*[18]

To fail to exercise the natural dominion of U.S. civilization over southern barbarism, Whipple warned, would be for the victorious nation to barbarize itself.

Of course, this notion—that the United States would join the ranks of European empire by conquering, acquiring, and reconstructing its South—could not be simply, suddenly, and unproblematically embraced.

The idea struck at the heart of American exceptionalism: if the nation was becoming *like* the extant European powers, was borrowing foreign forms, was progressing by analogy, how could it possibly stand alone and independent? Worse, the core of U.S. national identity itself—the republic—had been formulated from the start in opposition to European empires; to embrace empire would be to lose the identity of the United States. Celebrations of "the glory of conquest" at the close of the war thus always were shadowed by the fear that—as the former Confederate vice president Alexander Stephens succinctly formulated it—"all that is so glorious in the past and so hopeful in the future [of the nation] will, sooner or later, be lost in the same inevitable despotism of a Consolidated Centralized Empire, which eventuated in the overthrow and destruction of the liberties of Rome."[19]

This yoking of the ascendance of U.S. empire with the destruction of the republic became the theme of the penultimate poem of Melville's 1866 *Battle-Pieces,* which is perhaps the first literary treatment of Reconstruction. The poem meditates upon the uncanny appearance of "Lee in the Capitol" (its title), describing the defeated Confederate general Robert E. Lee testifying by command before the Joint Committee on Reconstruction. Melville's Lee appears simultaneously as an apotheosis of the formerly intact antebellum nation, and as an avatar of its destruction: "In his mien / The victor and the vanquished both are seen— / All that he is, and what he late had been." While Melville's yoking of incompatible terms—identity and opposition, present and past—identifies Lee as a classic southern figure, on the other side of the secession crisis the familiar figure has come to represent an unbearable paradox. Melville's Lee in the Capitol, on the one hand, embodies the mythic consensual origins of the republic—literally embodies them, through his Virginian bloodlines to George Washington, whom Melville terms "the Founder." On the other hand, Lee now sits subjected before what has become the coercive, conquering state. "Who looks at Lee must think of Washington," Melville emblematizes the paradox, "In pain must think, and hide the thought / So deep with grievous meaning is it fraught."[20]

For Melville, the spectacle of Lee in the Capitol registers the annihilation of "what [the United States] late had been," an annihilation that must be recognized and sublimated at the same moment.[21] This annihilation of the past existence of the nation is brought about not by the now-subdued threat of secession, but by the triumphant overcoming of that threat. The poet initially turns to the subjugated descendent of Washington for salvation, imploring him, "Ay, speak . . . [a]nd the flushed North from her own victory save." Melville then assumes Lee's voice, delivering a soliloquy to the Reconstruction Committee with a clear warning against the shift to empire—and he uses the Revolutionary-era term "tyranny" to emphasize the stakes: "'Shun / To copy Europe in her worst estate— / Avoid the tyranny you reprobate.'"[22]

Melville ends the poem, though, both by summarily disregarding the speech that he has required Lee to make and by asserting that the transformation of the United States from republic to empire has already been irremediably effected. Not Lee's imagined speech, but rather his forced appearance before the state, ultimately signifies here:

> But no. Brave though the Soldier, grave his plea—
> Catching the light in the future's skies,
> Instinct disowns each darkening prophecy:
> Faith in America never dies;
> Heaven shall the end ordained fulfill,
> We march with Providence cheery still.[23]

With this fantastically mediated interplay—of light and dark; nationalist "faith" and "instinctive" obliviousness; *Gott-mit-uns* "cheer" and the military "march" that continues incongruously after the ceasing of the declared war—Melville concludes the poem with both a rousing assurance of the survival of antebellum U.S. nationalism, and a sardonic stripping away of its republican illusions. He then abruptly hides the thought: he backs away from the ideological abyss he has opened with the last poem of *Battle-Pieces,* laboriously titled "A Meditation: attributed to a northerner after attending the last of two funerals from the same homestead—those of a National and a Confederate officer (brothers), his kinsmen, who had died from the effects of wounds received in the closing battles." Here, Melville beats a hasty retreat to what Anderson has termed "the official-nationalist reassurance of fratricide."[24]

This oscillation between embrace and denial of U.S. supremacy over its defeated South marked the initial conceptualization of the project of Reconstruction at the broadest cultural level. Was the war a national tragedy, a fratricidal calamity of self-wounding, or was it a national triumph, proving the civilizing might of the United States? Were the occupied former states to be considered temporarily alienated, intrinsic parts of the nation, or were they prototypically alien foreign possessions? Even the 1866 Report of the Joint Committee on Reconstruction tried to have it both ways. On the one hand, the report suggested that the former states should be treated as wayward members of the national family, along the well-established territorial model for admission to the Union that had been used for westward expansion since 1787: "The burden now rests upon them . . . to show that they are qualified to resume federal relations." But on the other hand, the same report suggested that the defeated states be considered "conquered enemies" who should have no "right . . . to participate in making laws for their conquerers." While administering "conquered enemies" and occupying their territory might seem a departure for the United States, without national historical precedent, the Joint Committee noted that the entire "history of mankind" beyond the exceptionalist borders of the Republic could provide examples of how it was done.[25]

The political architects of Reconstruction themselves relied heavily upon such extranational precedents, particularly the models provided by European imperial administration, and Reconstruction thus provided a training ground for U.S. administrative policies that would later be put into practice overseas.[26] An obvious instance of this methodological borrowing appeared in the first Reconstruction Act of 1867, which first of all *partitioned* the occupied former states: the borders of ten of the formerly belligerent states were declared void by the act and replaced with five "Military Districts" for the purposes of governmental administration. The administrative strategy of partition—the imposition of new boundaries that simultaneously acknowledged the way that local inhabitants had organized themselves prior to being conquered, and overruled that self-organization with a structure ostensibly more convenient or rational for the occupying forces—had been key to contemporaneous European imperial practices, and indeed would reach its peak with the partition of the entire continent of Africa after the Berlin Conference of 1880.[27]

In the sphere of national culture, though, such appropriated imperial practices were treated gingerly or, indeed, not at all. Although the partitioned map of the South was the law of the land for the period of Congressional Reconstruction, the U.S. government seems to have been loath to create representations of that partition—indeed, seems never to have commissioned an official map of the United States that illustrated the military districts.[28] An 1869 map of the United States, a detail from which is reproduced at the opening of this chapter, provides the rare example of even a glancing acknowledgement of the partition of the southern states. Even though it was produced by the U.S. War Department, the map first of all denotes the borders of all of the individual states in the nation, including the abolished antebellum borders of the southern states. Then, with a red overlay, the entire national map is divided into other sorts of districts. Over the former Confederate states, the red overlay indicates the borders of the First, Fourth, and Fifth Military Districts, while the Second and

Third are conflated and labeled simply, "The South." At the same time, though, as in some sort of weird solidarity, the rest of the map is also divided with overlaid red boundaries; these describe not legal administrative borders, but oddly defined "regions" that correspond roughly to landform features: "The Cumberland," "The East," "The Lakes," "The Platte."[29]

This blurring of imperial domination and impressionistic "regional" description is at the heart of "the Reconstruction South," a renovation of the internal other of national literature for the postwar purposes of U.S. writers and readers. This Reconstruction South drastically exceeds the exceptionalist narrative of U.S. cultural history that poses both the process of Reconstruction itself, and the so-called "local color" writing in which it was registered, against the golden age of European empire in the late Victorian era. Americans in the postwar decades often are imagined as turned inward: isolationist, recovering from their collective domestic trauma, interested only in the specificity and restriction of realist writing. Tracing the emergence of the Reconstruction South, though, highlights the formal kinship of regional fictions with imperial discourse, in terms of both protoethnographic narrative structure and exoticist aesthetics, and reveals that this new incarnation of the South allowed for a particularly potent literary projection of nascent U.S. empire. Initially confronting the question of empire on the terrain of a presumably "civil" domestic conflict facilitated a remarkably flexible simultaneous embrace and denial of U.S. global ascendancy in the years immediately following the Civil War.

Discovering Domestic Africa

As U.S. writers confronted the transformed relationship of the nation to its South after secession, the contemporaneous European imperial focus on Africa became their predominant analogy. The startlingly new idea of their South as a "transatlantic Africa" within the United States, as one essayist put it in 1861, had to do, certainly, with the African origins of much of the population of the southern states; and to this extent the geographic term served as a racial marker.[30] At the same time, though, "Africa" signified a specific pole in the high-imperial organization of the globe: the platonic form of barbarism, the site unequivocally destined for imperial administration from without, the ultimate challenge to the "Civilizing Mission." To conceptualize the Reconstruction South by reference to Africa was simultaneously to racialize the region and to colonialize it. The African analogy thus doubly placed the Reconstruction South in the global hierarchy of modern empire.

At the very outbreak of the war, both Union and Confederate partisans showed themselves well aware of these dual stakes of the "Africanization of the South." That term was coined by Louisiana medical doctor William H. Holcombe, who argued in the pages of the *Southern Literary Messenger* in February 1861—in the midst of secession—that with Lincoln's election to the presidency, the southern states found themselves "no longer partners to a federal compact, but the victims of a consolidated despotism." With this shift to an imperial United States, he argued, "the question is at length plainly presented: submission or secession. The only alternative left is this: *a separate nationality or the Africanization of the South.*" In Holcombe's usage, "Africanization" signified both local equality between the races and global colonial stature in the imperial order; indeed, to his mind, the two terms were inextricable. In the North, he complained,

> slavery is considered not only immoral but debasing to both owner and owned. It is, they say, a relic of barbarism and a disgrace to an enlightened people. We are not regarded as equals but are merely tolerated, as persons whom they in their wisdom may possibly reform and improve . . . [I]f [the North] has the power or can invent the means, it will be ready to reduce the South to the condition of Hayti and Jamaica, and expect the approval of God upon the atrocity.[31]

By using "Africanization" as his rubric, Holcombe equated emancipation with a "reduction" in political stature, from independent state to the "condition" of a colony like Jamaica, or an entity like Haiti that the United States refused to recognize as sovereign.

While Holcombe used the imperial analogy to support secession and the perpetuation of slavery, *North American Review* editor Charles Eliot Norton—writing in the same month—used precisely the same ideological paradigm for the opposite political program. In support of the Union and the abolition of slavery, Norton paradoxically joined Holcombe in conceptualizing the U.S. South as "this new Africa," constituted by "the ultimate and not distant ascendancy of the black race" in its "congenial climate":

> Free, civilized, and prosperous communities [of the North] are brought face to face, as it were, with the mixed and degenerating populations of the Slave country . . . Shall this new Africa push its boundaries beyond their present limits? Shall more territory be yielded to the already wide-spread African race? . . . . It is the question, whether New England or New Africa shall extend her limits,—whether the country shall be occupied a century hence by a civilized or by a barbarous race.[32]

This crystalline formulation of its South as explicitly a colony of the United States—the nation's black, "barbarous," "transatlantic Africa"—by contrast proved, in Norton's formulation, the Anglo-Saxon "civilization" of a "New England"—a new imperial incarnation of the United States.

At the close of the war, this placement of the "Africanized" Reconstruction South on the world map of modern empire strongly inflected literary portrayals of the U.S. military occupation of the former Confederate states. Walt Whitman, for instance, titled his poetic treatment of Sherman's march "Ethiopia Saluting the Colors": he personified the wartime act of conquest—"as under doughty Sherman I march toward the sea"—as a "dusky woman," garbed in the African colors of "yellow, red and green," genuflecting before the red, white, and blue of the U.S. flag.[33] As he presented the emblematic southerner in his account of the U.S. military domination of "Carolina" as essentially African rather than American, Whitman posited the U.S. occupation of its South as occupation of foreign territory, and the "dusky woman, so ancient hardly human," as the generic subject of modern empire. He thus suggested that the Reconstruction South was a site not of liberation but of renovated mastery—a suggestion borne out by the center stanza of the poem, rendered as the speech of "Ethiopia" herself. In answer to the question of the conquering U.S. speaker—"Why rising by the roadside here, do you the colors greet?"—"Ethiopia" replies, cryptically,

> Me master years a hundred since from my parents sunder'd,
> A little child, they caught me as the savage beast is caught,
> Then hither me across the sea the cruel slaver brought.[34]

The ideologically flattering interpretation of this speech, for a U.S. reader, is that "Ethiopia" welcomes the occupying forces because they put right the centuries-old original sin of American slavery. This interpretation hinges upon reading the first line of the stanza as "Me master years a hundred since / from my parents sunder'd [me]"—understanding it to mean, in paraphrase, "My [southern] master sundered me from my parents a hundred years ago." But Whitman's construction of the line with an internal rhyme—"*Me master years a hundred / since from my parents sunder'd*"—militates against this reading, instead suggesting that "Ethiopia" is addressing the occupying speaker of the poem himself as "me master." The Reconstruction South Whitman envisions, through its very "Africanization," emerges as a conversion of the patriarchal, local mastery of the Slave South into the institutional, foreign mastery of modern U.S. empire.

John W. DeForest, in his celebrated war novel *Miss Ravenel's Conversion from Secession to Loyalty* (1867), similarly posits Reconstruction as a regenerating exchange of Southern colonial masters for the modern imperial mastery of the U.S. government. At the close of the war, his Unionist character Dr. Ravenel expounds, "the question comes up, 'Which shall we hang, and which shall we pardon?' I say, hang Planter, and tell Cracker to get to work. Planter gone, some better man will occupy Cracker and make him live and speak virtuously." DeForest's focus on "Cracker"—as opposed to Whitman's "Ethiopia"—as the generic southerner to be "occupied" (and put to work) by U.S. forces reveals his interest in white rather than black southerners as the key subjects of the conquering United States. His conceptualization of the generic Reconstruction South subject, nonetheless, still relies upon the Africa analogy. In the first chapter alone, Dr. Ravenel informs readers that white southerners are "ill-informed as Hottentots"; "that they are barbarians, and that all barbarians are obstinate and reckless"; that their war for secession is a "stupid, barbarous Ashantee rebellion"; and that, given the infallible civilizationist hierarchy, these "Ashantee secessionists" are "doomed to perish by their own ignorance and madness."[35]

DeForest's unhesitating application of the African analogy to white— and indeed, white-supremacist—Confederates hearkens back to late-eighteenth-century postcolonial concerns about climatic determinism and heterogeneous population in tropical America. These venerable fears about degeneration and subordination, though, are reinvigorated for DeForest by contemporaneous British imperial ventures in Africa. Whitman's invocation of "Ethiopia" uses a term for Africa conventional in the eighteenth century, signifying ancient African language and culture; DeForest's denomination of Southerners as "Ashantees" and "Hottentots," by contrast, references both the colonial wars being prosecuted by Britain at the time he wrote and the racialist pseudoscience underwriting them.[36] By analogizing the Confederate rebellion against U.S. control to the Anglo-Asante Wars of the mid-1860s, DeForest's Dr. Ravenel suggests that self-rule for either "stupid, barbarous" population would violate the organic hierarchy of human civilization. In the same year that DeForest's novel appeared, Ralph Waldo Emerson made the identical analogy of the defeated Confederacy to contemporary Africa at a dedication of a Civil War monument in his hometown of Concord, Massachusetts. "The common people, rich or poor" in the former Confederate states "were the narrowest and most conceited of mankind, as arrogant as the negroes on the Gambia River," he reminded his auditors. "'This will be a slow business,' writes our Concord captain home, 'for we have to stop and civilize the people as we go along.'"[37]

This potent vision of the Reconstruction South as the nation's own private Africa—as the domestic site upon which the United States would take up the mantle of global empire—was institutionalized in U.S. letters by a monumental series titled *The Great South,* published in *Scribner's Monthly* magazine from 1873 to 1875 and thereafter as an eight-hundred-page, copiously illustrated volume. The series formalized the connection between representations of the Reconstruction South and contemporaneous imperial writing about Africa, explicitly replacing the venerable U.S. tradition of southern travel writing with a new European model: the interior-Africa exploration narrative.[38] At the same time, *The Great South* series has been credited with creating the national audience for what would become the most popular form of postwar literature, the so-called "local color" fiction championed in the pages of *Scribner's* (later *Century Magazine*).[39] Since this Reconstruction-era series made such a substantial impact on later-nineteenth-century U.S. letters, it is worth examining in some detail how it came into being.

In 1872, the magazine editor Josiah Gilbert Holland had found himself in something of a predicament. Just over a year earlier, he had persuaded the powerful publisher Charles Scribner to discontinue two of the magazines published by his firm and to consolidate their subscription rolls behind Holland's bold new venture: the filially named *Scribner's Monthly,* a magazine that aspired to be the cultural outlet for a nation aggrandized and consolidated by its Civil War, and taking up a new place on the world stage. Holland conceived of *Scribner's* as combining the moral and literary authority of the *Atlantic* or *North American Review,* with the illustration quantity and quality of the popular London magazines of the day; with the transatlantic fusion, he aspired to exceed the circulation figures of all previous or extant "high-toned" U.S. periodicals.[40] But Charles Scribner had died unexpectedly at age 50, control of his firm had passed to his young sons, whose dispensation toward the upstart magazine was unclear, and Holland had failed so far to generate much notice for *Scribner's Monthly* at home or abroad, or indeed to produce an increase in circulation substantially beyond that of the forty thousand subscriptions the elder Scribner had handed him in November 1870. Holland needed a major editorial innovation that would catapult his little-noticed new magazine to the position of prominence suited to the flagship periodical of a major publishing house; he needed a revolution in content that quickly would push his circulation closer to the goal of one hundred thousand he optimistically had proposed to Scribner pére.[41]

At this critical juncture, Holland took inspiration from the great U.S. periodical coup of the day. British expatriate and Civil War veteran Henry Morton Stanley, traveling on assignment for the *New York Herald,* had in November 1871 "discovered" the incommunicado British missionary David Livingstone in interior Africa.[42] Stanley's "expedition" into "darkest Africa" transfixed audiences around the English-speaking world, despite its origin as a bald publicity stunt designed by *Herald* publisher James Gordon Bennett to garner a European readership for his newspaper.[43] Stanley's climactic meeting with Livingstone was dubbed the scoop of the century by Bennett's paper; it also represented an American usurpation of the interior-Africa exploration narrative, the most popular form of British imperial travel writing. The *Herald* stunt arrogated the authority of the great empire on matters of African "discovery," figuratively transferring that authority to the United States—itself a former British colony just emerging from a political and military convulsion that almost had disassembled it. While the U.S. had no immediate material claim in the scramble for Africa among the European powers, Stanley and Bennett momentarily had bested Britain on the cultural field of empire, and both European and U.S. readers took notice. The Scribner firm rushed to secure the U.S. rights to publish the book version of Stanley's dispatches, *How I Found Livingstone,* as a copiously illustrated volume of over seven hundred pages produced by subscription in late 1872.

As he watched his own publisher angle for a piece of the Stanley sensation, Holland began plotting a parallel "expedition" for *Scribner's Monthly.*[44] Channeling Bennett's already oft-quoted charge to Stanley to "draw a thousand pounds now . . . and when you have finished that, draw another thousand, and so on; but, FIND LIVINGSTONE," Holland laid out "an enterprise involving an amount of labor and expense unprecedented in popular magazine literature . . . [with] neither pains nor money . . . spared to make it all that we promise it should be."[45] And as with the Stanley expedition, Holland projected that a year-long series of dispatches to the magazine would culminate in "a beautiful volume, in which the material will be newly arranged . . . and offered to the subscriptions of the public, not only in America, but in Great Britain and nearly all the British colonies." On Bennett's model, in other words, Holland laid out an expedition that both would boost magazine subscriptions as the story unfolded and, at its end, would consolidate the sensation it had garnered in book form—which would not only be more enduring but also generate higher profits. He followed Bennett as well in engaging an international, rather than purely domestic, English-speaking readership. At the same time, though, Holland sought to improve on the *Herald* stunt by using his magazine format to best advantage. In particular, he stressed the production of high-quality illustrations from direct artist observation; whereas the 1872 volume *How I Found Livingstone* was illustrated after the fact with artists' renderings ostensibly based upon Stanley's untrained sketches, Holland's *Scribner's Monthly* "expedition" was publicized from the first as a joint venture between correspondent and chief illustrator. A "band" of up to seventeen sketchers and engravers would accompany every leg of the journey, and fresh illustrations from the field would be included with each installment of the series. By the end of 1874, Holland's "enterprise" had "occupied, in all, about four hundred and fifty pages of the magazine and had involved the production of more than four hundred and thirty engravings."[46]

Holland's biggest innovation on Bennett's precedent, though, was his choice of "expedition" locale. Rather than follow the *Herald's* figurative competition with Britain on the final frontier of European empire—in the African interior where the United States had no present prospect of an actual material stake—Holland trained his sights on a territory the nation already possessed: an "immense tract of country" recently subdued in war, currently occupied by the U.S. military, and in the midst of a civilizing process called Reconstruction. *The Great South* would follow the basic ideological contours of British Victorian travel writing about Africa, positing discovery as the necessary predecessor to development as it boasted that the *Scribner's* team "penetrated regions rarely seen by Northern men."[47] It would evoke the transatlantic solidarity of British and U.S. imperial civilizations by "exhibit[ing], by pen and pencil, a vast region almost as little known to the Northern States of the Union as it is to England."[48] But the cultural authority of *The Great South* would dovetail, as it could not in Stanley's African writings, with real U.S. political and economic authority over the realm being "penetrated," "investigated," and "simultaneously offered to the English-speaking public on both sides of the Atlantic."[49]

As he presented the series with an appropriation of British imperial travel writing modes, Holland registered the extent to which secession, conquest, and occupation had transformed the internal relationship of the nation to its southern states. As he packaged the Reconstruction South for his readers as a domestic Africa—an imaginatively parallel field for the projection of imperial power *within* the United States—Holland built upon at least a decade of attempts by writers North and South to understand the domestic sectionalist crisis by global analogy to the relationships between European nations and their colonies. To represent the Reconstruction South as a colonized region of the United States, parallel to colonized regions of the European powers around the globe, was to assert a new stature of equality for the U.S. amongst the imperial nations of the world. This global reframing of the relationship between the nation and its Reconstruction South made *The Great South* series a revelation—and an education—for U.S. readers of the day.

Even Holland's selection of his correspondent for the series telegraphed to his readers the connection that he was making between British imperial writing about Africa and U.S. postwar writing about the southern states. Stanley himself might have been Holland's first choice, but the editor secured the next-best possibility: Edward King, a little-known, twenty-six-year-old aspiring journalist, whose sole claim to fame was having been Stanley's last press corps companion prior to the latter's secret departure for Africa and Livingstone. King had first appeared in *Scribner's Monthly* in late 1872 with the article "An Expedition with Stanley," and then in early 1873 with "How Stanley Found Livingstone," both of which sought to capitalize on his casual acquaintance with Stanley in Spain as the two covered the Carlist insurrection for different U.S. newspapers in late 1869.[50] In the first of these pieces, King wrote of his close associations with his "brother of the craft" in the tropical clime of southern Spain: "We slept; we waked; we ate pomegranates: and meantime the lusty sun poured down unrelentingly, waking the fair land into tropical fervor and voluptuousness . . . We had at last got beyond Europe." After lingering on the "haughty ancient Moorish look" "of these tall, voluptuously formed dark women, who . . . were not Europeans," King left *Scribner's* readers with the image of himself and Stanley standing side by side on the Mediterranean coast, "point[ing] carelessly beyond the throbbing rim of the purple sea" and breathing: "Africa!"[51] By the time those words appeared in the magazine, King was on his way to the stateside version of the dark continent as the "enterprising man" in charge of Holland's "unprecedented" southern expedition.[52]

King's last dispatch to *Scribner's* from Europe left him standing with his readers on the southernmost edge of Spain, gazing across the Mediterranean with eroticized longing toward the Africa his British-American companion soon would penetrate. The first installment of *The Great South* found King in a transatlantically transported but arrestingly analogous position: at the port of New Orleans, with illustrations and text calculated to direct the longing gaze of his readers across the Gulf of Mexico. (On the 1873 title page, Louisiana's emblematic pelicans seem to be pulling the words "THE GREAT SOUTH," dripping, out of the Gulf.) In moving from the rim of the Mediterranean to the rim of the Gulf of Mexico, King transposed a surrogate experience of European empire into a more immediate projection of United States empire to come. The southward gaze from Spain toward Africa became the southward gaze from domestic Africa toward Spanish America. Just so, the Reconstruction South entered U.S. literature as an imaginative geographic nexus for conceptualizing U.S. empire in the 1870s, the decade when the United States increasingly was "turning outward after the Civil War."[53] As federal administration of the underdeveloped and war-ravaged southern states allowed U.S. writers to draw parallels to European exertions in Africa, they asserted, through transatlantic analogy, the legitimacy and power of the United States on the world stage. Like King, they situated the Reconstruction South in a global context—as both the U.S. *(The Great South)* and London *(The Southern States of North America)* titles of his series attest—and they vaunted the imperatives of capitalist development and the trials of the "Civilizing Mission."[54]

This broader imperial discourse constructed geographical peripherality and biological inferiority in tandem, creating narratives that explained the underdevelopment of a region as the product of the inferiority of its native inhabitants. Such is the explanatory paradigm for a proper Reconstruction of the occupied southern states that King develops over the course of *The Great South,* a text that he describes in his authorial introduction to the book as "an exhaustive catalogue of the material resources of the South and the social condition of its people."[55] The initial title page for the series, published in *Scribner's Monthly* in 1873 but expurgated from the book versions of *The Great South,* encapsulates the paradigm of the Reconstruction South that King develops over eight hundred pages of description: Louisiana has "unlimited, enchanting, faery possibilities" for capitalist expropriation of its resources, precisely *because* it is populated with bizarre, half-human flying and crawling creatures. (The lead engraver for *The Great South,* J. Wells Champney, directly borrowed the pictorial conceit for depicting a subhuman population from the distinctive cartoons of colonial subjects that were being produced contemporaneously by Briton John Tenniel for *Punch* magazine.[56]) The link between subhuman population and unlimited potential on the first page of the series remains central to the explanatory paradigm King develops through its ninety descriptive installments, as he couples exuberant detail of the untapped natural resources of the Reconstruction South with repetitious evidence of the degeneracy of the people living there.

In his geographical descriptions, King situates the Reconstruction

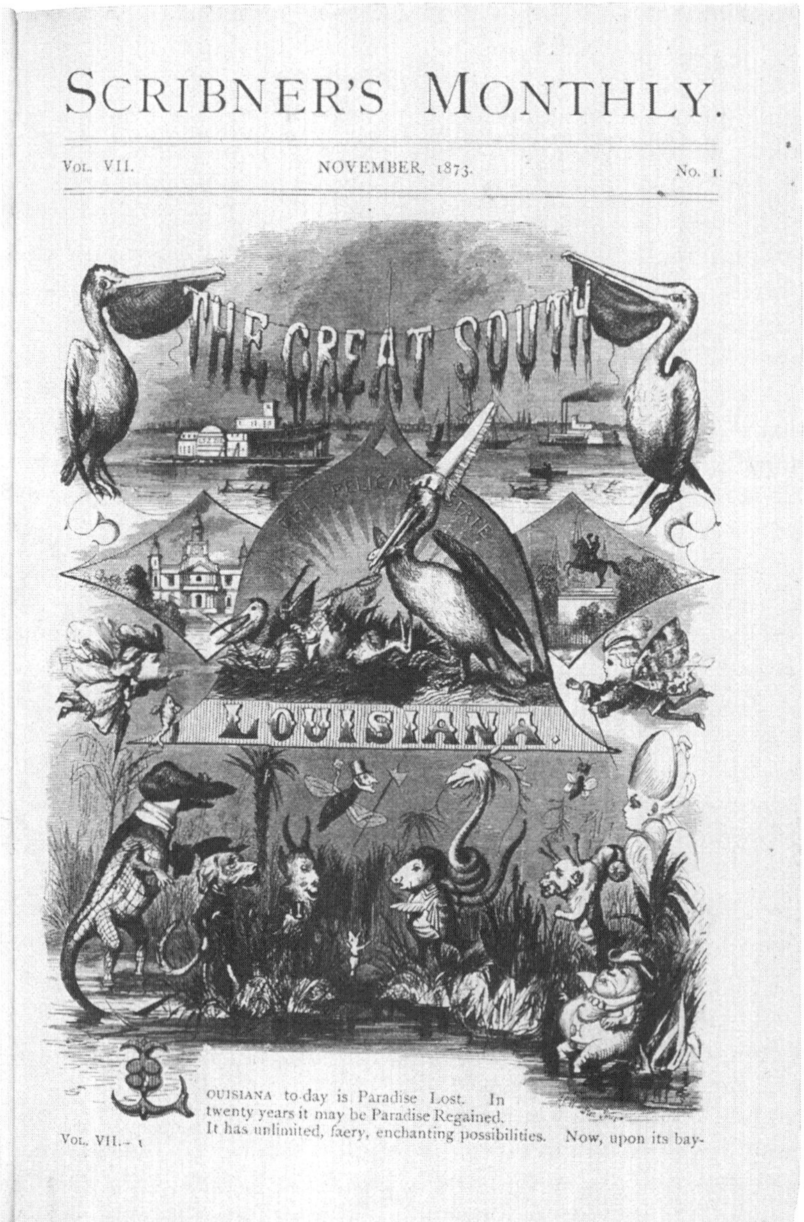

SCRIBNER'S MONTHLY.

VOL. VII. NOVEMBER, 1873. NO. 1.

THE GREAT SOUTH

LOUISIANA.

LOUISIANA to-day is Paradise Lost. In twenty years it may be Paradise Regained. It has unlimited, faery, enchanting possibilities. Now, upon its bay-

VOL. VII.—1

Figure 18. Series frontispiece, *The Great South, Scribner's Monthly,* Nov. 1873. Yale Collection of American Literature, Beinecke Rare Book and Manuscript Library.

South in the context of underdeveloped regions around the globe. Compared with any other desirable territorial possession in the world, the southern states are "inexhaustibly rich" in natural resources: King claims that mineral deposits, timber, and fertile soil are present in every nook of the region to a degree presumably incomprehensible to readers foreign and domestic, whose "wildest ideas" about southern wealth "can be none too exaggerated for the reality." Bolstered by more than one hundred site-specific engravings of unmined rock formations and uninhabited landscapes, King repetitiously claims that southern raw materials are unsurpassed: his "finds" range from a mythical "gold belt" stretching from North Carolina to Georgia—a story that gestures back to the earliest Old World designs on the American hemisphere—to a more up-to-date, industrial-age coal field in the Appalachians, which "considerably" exceeds "the entire coal area of Great Britain." Assessing the potential aids and impediments to extraction and improvement of the "riches" he details, King again echoes much earlier European colonialist promotions of America as "neu-gefundenes Eden": southern raw materials are unparalleled in their ease of access, as the soil requires "but little attention," the ore little smelting, and the coal little mining. Like diamonds in Africa, according to contemporaneous reports, Southern coal is located conveniently "at the surface" of the earth.[57]

Yet despite the ready availability of these sources of vast wealth, King repeatedly informs his readers that they have lain fallow prior to U.S. occupation of the southern states, for "the natives of the poorer class, who might make fortunes by turning their attention to it, are too idle to develop the country." King's figuring of the unequaled yet undeveloped riches of the peripheral South thus unfolds in tandem with his extensive proofs of the degeneracy of its local population, white and black. His account of "the old town of Alexandria [Va.]" is typical.

> It occupies a position admirably fitted for large industrial activity . . . and yet it languishes. Its inhabitants seem to lack the vigor and the enterprise needed to seize upon and improve their fine advantages. They are in the attitude of waiting for something to turn up . . . The streets were not paved until a Northern officer, during the occupation in war times, insisted upon having a pavement of cobble stones laid down, and met the expense by fines levied upon whiskey-selling . . . One sees nerveless unthrift in many small Virginian towns. It seems graven in the nature of whites and blacks. An occasional conversation with the negroes led me to believe that they offer as many hindrances to the advent of capital as their ex-masters do. Both seem suspicious that some improper and undue advantage is to be taken of them.

According to King's diagnosis, the incapability for improvement "graven in the nature" of southern "inhabitants" is partially due to climatic and historical determinism. "The aboriginal [white] Texan . . . is a child of the sun; he dislikes effort; it gives him no gratification to labor"; while "the tough moral fibre of the Anglo-Saxon . . . is not perceptible in the negro; neither could it be expected, considering that he was brought from the jungles of Africa into a comparatively wild region in America." Such characterizations, in turn, easily progress into biological determinism: King reiterates that "the rural Caucasian" is "lean and scrawny, without animation . . . all [with] the same dead, pallid complexion," while "the negro . . . lets the African in him run riot."[58] What sometimes reads as King's biracialization of southern incapacity for self-rule is, again, bolstered by visual evidence; the *Scribner's* engravers also produced more than one hundred "wayside sketches" of "Southern Types": physiognomic caricatures of slack-jawed southerners, white and black, that often exhibit distorted facial features (such as low foreheads and exaggerated noses and lips) and assume more or less bestial postures (such as slouching, crouching, and begging).

Taken together, the two organizing elements of King's "exhaustive" Reconstruction South account create a moral imperative for the U.S. occupation and administration of a populated and resistant territory—an imperative ideally suited to the postbellum needs of a national audience beginning to think of the United States as a modern imperial power on the European model, yet ambivalent about the prospect. The overarching claim of *The Great South* is that the most vital natural stores of the North American continent have until now been in the possession of "inhabitants" devoid of the productive capabilities that would allow them to make use of those resources. The fledgling imperative of United States empire proposed in King's catalogue of the Reconstruction South might best be described as an imperative of improvement: unless progress is imposed from outside of the region, its "riches" will continue to "languish" unused, its "natives" living "the very rudest and most incult life imaginable." But with "proper investment" of "Northern capital" trained on the harvesting of southern riches, King programatically and repetitiously counsels his readers, the nation "will find one of its most profitable fields" and will place itself "at that pinnacle of commercial glory" equivalent to the European nations that similarly harvest the riches of the globe. And while uplift of the "native" population is a priority clearly secondary to the attainment of national "commercial glory," King optimistically speculates that U.S. administration may even in the course of time civilize the degenerate southern peoples into worthy laborers in the modern order. "We may expect in a few years, as . . . the persistent idlers are crowded to the wall, to see [the negro and] the Southern poor white transformed into industrious and valuable members of society."[59]

King's imperial imperative of improvement—his certainty that the most efficient exploitation of both natural and human resources by capital is a positive good—taps into an American tradition of thought about the relationships between people and the land they inhabit that stretches back to the colonial era.[60] A similar ideological conflation of people and place was encapsulated in the formal name of the most important Reconstruction agency: the Bureau of Refugees, Freedmen, and Abandoned Lands, usually shorthanded as "the Freedmen's Bureau." The terms "Refugees" and "Freedmen" posited white and black southerners, respectively, as subjects of Reconstruction administration, while the term "Abandoned Lands" dissevered the occupied territory itself from propri-etary claims by either local group. (As W. E. B. Du Bois put it, the Freed-man's Bureau "had to do, not simply with emancipated slaves and poor whites, but also with the property of Southern planters.")[61] The term "Abandoned Lands" was especially suggestive for conceiving of an already-inhabited territory as nonetheless open for U.S. acquisition, since it hearkened back to the original use of "plantation" in English New World colonization: the ideological argument that the Indians inhabit-ing the land desired by the English were not properly "planting" or im-proving it, and thus that they had no rights of possession. Though populated, New World lands were understood according to this ideology as "abandoned"—or, in seventeenth-century terminology, "desert." At the same time, "Abandoned Lands" also signified in the more modern sense of the Slave South: abandoned of God and utterly given over to evil, the denizens of the Confederate states had invited their own conquest and expropriation. Conceptualizing Reconstruction under the aegis of "Abandoned Lands" extended the concept of righteous conquest in war (Lincoln's "right makes might") to a righteous and exceptionally Ameri-can form of imperial dominion over a populated and resistant territory. With Harriet Beecher Stowe, U.S. readers could find themselves "come out of one of the severest struggles that ever tried a nation, purer and stronger in morals and religion, as well as more prosperous in material things!"[62]

Even as King presented *The Great South* to his readers as a region of si-multaneously peripheralized and racialized "color," analogous to African and other colonial territories abroad, he used the claim of the "local"—the domestic, the intimate—to differentiate U.S. administration of its Reconstruction South from the forms of European empire. His magnum opus of the Reconstruction South thus did indeed pave the way for the most popular form of postwar fiction, "local color" writing—but it institutionalized "local color" as the preeminent site in U.S. letters for developing an exceptionalist imperial imaginary. In his introduction to the book version of *The Great South*, King most directly put forth the notion of an exceptional U.S. empire by pointedly diverging from the derivative appropriation of Victorian travel writing modes that had marked the installments of the series published in *Scribner's Monthly*. Instead, King offered a distinctively American colonial history of Louisiana.

> For a century and a-half [Louisiana] was coveted by all nations; sought by those great colonizers of America,—the French, the English, the Spaniards. It has been in turn the plaything of monarchs and the bait of adventurers. Its history and tradition are leagued with all that was romantic in Europe and on the Western continent in the eighteenth century.

By beginning his encyclopedic account of the Reconstruction South with American colonial history, and with the archetypal global opposition of "Europe" to "the Western continent," King resituated the United States as itself part of a colonized hemisphere that had been, for a century, unevenly throwing off the yoke of Old World empire. And thus he carefully distinguished both the federal occupation of Louisiana in 1875, and the original U.S. acquisition of the territory in 1803, from the long prior history of Louisiana's changing imperial masters. "Each building" in New Orleans "which confesses to an hundred years has memories of foreign domination hovering about it," he noted, implying that U.S. control of the territory since 1803 had involved the opposite of "foreign domination"—had involved Louisiana's domestic American liberation.[63]

Most important, the American-colonial-to-U.S.-liberated trajectory King recounted provided a template for further expansion into an evergreater South. As he summed up:

> To-day a tract of country which, two years ago, was comparatively as unknown to the masses of our citizens as Central Africa, is now easily accessible . . . and in a few years the outside world will suddenly discover that a journey to Mexico is no more difficult than the present journey to New Orleans, and that new lands and territories have been opened up to speculation and profit as if by magic.[64]

King's "expedition" and its "discovery" of *The Great South* played a central role in this inexorable southward expansion: rehearsing the global context of the nation's domestic possession of Louisiana became the first step in conceptualizing an expansion of the United States beyond territorial contiguity—an expansion that, nonetheless, could be distinguished signally from competing European designs on the peripheries of the globe. Like the "local color" fiction that flooded U.S. journals after his series appeared, King's intensive focus on the *locality* of Louisiana and its past allowed for a rehearsal of U.S. conquest as liberation—a story of how acquiring and administering previously colonial, semitropical territories had always been a part of U.S. history.

Thus while the Reconstruction South evoked a transatlantic transposition of the stature and practices of European empire, it also allowed for a hemispheric American exception from those practices. To the extent that the southern states under Reconstruction appeared to U.S. readers as conquered provinces, they constituted a sort of domestic Africa for the United States, a site upon which the nation proved its civilizing might equal to that of Europe. But to the extent that the southern states appeared as temporarily alienated, intrinsic parts of the nation—soon to reassume full standing as constitutive members of the Union—their Reconstruction attested to the role of the United States as anti-imperial liberator of the formerly colonial American hemisphere. In this sense, the Reconstruction South began to appear as a point of privileged and intimate access to Spanish America, as well as to other underdeveloped sites around the globe. When U.S. writers and readers saw their Reconstruction South as not only a conquered territory, but also an inherent part of their nation, they claimed as national heritage the shared inter-American experiences of colonization, slavery, defeat, occupation, and—improbably—resistance to Yankee (Yanqui) imperialism. From King's travel series to the so-called "local color" fiction that closely followed it, writing about the Reconstruction South fostered the development of stories about a projected U.S. empire that would be exceptional for its self-critical capacity, its empathy born of shared experience with those peoples it would dominate.

CHAPTER TEN

The Glory of Disaster

Romance and poetry, like ivy, lichens, and wall-flowers, need
Ruin to make them grow.

—Nathaniel Hawthorne, Preface to *The Marble Faun* (1860)

F
ROM "THE LITERARY POINT OF VIEW" of U.S. cultural nationalism, the ruin wreaked in the former Confederate States during
the war wasn't all bad. In fact, on the cusp of the secession crisis,
in 1860, Nathaniel Hawthorne had seemed almost to wish for more
"Ruin" in America, as he explained that he had had to set his most recent
novel in the Old World because of the lack of a historical atmosphere of
tragedy and disaster in the United States:

> No author, without a trial, can conceive of the difficulty of writing a Ro-
> mance about a country where there is no shadow, no antiquity, no mystery,
> no picturesque and gloomy wrong, nor anything but a common-place pros-
> perity, in broad and simple daylight, as is happily the case with my dear na-
> tive land. It will be very long, I trust, before romance-writers may find
> congenial and easily handled themes in either the annals of our stalwart Re-
> public, or in any characteristic and probable events of our individual lives.[1]

Hawthorne seemed to flaunt the act of repression in these lines. He had,
after all, spent most of his antebellum career writing about "picturesque
and gloomy wrongs" in colonial New England. And what reader in 1860
could credit his claimed "trust" that "our stalwart Republic" could not
possibly face imminent peril? Instead, on the eve of the rending of the republic, Hawthorne was offering a glance at the aesthetically generative
potential of destruction.

By war's end, audiences in the victorious North seemed to agree with
Hawthorne's assessment of the cultural value of disaster, as a market
quickly blossomed for representations of the ruins of the former Confederacy. From textual accounts like J. T. Trowbridge's *Tour Through the
Desolated States* (1866), to the many photographic images of ruins produced for viewing as entertainment, the first repossession of the South in
national culture after Appomattox involved assimilating the sheer destruction the United States military had wrought upon its enemy. With

Figure 19. "Charleston, S.C., 1865, Ruin." Left half of a commercial image designed for viewing with a stereoscope. Civil War Glass Negative Collection, Prints and Photographs Division, Library of Congress (LC-B811-3100).

these ruins, the United States had not simply proved its unparalleled might in warfare, "certif[ying] to earth a new imperial race." More, the nation had created a parallel in its landscape to classical antiquity. It had created, almost overnight, a deep past organized around a tragic episode of rupture, a past flaunted on the very face of its land.

Reconstruction as "Fool's Errand," ca. 1879

The Reconstruction South was defined from the very beginning by this ruin—it is, after all, destruction that necessitates reconstruction—but ruin quickly came to typify the *project* of Reconstruction itself by the mid-1870s. This project, the remaking of slave society into an order that guaranteed the equal rights before the law of all men, was arguably the most important and intensive reform ever undertaken in national life— and yet, the phrase "the failure of Reconstruction" comes to us today as pat, unavoidable, almost cliché. It is startling, indeed, to recognize how early this judgment on the project of Reconstruction was rendered in U.S. letters. Even the first novel on the topic—*A Fool's Errand, by One of the Fools* (1879)—bore a bitterly dismissive title that belied the passionate commitment to the best goals of Reconstruction held by its author. Ohioan Albion W. Tourgée had served for six years as a superior court judge in the Second Military District (North Carolina), and he was a staunch defender of equity for the recently emancipated people there.[2] When he created his fictional account of Reconstruction, though—for many years, the best-selling account—Tourgée produced a novel focused on the travails of the Reconstructor himself, rather than on the problems of the occupied southern states and their people. That this focus bears much in common with the British imperial writing of the day is borne out by reading the novel, which follows Tourgée's Michigan-born protago- nist, Comfort Servosse, through the various indignities he encounters while seeking both to develop the "subjugated territory" and to uplift "the African population" of the Reconstruction South.[3]

But in marked contrast to novels from the previous decade, such as De- Forest's *Miss Ravenel's Conversion from Secession to Loyalty,* Tourgée's plot template is not victory, but defeat. His hero proves quite incapable of "converting" any Reconstruction South character or institution into regenerate form; to the contrary, the Reconstruction South does the Re- constructor himself in. In the final pages, Tourgée dispatches Servosse by way of a sudden tropical illness and then employs a "poor white" local character to eulogize the Reconstructor as a martyr to his own cause. "There, son, . . . is where they laid away our Carpet-Bagger," the character memorializes colorfully, sounding, but for the dialect, rather as though he has been imported from a Walter Scott novel. "I want you should remember his grave; for he was a powerful good friend to your father, and the common people like him . . . The failure of what we called Reconstruction hurt him mighty bad, an', to my mind, hed more ter du with takin' him off than the fever."[4]

By 1879, the eulogy already seemed the appropriate form for dealing with Tourgée's subject, for with the end of Congressional Reconstruction in 1877, the Reconstruction South had become a historical rather than a contemporary construct for national literature. Before any histories of the period had been written, Tourgée's popular novel ensconced the just-ended project of remaking slave society as having been, from its start, the hapless "fool's errand" of a doomed idealism. With this characterization, he registered—quite earlier than did the political discourse of his day—the extent to which the Reconstruction South had been the site of an irresolvable collision between national ideals and national reality. On its terrain, the most cherished ideals of the republic—human equality, social justice, individual freedom—had run head-on into "the incorporation of America": the great era of capitalist consolidation in the United States, which had been made possible by the economic expansion of the war itself.[5]

> Two quite distinct but persistently undifferentiated visions of the future dominated the triumphant North after the war. One was the prolongation of Puritan idealism, transformed by the frontier into a theory of universal democracy . . . The other trend was entirely different and is confused with the democratic ideal because the two ideals lay confused in so many individual minds. This was the development of industry in America and of a new industrial philosophy.
>
> The new industry had a vision not of work but of wealth; not of planned accomplishment, but of power. It became the most conscienceless, unmoral system of industry which the world has experienced. It went with ruthless indifference towards waste, death, ugliness and disaster, and yet reared the most stupendous machine for the efficient organization of work which the world has ever seen.[6]

Thus W. E. B. Du Bois, assessing the broader national context of Reconstruction in his great 1935 history of the era.

The major historians of our own time have tended to agree with DuBois that, after the war, the emancipated people of the southern states "lost democracy in a new and vaster slavery," and that securing the rights of those workers would have required massive governmental land reform to transform the basic economic structure of the former Confederate states.[7]

It seems not even within the realm of counterfactual plausibility, though, to imagine that the same federal government that underwrote the rise of robber barons and the Gilded Age in its north and west might simultaneously have carried out the Bolshevik Revolution in its south. The yearning for land redistribution in the Reconstruction South to the workers who had improved it for generations—the aspiration for "forty acres and a mule" to be allotted to each emancipated person—remained "inaudible and illegible within the prevailing formulas of political rationality" because it was "so wildly utopian and derelict to capitalism."[8] The sort of sweeping, radical reformation of the U.S. economic system that would have enabled Reconstruction to achieve its ideals was never seriously on the table for its architects. Thus, the "fool's errand" of the project for sincere idealists like Tourgée: the nation demanded that Reconstruction produce "bricks without straw" (the title of Tourgée's best-selling 1880 sequel), that it conjure justice for the emancipated people of the South without the material commitment that would make such justice possible.

The sort of postwar property redistribution that *did* seem plausible to writers contemplating the Reconstruction South in the late 1870s is epitomized by an autobiographical sketch that Harriet Beecher Stowe published in the *Atlantic Monthly* in 1879. "Our Florida Plantation," as its title suggests, proposed that the United States had kept the plantation system firmly in place in its Reconstruction South, and institutionalized reform simply by changing mastery from the hands of southern to northern elites. In just a few pages, Stowe revisited her experience of visiting two of her sons, "fine Yankee officers—Connecticut men," in Florida in 1867, where they were "working a cotton plantation of a thousand acres."[9] "The history of 'our plantation' so far had been briefly this," she explained at the outset:

> The year of the closing of our war, two captains of the Union army, who had been serving in Florida, had conceived the bright idea of hiring a plantation and making their fortunes in raising cotton . . . And here is a plantation which may be hired for a very reasonable sum, and negroes versed in the processes of culture on all hands asking for work. So the valiant ex-captains rented the plantation . . . the moment peace was declared.[10]

Here Stowe writes the "history" of a seamless transition from Slave South into Reconstruction South, a transition that preserves the basic economic system of labor organization and profitable commodity production. Stowe and her "practical New England" protagonists, upon investigating this territory they have acquired, find no need to change the situation of the formerly enslaved people on the plantation, for "the negro quarter was a regular village of well-built and comfortable little houses, speaking favorably for the humanity of the former masters." Nor is there cause to change their disciplined labor: "The old plantation *régime* was adopted, because they were accustomed to working in that way, and in no other." As in Tourgée's novel, the characters who undergo transformation and trials in Stowe's Reconstruction South sketch are not the emancipated people, but the emancipators themselves, a point Stowe highlights by terming the carpetbaggers' journey southward from Connecticut to Florida "that provoking middle passage."

While the basic economic structure of the old Slave South remains in place, Stowe locates the epochal transformation of her Reconstruction South in the shift from local to foreign rule. Though she writes with a few years of hindsight, the ideological thrust of her sketch nonetheless shares much with King's prospective *The Great South* of the mid-1870s, as she spends most of her pages establishing the incapacity for self-governance shared by the various segments of the local population. The former local ruling class, the deposed southern planters, have evaporated entirely from the scene. In keeping with the notion of the former Confederate states as "abandoned lands," Stowe devotes a significant proportion of her sketch to reading the ruins of the "big house" occupied by her Reconstructors, searching for clues to the now-extinct people who formerly lived there. In the manner of an archeologist comparing physical evidence to local legend, she determines that although "the plantation, we were told, had been in former days the leading one in Florida," its local owners had never achieved a level of civilization that surpassed their peripheral situation. "There was no evidence of aesthetic taste in any of the grounds," she finds, and "hearing the tales of former grandeur, we could not but wonder at the primitive coarseness and ugliness of the construction of the house we lived in."[11]

After establishing the "barbarism" of the former masters of the plantation, Stowe introduces a second southern population type in a "very characteristic and rather picturesque personage whom we shall call Long John." This class of southerner Stowe typifies by his "wholly unintelligible . . . cracker dialect," and, essentially, his approach to economic transactions, which "[could not be] more unlike a Northerner's ideas of property management."[12] Clearly this category of local resident is unfitted not only for home rule, but also for acquiring the abandoned lands of the evaporated master class. And when Stowe at last turns her attention to the formerly enslaved workers still providing all of the labor upon which "our Florida plantation" runs, she seems to revise her best-known creation of a quarter-century earlier in a frankly regressive direction.

> We have before us now a picture of our "Tom," a great Hercules of a fellow, lying on the ground in his nooning, with the spelling-book before him, and the sweat starting out on his forehead, as he puzzled his patient way through the *ab, ib, ob,*—cabalistic signs on the lowest door step of knowledge.

This is the unkindest blow in Stowe's brief "history" of the Reconstruction South: her metamorphosis of "our 'Tom'"—surely there might have been another name?—from the fully literate theologian, patriarch, and community leader of her 1852 novel, into a prone, illiterate figure plainly suited only for physical labor. Stowe had introduced the 1852 Tom in the first chapter of *Uncle Tom's Cabin* as already "running" the plantation upon which he was enslaved "like a clock." From the vantage of her Reconstruction South, such a proposition is unimaginable—or, at least, it is against the interests of her Reconstructor protagonists.

Those interests—"making their fortunes in raising cotton"—seem to give Stowe increasing pause as her sketch progresses. Halfway through, she notes that "the whole establishment" of her protagonists at their plantation is "like a lair of banditti rather than a home for settled Christian people." To the image of her Reconstructors as roving thieves, she adds the disturbing resonance of an occupying army still in a state of war. "The plantation house, be it known, was yet unfurnished, except as a soldier's bivouac"; the womenfolk "pitch our housekeeping tent," and the entire group are continually concerned to "reinforce their numbers and capital." Stowe's figures register uneasiness with the collision of ideals and material realities in the project of Reconstruction, but she ultimately resolves that uneasiness with an oddly assuaging failure *ex machina*. In the last paragraphs, the first crop of cotton raised by these "practical New England farmers" on "our Florida plantation" suddenly is destroyed by an "Army Worm" infestation:

> We made in all, perhaps, two bales of cotton! Our scheme was over, our firm dissolved . . . But as at the bottom of Pandora's box there was a grain of comfort, so there was in ours. Though *we* made nothing, and lost all we invested, our hands were all duly paid, scot and lot,—in many cases with the first money they ever earned, and it gave them a start in life. That has been the one consoling reflection when we recall the tragedy of *Our Plantation*.[13]

In this conclusion may be glimpsed the remarkable ideological utility of the requisite failure of Reconstruction, the inevitable "tragedy of *Our Plantation*." The material aims of the Reconstructors—making a fortune raising cotton—are thwarted by an impartial (or, perhaps, just) Fate, and as this happens their places as the tragic heroes of the story are cemented. Suddenly the repressed idealistic aims of Reconstruction return to the fore, as Stowe adjudges the only beneficiaries of the failed capitalist "adventure" to be the local population who have been occupied, particularly the formerly enslaved plantation hands. As an integral part of the tragic failure of the Reconstructors—"though *we* made nothing, and lost all we invested"—the passive local population are "all duly paid" for their unasked participation in "the tragedy of *Our Plantation*."

Bolstered by this moral triumph, and assuaged by the proclaimed cost to themselves, Stowe's Reconstructors do not abandon their "tragic" imperial project. Rather, they *expand* it, taking it still farther south. "As for us, we and ours bought an orange grove on the other side of the St. John's," she concludes, using every form of the first person plural to consolidate the sense of her protagonists as an embattled, exogenous, civilizationist vanguard. These metropolitan U.S. Reconstructors are bound to a self-immolating and impossible, yet ever-enlarging uplift mission, in the underdeveloped lands and amongst the barbaric peoples of the semitropical, commodity-producing periphery. The civilizing mission of the Reconstruction South is one in which material gain could not possibly compensate for the selfless and costly exertions of occupation. Two decades before Rudyard Kipling invited the United States to join Britain in assuming "the white man's burden" of global empire, Stowe's account of "the tragedy of *Our Plantation*" limned a similar ideological register.

The Global Scope of Local Color

Yet Stowe's account of "Our Florida Plantation" located the recognizably imperial register on ground that bore a politically exceptional relation to the nation. Reconstruction Florida, as she recalled it in the sketch, circa 1867, was characterized by foreign rather than domestic rule; by 1879, though, the state of Florida had been fully restored to the Union. From the post-Reconstruction vantage of the sketch, Stowe's account perhaps looked less like contemporaneous British imperial writing and more like the most popular form of late-nineteenth-century U.S. fiction.[14] "Local color" fiction, as it was termed, usually was produced in short sketches or stories like Stowe's, rather than in book-length prose narrative; its métier was the vignette rather than the complex and developing social or psychological scene of the novel. Like "Our Florida Plantation," "local color" stories were structured around the encounter of a metropolitan narrator with a peripheral territory that had until recently been closed to the outside world. Because of this defining metropolitan/peripheral tension, though, "local color" fiction exploded the notion of the "local" that was its ostensible subject. Instead, it dramatized the incorporation of America, the opening of the hinterlands of the nation to capital and to standardization.[15] The metropolitan narrator, acting as interpreter of the "local" site for putatively metropolitan readers, further highlighted the geographical unevenness of U.S. literary production.[16] With its very form producing the "local" for consumption by a supralocal audience, "local color" fiction necessarily exceeded its geographical designation.[17]

The metropolitan/peripheral counterpoint in "local color" fiction could have worked with settings in any hinterland region of the United States, and indeed authors made forays into the genre from locations ranging from the West to the Middle West to rural New England as the century neared its close.[18] Nevertheless, the earliest portrayed, most often represented, and most popular locality for "local color" fiction was, hands down, the South—for the Reconstruction South crossed and re-crossed the border between domestic and foreign. By setting stories there, writers melded concerns about national standardization with increasingly aggressive visions of U.S. power projected outward, from a metropolitan center into a peripheral world.

The term "local color" itself originated in the broader Western impe-rial discourse invested in maintaining and relating hierarchies based upon geographical peripherality *(locality)* and racial categorization *(color)*. When the term emerged in U.S. letters in the late 1870s, it characterized the Reconstruction South by denoting a mutually constitutive narrative process of peripheralization and racialization. In a very early usage in the *Atlantic Monthly,* for instance, a description of regional peculiarity in matters of dialect, labor organization, and population shaded easily into an account of racial intermixing or indeterminacy: "What gives an oddly contrasting local color to this dignified speech [of the Southern ladies] is the pronunciation of certain words,—a pronunciation probably caught in childhood from negro nurses."[19] Here a local deviance from a metro-politan standard of speech was posited as also, inextricably, a deviance in color from an Anglo-Saxon norm.[20] In a similar vein, Joel Chandler Har-ris remarked, in the 1880 introduction to his first volume of exception-ally popular "Uncle Remus" tales, that these folk tales were both of African origin and "a part of the domestic history of every Southern family"—thereby equating the "local" distinctiveness of southern cul-ture with the "color" distinctiveness derived from African as opposed to Anglo-Saxon genealogy.[21] Recovering the initial conceptualization of "local color" within the ideological framework of Western empire helps to explain why this writing—often thought of as xenophobic and backward-looking—so perfectly spoke to the expansionist and forward-marching temper of the times.

The breakthrough writer of "local color" fiction was George Washington Cable, a native Louisianan, Confederate veteran, and progressive local newspaperman who rapidly became the most-read U.S. fiction writer of the 1870s and 1880s. In the midst of Reconstruction, and as Josiah Holland of *Scribner's Monthly* was just beginning to plot his *Great South* series, Cable exhorted readers of the New Orleans *Times-Picayune* to think of their local culture as an exploitable and exportable resource, analogous to their land, labor, and crops. With recourse to the familiar African analogy, he proposed that Louisiana's "peculiar" history would be excavated, refined, and converted into the stuff of metropolitan literature: "Here lie the gems, like those new diamonds in Africa, right on top of the ground. The mines are virgin."[22] Foretelling the extraction of local culture—and the production of regional/racial difference—that would soon become the central obsession of U.S. literature, Cable encouraged Louisianans themselves to capitalize upon the exoticist appetites of the metropolitan market.

In his ascent to national literary stardom, though, Cable was cast less in the role of the miner of gems, and more in the role of the extracted diamond itself. Soon after writing the newspaper column quoted above, the aspiring writer himself became the most famous "discovery" of Edward King's *Great South* expedition.[23] His first stories appeared in *Scribner's Monthly* alongside King's Reconstruction South series installments, as nuggets of the southern richness King described served up to metropolitan readers by subscription. During the zenith of his popularity, Cable showed himself equally able to act as a cultivated guide to those metropolitan readers and to play the object of their exoticism. On his "Twins of Genius" tour with Mark Twain in the winter of 1884–1885, Cable drew most acclaim from reviewers not for the fiction he read but for his performance of Creole dialect and, especially, for his performance of "African Creole songs" and "Negro spirituals," during which he often accompanied himself with a banjo.[24] A new popular notion of a "Southern author" was coming into being in U.S. letters, and it seemed to be inextricable from the expectations of an entertaining, consumable "Southernness" that had evolved on metropolitan minstrel stages.[25]

Despite operating within this overdetermined field, the stories Cable published in *Scribner's Monthly* in the 1870s generated a rapture among metropolitan literary critics and readers that set the expectations for what a Reconstruction South story should entail. Against King's encyclopedic account, Cable's "local color" stories operated within an extremely limited setting: a markedly liminal version of New Orleans. Cable stressed the geographical liminality of his home city, its situation at the southernmost limit of the U.S. but at the center of the American hemisphere. He also revisited a particular moment of temporal liminality in its history: the early-nineteenth-century transition from European imperial rule to U.S. acquisition. The opening sentence of "Jean-Ah Poquelin," a much-remarked 1875 story in *Scribner's* that set the standard for "local color" fiction, demonstrates Cable's typical historical orientation of the reader:

> In the first decade of the present century, when the newly established American Government was the most hateful thing in Louisiana—when the Creoles were still kicking at such vile innovations as the trial by jury, American dances, anti-smuggling laws, and the printing of the Governor's proclamation in English—when the Anglo-American flood that was presently to burst in a crevasse of immigration upon the delta had thus far been felt only as slippery seepage which made the Creole tremble for his footing—there stood . . . an old colonial plantation-house half in ruin.[26]

Cable's historical setting appears overtly isolated in time and space, designed to produce nostalgia by documenting a regionally specific way of life that already has been lost to the standardizations of modernity. It is easy to perceive, though, that he uses this setting in the past to imply an analogue for his present, routing the postbellum conflicts between the deposed local elites of Louisiana and the "newly established American Government" of the state under Reconstruction through a story about the original U.S. acquisition of the territory after 1803.[27] Most important, his setting in the past directs the reader's gaze forward, beyond the soon-to-end Congressional Reconstruction of Louisiana and toward future occupations and administrations of underdeveloped, tropical territory beyond the U.S. borders.

The opening sentences of "Jean-Ah Poquelin" alone realize Edward King's imperial imperative of improvement, cast into an inexorable narrative trajectory. A requisite background for the plot is the "old colonial plantation-house half in ruin," a reminder that the colonial system of plantation production, for which tropical America was valued during the first centuries of European New World empire, has become outmoded, no longer profitable or competitive in the modernizing world economy.[28] Hand in hand with this note of changing economic exigency comes the certainty that the "Creole" locals of tropical America are not able to transform their own colonial way of life in order to participate in historical progress and develop their own territory:

> The indigo fields and vats of Louisiana had been generally abandoned as unremunerative. Certain enterprising men had substituted the culture of sugar; but while [his brother] was too apathetic to take so active a course, [Jean

Poquelin] saw larger, and, at that time, equally respectable profits, first in smuggling, and later in the African slave trade. What harm could he see in it?[29]

"Certain enterprising men"—the vanguard of the coming "Anglo-American flood" of immigration from the North—will transform the defunct colonial means of production in order to render local resources again profitable under changing economic conditions. But Cable's Creoles, like King's Reconstruction South "natives," "lack the vigor and the enterprise needed to seize upon and improve their fine advantages."[30] While his brother does nothing at all, Cable's title character—rather like a Confederate partisan—perversely invests himself even more fully in the passing colonial order by outfitting himself for the last days of the Atlantic slave trade. More disturbing than his colonial lack of economic foresight is his colonial lack of metropolitan ethics—his degenerate inability, diagnosed by Cable's rhetorical question, to "see harm in" his course of action.

Precisely because of their perverse inability or unwillingness to evolve with the changing times, Cable's colorful local characters enter his stories mired in a nonproductive way of life, one marked by repetitive compulsions, mental and physical disease, and decay. On Jean Poquelin's last voyage to Africa, his brother contracts leprosy; when the two return to their rotting plantation, Jean seals off his land and allows it to revert to swamp in order to hide the fact that his brother—now equally rotting—is illegally concealed there rather than banished to the "*Terre aux Lépreux.*" Thus one of the Poquelin brothers is rendered a social outcast, and the other a walking corpse, by their attempt at slave-trading; by the second page of the story they have come to embody and perpetually live out the evil excesses of the colonial order that produced them. The Creoles achieve no expiation or redemption from their tropical stasis, though; it is only the U.S. takeover of Louisiana that advances the plot of the story, interrupting what would otherwise become a stagnant cycle. The "newly established American government" intervenes in Jean's willful neglect of his land by building a new municipal street through his plantation, draining his swamp, and filling in the canal that cuts his plantation off from the growing New Orleans suburbs that surround it. Despite Poquelin's colorful "curses upon the United States, the President, the Territory of Orleans, Congress, the Governor and all his subordinates,"[31] this forced development finally exposes the secret of his brother's whereabouts and his own strange behavior, and brings the narrative to its resolution.

Set in the early national past, Cable's Creole stories are investigations of the modern Reconstruction project writ large: of U.S. intervention, in the name of progress, into underdeveloped, foreign territory—even when such intervention is vehemently opposed by the "native inhabitants." Structurally, the stories present the U.S. takeover of Louisiana as a narrative inevitability, given the characterological stasis of the locals; without the U.S. occupation, there simply would be no plot. Yet this means that Cable necessarily casts "les Américains"—the metropolitan analogues to his own intended readers—in the role of invaders and occupiers who orchestrate both the political disempowerment and the wholesale dispossession of his Creoles. Brilliantly, though, he soft-pedals the new (and not altogether flattering) role into which he casts U.S. readers by bringing cultural expropriation, rather than material expropriation, to the fore in his stories. While "the fertile birthright arpents . . . tricked away from dull colonial Esaus by their blue-eyed brethren of the North" remain his essential background, Cable presents the expropriation of the Poquelin *marais* by bureaucratic U.S. administrators as primarily a cultural, rather than material, loss to the native Creoles—and primarily a cultural, rather than material, gain to the United States.[32] As the "new American government" takes control of Jean Poquelin's land, its enforced improvements crowd out the colorful local tales about ghosts, haunting, witchery, and murder that have arisen to explain Poquelin's reclusion and his brother's disappearance. These endangered tales, themselves artifacts of "local color," are, of course, precisely what Cable's story purports to mine, refine, and deliver to its U.S. readers; indeed, it is the destruction of the mystery undergirding the local lore that provides the rewarding resolution of Cable's plot. Cable thus aligns his delivery of the locally colored story to metropolitan readers with the delivery to them of other sorts of Reconstruction South treasures—cotton, oranges, heart-pine flooring. By reading Cable's Creole stories, the readers of *Scribner's Monthly* participate in Southern expropriation in a cultural register; at the same time, they register Reconstruction as a destructive project. To improve the locality, to bring it into modernity, is to destroy what makes it distinct.

Herein lies the powerful relevance of a "local color" story like "Jean-Ah Poquelin" in the late 1870s: it places metropolitan readers in the rather comfortable position of both claiming and deploring U.S. dominion over peripheral territory and the people who inhabit it. When the title character expires, along with the tales and rumors that have sheltered him, Cable cedes narration of the story to its only substantial U.S. character: a minor development official called "little White." "Little White"—nonthreatening, though morally and racially superior to the Creoles, as his name suggests—creates an ad hoc funeral for Poquelin and becomes the author of the exposé of his secret. "'Gentlemen,'" he declaims, "'here come the last remains of Jean Marie Poquelin, a better man, I'm afraid, with all his sins, than of you will ever be.'"[33] The stagy valedictory to an anachronistic native whose human value can be recognized only after his demise becomes quite typical of later "local color" fiction; with it Cable again puts metropolitan readers at center stage, offering them an elegiac mode for expressing the pain of being in civilization's vanguard. He allows his readers simultaneously to remember and to forget that the capture of the southern legend that entertains them requires the destruction of its southern protagonist—and that the acquisition of the southern tale cannot be extricated from the takeover of southern land by "little White's" "Building and Improvement Company."

Cable's "local color" stories transformed the Reconstruction South, making an episode of recent national history into a widely applicable paradigm for U.S. empire. As southern planters became Creoles, and the antebellum focus on the upper southern states shifted to the rim of the Gulf of Mexico, Cable recast the Reconstruction South in an explicitly global context. His many laudatory critics praised him for creating stories with geographic resonance that extended far beyond the bounds of Reconstruction Louisiana. The author of a *Harper's* lead essay on "The Recent Movement in Southern Literature," for instance, found a protoimperial pedagogical function in the stories: Cable was "the recognized master over the enchanted, semitropical realm, beautiful with flowers, yet marked by the trail of the serpent." His Creole stories, in other words, taught not only the Edenic promise of underdeveloped, fertile lands, but also their fallen stature—the original sin of their coloniality and, implicitly, the possibility of their redemption with proper management by the United States.[34] In another vein, Lafcadio Hearn, the essayist who would become the preeminent U.S. Orientalist of the later nineteenth century, attributed to his reading of "Jean-Ah Poquelin" a wholesale awakening of his desire for the global exotic; in an 1883 essay, he claimed that "that strange little tale . . . and its exotic picturesqueness had considerably influenced my anticipations . . . and prepared me to idealize everything peculiar and semi-tropical that I might see."[35]

The assurance of Cable's contemporaries that his "local color" stories were globally exportable may be traced to his pitching of the conflict between southern natives and their U.S. administrators as one between "Creoles" and national citizens. Cable refused the biracial approach to the Reconstruction South typical of metropolitan writings on the subject, as well as its three-pronged (planter-cracker-freedman) variant. Instead of divvying up the subjects of Reconstruction into competing groups jockeying for the favor of their metropolitan masters, Cable—like the "domestic Africa" writers who immediately preceded him—foregrounded the shared, cohesive southernness of the Louisianan population. By focusing on southerners as Creoles in the post-Louisiana-Purchase days of the early nineteenth century, he defined southernness as, fundamentally, a subordinate colonial stature in the imperial world order. Cable's Louisianans share in common only their colonial American nativity; according to other markers of cultural belonging, they are wildly indeterminate, of no extricable linguistic, national, or racial origin. His Creoles are always multilingual—though, significantly, never fluent speakers of standard English—and they are of hopelessly tangled genealogy.[36] French and Spanish, African and Choctaw heritages intermingle inseparably, as in the story "Belles Demoiselles Plantation" (1873), in which the lineal descendants of a seventeenth-century French nobleman have assumed, after a century of colonial American life, the various names De Charleu, De Carlos, and "Injun Charlie."[37]

The hybridity of Cable's Creoles bore subversive potential in an increasingly white-supremacist nation, for his characters prove racially as well as nationally indeterminate.[38] The De Charleu descendant referred to as "half-caste" on one page becomes "plainly a dark white man" on the next. Likewise, the title character of " 'Tite Poulette" (1874) is at the beginning of the story the daughter of a woman "[y]ou would hardly have thought of . . . as being 'colored'"; at the end of the story instead the "Spaniards' daughter"; and throughout an epitome of Creole beauty, "her great black eyes made tender by their sweeping lashes, the faintest tint of color in her Southern cheek."[39] Yet the potentially revelatory racial politics of this Creole hybridity is undercut by its geopolitical liability. When Cable's fellow New Orleanians in the 1870s protested that he portrayed them as "ignobl[y] descen[ded] from the ill specimens of three races—Indian, African, and French prostitutes," they were of course betraying their own investment in white supremacy.[40] But they also were registering their understanding of the broader imperial order that white supremacy underpinned.[41] When Cable characterizes his Creoles as hybrid, he obviates the notion that an identifiable class of Southern elites exists to be dispossessed by U.S. rule.[42] While he records local preoccupations with caste, Cable implies that caste distinctions are simply another form of colorful local folklore, that a master class cannot be extricated from a slave class in Louisiana, nor a "white" (by Anglo-Saxonist standards) group of Creoles cordoned off from the heterogenous Reconstruction South population. His subsumption of "Southerner" under the aegis of "Creole" produces a popular version of the Reconstruction South that invites projections of U.S. empire.

Against the colonial hybridity of his Creoles, Cable's U.S. characters appear homogenous, coherent—natural imperial masters. They are monolingual anglophones to the point of comedy; they are unimpeachably "Anglo-Saxon" in descent. These linguistic and racial markers legitimate the political and military might of the United States in Cable's stories, even to the Creoles who resent that power. (Jean Poquelin himself concedes, at the height of his protest against U.S. incursion on his land: "'Mais, I know; we billong to Monsieur le Président.'") As "Creoles, Cubans, [colonial] Spaniards, St. Domingo refugees, and other loungers"— as "amigos . . . Creoles, Irishmen, and lovers"—Cable's southerners do not rule themselves, they have no coherent affiliation to another imperial nation, and thus they are entirely open to acquisition by the United States.[43] Locally colored, creolized Louisiana finally validates the imperial nationhood of the United States.[44] Poised on the edge of the Gulf of Mexico, Cable's enormously influential fiction offers the Reconstruction South as a stepping stone to U.S. occupation, intervention, and improvement further south, beyond the territorial contiguity of the national borders.

Soon after the sensational success of his stories in Scribner's made him a household name, Cable cannily assessed his own place in the world of U.S. letters: "I am a Creole myself."[45] As he knew, this was not a desirable position to occupy in the globally ascendant United States, and he used his unmatched fame as a southern writer over the subsequent decade to exhort residents of the southern states, particularly local elites, to throw off the locally colored—and necessarily subordinate—stature that his stories had done so much to institutionalize in national culture. Rather than romanticize their southernness and cherish their past, Cable urged people living in the post-Reconstruction southern states to embrace the modernization of their region: to do all they could to join the metropolis, to hasten the destruction of their local distinctiveness. Ironically, Cable couched even his arguments for local racial equality in the civilizationist language of empire. "The plantation idea is a semi-barbarism," he chided recalcitrant southern elites, while white supremacy (or "caste prejudice") is "an unmanly and inhuman tyranny" that should be sent "back to India and Africa."[46]

In a commencement address at the University of Mississippi in 1882, Cable warned students that to identify with a distinctive "South" was to choose to assume a subordinate status in the imperial order of the globe.

Instead, he exhorted the rising generation, they must pledge allegiance to the full stature of the metropolitan United States:

> I trust the time is not far away . . . when you shall say, "Southerners? South? New South? Sir, your words are not for us . . . We are Americans. Go you to Mexico. That is the New South. And make haste, friend, or they will push you on into South America, where we have reshipped the separate sort of books printed for the Southern market."[47]

Southerners must either become agents, or else remain subjects, of a rising U.S. empire. His Creole stories had held out the promise of delicate shading and hybrid variety, but in the evolution of national life after Reconstruction, Cable saw no middle ground.

The Uses of "Confederate Sympathy"

At the moment that the Reconstruction South became a historical setting for U.S. literature, it was fixed as a site of betrayal of the principles of the republic. Yet despite its identification with national failure and doom—indeed, *because* of that identification—the Reconstruction South became an astonishingly fertile imaginative location for writers in the United States. In the failure itself, in the ruin, writers from many different vantages found a new sort of national romance shadowed by tragedy and guilt, a national romance that would provide a powerful emotive register for conceptualizing the frank and rapid expansion of U.S. power beyond both the borders of the nation and the rubrics of the republic. Indeed, the complex pull of the Reconstruction South on U.S. letters was such that, by 1888, Albion Tourgée observed that national literature had "become not only southern in type, but distinctly Confederate in sympathy."[48] Tourgée had hardly become a "Redemptionist" in the decade since he published *A Fool's Errand;* to the contrary, he had continued to agitate for equal rights in the southern states and he would go on to provide a Supreme Court brief in support of Homer Plessy in 1896. Yet he did not perceive the growing "Confederate sympathy" in U.S. imaginative life to be a bad thing. Instead, he judged it a boon for national culture, proposing that the Reconstruction South had achieved its central cultural place in a different form from the one he had pioneered in his own first novel. Whereas the hero of *A Fool's Errand* had been the metropolitan agent of "'progress,'" Tourgée now proposed that the hero of the Reconstruction saga was the dispossessed southerner, white or black. And rather than a chronicle of the travails of the civilizing process, he asserted, the story of the conquest and reconstruction of its South should provide the literature of the nation with its formative episode of historical tragedy. The tragic story could be told equally well from the vantage of either the ex-slaves or the ex-masters of the south, Tourgée postulated ecumenically. On the one hand, since "[t]o the American Negro the past is only darkness replete with unimaginable horrors," his life "as a slave, freeman, and racial outcast offers undoubtedly the richest mine of romantic material that has opened to the English speaking novelist since the Wizard of the North discovered and depicted the common life of Scotland." On the other hand, since "[t]he level of Caucasian life at the South must hereafter be run from the benchline of the poor white, and there cannot be any leveling upward . . . the dominant class itself presents the accumulated pathos of a million abdications" around whom "will cluster the halo of romantic glory."[49]

Tourgée seemed to identify, once again presciently, what would come to serve as a corollary truism to the "failure of Reconstruction": the notion that "the South won the War" on the cultural front. His unconcern about this development—or, even, his enthusiasm for it—should remind us that in its first iteration, the turn to Reconstruction South romance in U.S. fiction was not engineered by former Confederates. Rather, as C. Vann Woodward pointed out fifty years ago, the most enduring of these romances in the 1870s and 1880s were penned by Herman Melville, Henry Adams, and Henry James—and Woodward adjudged the topical fixation among these metropolitan writers to be "one of the most curious phenomena in the intellectual history of the period." It seems plain that metropolitan writers and readers were producing and consuming Reconstruction South romances "Confederate in sympathy" not because they had been brainwashed by elites from the southern states, but because these stories were useful somehow for national culture more broadly. For his part, Woodward proposed that the tragic Reconstruction South heroes in these stories provided their metropolitan authors with a critical vantage on the Gilded Age—on "the mediocrity, the crassness, and the venality" that "had overtaken their own society since the Civil War."[50]

But these works formative in U.S. literary history do more than provide a resentful backward glance for metropolitans flummoxed by their own accelerating modernity. The books by Melville, Adams, and James also marshal "the South or the Southern hero" as a bridge to a new national future—as a vehicle for limning the conversion of the nation from soi-disant republic into self-confessed empire. Indeed, each writer presents a tragic, former Confederate character as an allegorical figure for the republic's demise. In Melville's epic poem *Clarel,* published in 1876, this figure is Ungar, a battle-scarred veteran met by a party of "pilgrims" from Europe and the postbellum United States touring the Holy Land.[51]

Upon encountering him, Rolfe, a protagonist in the poem often identified as a figure for Melville himself, asks himself, "Ay me, / Ay me, poor Freedom, can it be / A countryman's a refugee?" Then wondering "what maketh [Ungar] abroad to roam," Rolfe easily fills in possible answers: the war's destruction ("the immense charred solitudes / Once farms"), or the military occupation of Reconstruction ("misrule after strife? And dust / From victor heels"). Rolfe settles, though, on the transformation of the United States itself as the plausible cause for Ungar's "self-exile"; the ex-Confederate must be filled with "disgust / For times when honor's out of date / And serveth but to alienate." Rolfe then concludes that Ungar's expatriated, "refugee" status proves that the promise of the exceptional American republic has expired and that the United States has chosen the way of European tyranny:

> Oh, but it yields a thought that smarts,
> To note this man. Our New World bold
> Had fain improved upon the Old;
> But the hemispheres are counterparts.[52]

Similarly, Adams's *Democracy: An American Novel* (1880) asks readers to consider the Virginian John Carrington as a "type" that combines the "idea of General Washington restored to us in his prime"—a figurehead of the original republican ideal—with the stature of being "a traitor" to the present-day United States. Faced with the paradox of Carrington, Adams's protagonist Madeleine Lightfoot Lee—herself a hybrid of North and South "more often blue than gray"—bemoans the fallen stature of the postbellum nation, asking, "Why do I feel unclean when I look at Mount Vernon?"[53] Not to be outdone, James introduces Basil Ransom, the "most important personage" in his novel *The Bostonians* (1885–1886), thus:

> The young man looked poor—as poor as a young man could look who had such a fine head and such magnificent eyes . . . These things, the eyes especially, with their smouldering fire, might have indicated that he was to be a great American statesman; or, on the other hand, they might simply have proved that he came from Carolina or Alabama. He came, in fact, from Mississippi.

To be marked for "a great American statesman" in the republican line— to possess "a head to be seen . . . on some judicial bench or political platform, or even on a bronze medal"—is synonymous, James posits, with a southern origin. And thus in the age of Reconstruction, republican statesmanship is, like young Ransom himself, "blighted," "ruined," and "without prospect."[54]

These early Reconstruction South romances do not simply use the tragic Confederate characters to figure the expatriation, marginalization, and shutting out of the ideals of the republic from the postbellum nation. They also put forth their stories of trauma and disillusionment as a distinctly American register for stepping into the stature of empire. It is no accident that both Melville's "pilgrims" and Adams's protagonist Madeleine Lee end up on the stomping grounds of the Crusades, at the origin point of Western empire. Only their tragic "Confederate sympathy," their melancholic nihilism, preserves a kernel of New World exceptionalism in their embrace of a very Old World global role. Working as an imperial mercenary near Bethlehem, Ungar is approached by a monk who, noting the "favorable frame . . . within the soldier's thought," remarks to him: "'True sign you bear: your sword's a cross.'" Ungar assents—"''Tis true; / A cross, it is a cross,' he said": his taking up of arms on foreign soil, against the local people, is actually a martyr's burden.[55] In a not-unrelated vein, when Adams's Madeleine Lee gives up on finding republican virtue in Reconstruction-era Washington, her next stop is the Holy Land as well. In the last lines of his last chapter, though, Adams indicates that she will turn abroad as an almost-suicidal nihilist rather than a triumphant imperialist.

> "I want to go to Egypt," said Madeleine, still smiling faintly; "democracy has shaken my nerves to pieces. Oh, what rest it would be to live in the Great Pyramid and look out for ever at the polar star!"[56]

These first, most important Reconstruction South romances provide the emotive backstory for an exceptionalist idea of U.S. empire. Adams even records the deployment of sympathetic Confederates as a foreign policy strategy in Washington: when the assistant secretary of state needs to appoint "a counsel to the Mexican claims-commission"—the body for hearing Mexican grievances against the United States—he taps Carrington, noting, "We want a Southern man." Void as he is of Union triumphalism, the defeated Reconstruction South hero already appears, in the late 1870s, a peculiarly effective imperial functionary.[57] In the power struggle that James figures as a romance plot in *The Bostonians,* on the other hand, the taciturn and dispossessed southerner Ransom faces off against his rival, Olive Chancellor, who serves as a figure for Old World empire.[58] (James introduces her with a description that foretells one of Cecil Rhodes's most famous statements: "She would reform the solar system if she could get hold of it."[59]) Provoked by Chancellor's feminized and thus (to James) unnatural bid for power over the weak and unprotected maiden in question, Ransom ultimately carries the maiden off—as his name has indicated from the outset he will do. Given his dispossession against Chancellor's great wealth, James's Reconstruction South hero is simply required by his circumstances to loose his New World, new kind of "muscular force"—even though it leads, in the memorable last words of the novel, to "a union so far from brilliant."

It is this emotive story about a desparate, nihilistic embrace of empire that so captivated Tourgée as he considered "The South as a Field for Fiction" in 1888. Finding a ground for national tragedy in the Reconstruction South was essential for U.S. literature, he proposed, not only because tragedy is the stuff of great art ("The ills of fate, irreparable misfortune, untoward but unavoidable destiny: these are the things that make for enduring fame"); but also, and more important, because a tragic past ennobles a nation: "The brave but unfortunate reap always the richest measure of immortality." A U.S. national mythology that claimed its defeat and occupation of its South as its own would stake out a place for the nation in "the epoch of romance"—would canonize its people as "glorified by disaster."[60]

Eleven years after the end of Reconstruction, Tourgée argued that the most valuable resource still to be extracted by the U.S. from its southern states was not King's gold and coal, not Cable's local history and legend, but instead the distinctive experience of *being reconstructed*. With his language of mines, fields, discovery, development, and "the almost unparalleled richness of Southern life," Tourgée exhorted his metropolitan readers, poised on the threshold of empire, to expropriate the defeat and occupation of the former Confederate states as the central tragic episode of national life. "[A] vigorous people," Tourgée wrote, channeling the language of Anglo-Saxonist expansionism, "demand a vigorous literature."[61] Placing the humiliated Reconstruction South at the center of that literature would enable the nation's outward projection of coercion and force—precisely by allowing U.S. readers to feel themselves the empathetic, self-critical, and righteous founding victims of their own nation's power.

CHAPTER ELEVEN

Internal Islands and the American Scene, 1898–1905

The "other side" has not been represented by one who "lives
there."

> —A Black Woman of the South [Anna Julia Cooper], *A Voice
> from the South* (1892)

N JUST A FEW YEARS at the turn of the twentieth century, the Reconstruction South was institutionalized in U.S. culture in the
form that is still familiar to us today. In place of the "transatlantic
Africa" of the 1860s, or the locally colored Creole zone of the 1870s, a
rigidly biracial story of the Reconstruction South took hold, rapidly becoming so dominant as to admit of almost no alternative interpretation.
This story pitted black and white southerners against one another as its
major antagonists, vying for the soul of the United States. It held the
claims of these opposed parties upon the nation—their claims to full citizenship, equal rights before the law, and participation in government—
to be mutually exclusive. This story of the Reconstruction South asked
U.S. readers, who implicitly stood above the fray, to choose between the
ostensibly opposed interests of black and white southerners.[1] Were black
or white southerners properly citizens of the nation? And were black or
white southerners properly its subjects? Retelling the Reconstruction
South in this form, a generation after the end of Reconstruction itself, became a way of gauging, explaining, and historicizing the dominant national stance on race that had emerged at the end of the century—the
increasingly hegemonic belief that the United States was, explicitly, a
"white man's nation."[2]

This belief was part and parcel of the United States stepping self-
consciously into the role of empire. Political historians consider the
epochal shift to have taken place roughly in the years between 1898 and
1905, as the United States first declared war on Spain over the administration of Cuba, and then took over the Philippine Islands in order
to secure a gateway to Pacific trade.[3] It is in precisely these years that
the revision of the Reconstruction South became a central obsession in
U.S. culture. In historiography, the infamous "Dunning school" coalesced

around William A. Dunning of Columbia University; this influential group of historians argued, from their ivied towers, that the noblest aim of the Reconstruction project—establishing equality before the law for all people regardless of race—had itself been a mistake. As Pennsylvania scholar Ellis Paxson Oberholtzer put it in a typical formulation, Reconstruction necessarily failed because southern African Americans were incapable of citizenship, since they were "as credulous as children, which in intellect they in many ways resembled."[4] This aggressive reinterpretation of the Reconstruction South was ensconced in mainstream discourse when the *Atlantic Monthly* devoted its entire 1901 volume to articles on the subject by Dunning's adherents. Dunning himself appreciated the irony that the *Atlantic* should provide the venue through which he grasped the reins of public opinion; this was, after all, the very New England journal that had been founded to support the Unionist cause, that had called for the execution of surrendered Confederate leaders in 1865, and that had printed Stowe's account of the tragic heroics of reconstructing "Our Florida Plantation" just twenty years earlier.[5] "Lord, how the reconstructors have been reconstructed!" Dunning crowed to fellow historian Frederic Bancroft, in a letter written as the 1901 volume concluded. "I'm going to . . . take the ground that the whole business was ethically, socially, and politically right; that's the only way in which a man can attract any attention now."[6]

Alongside the revisionist history, a veritable flood of literary portrayals of the Reconstruction South swamped the U.S. cultural marketplace. Several dozen fictional accounts of the era, along with dozens more memoirs, appeared in the years between 1898 and 1905—and a respectable number of these books became bestsellers. While the "Dunning school" historians marched in interpretive lockstep, the literary authors proved far more diverse: male and female, African American and white, most of them were natives of southern states but were published through metropolitan publishing houses. These writers retold the Reconstruction South from a variety of ideological perspectives, ranging from white supremacy to black nationalism, from progressivism to romantic racialism.[7] From the point of view of national literary production and marketing, though, the plethora of Reconstruction South writing was all part of the same conversation: Booker T. Washington's *Up From Slavery* and Thomas Dixon's pro–Ku Klux Klan novel *The Leopard's Spots,* for instance, shared a New York–based publisher, Doubleday, in 1901–1902.

In the lead *Atlantic Monthly* article of January 1901, Princeton historian Woodrow Wilson explained that Americans were revisiting their Reconstruction South en masse precisely because of the self-confessed turn to empire through which they were living. "A new age gives [Recon-struction] a new significance," Wilson proposed. "The revolution"—the transformation of the United States from republic to empire—"lies there."[8] In common with both the "Dunning school" historians and the vast ma-jority of the historical novelists of Reconstruction, Wilson was proposing that the U.S. war in and occupation of the Philippines—which seemed a radical departure in national mission to his contemporaries—was simply the latest manifestation of a process that had in fact begun with the Civil War and developed steadily through Reconstruction. "The real change" had happened in the 1860s, with a transformation in the perceived "rela-tion of the life of the land to the supremacy of the national lawmaking body." "Empire is an affair of strong government," he concluded; and as such, U.S. empire was "a direct result of that national spirit which the war between the states cried so wide awake, and to which the process of Reconstruction gave the subtle assurance of practically unimpeded sway."[9] Thomas Dixon's subtitling of his 1901 novel made a similar point: the British writer Rudyard Kipling had written an instantly classic poem in 1899, encouraging the United States to follow through on its exploits in Cuba and the Philippines and join Britain in bearing "the white man's burden" of empire; Dixon shot back that his Reconstruc-tion South historical novel was a "Romance of the White Man's Burden, 1865–1900." Wilson and Dixon rewrote the Reconstruction South to ar-gue that the United States had been in the empire business already for decades.

The end of Congressional Reconstruction in 1877 had hardly marked the end of colonialism in the southern states, and the events of the interven-ing decades had only cemented the relevance of the Reconstruction South as a site for conceptualizing U.S. empire. At the same time that the end of Reconstruction restored the local political autonomy of white south-erners, it only marked the beginning of the massive state-countenanced disenfranchisement of southern African Americans and the institutional-ization of the state-sanctioned system of racial apartheid in the southern states that remained in place until the Civil Rights Movement. To the extent that racialist ideas about citizenship became the foundation for the reintegration of its Reconstruction South into the body politic of the United States, the end of Reconstruction marked a significant turn toward modern white supremacy in U.S. nationalism.[10] Whereas King in *The Great South* had been perfectly clear that all local inhabitants of the Reconstruction South, white and black, were rightly subjects of the United States under Reconstruction, and whereas Cable had put forth a "Creole" model of southern population that undermined the very notion of biracial categorization, in the years after 1877 it came to be only African Americans—objects of the offices of the abbreviated "Freedman's Bureau"—who were seen in dominant U.S. discourse as appropriately subjects, rather than citizens, of the nation-state.

The "Republic-or-Empire?" debate of the turn of the century readily demonstrates that administration of African Americans in the Reconstruction South had been linked indelibly to imperial dominion over peoples of color abroad in U.S. discourse of all political persuasions—imperialist or anti-imperialist, white supremacist or anti-racist.[11] The precedent of Reconstruction set the very horizon of possibility for envisioning the relationship the United States should assume vis-à-vis its new island possessions: should they be territories on the way to statehood? or indefinitely held "conquered provinces"? Pro-imperialist Republicans, such as Elihu Root, President McKinley's secretary of war, claimed that denying the Filipinos self-rule was just common sense, because "in view of the failure of Reconstruction, it would be foolish to enfranchise any non-white people."[12] Anti-imperialists cited the same precedent to voice their opposition to the occupation, as when Booker T. Washington asked, "Can this Government do for the millions of dark–skinned races to be found in Cuba . . . and the Philippine Islands that which it has not been able to do for the now nearly 10,000,000 negroes" within its borders?[13] As visions of the future of the United States in the world were, inexorably, routed back through understandings of the domestic past, the fixation of turn-of-the-century thinkers on the Reconstruction South seemed to deaden the political discourse of the day.

The *literary* reimagination of the Reconstruction South at this time, however, was more generative. In 1892, a few years before the flood of Reconstruction South fiction burst forth upon the scene of U.S. culture, North Carolinian educator Anna Julia Cooper hypothesized that the emergence of a literary *Voice from the South*—as her volume was titled— could intervene in the life of an increasingly imperial nation. "One phase of American Literature" was ending, Cooper proposed, and good riddance to it: for this phase had consisted of metropolitan writers seeking to depict southern African Americans from a position of "sheer ignorance" and with "their art . . . almost uniformly perverted to serve their [civil and political] ends."[14] This particular failure of national literature, Cooper explained, was itself evidence of an imperial mindset. "It seems an *Anglo Saxon characteristic*," she quipped, "to publish any such sweeping generalizations . . . on [the basis of] such meager or superficial information." This "spirit" of mainstream authorship must "come with the blood of those grand old *sea kings* (I believe you call them) who shot out in their trusty barks speeding over unknown seas and, like a death-dealing genius, with the piercing eye and bloodthirsty heart of hawk or vulture killed and harried, burned and caroused."[15]

In opposition to and in place of this "death-dealing" phase of American literature, Cooper called for more voices from the South, more writings by, as her subtitle put it more specifically, "a Black Woman of the South." The new phase of American literature she envisioned would construct a revised national literary history upon which to draw. For their deep national past, writers would be informed by the fraught proximity of unlettered African American folk culture to Thomas Jefferson's Revolutionary rhetoric. Blending a paean to the folk as America's "Homer or Caedmon," with a silent quote from the Declaration of Independence, Cooper exhorted writers to take inspiration from the "original lispings of an unsophisticated people while they were yet close—so close—to nature and to nature's God."[16] (In a controversial move for 1892, Cooper also suggested that Poe should hold the place of Shakespeare in the U.S. literary canon.[17]) Most important in the new age of national literature Cooper envisioned, though, was the way that voices from the South would mount a challenge to U.S. imperialism. As "our raison d'être" in the opening lines of the book, she presented a deceptively straightforward assertion: "The 'other side' has not been represented by one who 'lives there.'"[18] With the parallel scare-quotes, Cooper marked both otherness ("other side") and geographical difference ("lives *there*") as constructed terms—and, more, as terms constructed in tandem. Her single sentence named the geographical and racialized distancing that was the basis of imperial culture. But at the same time, Cooper's "raison d'être" promised that the seemingly indomitable, "death-dealing" cultural formation could be undermined from within—through the raising of "a voice from the South," through the authorship of "a black woman of the South."

Retelling Reconstruction during the Spanish-Philippine-American War

Cultural historians have taken note of the unprecedented number of historical romances of the Reconstruction South that flooded the national market at the turn of the century; but, generally, they have interpreted the phenomenon as a psychological working-out of domestic conflicts. Sons and daughters of the Confederacy were refighting the Civil War on a cultural front, one hypothesis has it; or, metropolitan readers were becoming imaginatively reconciled with their fictionalized South; or, more broadly, the nation was in the throes of "plantation nostalgia," longing for an idyllic, premodern rural past.[19] But since Walter Benn Michaels proposed that Thomas Nelson Page's formative *Red Rock: A Chronicle of Reconstruction* (1898) is "an anti-imperialist novel," literary historians have begun to attend to the connections between the turn-of-the-century romances and the wars and occupations the United States was actively waging overseas when they appeared.[20] These books now appear to us not simply as revisions of domestic history, but also as prescriptions for the future course of the nation on the world stage.[21]

Many of the writers themselves were quite clear on this point. Thomas Dixon, for whom subtlety was never a goal, closed *The Leopard's Spots* by lecturing his readers on how to apply what they had learned about their failed reconstruction of North Carolina to their present-day political scene. "In this hour of crisis, our flag has been raised over ten millions of semi-barbaric black men in the foulest slave pen of the Orient," he hectored his readers. "Shall we repeat the farce of '67, reverse the order of nature, and make these black people our rulers?"[22] In the same year that Dixon's racist novel was published, the most prominent African American variety troupe of the day—the Black Patti Troubadours, led by classically trained Virginian soprano Sissieretta Jones—designed their touring show around another take on the same conjuncture. According to the program of the play, which was titled *Filipino Misfit,* the Troubadours organized their show around another take on the stylized representation of African American life in the post–Emancipation South, as codified by decades of minstrel performance: "the cake walk," "the buck dance," and songs such as "My Alabama Lady Love" received pride of place. In the dramatic narrative of the play, though, the troupe members played both Filipinos and U.S. occupying forces in a romantic "farce" centered on the island ruler's daughter who is "looking for a husband"— who, in other words, is open for acquisition.[23]

Both Dixon and the Troubadours routed the issues of political domination and subjection they addressed through a romance plot, which was based upon the presumably natural subordination of women to men.[24] The strategy is one that they shared with the great majority of the turn-of-the-century Reconstruction South novelists. Taking up the assertion in the historiography and political discourse of their moment—that U.S. imperialism had begun at home, and that thus the uncertain role of the nation abroad in the present could be predicted and prescribed by revisiting the domestic past—writers doubly domesticated the question of empire by moving it into the realm of intimate relationships between men and women. Virginian Thomas Nelson Page in many ways set the standard for the genre with his influential *Red Rock,* published in 1898. Despite the staid historical sound of his subtitle (*A Chronicle of Reconstruction*), the primary motivators of Page's plot are two parallel courtships: while the major political events of the novel take place offstage, Page relates the romantic pursuits of his male protagonists in excruciating detail. By writing a romance in place of a chronicle, Page maps the imperial relationship of colonizer and colonized onto the domestic relationship of husband and wife, just as the broader discourse of his moment maps the global question of U.S. empire overseas onto the domestic territory of the conquered Reconstruction South. If the novel may be construed as anti-imperial, because Page's heroes champion home rule against the forces of foreign occupation, *Red Rock* must simultaneously be seen as thoroughly imperial, thanks to Page's handling of the romance plot. Who better than a scion of Virginia, that bastion of the slaveholding republic, to provide the nation with a primer on being anti-imperial and imperial at the same time? Page's popular Reconstruction South novel, and the many imitations and variations it spawned, created forms for the affective assimilation of the occupation of the Philippines into U.S. national culture.

To begin the novel, Page gives an account of the founding of the Red Rock plantation, the contested ground of the novel, by the Gray family—his rather obviously named, defeated Confederate protagonists. The account conflates colonization and marriage, possession of land and possession of women, in a transitive logic of ownership peculiar to the turn of the century:

> [The plantation] took its name from the great red stain which appeared on the huge bowlder in the grove . . . That stain was the blood of the Indian chief who had slain the wife of the first Jacquelin Gray who came to this part of the world . . . The bereft husband had exacted swift retribution of the murderer, on that very rock, and the Indian's heart blood had left that deep stain . . . as a perpetual memorial of the swift vengeance of the Jacquelin Grays.[25]

Page begins at the very beginning, at the origin story of American empire—New World colonization—but he retells it in terms of 1898 U.S. ideology: specifically, the specious argument, put forth by apologists for southern lynching, that alleged violence against white women justified all repressive actions taken by white men against people of color.[26] Page's aspiring New World colonialists, the Grays, begin with no direct ownership of land or of the bodies of people of color, but they do own their wives; and white women become the primary terrain upon which their claims to dominion are staked.

With this focus on courtship, Reconstruction South novelists not only demonstrate how their heroes "win" their primary possessions, but they

SHE GAVE HIM A ROLLING-PIN AND HE SET TO WORK.

Figure 20. Frontispiece ("She gave him a rolling-pin and he set to work"),
Thomas Nelson Page, *Red Rock: A Chronicle of Reconstruction,* 1898.
Courtesy of the Yale University Library.

also create dramas of consent, proving that their female characters freely choose to submit to (as Page puts it) "their higher powers." By consenting to marriage in these novels, a woman attests to her husband's fitness as a master; thereby, she sanctions his transitive dominion over others. The frontispiece of Page's novel illustrates this use of courtship as moral sanction for domination, and indeed this image could be read as another satiric rendering of "the white man's burden." As the occupying U.S. officer in uniform gallantly performs kitchen duties to woo the nubile southern woman under his command, his military occupation of her home and person is domesticated: she is pictured as "ruling" him just as surely as the kittens on the floor control his officer's cap. This scene takes place, though, in a plantation kitchen—and so the white woman is there in the first place because her formerly enslaved African American cook is absent. Just as the nubile young woman here stands in for the laboring cook, so throughout Page's novel, white women replace people of color in their interactions with white men. As the relation between suitor and object of his affection replaces and mimes the relation between imperial nation and objects of its colonization, the intrinsic coerciveness of the unequal relationship is only thinly veiled by Page with chivalric niceties. Throughout the novel, he incessantly describes courtship, from the point of view of his male protagonists, as a military engagement with a weak opponent whose surrender is inevitable. "She will not?'" one suitor asks indignantly. "I'll make her. Whether she speaks or not, I'll win her." Assured of their natural superiority to the women they seek to acquire, Page's protagonists approach their beloveds as imperial administrators manipulating their charges: one calls himself "a diplomatist," and goes on to assert, "It's necessary, to accomplish anything with the dear creatures." By replacing conquest with courtship, Page implies that the actions of his ascendant white male characters are inspired not by power over their subjects, but by affection for them. *Red Rock* thus prefigures the ideological catchphrase that the McKinley administration would choose, several months after its publication, to characterize U.S. occupation of the Philippines: "benevolent assimilation."[27]

Necessarily, then, Page must assure his readers that his female characters joyously accede to their subordinate role in this unequal relationship. Indeed, the climax of *Red Rock* comes when Ruth Welch, the daughter of a northern carpetbagger, begs hero Steve Allen, a Gray cousin, to marry her—so that she will not have to testify against him in court, where he is on trial for leading a Klan raid. In other words, Ruth begs Steve to take control of her and to relieve her of her civic and citizenship rights; and thus she performs exactly the consent of the governed whose lack in the

Philippines so bedeviled American consciences. To her plea, Steve first answers with republican restraint: "No . . . I could not let you do that, Ruth. I could not let you sacrifice yourself." But Ruth "suddenly sinks in a heap on the floor," and Steve "stoops and lifts her, as though she were a child." (The image resonates with the "little brown brother" formulation applied—again, slightly later—to the Filipinos subject to U.S. rule.) As he holds her in his arms, Ruth reiterates her desire for submission to him: "It is no sacrifice. Do you not see? Oh! Can you not see that—I—love . . ."—and she trails off, never to speak again in the novel.[28] By retelling Reconstruction as a love story, Page and his fellow novelists recast the issue of subjugation at the heart of the imperial question as a matter of the heart. The relationship of the United States to the larger world stays, through the Reconstruction South, in the national family and within the realm of national precedent.

But what if there is no love in the imperial romance? What if the weak do not consent to their subjugation? In her 1900 novel *Contending Forces: A Romance Illustrative of Negro Life North and South,* Bostonian Pauline Hopkins poses precisely these demystifying questions, drawing back the thin veil with which Page had masked the coercion at the heart of his "fairy tale of love and chivalry." The southern "romance" of Hopkins's subtitle is a violent story of the brutal destruction of the Montfort family by a secret "committee on public safety" obviously meant to conjure the Ku Klux Klan. But Hopkins carefully constructs this Reconstruction South plot with international as well as regional dimensions, beginning the novel by positioning the Montforts at the juncture of the forces of foreign and domestic empire in the United States. On the domestic side, the patriarch of the family, Charles Montfort, appears in the plot in the capacity of an incoming Reconstruction official: he moves to New Bern, North Carolina, with the express purpose of freeing his slaves; once there he takes over the family "homestead" of local landowner Anson Pollock, the primary villain of the novel; and his great possession of capital is symbolized by the (Federal) "golden eagles" he gives his young son to play with as toys.[29] The reformist, capitalist Montforts, however, come to New Bern not from the metropolitan North but from a colonized island, making their identity resonant with that of Filipinos and other Pacific islanders. Indeed, when Hopkins has Grace Montfort, the wife and mother of the family, arrive in North Carolina on a ship named the "Island Queen," she well foreshadows Grace's fate by aligning her with deposed Queen Lilioukalani of Hawai'i, another island officially acquired by the United States in 1898.

These island origins are exploited by Hopkins's villain, Pollock, who for-

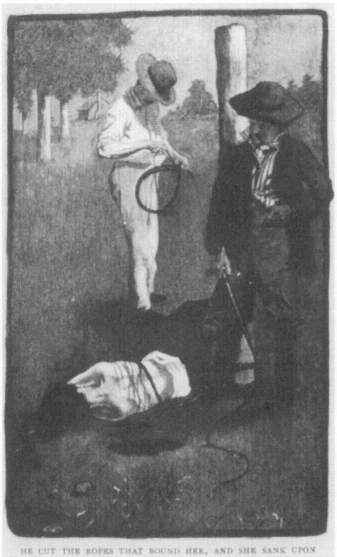

HE CUT THE ROPES THAT BOUND HER, AND SHE SANK UPON
THE GROUND AGAIN. (See page 69.)

Figure 21. Frontispiece ("He cut the ropes that bound her, and she sank upon the ground again"), Pauline Hopkins, *Contending Forces: A Romance Illustrative of Negro Life North and South,* 1900. Courtesy of the Yale University Library.

mulates a foolproof plan to rid New Bern of the interlopers—foolproof, that is, according to the turn-of-the-century gendered ideology of imperialism. Pollock spreads a rumor that Grace Montfort is not in fact "white," but that she is of mixed blood; and once Grace is deemed "black" in the eyes of the New Bern community, her husband's claim on her body is rendered void—and thereby also are nullified his transitive claims on his land, property, and slaves. Two pages after Pollock concocts the rumor, he is able to lead a mass raid on the Montfort household. While Charles is quickly shot and killed, the mob ritualistically performs their repossession of Montfort's land and property by torturing his wife. In the graphic scene illustrated in the frontispiece, two members of the "committee on public safety" strip Grace, tie her to a post, and take turns "whipping" her until "the blood stood in a pool around her feet," a violation of her body that conflates lynching and rape and leaves her "outraged . . . bleeding, friendless, alone"—and in the same prone position, we might note, that had been voluntarily assumed by Ruth Welch in Page's novel.[30] Thinking back to the opening scene of Page's novel, the story of how Red Rock got its name, makes clear that Hopkins carries the imperial logic of the Reconstruction South romance to its logical conclusion in her alternative story of national origins. If white women's bodies are the terrain upon which white men prove their dominion in the world of empire, then this is how land and power change hands.

Much like Cable before her, though, Hopkins remains notably agnostic on the question of whether Grace is "black" or "white." All the phenotypically white southern women of *Contending Forces* share Grace Montfort's "most lovely"—and indeterminate—"type of Southern beauty," and when describing the Montforts' island heritage, Hopkins mentions, tongue-in-cheek, the possibility that "there might even have been a strain of African blood polluting the fair stream."[31] But by ultimately refusing to race Grace, even as she makes Grace's race central to her plot, Hopkins rejects the binary categories to which her villains subscribe. In Hopkins's formulation, Grace's racial indeterminacy takes on an aggressive political thrust that Cable's exotic Creoles had lacked: through this indeterminacy, Hopkins shows that "white" women in the Reconstruction South romance cannot be held apart from the extent to which their embodiment and their actions directly impact the status of peoples of color under U.S. imperialist ideology. (Her implicit critique illuminates even so early a Reconstruction South novel as DeForest's *Miss Ravenel's Conversion from Secession to Loyalty* (1866): DeForest compulsively describes Lillie Ravenel, the Confederate-sympathizing love object of his occupying Union Army hero, as an "Ashantee" in the early chapters of the book.) The moral of Hopkins's Reconstruction South romance thus appears the inverse of Page's. Civilization does not begin at home, in the "redeemed" South or in the relation between men and women. Instead, barbarism begins at home, and an imperial United States trained by domestic example will export not love and benevolence, but savage subjugation.

Page and Hopkins do have something important in common, though. Their romances of the Reconstruction South irremediably subvert the organizing binary of the political debate of the period: "America—Republic or Empire?" Novelists who retell Reconstruction recognize an internal empire domestic to the United States, propose that the United States already is a colonizing and coercive nation, and thus implicitly require a fundamental reevaluation of the idea of the republic itself. American queasiness about imperialism abroad at the turn of the century had at its base an idea which proved surprisingly durable through the twentieth century: that the United States had always been a nation based upon consensus, and that its virtuous innocence was about to be corrupted by foreign entanglements. The Reconstruction South challenges that notion of consensus, stripping away the illusions of an exceptional republic standing alone on a corrupt globe. And with disillusion comes the possibility of enlightenment, of discerning a path toward redemption and reform. In a ringing declaration at the heart of her Reconstruction South romance, Hopkins implies that achieving a balance between national interest and national morality will entail as well a revision of presumably natural domestic relationships: "Expediency and *right* must go *hand in hand*. There is no room for compromise."[32]

An American Universal Geography for the American Century

At the dawning of the twentieth century, Reconstruction South stories retold the history of the United States in the context of the rapid ascendance of the nation on the world stage. The subsequent decades would see both the decolonization of the globe and the rise of the United States to the stature of global superpower, and Reconstruction South romances as they were institutionalized in U.S. culture during the Philippine-American War would continue to process and facilitate this rise. Indeed, these romances were cemented in the national popular imaginary in 1915 with D. W. Griffith's *The Birth of a Nation*: as American audiences watched the European imperial powers immolating themselves in the First World War, Griffith founded American cinema with a film that dramatized Thomas Dixon's 1905 novel *The Clansman*. (The conjuncture would repeat itself in 1939, on the brink of the even more decisive U.S. intervention in European affairs, with the blockbuster film of the Reconstruction romance redux *Gone With the Wind*.) As a new scope for the international exertion of U.S. power became apparent, the alchemy of the Reconstruction South story explained the unique intervention that Americans could make in a world of fallen empires: the United States knew how to play both sides of the inherited binary of nineteenth-century empire at the same time. Dixon's pro-Klan plot proposed that anti-imperial self-defense was simultaneously imperial supremacy: to restore "home rule" and throw off foreign occupation in the Reconstruction South, he asserted, was to institutionalize apartheid and strip half the local population of citizenship rights. President Woodrow Wilson, three years away from his plan for the League of Nations, memorably found watching *The Birth of a Nation* to be "like writing history with lightning."[33]

This turn-of-the-century incarnation of the South was not just about the historical problematic of Reconstruction, nor simply about the ways that the past event in national life could be reinterpreted and its relevance extended. It was also the latest installment in the one hundred and twenty-five year-long literary history of figuring the connection of the United States to the world through its South. With their Civil War and Reconstruction behind them, Americans found themselves poised on the threshold of the "American Century," wielding an "American Universal Geography" like never before. Their nation was now a metonym for the world, encompassing within its borders all of the oppositions and warring interests of the globe: colonizer and colonized, industrial and peripheral, civil and savage, brown and white, rich and poor. Both Henry James, at the end of a long nineteenth-century career that stretched back to the 1860s, and W. E. B. Du Bois, at the beginning of a long twentieth-century career that would reach to the 1960s, had ready access to this cultural formation, although they wielded it to different ends. In *The American Scene* (1907) and *The Souls of Black Folk* (1903), the two writers took as their topic the remaking of U.S. nationalism to comport with the newly central place of the United States on the globe; and both structured their inquiries around the relay between the nation and its Reconstruction South. Looking forward and looking back, looking outward and looking South, their famous observations provide a resting point for this study.

When James returned to the United States in 1904, after decades of expatriation in Europe, the fact that the United States was a global power was already firmly established. With colonies in both the Atlantic and the Pacific Oceans, his native land had begun to stake an expanding claim on the map of Western empire. To gauge the changes in the nation wrought by this modernization, though, James turned to a venerable form: the north-to-south, eastern-seaboard travelogue that had been one of the central genres of U.S. literature since the founding. Much like the writers of the early republic, James began *The American Scene* with essays on the metropolitan northeastern regions of the nation, and then journeyed southward away from the national norm he had established, with his observations sharply punctuated by his textual encounter of the Mason-Dixon line.[34]

At the opening of his chapter on Richmond, Virginia, James explains that he has returned to "American civilization" with the "fond calculation" of finding there the "[r]omance and mystery" that a declining Europe has ceased to hold for him. And "[i]t was in respect to the South . . . that the calculation had really been fondest—on such a stored, such a waiting provision of vivid images, mainly beautiful and sad, might one surely there depend."[35] Confronted with the city of Richmond itself, though, James registers the gap between the South he had expected to find, and the abandoned land that instead greets him: "One had counted on a sort of registered consciousness of the past, and the truth was that there appeared . . . on the face of the scene, no discernible consciousness, registered or unregistered, of anything." (James's contemporary, Henry Adams, was revising his 1880s perception of the tragic Confederate in strikingly similar terms in his own 1907 volume, *The Education of Henry Adams:* "Strictly, the Southerner had no mind."[36]) This mindless, unconscious South, James presciently explains, is not a place, not a site of events, not *content*; it is pure *form*—a rhetorical structure, an empty sign. This South provides above all a passive occasion for the meditation of the metropolitan author: "Richmond, in a word, looked to me simply blank and void—whereby it was, precisely, that the great emotion was to come."[37] The nationalist clarity, the "great emotion" for which this South is a vehicle inheres in precisely its function as "a pale page into which [the author] might read what he liked."[38]

Filling the blank with what meaning he will, James calibrates his turn-of-the-century South precisely to the question of empire that would seem to be beyond the ken of his domestic travelogue. In four short pages, he moves to an all-encompassing verdict on "the budding Southern mind," which

> strikes us to-day as beyond measure queer and quaint and benighted—innocent above all; stamped with the inalienable Southern sign, the inimitable *rococo* note. We talk of the provincial, but the provinciality projected by the Confederate dream . . . looks to our present eyes as artlessly perverse,

as untouched by any intellectual tradition of beauty or wit, as some exhibited array of the odd utensils or divinities of lone and primitive islanders.[39]

Being "blank and void" allows James's South to become, paradoxically, an "inalienable . . . sign"; and for the American scene of the moment, his South is the sign of the colonial subject, of the "lone and primitive" other whose subordinate status is justified and prescribed by an utter lack of civilization, consciousness, and culture. James's introjection of the Philippines into the provincial in this passage—with "islanders" as the preferred simile for "Virginians"—would suggest that his homeland has not been changed by assuming its new place in the order of empire. Instead, his encounter with Richmond proposes that the world has always been in the nation, and that the United States has from its beginnings negotiated a more or less effective hierarchical relationship with its internal islanders.

The most famous pronouncement of Du Bois's most often-read book operates around an identical yoking of terms.

> The problem of the twentieth century is the problem of the color-line,—the relation of the darker to the lighter races of men in Asia and Africa, in America and the islands of the sea. It was a phase of this problem that caused the Civil War. . . . No sooner had Northern armies touched Southern soil than this old question, newly guised, sprang from the earth,—What shall be done with Negroes?[40]

The problematic Du Bois formulates is preeminently global in the first sentence, spanning continents, circling the globe, and extending even to the nameless "islands of the sea." (Some names might have sprung easily to American minds in 1903, such as "Cuba," "Hawai'i," "Luzon," or "Visayas.") In the next sentence, though, Du Bois's problematic becomes profoundly domestic: it was the cause of the U.S. Civil War. Du Bois's "color-line" is a universal, present everywhere; it is simultaneously the particular internal divide, the Mason-Dixon, across which "Northern armies touched Southern soil."

With the interpolation of global and domestic, universal and particular, Du Bois effects not only a geographic, but also a temporal translation. The problem of the color-line may be in the world's *future,* but it is a central fact of the nation's *past.* The prophecy for the coming century of the globe becomes, through its domestication on the field of the Reconstruction South, an "old question" for Americans. Where the rest of the world is going in the twilight of the great European empires, the United States—thanks to its South—has always already been. "Merely a concrete test of the underlying principles of the great republic is the

Negro Problem," Du Bois remarks dryly, converting the global "problem of the twentieth century" into simply another test of U.S. national ideals, the latest in a long line of tests stretching back to the nation's founding. By "study[ing] the period of [U.S.] history from 1861 to 1872," Du Bois deconstructs the turn-of-the-century opposition of republic and empire, offering an expanded South—"in Asia and Africa, in America and the islands of the sea"—as the field upon which the imperfect, aspirational republic of 1776 must finally prove itself.[41]

For a new era, Du Bois summons yet again the complex and visceral connection to the world, and to the past, that our South has always provided to U.S. literature. Against official-nationalist pronouncements of the new and unencumbered United States standing alone on the planet, our South makes available an alternate story of U.S. origins: a story of a nation that has emerged out of the ideological and material matrices of New World empire, and has carried that inheritance forward into its subsequent phases of modernity. Against narratives of independence and exceptionalism, our South inscribes counter-narratives of contiguity and continuity. This connection of the republic back to its origins can simply reassert the deadly hierarchies of imperialism, as in *The Birth of a Nation*; but our South also holds out the potential of making something new, of getting beyond the inherited power binaries by seeing from both sides and drawing syntheses out of oppositions.[42]

From the perspective of the decolonizing world in the American Century, certainly, the closeness and intimacy of its South to the United States—the internalization in U.S. culture of that which is openly disavowed—has seemed to promise an American progression away from Old World business-as-usual. At the end of his influential inquiry into the aftermath of French imperialism, *Black Skin, White Masks* (1952), Frantz Fanon turns for a moment to "the American Negro," who "is cast in a different play." Watching the early days of the Civil Rights Movement unfold from abroad, Fanon sees a different Civil War: "In the United States, the Negro battles and is battled. . . . There is war, there are defeats, truces, victories."[43] Precisely because this conflict is inside the nation, though, Fanon envisions a resolution in the United States that he cannot see elsewhere in the world. "On the field of battle," he writes, his imagery resonant with Pauline Hopkins's Reconstruction romance of half a century earlier, "a monument is slowly being built that promises to be majestic.

"And, at the top of this monument, I can already see a white man and a black man *hand in hand*."

Notes

Introduction: Magnet South

1. Although I do not use a psychoanalytic theoretical framework in this study, both Freud's sense of the fantasy as an imagined scene that stages an unconscious desire and Lacan's sense of fantasy as a fundamental mode of psychological defense are not irrelevant to what I see as the workings of the South in U.S. nationalism.

2. I take the term "ideological juxtaposition" from Raymond Williams, *The Country and the City* (New York: Oxford University Press, 1971), esp. 46–54 and 289–306. Williams warns that the "fiction" of the ideological juxtaposition "promote[s] superficial comparisons and prevent[s] real ones" (54).

3. Edward Said, in *Orientalism* (New York: Pantheon, 1978), provides the classic argument that representation of the periphery underwrites the culture of the capital in the modern era. Peter Stallybrass and Allon White, in *The Politics and Poetics of Transgression* (Ithaca: Cornell University Press, 1986) discuss more globally the high/low distinction in Western culture and the extent to which the dominant cultural tradition is underwritten by that which it spurns.

4. I am grateful to Wai Chee Dimock for this phrasing.

5. Studies along this line include Sandra M. Gustafson, "Histories of Democracy and Empire," *American Quarterly* 29:1 (Mar. 2007): 112; Sandhya Shukla and Heidi Tinsman, editors' introduction to "Our Americas: Political and Cultural Imaginings," *Radical History Review* 89 (Spring 2004): 3, 5; and the classic by William Appleman Williams, *Empire as a Way of Life* (New York: Oxford University Press, 1980).

6. On U.S. slavery and apartheid as internal colonization, see Leigh Anne Duck, *The Nation's Region: Southern Modernism, Segregation, and U.S. Nationalism* (Athens: University of Georgia Press, 2006). On the paradox of the postcolonial nation that is "colonized and colonizing, sometimes at the same time," see Étienne Balibar, "The Nation Form: History and Ideology," in *Race, Nation, Class: Ambiguous Identities* (London: Verso, 1991), 341.

7. Benedict Anderson has theorized that the "principle of exclusion," a sense of the limitation and boundary of the imagined community, is intrinsic to formation of national identity (*Imagined Communities*, rev. ed. [London: Verso, 1991]); Terry Eagleton has used the same term to describe the privileging of subject-object over dialogical subject-subject relations in myths of national identity (*Nationalism, Colonialism and Literature—Nationalism, Irony and Commitment* [Derry, Ireland: Field Day, 1988]).

8. See for instance, Roy Harvey Pearce, *Savagism and Civilization: A Study of the Indian and the American Mind* (Baltimore: John Hopkins University Press, 1967); Elizabeth Dillon, *The Gender of Freedom: Fictions of Liberalism and the Literary Public Sphere* (Stanford: Stanford University Press, 2004); and Bruce A. Harvey, *American Geographics: U.S. National Narratives and the Representation of the Non-European World, 1830–1865* (Stanford: Stanford University Press, 2001).

9. This observation was made in 1961 by C. Vann Woodward in *The Burden of Southern History*, 3rd ed. (Baton Rouge: Louisiana State University Press, 1993). Recently, Jon Smith and Deborah Cohn have put Woodward's insight into the frame of transnational American Studies, revealing its applicability to current intellectual concerns ("Introduction: Uncanny Hybridities," in *Look Away! The U.S. South in New World Studies* [Durham, N.C.: Duke University Press, 2004]).

10. Jon Smith has made the most lucid call for this transnational conceptualization in his review essay "Postcolonial, Black, and Nobody's Margin: The U.S. South in New World Studies," *American Literary History* 16:1 (2004): 144–161.

11. Henry Nash Smith, *Virgin Land: The American West as Symbol and Myth* (Cambridge, Mass.: Harvard University Press, 1950); and R. W. B. Lewis, *The American Adam: Innocence, Tragedy, and Tradition in the Nineteenth Century* (Chicago: Chicago University Press, 1955).

12. Timothy Dwight, "Valedictory address to the Young Gentlemen, who commenced Bachelors of Arts, at Yale College, July 25th 1776," *American Magazine* 1:1 (Dec. 1787): 42. A particularly galvanizing critique has come from Amy Kaplan, "'Left Alone with America': The Absence of Empire in the study of American Culture," in *Cultures of United States Imperialism*, ed. Amy Kaplan and Donald E. Pease (Durham, N.C.: Duke University Press, 1993), 3–21.

13. Jon Smith improves upon the reading of Perry Miller that Kaplan offers in "'Left Alone with America,'" proposing that "marginalization of the South has had disastrous consequences for American studies, unnecessarily prolonging ideas of American exceptionalism and deferring genuine engagement with the African origins of the American self" ("Postcolonial," 144–145).

14. Henry Adams, *The Education of Henry Adams* (Boston: Houghton Mifflin, 1918), 47.

15. "[L]'essence d'une nation est que tous les individus aient beaucoup de choses en commun et aussi que tous aient oublié bien des choses . . . Tout citoyen français doit avoir oublié la Saint-Barthélemy, les massacres du Midi au XI-

IIe siècle." Ernest Renan, "Qu'est-ce qu'une nation?" in *Oeuvres Complètes* ed. Henriette Psichari (Paris: Calmann-Levy, 1947), 1:892.

16. Adams, *Education,* 44.

17. I mean the title to resonate as well with José Martí's "Nuestra America" (1892), particularly as it has been reconceptualized recently by Susan Gillman: "Rather than a geographically or culturally specific term, Our America is a rhetorical phrase dependent on the shifting referent of the linguistic signifier 'our.' As the reference changes from one context to another, a multidimensional, multidirectional comparativism develops" which can register "the different regional, national, imperial, and neocolonial histories" of the hemisphere ("Otra vez Caliban/Encore Caliban: Adaptation, Translation, Americas Studies," *American Literary History* 20:1–2 [2008]: 187–209).

18. The poem was originally published in the *Saturday News* of New York City and was included under its original title in the 1860, 1867, and 1871–1872 editions of *Leaves of Grass.* For the 1881–1882 edition, Whitman changed the title to "O Magnet-South," and it is included in the 1891–1892 "deathbed" edition under that name.

19. René Girard's proposition that any entity conceptualized as "other" and disavowed actually functions simultaneously as a mediator and source of desire is relevant here: "[Through disavowal] the secondary role of the mediator becomes primary . . . Everything that originates with this mediator is systematically belittled although still secretly desired" (*Deceit, Desire, and the Novel: Self and Other in Literary Structure,* trans. Yvonne Freccero [Baltimore: Johns Hopkins University Press, 1965], 10–11).

20. Whitman, "Longings for Home," *Leaves of Grass* (1891–1892) (New York: Vintage Books; The Library of America, 1992) 584. See Michael R. Dressman, "Goodrich's Geography and Whitman's Place Names," *Walt Whitman Review* 26 (June 1980), 64–67; and Mary Louise Pratt, *Imperial Eyes: Travel Writing and Transculturation* (London: Routledge, 1992), 9.

21. Whitman had done enough self-promotion by 1860 that it was obvious to his readers that he was not a native southerner; the editor of the *Southern Literary Messenger* called the claim "a Whitmaniacal license, accent on the first vowel in *license*" (31:1 [Jul. 1860]: 75).

22. Edward Said, *Culture and Imperialism* (New York: Vintage, 1993), 63.

23. Ralph Waldo Emerson, "The Young American" (1844), in *The Complete Works of Ralph Waldo Emerson,* centenary ed. (Boston: Houghton Mifflin, 1903) 1:379.

24. Trowbridge, *The South: A Tour of Its Battlefields and Ruined Cities, A Journey through the Desolated States, and Talks with the People* [etc.] (Hartford: L. Stebbins, 1866).

25. A Virginian spending July in Vermont [Herman Melville], "Hawthorne and His Mosses," *Literary World* (Aug. 17, 1850), reprinted in *Herman Melville,* vol. 3 (New York: Library of America, 1984), 1164.

26. Much of the most important scholarship in southern literary studies in the past decade or so has been devoted to exposing the exclusionary ideological dimensions of a monolithic idea "the South." See especially Michael Kreyling, *Inventing Southern Literature* (Jackson: University Press of Missis-

sippi, 1998); Scott Romine, *The Narrative Forms of Southern Community* (Baton Rouge: Louisiana State University Press, 1999); and Patricia Yaeger, *Dirt and Desire: Reconstructing Southern Women's Writing, 1930–1990* (Chicago: University of Chicago Press, 2000).

27. Letter from the First International Workingmen's Association (founded in London by Karl Marx) to Lincoln after his re-election in 1864, quoted in W. E. B. Du Bois, *Black Reconstruction in America, 1860–1880* (1935; repr., New York: Free Press, 1998), 218. Less pernicious than proslavery politics in this era is the rise of "southern literature" as a self-conceived countertradition characterized by a defensive impulse that Richard Gray has called "beginning from a consciousness of its own marginality" (*Southern Aberrations: Writers of the American South and the Problem of Regionalism* [Baton Rouge: Louisiana State University Press, 2000], xvii), and Fred Hobson has called "the southern rage to explain" (*Tell About the South: The Southern Rage to Explain* [Baton Rouge: Louisiana State University Press, 1983].

28. See especially the world-systems theorist Immanuel Wallerstein, *The Modern World-System*, vol. 1 (New York: Academic Press, 1974), and the social geographer D. W. Meinig, *The Shaping of America*, vol. 1 (West Haven: Yale University Press, 1988).

29. Sir William Berkeley quoted in Edmund S. Morgan, *American Slavery, American Freedom: The Ordeal of Colonial Virginia* (New York: W. W. Norton, 1975), 187.

30. Timothy Dwight, *Greenfield Hill: A Poem in Seven Parts* (New York: Childs and Swaine, 1794), 7.

31. On this point, see Martin Brueckner and Hsuan Hsu, introduction to *American Literary Geographies: Spatial Practice and Cultural Production, 1500–1900* (Dover: University of Delaware Press, 2007), 11–29.

32. The classic attribution is Lincoln's supposed (almost certainly apocryphal) statement upon meeting Stowe in 1862: "So you're the little woman who wrote the book that started this great war."

33. On the former point, see Harilaos Stecopoulos, *Reconstructing the World: Southern Fictions and U.S. Imperialisms, 1898–1976* (Ithaca, N.Y.: Cornell University Press, 2008); on the latter, Edward L. Ayers, "The First Occupation," *New York Times Magazine*, May 25, 2005.

34. The definitions of "North" and "South" in the *Oxford English Dictionary* are instructive on this point.

35. Jedidiah Morse's *American Universal Geography* (1st ed. 1790) was the most important geography textbook of the early republic; I discuss it in chapter 1.

36. Douglas Brinkley, *The Great Deluge: Hurricane Katrina, New Orleans, and the Mississippi Gulf Coast* (New York: HarperCollins, 2005), 204.

37. Brinkley, *The Great Deluge*, 204, 454. Both Anna Brickhouse, in "'L'Ouragan de Flammes': New Orleans and Transamerican Catastrophe, 1866/2005" (*American Quarterly* 59:4 [Dec. 2007]: 1097–1127), and Wai Chee Dimock, in "Afterword" (*ESQ: A Journal of the American Renaissance* 50 [Feb. 2006]: 226), have written incisively about the collisions of national and transnational interpretations of the Katrina catastrophe.

38. One classic formulation of the here/now, there/then dyad may be found in Johannes Fabian, *Time and the Other: How Anthropology Makes Its Object* (New York: Columbia University Press, 1983); another is Mikhail Bakhtin's idea of the chronotope, which I discuss at more length in chapters 1 and 2.

39. *A Fool's Errand, By One of the Fools* (1879), by Albion Tourgée, is the title of the first historical novel of Reconstruction.

40. On Cooper, see William R. Taylor, *Cavalier and Yankee: The Old South and American National Character* (New York: Brazillier, 1961); on Twain, see Amy Kaplan, *The Anarchy of Empire in the Making of U.S. Culture* (Cambridge, Mass.: Harvard University Press, 2002); on southwestern humor writing, see Jonathan Arac, *The Emergence of American Literary Narrative, 1820–1860* (Cambridge, Mass.: Harvard University Press, 2005); on southern travel writing, see John D. Cox, *Traveling South: Travel Narratives and the Construction of American National Identity* (Athens: University of Georgia Press, 2005).

41. Said, *Culture and Imperialism*, 65. Katie Trumpener brilliantly addressed the relation of internal and external colonialism in the British context in *Bardic Nationalism: The Romantic Novel and the British Empire* (Princeton: Princeton University Press, 1997).

1. The Problem of the Plantation

1. Thomas Jefferson, *Notes on the State of Virginia* (1787), ed. William Peden (Chapel Hill: University of North Carolina Press, 1982), 164–165. For the sequence of political and military events surrounding Jefferson's composition of the *Notes,* see Peden's indispensable introduction (xii–xv).

2. As Edmund S. Morgan puts it at the end of his landmark study *American Slavery, American Freedom* (New York: Norton, 1975): "And could the new United States have made a go of it in the world of nations without Virginia and without the products of slave labor?" (387).

3. In our time, Jefferson's opposition of agrarian virtue and commercial corruption was especially central to a generation of intellectual histories of republicanism published in the late 1970s by J. G. A. Pocock, Bernard Bailyn, Gordon Wood, and others. More recently, the agrarian/commercial opposition has been pushed toward a synthesis, notably in Joyce Oldham Appleby, *Liberalism and Republicanism in the Historical Imagination* (Cambridge, Mass.: Harvard University Press, 1992).

4. An authoritative biography of Crèvecoeur does not yet exist; this schematic outline of his movements is fairly well agreed upon and is taken here from Julia Post Mitchell, *St. John de Crèvecoeur* (New York: Columbia University Press, 1916), and Gay Wilson Allen and Roger Asselineau, *St. John de Crèvecoeur: The Life of an American Farmer* (New York: Viking Penguin, 1987).

5. J. Hector St. John [de Crèvecoeur], *Letters from an American Farmer; describing certain provincial situations, manners, and customs, not generally known; and conveying some idea of the late and present interior circumstances of the British Colonies in North America. Written for the information of a friend in England* (London: Thomas Davies and Lockyer Davis, 1782).

6. Dennis Moore gives an excellent account of the full body of Crèvecoeur's

manuscripts in English in his introduction to *More Letters from the American Farmer* (Athens: University of Georgia Press, 1995), xi–lxxvi.

7. Jean-Jacques Rousseau, *Du Contrat social, ou, Principes du droit politique* (Strasbourg: Societé Typographique, 1791).

8. A first "Crèvecoeur revival" in the United States was part of the great literary nationalist movement during and following World War I and likely was encouraged by D. H. Lawrence's giving the *Letters* pride of place in his *Studies in Classic American Literature* (London: M. Secker, 1924). Anthologies intended for classroom use that begin with "Letter III" include the *American Literary History Reader,* ed. Gordon Hutner (New York: Oxford University Press, 1995).

9. The painting (full title: "The Plantation of Pine-Hill. The first tree of which was cut down in ye year of our Lord 1770. County of Orange, Colony of New-York.") is described in thorough and minute detail by its former owner, Robert de Crèvecœur, in his biography of his great-grandfather, *Saint John de Crèvecoeur: Sa Vie et Ses Ouvrages* (Paris: Librairie des Bibliophiles, 1883), 24–25. I use this description to supplement the black-and-white detail of the aquarelle, reproduced as figure 1 from the *Pennsylvania Magazine of Biography and History* 30 (1906): opp. 257. According to the accompanying text, this illustration was reproduced from a black-and-white photograph of part of the painting taken by Robert's son for F. B. Sanborn, an American scholar attempting to popularize Crèvecoeur in the United States. I estimate the date of the painting on the basis of the age of the child and on Howard C. Rice's dating of the original manuscripts of the *Letters* (*Le Cultivateur Américain: Etude sur L'Œuvre de Saint John de Crèvecœur* [Paris: Librairie Ancienne Honoré Champion, 1933]).

10. Patricia Seed, *Ceremonies of Possession in Europe's Conquest of the New World, 1492–1640* (Cambridge: Cambridge University Press, 1995), 25–35.

11. Crèvecoeur was master of both Pine Hill in Orange County, New York, and Greycourt, a second plantation in Sussex County, New Jersey; Allen and Asselineau estimate that he owned more than four hundred acres of land (*St. John de Crèvecoeur,* 35).

12. This is a key element of the "Black Legend" of Spanish New World imperialism, revivified in eighteenth-century British literature. See David Shields, *Oracles of Empire: Poetry, Politics, and Commerce in British America, 1690–1750* (Chicago: University of Chicago Press, 1990), 175–194, and Roberto Fernández Retamar, "Against the Black Legend," in *Caliban and Other Essays,* trans. Edward Baker (Minneapolis: University of Minnesota Press, 1989), 56–73.

13. Crèvecoeur, "Sketch of a Contrast between the Spanish & English Colonies," in *More Letters from the American Farmer,* 88.

14. As Robert de Crèvecoeur describes the scene: "C'est un vrai paysage américain. L'habitation . . . domine des prairies onduleuses . . . À gauche, un jardin; à droite . . . une dizaine de cases de nègres . . ." (*Saint John de Crèvecoeur,* 24–25).

15. "The Plantation of Pine-Hill" exhibits many of the characteristics John Michael Vlach has attributed to nineteenth-century plantation landscape

paintings in the southern United States, produced when planters "commission[ed] images that focused solely on themselves, their families, and their buildings and spaces" (*The Planter's Prospect: Privilege and Slavery in Plantation Paintings* [Chapel Hill: University of North Carolina Press, 2002], 1).

16. Crèvecoeur, *Letters,* 26–27, emphasis mine.

17. On the transitional representation of the United States during Revolution and Confederation, see especially Gordon S. Wood, *The Creation of the American Republic* (Chapel Hill: University of North Carolina Press, 1969); Morgan, *American Slavery, American Freedom;* Jack P. Greene, *Peripheries and Center* (Athens: University of Georgia Press, 1983); Bernard Bailyn, *The Ideological Origins of the American Revolution* (1976; enl. ed., Cambridge, Mass.: Harvard University Press, 1992); and Joyce Oldham Appleby, *Without Resolution* (New York: Oxford University Press, 1992).

18. [Guillaume Thomas François] Raynal, *A Philosophical and Political History of the Settlements and Trade of the Europeans in the East and West Indies. To Which is Added, The Revolution of America. A New Translation,* 6 vols. (Edinburgh: Gordon, Donaldson, Gray, Bell, Dickson and Anderson, 1782). In vol. 5, Raynal narrates the aftermath of a failed slave rebellion in Jamaica: "Those who were supposed to be the ringleaders of the conspiracy were tied alive to gibbets, and there left to perish slowly, exposed to the scorching sun of the torrid zone: a far more painful and more terrible death than that of being burnt alive" (48).

19. Crèvecoeur, *Letters,* 225–231, emphasis mine.

20. Montesquieu, *The Spirit of the Laws,* trans. and ed. Anne Cohler et al. (Cambridge: Cambridge University Press, 1989). Christopher Iannini gives Montesquieu a central place in the development of Crèvecoeur's "cultural geography" in "'The Itinerant Man': Crèvecoeur's Caribbean, Raynal's Revolution, and the Fate of Atlantic Cosmopolitanism," *William and Mary Quarterly* 61 (2004): 201–234.

21. Crèvecoeur, *Letters,* 230–231.

22. On the conflation of American tropical productivity with moral and biological inferiority in European imperial discourse, see Louis B. Wright, *The Colonial Search for a Southern Eden* (Tuscaloosa: University of Alabama Press, 1953); Leo Marx, *The Machine in the Garden* (New York: Oxford University Press, 1964); Peter Hulme, *Colonial Encounters* (London: Methuen, 1986); and Edouard Glissant, *Caribbean Discourse: Selected Essays,* trans. J. Michael Dash (Charlottesville: University Press of Virginia, 1989).

23. Crèvecoeur, *Letters,* 219–224.

24. By including this sensational chapter, Crèvecoeur met the expectations of his European readers; on the form of later, but similar, sentimental travel writing by Europeans visiting colonies, see Mary Louise Pratt, "Scratches on the Face of the Country; or, What Mr. Barrow Saw in the Land of the Bushmen," *Critical Inquiry* 12:1 (Autumn 1985): 119–143.

25. Rice concludes that "En somme, dans cette lettre . . . il n'y a presque rien d'original, rien qui démontre une observation directe et personelle" (*Le Cultivateur Américain,* 108–109, 113).

26. The full title of the renamed chapter is "Lettre d'un Voyageur Européen, sur la situation de Charles-Town, sur son commerce et les Mœurs de ses Habitants, et ceux des Campagnes: Pensées sur l'Esclavage, sur le mal Physique: barbarie des Planteurs," in *Lettres d'un Cultivateur Américain* (Paris: Chez Cuchet, Libraire, 1784), 2:361.

27. Crèvecoeur, *Letters,* 233–234.

28. According to the biographers who have worked with his manuscripts and correspondence, there exists no evidence that Crèvecoeur ever traveled south of northern Virginia on the North American continent, even though his other travels in both America and Europe are well documented.

29. Rice quotes Brissot de Warville on Crèvecoeur's rationale for omitting the Charles-Town letter from the second and subsequent French editions of the *Lettres:* "Il ne l'a pas inséré dans sa nouvelle édition qu'on l'a prié de le supprimer, pour l'honneur des Caroliniens . . . Il a supprimé l'anecdote, et cette suppression prouve tout à la fois la bonté de son âme et son patriotisme" (*Le Cultivateur Amèricain,* 120). Iannini makes the compelling point that Crèvecoeur's sketch of Jamaica, included in the French editions, works in important ways with the omitted Charles-Town letter while also expanding "the face of America" south beyond the borders of the United States ("'The Intinerant Man'").

30. Thus Teresa Goddu rightly identifies this excessive irruption of violence as a "gothic scene" that "upsets James's tidy classifications, forcing him to see what they repress," while Dana D. Nelson, also rightly, sees the scene as a site of consolidation for national identity: an example of how "(t)he disembodied, objective, and universalized standpoint offered by Enlightenment science became useful for consolidating a perspective for 'white' [national] manhood" (Goddu, *Gothic America: Narrative, History, and Nation* [New York: Columbia University Press, 1997], 18–21; and Nelson, *National Manhood: Capitalist Citizenship and the Imagined Fraternity of White Men* [Durham, N.C.: Duke University Press, 1998], 7–10).

31. Crèvecoeur, *Letters,* 234–235.

32. Ibid., 221–222. Robert de Crèvecoeur reports that his great-grandfather "a écrit les lignes . . . au revers du cadre" (*Saint John de Crèvecoeur,* 24).

33. Crèvecoeur, *Letters,* 235.

34. Ibid.

35. John Keane details Paine's "fifteen months as executive editor" of the magazine and identifies Paine as the author of "at least seventeen and perhaps as many as twenty-six essays, poems, and reports" in its pages (*Tom Paine: A Political Life* [Boston: Little, Brown, 1995], 95–96). Edward Larkin suggests that Paine stopped working as editor and author for the magazine around August or September of 1775 (prior to writing *Common Sense*), but Keane nonetheless attributes to Paine many articles published in the first half of 1776 (Edward Larkin, "Inventing an American Public: Thomas Paine, the *Pennsylvania Magazine,* and American Revolutionary Political Discourse," *Early American Literature* 33:3 [Fall 1998]: 250–276).

36. "Proposals for Printing by Subscription The Pennsylvania Magazine," *Pennsylvania Packet,* November 21, 1774; quoted in Keane (*Tom Paine,* 92–93).

37. [Thomas Paine], "To the Publisher of the Pennsylvania Magazine: Utility of this Work Evinced," *Pennsylvania Magazine, or, the American Monthly Museum* 1:1 (Jan. 1775): 9.

38. Frank Luther Mott, *A History of American Magazines* (New York: D. Appleton, 1930), 1:89. The list of subscribers included with the first volume of the *Pennsylvania Magazine* boasts a circulation from Charleston to Portsmouth, New Hampshire.

39. [Paine], "To the Publisher," 10.

40. Johann Gottlieb Fichte, "Reden an die deutsche Nation," in *Werke*, vol. 2, ed. Peter Lothar Oesterreich (Frankfurt am Main: Deutscher Klassiker Verlag, 1997), 539–788.

41. One of the most striking things about early U.S. print production—since theories of nationalism almost inevitably see representational power as geographically aligned with material power—is that the cultural center of the nation was not, in the first years of the republic, also its economic and political center. According to classic assumptions about how modern nationalism operates, the first two decades of U.S. print culture were significantly anomalous. On the location of nationalism in print culture, the geographical alignment of cultural production with the national economic/political core, and the "centripetal" nature of nationalism, see respectively Benedict Anderson, *Imagined Communities,* rev. ed. (London: Verso, 1995); Immanuel Wallerstein, *The Modern World-System,* vol. I (New York: Academic Press, 1974), 349; and D. W. Meinig, *The Shaping of America: A Geographical Perspective on 500 Years of History,* vol. 1, *Atlantic America, 1492–1800* (New Haven: Yale University Press, 1988), 395–418.

42. No novel was published in a southern state until 1809, and only one magazine before 1800: Baltimore's quarterly *Free Universal Asylum* (1793–1797); see Cathy N. Davidson, *Revolution and the Word* (New York: Oxford University Press, 1984), 20–25, and Mott (*A History of American Magazines,* 1:31–33).

43. The material Paine *did* receive from south of Philadelphia perhaps was out of sync with his centralizing nationalism. In a "Supplement" to the 1775 volume produced at year-end, Aitken included as "Articles of Intelligence formerly omitted" a lengthy exchange of letters submitted from Charleston protesting the protection of a "negro man named Shadrack" by a British captain and analyzing this "infraction" as an affront against the property rights of the South Carolinian planter class. Although Paine forebore from addressing slavery anywhere in the magazine, it is easy to imagine why this particular "article of intelligence," direct from a southern state, would not have found a place in his pages.

44. Figure 3 is reproduced from the *Pennsylvania Magazine:* "A Perspective View of the Salt Works in Salisbury New England" 2:3 (Mar. 1776): opp. 146; "The Art of Making Common Salt" 2:3 (Mar. 1776): 128–133.

45. Figure 4 is reproduced from the *Pennsylvania Magazine:* "A New Map of North & South Carolina & Georgia," 2:6 (Jun. 1776): frontispiece. See also "An Accurate Map of the Colony of Virginia" 2:4 (Apr. 1776): frontispiece.

46. "Map of the British and French Dominions in North America, 1755," was

produced by the Virginian cartographer John Mitchell and engraved and published in London. For the significance of the map through the Revolutionary War, see Walter Ristow, *American Maps and Mapmakers: Commercial Cartography in the Nineteenth Century* (Detroit: Wayne State University Press, 1985), 25–32.

47. "An Account of the Colonies of North and South Carolina, with Georgia," *Pennsylvania Magazine* 2:6 (Jun. 1776): 268–277.

48. "An Aggregate and Valuation of the Produce of the Colony of Georgia" originally was published in the *Pennsylvania Magazine* the previous year (1:7 [Jul. 1775]: 306–307).

49. "Some Account of the Colony of Virginia," *Pennsylvania Magazine* 2:4 (Apr. 1776): 184–186. It is noteworthy that when the rebelling colonies were contemplating conquering the British colony of Québec, maps and financial accounts of Montréal and Québec City similar to those of the southern states appeared in the *Pennsylvania Magazine* as well (see 1:11 and 1:12 [Nov. and Dec. 1775]).

50. "A Correct View of the Late Battle at Charlestown," *Pennsylvania Magazine* 1:9 (Sept. 1775): frontispiece; "Lord Dunmore's depradations," *Pennsylvania Magazine* 2:4 (Apr. 1776): frontispiece.

51. Michael J. Gilmore, *Reading Becomes a Necessity of Life* (Knoxville: University of Tennessee Press, 1989), 18–27; Russel B. Nye, *The Cultural Life of the New Nation* (New York: Harper and Row, 1960), 250.

52. Carroll Smith-Rosenberg, "Dis-Covering the Subject of the 'Great Constitutional Discussion,'" *Journal of American History* 78:3 (Dec. 1992): 841–872. See also Yehoshua Arieli, *Individualism and Nationalism in American Ideology* (Cambridge, Mass.: Harvard University Press, 1964).

2. Putting the Colonial Past in Its Place

1. Immanuel Wallerstein, *Modern World-System II: Mercantilism and the Consolidation of the European World-Economy, 1600–1750* (New York: Academic Press, 1980), 157, 166–167, 179; and *Modern World System III: The Second Era of Great Expansion of the Capitalist World-Economy, 1730–1840s* (New York: Academic Press, 1989), 141, 236–237; D. W. Meinig, *The Shaping of America,* vol. 1 (New Haven: Yale University Press, 1988), 144–202, 244–254, 270–288, 395–418, 421–454.

2. On the conflation of American tropical productivity with moral and biological inferiority in European imperial discourse, see Louis B. Wright, *The Colonial Search for a Southern Eden* (Tuscaloosa: University of Alabama Press, 1953); Leo Marx, *The Machine in the Garden* (New York: Oxford University Press, 1964); Peter Hulme, *Colonial Encounters* (London: Methuen, 1986); and Edouard Glissant, *Caribbean Discourse: Selected Essays,* trans. J. Michael Dash (Charlottesville: University Press of Virginia, 1989).

3. Johann Gottfried Herder, "Ideas for a Philosophy of the History of Mankind" (1784), quoted in Carlton J. Hayes, "Contributions of Herder to the Doctrine of Nationalism," *American Historical Review* 32:4 (1927): 722.

4. Figure 5 is reproduced from the *Columbian Magazine, or Monthly Miscellany* (Philadelphia: Printed for Seddon Spotswood Cist and Trenchard, 1789), vol. 3 frontispiece. The allegorical frontispiece for vol. 2 (1788) similarly uses a palm tree as a framing device; after 1789, palm trees disappear from the magazine.

5. On the evolution around the Revolutionary War of the iconographic image of America as a woman, and the relationship of this image to Britannia, see E. McClung Fleming, "The American Image as Indian Princess, 1765–1783," *Winterthur Portfolio* 2 (1965): 65–81. Fleming notes that the "Caribbean attributes" of this iconographic woman were quickly dispensed with by U.S. artists after independence.

6. Figure 6 is reproduced from l'Abbé Raynal, *Histoire philosophique et politique des établissements et du commerce des Européens dans les deux Indes* (La Haye: 1774), vol. 4 frontispiece.

7. Thomas Jefferson, *Notes on the State of Virginia* [1787], ed. William Peden (Chapel Hill: University of North Carolina Press, 1982), 63.

8. Ibid., 23, 59, 38.

9. For an account of the development of encyclopedic Enlightenment natural history and geographical writing, see Anne Marie Claire Godlewska, "From Enlightenment Vision to Modern Science? Humboldt's Visual Thinking," in *Geography and Enlightenment,* ed. David N. Livingstone and Charles W. J. Withers (Chicago: University of Chicago Press, 1999), 236–275.

10. On Jefferson's attribution of significance to the map vs. his book, see Peden (*Notes,* xviii), and Dumas Malone, introduction to *The Fry and Jefferson Map of Virginia & Maryland* (Princeton: Princeton University Press, 1950), 1–12.

11. For instance, Jack P. Greene, "The Constitution of 1787 and the Question of Southern Distinctiveness," in *Imperatives, Behaviors, and Identities: Essays in Early American Cultural History* (Charlottesville: University of Virginia Press, 1992), 327–347; and Edward Ayers, "What We Talk About When We Talk About the South," in *All Over the Map: Rethinking American Regions* (Baltimore: Johns Hopkins University Press, 1996), 62–82. A dissenting view, championed foremost by John Richard Alden in a series of lectures, holds that the "seeds of [North/South] sectionalism" may be discerned as early as the war for independence (Alden, *The First South* [Baton Rouge: Louisiana State University Press, 1961], 4).

12. Jefferson quoted in Greene, "The Constitution of 1787"; Madison, *The Papers of James Madison,* ed. William T. Hutchinson (Chicago: University of Chicago Press, 1962), 10:88; emphasis in original.

13. For instance, Dumas Malone, *Jefferson and His Time,* vol. 1, *Jefferson the Virginian* (Boston: Little, Brown, 1948), 378.

14. Jefferson, *Notes,* 4, 8, 15.

15. I am drawing here on Peter S. Onuf's definition of Jefferson's "republican empire" (*Jefferson's Empire: The Language of American Nationhood* [Charlottesville: University of Virginia Press, 2000], 67).

16. Jefferson, *Notes,* 165. As Onuf puts it, Jefferson's conceptualization of Virginia in the *Notes* "was premised on his profound hostility to metropolitan domination" (*Jefferson's Empire,* 70).

17. For these "paradoxical" readings of Jefferson, see, respectively, Joyce Oldham Appleby, *Without Resolution: The Jeffersonian Tensions in American Nationalism* (Oxford: Clarendon Press, 1991); David Kazanjian, *The Colonizing Trick: National Culture and Imperial Citizenship in Early America* (Minneapolis: University of Minnesota Press, 2003); and Onuf, *Jefferson's Empire*.

18. Lewis P. Simpson notes the literariness of the subject matter of the query on manners; he also points out that Jefferson's paean to the yeoman farmer directly follows it, and thus that "the vision of the yeoman farmer represents not only a pastoral purification of European influences but of the influence of slavery" (*The Dispossessed Garden: Pastoral and History in Southern Literature* [Athens: University of Georgia Press, 1975], 30–33).

19. Jefferson, *Notes,* 162. Locke had stated: "This is the perfect condition of Slavery, which is nothing else, but the State of War continued, between a lawful Conquerour, and a Captive" (John Locke, *Two Treatises of Government,* ed. Peter Laslett [Cambridge: Cambridge University Press, 1988], 284).

20. Jefferson, *Notes,* 163.

21. [Guillaume Thomas François] Raynal, *A Philosophical and Political History of the Settlements and Trade of the Europeans in the East and West Indies* (Edinburgh: Silvester Doig, 1792), 4:81.

22. Jefferson, *Notes,* 163.

23. Ralph Bauer finds that what seems Jefferson's precocious modern racism in the *Notes* is directly tied to his spurning of Raynal's indictments of creole degeneracy: to reject the validity of environmental influence on organisms as a source of hierarchy between peoples, Bauer proposes, lends credence to the validity of organic biological difference as just such a hierarchical marker ("The Hemispheric Genealogies of 'Race': Creolization and the Cultural Geography of Colonial Difference across the Eighteenth-Century Americas" in *Hemispheric American Studies,* ed. Caroline F. Levander and Robert S. Levine [New Brunswick: Rutgers University Press, 2008], 48–54).

24. In his more extensive studies of early nationalist "geographic literacy," Martin Brückner concurs that "the early national geography textbooks inculcate a perspective that follows the classical geodeterminism prescribing a North-South gradient of moral-ethnic distinction . . . a geographic scale designed to admeasure and ascribe moral value to local places . . . [B]ooks persistently privilege white Americans living in the North over those in the South" ("Lessons in Geography: Maps, Spellers, and Other Grammars of Nationalism in the Early Republic," *American Quarterly* 51:2 [Jun. 1999]: 338).

25. Jedidiah Morse, D. D., *The American Universal Geography, or, a View of the Present State of all the Empires, Kingdoms, States, and Republics in the known world, and of the United States of America in particular,* 4th ed. (Boston: Isaiah Thomas and Ebenezer T. Andrews, 1802), 1:vii.

26. Ibid., iii–vii. Brückner makes a similar point about the "New World order" of Morse's *American Universal Geography;* he also usefully discusses the "geographic reading protocol" shaped by early national textbooks (*The Geographic Revolution in Early America: Maps, Literacy, and National Identity* [Chapel Hill: University of North Carolina Press, 2006], 164).

27. A Hawk [Noah Webster], "Letters on Education," the *American Magazine* 1:6 (May 1788): 367–374.
28. On the London vantage, Greene quotes John Fothergill's prescient 1765 diagnosis of the nascent metropolitanism of the northern colonies versus the entrenched colonialism of their southern counterparts, in "The Constitution of 1787," 327–347. On the Nova Scotia-Massachusetts connection, see Stephen Nissenbaum, "New England as Region and Nation," in *All Over the Map*, 38–61; on the Barbados-South Carolina connection, see Greene, "Colonial South Carolina and the Caribbean Connection," in *Imperatives, Behaviors, and Identities*, 68–86.
29. [Webster], "Letters on Education," 368.
30. Webster, *An American Selection of Lessons in Reading and Speaking* (Philadelphia: Young and McCulloch, 1787), 141.
31. Warner, "What's Colonial about Colonial America?" in *Possible Pasts: Becoming Colonial in Early America*, ed. Robert Blair St. George (Ithaca, N.Y.: Cornell University Press, 2000), 63.
32. Webster, *An American Selection*, 147, 145, 149.
33. Morse, *American Universal Geography*, 302, 304.
34. Ibid., 458.
35. On the history of reception of the maps, see Ralph H. Brown, "The American Geographies of Jedidiah Morse," *Annals of the Association of American Geographers* 31:3 (Sept. 1941): 188–205.
36. Morse, *American Universal Geography*, 580, 583, 619; Morse, *Geography Made Easy*, (his abridgement of the volume), 8th ed. (Boston: I. Thomas and E. T. Andrews, 1802), 223.
37. Morse, *American Universal Geography*, 650, 655; Morse, *Geography Made Easy*, 234–235; Morse, *American Universal Geography*, 694, 696.
38. Webster was criticized scathingly for his New England prejudices against the southern states by the *Columbian Magazine* editors in 5:4 and 5:5 (Oct. and Nov. 1790)—and again in 7:4 (Oct. 1791) when he attempted to reply.
39. A Citizen of Williamsburg, *A Letter to the Rev. Jedediah Morse, A. M.* (Richmond: Thomas Nicolson, 1795) (The author has been variously identified as either St. George Tucker or James Madison). J[ames] F[reeman], *Remarks on the American Universal Geography* (Boston: Belknap and Hall, 1793), 59, 12.
40. On Webster's textbook-hawking travels, see Harlow G. Unger, *Noah Webster: The Life and Times of an American Patriot* (New York: John Wiley, 1998). According to the publication information given on the title pages of the 1793, 1796, and 1802 editions of Morse's *American Universal Geography*, the textbook was published in Boston, Worcester, Philadelphia, and New York, and progressively added a southern city to this roster with each edition: first Charleston, then Baltimore, then Savannah.
41. M. M. Bakhtin, "Forms of Time and of the Chronotope in the Novel: Notes Toward a Historical Poetics," in *The Dialogic Imagination: Four Essays*, ed. Michael Holquist, trans. Caryl Emerson and Michael Holquist (Austin: University of Texas Press, 1981), 84, 158.

42. For instance, Sean X. Goudie, *Creole America: The West Indies and the Formation of Literature and Culture in the New Republic* (Philadelphia: University of Pennsylvania Press, 2006); Eric Wertheimer, *Imagined Empires: Incas, Aztecs, and the New World of American Literature, 1771–1876* (Cambridge: Cambridge University Press, 1998); and Henry Nash Smith, *Virgin Land: The American West as Symbol and Myth*, new ed. (Cambridge, Mass.: Harvard University Press, 2005).

3. Domestic Possession and the Imperial Impulse

1. Ralph Bauer makes a similar observation about the strategies of Crèvecoeur and Alonso Carrió de la Vandera in the concluding chapter of *The Cultural Geography of American Literatures* (Cambridge: Cambridge University Press, 2003), 216–217, 232–233.

2. [Noah Webster, jun., esq.], *The American Magazine*, vol. 1 (New York: Samuel Loudon, Dec. 1787–Nov. 1788). Webster's personal copy is held with his papers at the Beinecke Rare Book and Manuscript Library.

3. I have not ascertained conclusively whether or not Webster actually distributed copies of this map to his subscribers, either with the original first issues or with the year-end supplement. Certainly the synchronous production of magazine and map makes this a possibility. Since there are no instructions to binders printed as part of the volume, and since I have not located a second full-volume copy that includes the frontispiece, I assume here that this illustration appears only in Webster's personal copy.

4. Timothy Dwight, "A Valedictory address To the Young Gentlemen, who commenced Bachelors of Arts, at Yale College, July 25th 1776. By the Rev. Dr. Dwight," *American Magazine* 1:1 (Dec. 1787): 42.

5. Webster included George Washington's "Circular Letter of June 18 1783" in the third volume of his *Grammatical Institute, An American Selection of Lessons in Reading and Speaking* (ed. Noah Webster, jun Esq., 3rd ed. [Philadelphia: Young and McCulloch, 1787], 203); Dwight, "A Valedictory address," 42, 45.

6. Dwight, "A Valedictory address," 44.

7. Ibid., 44.

8. Morse's section on the "Third [Southern] Grand Division" of the United States ends with his musings that "we cannot but anticipate the period, as not far distant, when the *American Empire* will comprehend millions of souls west of the Mississippi" (Jedidiah Morse, D.D., *The American Universal Geography, or, a View of the Present State of all the Empires, Kingdoms, States, and Republics in the known world, and of the United States of America in particular*, 4th ed. [Boston: Isaiah Thomas and Ebenezer T. Andrews, 1802] 630).

9. For an incisive summary of this turn, see Sandra M. Gustafson, "Histories of Democracy and Empire," *American Quarterly* 59:1 (Mar. 2007): 107–133.

10. See, for instance, Thomas Kitchin's "New and General Map of the Southern Dominions Belonging to the United States of America, viz: North Carolina, South Carolina, and Georgia," (London: Laurie and Whittle, 1794).

11. "The Present State of the American Nation," *New-York Magazine, or, Literary Repository* 2:2 (Feb. 1791), 89–93.

12. M. M. Bakhtin, "Forms of Time and of the Chronotope in the Novel: Notes Toward a Historical Poetics," in *The Dialogue Imagination: Four Essays,* ed. Michael Holquist, trans. Caryl Emerson and Michael Holquist (Austin: University of Texas Press, 1981), 251, 250.

13. On the issue of centralization in the Constitutional debates and its transmogrification into the Federalist/Republican standoff of the 1790s, see Peter S. Onuf "The Origins of American Sectionalism," in *All Over the Map: Rethinking American Regions* (Baltimore: Johns Hopkins University Press, 1996), 11–37; on comparative total wealth production by region, see Joyce Oldham Appleby, *Capitalism and a New Social Order* (New York: New York University Press, 1983).

14. On the hegemonic function of national culture, specifically in situations of internal colonization, see Immanuel Wallerstein: "World-economies then are divided into core-states and peripheral areas . . . In a world-economy the political structure tends to link culture with spatial location . . . [I]n core-states, the creation of a strong state machinery coupled with a national culture, a phenomenon often referred to as integration, serves as an ideological mask and justification for these disparities" (*Modern World-System I,* [New York: Academic Press, 1974] 349).

15. [Charles Brockden Brown], "On the State of American Literature," *Monthly Magazine, and American Review* 1:1 (Apr. 1799): 15–19.

16. Classic readings include Gayatri Spivak, "Three Women's Texts and a Critique of Imperialism" (*Critical Inquiry* 12:1 [Autumn 1985]: 243-261); Edward Said, "Jane Austen and Empire," *Culture and Imperialism* (New York: Knopf, 1993); Fredric Jameson, *Nationalism, Colonialism, and Literature—Modernism and Imperialism* (Minneapolis: University of Minnesota Press, 1996); Firdous Agim, *The Colonial Rise of the Novel* (London: Routledge, 1993); and Homi Bhabha, *The Location of Culture* (London: Routledge, 1994).

17. *Columbian Magazine* 8:2 (Feb. 1792): 121–123.

18. Ibid., 122–123. For a contemporaneous survey of 1790s theories on the origins of the yellow fever epidemics, see [Charles Brockden Brown], "On American Literature," *Monthly Magazine* 1:8 (Nov. 1799): 339–342.

19. A biographical sketch is given by W. B. Chittenden in *The Literary Remains of Joseph Brown Ladd, M.D.* (New York: H.C. Sleight, 1832).

20. "If we may judge by the poems which Mathew Carey reprinted in the *American Museum*," writes Jay B. Hubbell, "Ladd's verses were in greater demand than those of Freneau, Francis Hopkinson, or the Connecticut Wits. His poems are easy, facile, and timely. They are a good index to what American readers liked in the closing years of the eighteenth century" (*The South in American Literature, 1607–1900* (Durham, N.C.: Duke University Press, 1957), 164).

21. "Prospect of Carolina. For July.—by the late dr. Ladd," *American Museum* 2:5 (Nov. 1787): 516–517.

22. See, for instance, "The State of Slavery in Virginia and other parts of the

Continent," *Columbian Magazine* 1:6 (Jun. 1787): 479–481; "Anecdotes of Pocahunta, an Indian Princess, from whom several respectable families in Virginia are descended," *Columbian Magazine* 1:7 (Jul. 1787): 548–551; "Thoughts on the Probable Termination of Negro Slavery in the United States of America," *Monthly Magazine* 2:2 (Feb. 1800): 81–84.

23. "Comparative View of the number of Males and Females in the several districts of the United States, excepting South-Carolina, from which returns have not yet been made," *Columbian Magazine* 8:1 (Jan. 1792): 12–14.

24. "The analogy between the respective forms of Government, and the origins of the several states of North America, taken from the entertaining Travels of the Marquis de Chastelleux," *Columbian Magazine* 1:6 (Jun. 1787): 477–478.

25. "Essay on negro slavery," *American Museum* 4:6 (Dec. 1788): 509–511.

26. Charles Brockden Brown, "[Review of] The History of America, Books IX and X. Containing the History of Virginia to the Year 1688, and of Connecticut to the Year 1652. By William Robertson," *Monthly Magazine* 1:2 (May 1799): 130–131.

27. On the anti-southern dimensions of Federalist rhetoric, see Linda K. Kerber, *Federalists in Dissent: Imagery and Ideology in Jeffersonian America* (Ithaca, N.Y.: Cornell University Press, 1970), 23–66.

28. "An Essay intended to shew that Necessaries are the best Productions of Land, and the Best Staple of Commerce," *Columbian Magazine* 6:5 (May 1791): 320–326.

29. "Character of the Virginians," *Massachusetts Magazine: or, Monthly Museum of Knowledge and Rational Entertainment* 3:7 (Jul. 1791): 409–410.

30. Joanne Pope Melish closely investigates this active amnesia in her indispensable *Disowning Slavery: Gradual Emancipation and "Race" in New England, 1780–1860* (Ithaca, N.Y.: Cornell University Press, 1998). On the progress of abolition of slavery in the northern and middle states, see David Brion Davis, *The Problem of Slavery in the Age of Revolution* (Ithaca, N.Y.: Cornell University Press, 1975), 85–89, and Edgar J. McManus, *Black Bondage in the North* (Syracuse, N.Y.: Syracuse University Press, 1973).

Before 1800, only Vermont outlawed slavery in its state constitution; the Massachusetts and New Hampshire legislatures had taken no action to restrict slavery; and Pennsylvania (1780), Connecticut (1784), Rhode Island (1784), and New York (1799) had passed gradual (*post nati*) emancipation laws applicable only to enslaved persons born after the date of the law and then only when they had reached a specified age (usually twenty-five or older). Slavery remained legal in effect in these states well into the 1820s; slaves were held legally in New Jersey and Delaware until the Civil War.

Given what historians of slavery in the northern states (such as Edgar J. McManus, *A History of Negro Slavery in New York,* and Lorenzo Johnston Greene, *The Negro in Colonial New England, 1620–1776*) have shown us about the employment of enslaved workers in the printing industry, particularly in cities like Philadelphia and New York, I wonder how many of the magazines and books quoted in this chapter—in which authors and editors

denied the existence or significance of slavery beyond the Plantation South—
might themselves have been physically produced by slave labor.

31. H. Trevor Colbourn, "*New Travels in the United States of America,* 1788,"
Journal of Southern History 31:4 (Nov. 1965): 453–455.

32. Brissot de Warville, "On the Laws of the different American States for the
Manumission of Slaves. From M. Brissot de Warville's Travels in the United
States," *Columbian Magazine* 9:5 (Nov. 1792): 311–314.

33. Ibid. Eric Williams provides a classic discussion of the imagined geography
of British abolitionism in the tenth and eleventh chapters of *Capitalism and
Slavery* (1944): "[S]lavery to [metropolitan British capitalists] was relative
not absolute, and depended upon latitude and longitude" (new ed. [Chapel
Hill: University of North Carolina Press, 1994], 169).

34. Thomas Clarkson "A fancied scene in the African slave trade," *New-York
Magazine,* 1:8 (Aug. 1790): 464–467.

35. "A Georgia planter's method of spending his time," *American Museum* 8:5
(Nov. 1790): 243–244.

36. For information on Smyth's wartime activities in America, see Charles R.
Hildeburn, *Sketches of Printers and Printing in Colonial New York* (New
York: Dodd, Mead, 1895), 82–83; for his claims to descent from the Stuart
line, see the *Dictionary of National Biography,* ed. Sidney Lee (New York:
Macmillan, 1898), 102–103.

37. J. F. D. Smyth, "Manner of Living of the inhabitants of Virginia," *American
Museum* 1:3 (Mar. 1787): 214–216; republished as "Satirical Character of the
Virginians. Written in 1686," *Massachusetts Magazine* 4:4 (Apr. 1792): 38–40.
Other examples of the genre, not authored by Smyth, include "Sketch of the
Character of the South Carolinians—their Luxury and Dissipation—Fatal ef-
fects of Luxury—Hospitality of South Carolina," *Massachusetts Magazine* 3:6
(Jun. 1791): 343–345; "Character of the Virginians. Written in 1720," *Massa-
chusetts Magazine* 3:7 (Jul. 1791): 409–410; "On the Climate of South Car-
olina. By Dr. Budd," *Massachusetts Magazine* 4:1 (Jan. 1792) 38–40;
"Character of the Virginians," *American Museum* 7:4 (Apr. 1790): 215–216.

38. "They spunge," in "Character of the Virginians," *New-York Magazine* 3:5
(May 1792): 38–40; shooting anecdote in "A Georgia planter's method of
spending his time"; "savage brutality" in "Sketch of the Character of the
South Carolinians."

39. Hazel Carby has alerted me to the similarity of these 1790s planter sketches
to characterizations developed fifty years later on blackface minstrel show
stages.

40. On the alienation of the southern states from the consolidating core of the
U.S. in the early national era, see D. W. Meinig: "Geographically a national
core was taking shape quite at variance from the delicate balances of feder-
alism . . . The alienation of Virginia from the integrative processes and formative patterns of the national core, given that state's great political prestige
and power and its geographical position in the emerging American nation,
was a sign of impending geopolitical stress" (*The Shaping of America: A Geographical Perspective on 500 Years of History* vol. 1, *Atlantic America,
1492–1800* [New Haven: Yale University Press, 1988], 404, 406).

41. A conversation with Jennifer Baszile helped me to clarify this key point. Orlando Patterson instructively interrogates the concept of "freedom" as dependent on the existence of slavery, in *Slavery and Social Death: A Comparative Study* (Cambridge, Mass: Harvard University Press, 1982).

42. On the dialectic of republican freedom and imperial mastery, see especially Edmund S. Morgan's analysis of the symbiotic relationship of slavery and freedom in colonial Virginia (*American Slavery, American Freedom* [New York: Norton, 1975]) and Joyce Oldham Appleby's reading of the equality/liberty dialectic in Jefferson (*Without Resolution* [New York: Oxford University Press, 1992]).

43. Thomas Dawes, jun. Esq., *American Magazine* 1:9 (Aug. 1788): 619–623.

44. Tyler's text long was thought to have been the first U.S. novel republished in London; it was published there as a novel in 1802 and serialized with illustrations in the *Lady's Magazine* in 1804. (Charles Brockden Brown's *Ormond* was published in London in 1800.) On the stature of *The Algerine Captive* among U.S. literary critics, see Cathy Davidson, *Revolution and the Word* (New York: Oxford University Press, 1986) 192–194.

45. For a complete list of ships and crewmen captured, crewmen who died in captivity, and the precise events of negotiation and ransom for the freedom of the U.S. slaves, see John Foss, appendix to *A journal of the captivity and sufferings of John Foss, several years a prisoner at Algiers* (Newburyport, Mass.: Angier March, 1798).

46. "Essay on negro slavery," *American Museum* 4:6 (Dec. 1788): 509–511. In a similar vein, but with West Indian rather than North American slavery as its point of comparison, an ostensible "Copy of a letter from an English Slave-driver at Algiers" remarks that "People may say this or that of the infidels; but sure am I they do not deserve to be extirpated any more than the English themselves . . . for we just do here to the whites what the whites do to the blacks in the West-Indies; only we use them more mercifully" (*New-York Magazine* 2:10 [Oct. 1791]: 584). Also drawing on this conjuncture is Franklin's famous 1790 letter to the *Federal Gazette* claiming to cite an excerpt from "Sidi Mehemet Ibrahim" in order to comment on the congressional debate on abolishing the slave trade.

47. Through the late 1780s, antislavery magazine commentators of the middle states explicitly criticized the continued participation of New England shippers in the African slave trade. See, for example, "A Tour to the Eastern States," *Columbian Magazine* 3:7 (Jul.): 531–534.

48. Tyler's literary treatment of the Algerian enslavement of white Christians was a true innovation in the portrayal of this subject matter. Previous U.S. treatments of the topic—such as the story "Louisa" (printed without attribution in the *Massachusetts Magazine,* 1790) and Susanna Rowson's play *Slaves in Algiers* (1794)—had followed the lead of English author Penelope Aubin's popular *The Noble Slaves* (1722), using the exotic setting of Algerian harems and mines to unfold courtly romance tales with a racy edge of threatened miscegenation (Anon., "Louisa, A Novel," *Massachusetts Magazine* 2:2 and 2:3 (Feb. and Mar. 1790): 78–82 and 147–151, respectively; Rowson, *Slaves in Algiers; or, a Struggle for Freedom* (Philadelphia; Wrigley

and Berriman, 1794); Aubin, *The Noble Slaves: Being an entertaining history of the surprising adventures and remarkable deliverances from Algerine slavery of several Spanish noblemen and ladies of quality* [New Haven, Conn.: George Bunce, 1798]).

49. In her important reading of the novel in the context of U.S. orientalisms, Malini Johar Schueller, too, focuses on Tyler's "strategic" placement of the slave ship scenes at the center of the text, finding that in these passages Tyler effects the major transition of the novel: here Updike's role as narrator shifts from "bumbling comic hero searching for himself in a new country" to "wise reporter acting as the agent of the new empire" (*U.S. Orientalisms: Race, Nation, and Gender in Literature, 1790–1890* [Ann Arbor: University of Michigan Press, 1998], 50–55).

50. Tyler names his protagonist after Captain John Underhill, Puritan prosecutor of the Pequot War, then ridicules the weighted name by punning on it. The notion that New Englanders were the colonizing and civilizing vanguard of U.S. expansion is evident even in 1780s print: see, for instance, Morse's thoughts on New England emigration to the southern states, the "Spanish dominions," and beyond (*American Universal Geography*, 480, 499, 554, 568, 613, 630).

51. Royall Tyler, *The Algerine Captive; or, the Life and Adventures of Doctor Updike Underhill, Six Years a Prisoner Among the Algerines* (Walpole, New Hampshire: Daid Carlisle, 1797), 151, 66, 74, 67.

52. Ibid., 102–103.

53. Beginning in the 1790s, dueling and concepts of "honor" in general were widely reviled in the national magazines as pre-Revolutionary, aristocratic hangovers from the colonial past that could not be purged quickly enough from the United States; towards the end of the decade, these activities not surprisingly began to be aligned with the southern states. See, for instance, "The Point of Honour in America," *Monthly Magazine* 3:6 (Dec. 1800): 408–409. The idea that indifference or recklessness about death was a sign of savagery was also widespread in the magazines of the period; for an early example, see "Indians Indifferent to Dying," *American Museum* 1:3 (Mar. 1787): 216–222.

54. Tyler, *The Algerine Captive*, 81.

55. Ibid., 152. Another model for the imperiled New England intellectual in the tropical Plantation South would have been William Hill Brown, the Bostonian author of *The Power of Sympathy* (1789), conventionally credited as the first U.S. novel; he moved to Halifax, North Carolina, in 1792 and promptly died of a fever the following year (Lewis Leary "1776–1815," in ed., Louis D. Rubin, Jr., *The History of Southern Literature* [Baton Rouge: Louisiana State University Press, 1985], 74).

56. Tyler, *The Algerine Captive*, 62.

57. Ibid., 163–164, emphasis mine.

58. Letter to the editor, *Farmer's Weekly Museum* (24 April 1798).

59. Tyler, *The Algerine Captive*, 167–168.

60. It is in the London edition that this geographical specification of "Barbadoes and South-Carolina" is made (Tyler, *The Algerine Captive; or, the Life and*

Adventures of Doctor Updike Underhill, Six Years a Prisoner Among the Algerines [London: G. and J. Robinson, 1802]) 92; the American edition simply reads, "West-Indies" (169–170).

61. An earlier short story treatment that shares Tyler's moral-geographic narrativization of Algerian captivity is "History of Mr. Wilfort (A True Narrative)," *Columbian Magazine* 4:4 (Apr. 1790): 231–233; in this story, a protagonist bored with New England abstemiousness emigrates, instead of to a southern state, to Jamaica, where he takes on aristocratic ways ("extravagancies and dissipation"), and then immediately boards a ship that is "taken by an Algerine corsair, and he (is) sold to slavery."

62. Tyler, *The Algerine Captive*, 201, 189, 166.

63. Attributed to Lincoln in "Lincoln's Definition of Democracy: As He Would Not Be a Slave, So He Would Not Be a Master," the *New York Times*, Sept. 13, 1895: 10.

64. Tyler, *The Algerine Captive*, 190, 204. Tyler ultimately makes Updike's expiation explicit: "I have deplored my conduct [on board the slaver] with tears of anguish; and I pray to a merciful God . . . that the miseries, the insults, and cruel woundings I afterwards received when a slave myself may expiate for the inhumanity I was necessitated to exercise towards (the African captives), MY BRETHREN OF THE HUMAN RACE" (110).

65. See the *Lady's Magazine; or Entertaining Companion for the Fair Sex* (London: G. and J. Robinson, 1770–1837). Tyler's novel was serialized in 35:4–11 (Apr.–Nov., 1804).

66. Tyler's last produced play, *The Georgia Spec, or Land in the Moon* (1797–1798), revived twice in New York under the revised title *A Good Spec: Land in the Moon, or the Yankee turn'd Duelist*, satirized the corruptions of U.S. expansionist ambitions (Marius B. Péladeau, "Royall Tyler's Other Plays," *New England Quarterly* 40:1 (Mar. 1967): 48–60).

4. The Enemy Within

1. Many literary historians have written insightfully about the U.S. adaptation of these genres. See especially Leslie Fiedler, *Love and Death in the American Novel* (New York: Criterion, 1960), and Leonard Tennenhouse, *The Importance of Feeling English: American Literature and the British Diaspora, 1750–1850* (Princeton: Princeton University Press, 2007).

2. [Charles Brockden Brown], "On a Scheme for describing American Manners. (Addressed to a Foreigner.)," *Monthly Magazine* 3:1 (Jun. 1800): 7–10.

3. Two enduring motifs for national literature are foretold in this image: the early portrayal of the Southerner as a *double* for a national character—a copy with a difference, in Otto Rank's definition (Rank, *Der Doppelgänger: eine psychoanalytische Studie* [1925; reprint, Vienna: Turia & Kant, 1993]); and the use of a river to organize an internal, as opposed to an external, geographic contrast. In the nineteenth century, the Hudson would mark the boundary between country and city; the Mississippi between East and West; and rivers such as the Ohio (in Eliza's dash across the ice floes) and the Po-

tomac (in Clotel's suicidal plunge) would continue to mark the divides between South and nation.

4. "Arguments drawn from interest, as well as humanity, against the practice of SLAVERY in the French Colonies," *Columbian Magazine* 3:6 (Jun. 1789): 361–363.

5. See Timothy Morton on "the function of the 'blood sugar' topos in 1790s" British poetry and addresses (*The Poetics of Spice* [Cambridge: Cambridge University Press, 2000], 174).

6. William Dunlap, *The Life of Charles Brockden Brown* (Philadelphia: James P. Parke, 1815), 1:44–45.

7. "Remarks on Cock-Fighting," *New-York Magazine* 2:3 (Mar. 1791): 158.

8. Although they are in the minority, major critics including Jay Fliegelman have rejected the "gothic" label for Brown's novels (introduction to *Wieland and Memoirs of Carwin the Biloquist* [New York: Penguin, 1991], x).

9. Peter Kafer makes this argument most convincingly in *Charles Brockden Brown's Revolution and the Birth of American Gothic* (Philadelphia: University of Pennsylvania Press, 2004), esp. 17–65.

10. Wai Chee Dimock, lecture for English 280a, Yale University, September 1997.

11. Dunlap, *The Life of Charles Brockden Brown*, 1:19–22. Steven Watts has proposed that Brown's Carsol sketches explain the "ideological condition" of the author in the first decade of the nineteenth century: "The author's long struggle (in the novels) with liberalizing individualism gave rise to a fictional hero whose unrestrained power imposed order upon chaos" (*The Romance of Real Life: Charles Brockden Brown and the Origins of American Culture* [Baltimore: Johns Hopkins University Press, 2004], 175).

12. Quoted in Dunlap, *The Life of Charles Brockden Brown*, 2:50.

13. Charles Brockden Brown, *Wieland, or, the Transformation* (New York: T. and J. Swords, 1798), 34.

14. Ibid.

15. Ibid., 37, 52–53. About precisely this passage, Ed White has argued that "we (should) find . . . a historical, geographical problem, one concerned with the elusive cultural dynamics of the material landscape of Pennsylvania," though his focus is on the looming presence of the "backcountry" rather than the South ("Carwin the Peasant Rebel," in *Revising Charles Brockden Brown,* ed. Philip Barnard, Mark L. Kamrath, and Stephen Shapiro [Knoxville: University of Tennessee Press, 2004], 48).

16. Charles Brockden Brown, *Ormond, or, the Secret Witness* (New York: H. Caritat, 1799); *Arthur Mervyn, or, Memoir of the year 1793* (Philadelphia: H. Maxwell, 1799); and *Arthur Mervyn, or Memoirs of the Year 1793, Second Part* (New York: George F. Hopkins, 1800), 138–147.

17. Brown, *Ormond,* 40. Robert S. Levine has noted that "during the 1790s, the fever was regularly portrayed as a duplicitous form of foreign infiltration and subversion" (*Conspiracy and Romance* [Cambridge: Cambridge University Press, 1989], 34).

18. Brown, *Ormond,* 242.

19. Brown, *Arthur Mervyn, Second Part*, 162.
20. Brown, *Arthur Mervyn, Second Part*, 162. With the monkey in the scene, Brown channels a major natural history debate of the period over whether African peoples were more closely related to "humans" (that is, European peoples) or "ourang-outangs." See, for instance, "Observations on the Gradation in the Scale of Being between the Human and Brute Creation. Including some Curious Particulars respecting Negroes," *Columbian Magazine* 2:1 (Jan. 1788): 14–22.
21. Sean X. Goudie aptly calls the southbound stage in this passage an "ethnolaboratory," although because of his focus on the West Indies rather than on the U.S. South, Goudie sees Baltimore as equivalent to Philadelphia—"another of the United States' heterotopic commercial ports"—and so why this short trip spurs Mervyn's "awakening to a racially supremacist consciousness" remains mysterious ("On the Origin of American Specie(s): The West Indies, Classification, and the Emergence of Supremacist Consciousness in *Arthur Mervyn*," in *Revising Charles Brockden Brown*, 73).
22. On Americans as agents of European natural history, see Andrew Lewis, *A Democracy of Facts: Natural History in the Early Republic* (Philadelphia: University of Pennsylvania Press, 2010), and Susan Scott Parrish, *American Curiosity: Cultures of Natural History in the Colonial British Atlantic World* (Chapel Hill: University of North Carolina Press, 2006).
23. Brown, *Arthur Mervyn, Second Part*, 162, 184, emphasis mine.
24. Ormond, who resides at the "Indian Queen" hotel in Philadelphia, transmits money to Jamaica through Baltimore; in this endeavor he trusts Craig, who has relocated to Baltimore after embezzling the family fortune of the Dudleys and absconding with it to Jamaica; the original Dudley fortune came from a union of a Tobago planter with a wealthy Baltimorean; unbeknownst to Ormond, his sister, Martinette, has entered Philadelphia from St. Domingo via Richmond; and the evil mother of the narrator of the novel, Sophia Westwyn (the "secret witness"), uses Charleston for her disruptive reentry into the plot.
25. Brown, *Ormond*, 155. In her excellent reading of Ormond's blackface masquerade, Julia Stern has argued that "it is precisely in the novel's representation of slavery, a distinctly domestic crisis, [and] not in the villain's phatasmagoric international schemes that *Ormond's* real 'political' interest lies" ("The State of 'Women' in *Ormond*; or, Patricide in the New Nation," in *Revising Charles Brockden Brown*, 196; see also Stern's *The Plight of Feeling: Sympathy and Dissent in the Early American Novel* [Chicago: University of Chicago Press, 1997], 153–238).
26. Brown, *Ormond*, 244.
27. Ibid., 62, 63, 291.
28. Charles Brockden Brown, *An Address to the Government of the United States, on the Cession of Louisiana to the French, and on the Late Breach of Treaty by the Spaniards: including the Translation of a Memorial, on the War of St. Domingo, and Cession of the Mississippi to France, Drawn up by a French Counsellor of State* (Philadelphia: J. Conrad, 1803), 2. As the title indicates, the pamphlet describes a counterfactual event.

29. Ibid.
30. C. F. Volney, *A View of the Soil and Climate of the United States of America*, trans. C. B. Brown (Philadelphia: J. Conrad, 1804), xii. Compare Brown's translation with the original French : "les differences d'opinion et meme d'intérêt qui partagent *l'union* en *États de l'Est*, et en *États du Sud* . . . la faiblesse de ceux/ci, causée par les esclaves; la force de ceux-là, causée par leur population libre et industrieuse" (*Tableau du climate et du sol des États–Unis d'Amérique* [Paris: Chez Courcier, 1803]).
31. Ibid., 3–4, 2.
32. An early English translation, published in Philadelphia, was C. F. Volney, *The Ruins: or, A Survey of the Revolutions of Empires* (Philadelphia: J. Lyon, 1799).
33. [Charles Brockden Brown], "The Point of Honour in America," *Monthly Magazine* 3:6 (Dec. 1800): 408–409.
34. Jay Fliegelman, *Prodigals and Pilgrims: The American Revolution against Patriarchal Authority* (Cambridge: Cambridge University Press, 1982); Ruth Bloch, "The Gendered Meanings of Virtue in Revolutionary America," in *Signs* 13:1 (Autumn 1987): 37–59; and Elizabeth Barnes, *States of Sympathy: Seduction and Democracy in the American Novel* (New York: Columbia University Press, 1997).
35. [Brown], "The Point of Honour in America," 408–409.
36. Although it was not published in book form until 1798, *Amelia, or the Faithless Briton* (anon.) was serialized widely in the literary magazines, beginning perhaps with the *Columbian Magazine* of October 1787 (1:10). Rowson's *Charlotte, A Tale of Truth* was first published in London, and its protagonist is a native Briton, but the novel did not achieve success until it was published in the U.S. the next year, where it quickly was assimilated as an "American" book and Charlotte adopted as an "American" heroine.
37. Anon., "Fatal Effects of Seduction. A Story founded on Fact, veiled only under a fictitious Name," *New-York Magazine* 1:1 (Jan. 1790): 22–23, emphases mine.
38. Constantia [Judith Sargent Murray], *The Gleaner. A Miscellaneous Production in Three Volumes* (Boston: I. Thomas and E. T. Andrews, 1798); Charles Brockden Brown, *Jane Talbot: A Novel* (Philadelphia: John Conrad, 1801).
39. A Lady of Massachusetts [Hannah Webster Foster], *The Coquette; or the history of Eliza Wharton: a novel, founded on fact* (Boston: E. Larkin, 1797), 140, 138, 172–73, 174.
40. Whereas Charlotte Lennox's 1752 novel of almost the same title negotiates the divide between romance and novel, as Margaret Anne Doody has argued, in her entry into the field a half-century later Tenney is uninterested in the courtly romance of Cervantes's original, firmly setting her critical sights on the modern English and American fiction of her day (Doody, introduction to Lennox, *The Female Quixote or the Adventures of Arabella* [Oxford: Oxford University Press, 1989], xi–xxxi).
41. Tabitha Tenney, *Female Quixotism: exhibited in the romantic opinions and extravagant adventures of Dorcasina Sheldon* (Boston: I. Thomas and E. T. Andrews, 1801), 9, 13, 324.

42. For the fraught debates about the place of fiction in the early republic, see Cathy Davidson, "Ideology and Genre," *Revolution and the Word,* 38–54.
43. Tenney, *Female Quixotism,* 4, 6, 7, 11, 10.
44. Ibid., 8–9.
45. Ibid., 8, 13, 9.
46. Acts 9:36: "Now in Joppa there was a disciple whose name was Tabitha, which in Greek is Dorcas." I am grateful to Candace Waid for this insight.
47. In the prior years, Samuel Tenney was an important supporter of the Alien and Sedition Acts (1798), the greatest governmental abridgement of free speech in U.S. history. Jean Nienkamp and Andrea Collins, introduction to *Female Quixotism,* by Tabitha Tenney (New York: Oxford University Press, 1992), esp. xxiv–xxvi.
48. Brown, *Ormond,* 205–206.
49. Timothy Dwight, D.D., *Greenfield Hill: A Poem in Seven Parts* (New York: Childs and Swaine, 1794), 7. The paraphrase is from a pamphlet on British federation by Scottish politician Andrew Fletcher: "[I]f a man were permitted to make all the Ballads, he need not care who should make the Laws of a Nation" (*An Account of a Conversation concerning a Right Regulation of Government* [Edinburgh, 1704], 10).

5. Underwriting Free Labor and Free Soil

1. On the "magisterial gaze" in painting of the era, see Albert Boime, *The Magisterial Gaze: Manifest Destiny and American Landscape Painting, c. 1830–1865* (Washington, D.C.: Smithsonian Institution Press, 1991). On stadial theory and the "vanishing Indian" narrative of the 1830s, see Lucy Maddox, *Removals: Nineteenth-Century American Literature and the Politics of Indian Affairs* (New York: Oxford University Press, 1991); and Bruce A. Harvey, *American Geographics: U.S. National Narratives and the Representation of the Non-European World, 1830–1865* (Stanford: Stanford University Press, 2001).
2. William Cullen Bryant, "The Prairies," *Poems* (Boston: Russell, Odiorne, and Metcalf, 1834), 39–43.
3. Kirsten Silva Gruesz also notes this directional "mutability in territorial borders" in Bryant's poem (*Ambassadors of Culture: The Transamerican Origins of Latino Writing* [Princeton: Princeton University Press, 2002], 49).
4. I take the term from Charles Sellers, who argues that the boom that followed the War of 1812 ignited a generational conflict over the destiny of the republic, in which democracy was born in tension with capitalism rather than as its natural political expression (*The Market Revolution: Jacksonian America, 1815–1846* [New York: Oxford University Press, 1994]).
5. Sean Wilentz offers a detailed analysis of this ideological shift in the meanings of republicanism under industrialization in *Chants Democratic: New York City and the Rise of the American Working Class, 1788–1850* (New York: Oxford University Press, 1985).
6. [Francis Scott Key], "Defense of Fort M'Henry" [broadside] (Baltimore, 17 September 1814).

7. Eric Foner charts this transformation in *Free Soil, Free Labor, Free Men: The Ideology of the Republican Party Before the Civil War* (New York: Oxford University Press, 1970).

8. Jay B. Hubbell, *The South in American Literature, 1607–1900* (Durham, N.C.: Duke University Press, 1954), 444.

9. Foner organizes his study of U.S. history on these lines in *The Story of American Freedom* (New York: W.W. Norton, 1999).

10. The vexed ideological relationship of industrial capitalism and slavery in the Anglo-American world has been a subject for intellectual history since the publication of Eric Williams's *Capitalism and Slavery* (Chapel Hill: University of North Carolina Press, 1944), which argued that British abolitionists consciously used antislavery politics to create ideological hegemony for the industrial order. Williams's thesis was tempered, though not entirely rejected, by later historians, notably David Brion Davis, who found his conclusions too cynical. See particularly Davis's "Reflections on Abolitionism and Ideological Hegemony," in *The Antislavery Debate: Capitalism and Antislavery as Problems in Historical Interpretation* (Berkeley: University of California Press, 1992), 161–179. Philip S. Foner and Herbert Shapiro provide an overview of several decades of subsequent debate in their introduction to *Northern Labor and Antislavery: A Documentary History* (Westport, Conn.: Greenwood Press, 1994), ix–xxx.

11. As well, the practice of slavery in the southern states underwent significant change in the 1830s, due to both the rapid expansion of slavery into the southwest and the increased severity of slave law in reaction to the rebellions at the turn of the decade. See U. B. Phillips, "The Origin and Growth of the Southern Black Belts," *Slave Economy of the Old South* (1906; repr., Baton Rouge: Louisiana State University Press, 1968), 95–116; and Eugene D. Genovese, "The Turning Point," *From Rebellion to Revolution: Afro-American Slave Revolts in the Making of the Modern World* (Baton Rouge: Louisiana State University Press, 1979), 82–125.

12. On urbanization and the exposé mode in England and France, see Raymond Williams, *The Country and the City* (New York: Oxford University Press, 1971), 153–164 and 213–232; and Richard Maxwell, *The Mysteries and Miseries of Paris and London* (Charlottesville: University Press of Virginia, 1992). On the rise of reformist exposé in the United States, see Stuart Blumin, introduction to *New York by Gas-Light and Other Urban Sketches* (Berkeley: University of California Press, 1990); Paul Boyer, *Urban Masses and Moral Order in America* (Cambridge, Mass.: Harvard University Press, 1978); and Timothy Gilfoyle, *City of Eros: New York City, Prostitution, and the Commercialization of Sex, 1790–1920* (New York: Norton, 1992).

13. Ronald Walters has observed that urban reformist discourse (especially its temperance and antiprostitution strains) used the same categories and registers as the new abolitionist discourse, that it predated the new abolitionist discourse by several years, and that prominent abolitionists worked in the urban reform movement before or simultaneously with the beginning of their involvement in abolitionism—but he finds this overlap to be mere "coincidence"; seeking to uncover the "conditions in the North that gave urgency to

concern for licentiousness," he finds only the seemingly spontaneous appearance of "a more general revulsion against domination and possession" (*The Antislavery Appeal: American Abolitionism after 1830* [Baltimore: Johns Hopkins University Press, 1976], 169, 76).

14. Quoted in Russel B. Nye, *William Lloyd Garrison and the Humanitarian Reformers* (Boston: Little, Brown, 1955), 31.

15. Following Lauren Berlant, Christopher Castiglia calls this Garrisonian shift in antislavery politics an "inward turn" ("Abolition's Racial Interiors and the Making of Civic Depth," *American Literary History* 14:1 [Winter 2002]: 35–36).

16. The sectionalist debate over slavery was posed, as early as the late 1830s, as an explicit struggle for empire within the United States. See, for instance, Richard Hildreth, *Despotism in America* (Boston: Whipple and Donnelly, 1840); and Calvin Colton, *Abolition a Sedition* (Philadelphia: George W. Donohue, 1839), esp. 184–187.

17. For the shift to immediate abolitionism and its consequences, see David Brion Davis, "The Emergence of Immediatism in Anti-Slavery Thought," in *From Homicide to Slavery: Studies in American Culture* (New York: Oxford University Press, 1986).

18. Nye, *William Lloyd Garrison*, 30–35; Walter M. Merrill, *Against Wind and Tide: A Biography of William Lloyd Garrison* (Cambridge, Mass.: Harvard University Press, 1963), 40–45; Henry Mayer, *All on Fire: William Lloyd Garrison and the Abolition of Slavery* (New York: St. Martin's Press, 1998), 100–105.

19. William Lloyd Garrison, editorial, *Liberator* 1:1 (Jan. 1, 1831): 1.

20. The first illustration in the newspaper was an engraving of the Massachusetts statehouse as the heading for "Boston" local news; it appeared in January 1831, though not in the first issue, and was included each week for several months. The masthead illustration appeared for the first time later that year and was included in each issue through the end of 1837. The departmental heading engravings described below first appeared in 2:1 (Jan. 7, 1832), and ran weekly through 1833.

21. At least Garrison's readers received the illustrations in this way; the writer of one letter to the editor echoed the sentiments of several others when he meditated upon the distant operations of slavery as proceeding "in the manner, I presume, which is represented in your vignette[s]" (*Liberator* 1:19 [May 7, 1831]: 74).

22. On the development and deployment of the supplicant-slave icon in the colonizationist movement, see Marcus Wood, *Blind Memory: Visual Representations of Slavery in England and America, 1780–1865* (New York: Routledge, 2000), 21–23.

23. Jo-Ann Morgan cites the first Johnston masthead as an important early example of the use of Madonna iconography in abolitionist visual culture ("Thomas Satterwhite Noble's Mulattos: From Barefoot Madonna to Maggie the Ripper," *Journal of American Studies* 41:1 [2007], 90–93).

24. "The Working Classes," *Liberator* 1:5 (Jan. 29, 1831): 19.

25. See, for instance, "The British India Society," in *The Liberty Bell,* ed. Friends of Freedom [Maria Weston Chapman] (Boston: American Anti-Slavery Society, 1839), 81–83. For a clarifying overview, see Eric Foner, "Abolitionists and the Labor Movement in Ante-Bellum America," in *Politics and Ideology in the Age of the Civil War* (New York: Oxford University Press, 1980).

26. I take the term "ultraist" from David S. Reynolds, *Beneath the American Renaissance: The Subversive Imagination in the Age of Hawthorne and Melville* (New York: Knopf, 1988), 54–91.

27. On the social significance of the exposé mode, see Blumin, *New York by Gas-Light*; Boyer, *Urban Masses and Moral Order in America*; Michael Denning, *Mechanic Accents: Dime Novels and Working-Class Culture in America* (London: Verso, 1987); Gilfoyle, *City of Eros*; and Marilynn Wood Hill, *Their Sisters' Keepers: Prostitution in New York City, 1830–1870* (Berkeley: University of California Press, 1993).

28. Ira Rosenwaike, *Population History of New York City* (Syracuse: Syracuse University Press, 1972), 20.

29. Wilentz: "[A] revolution, and not just an expansion of production, took place in New York's workshops" between 1825 and 1850, one that "transformed the very meaning of labor and independence in the city's largest trades" (*Chants Democratic,* 108).

30. The phrases quoted here appear ubiquitously in antebellum exposé discourse; all are included in the watershed text that I discuss in the next paragraphs, the *First Annual Report of the Executive Committee of the New-York Magdalen Society. Instituted, January 1, 1830* (New York: John T. West, 1831).

31. The significance of the *First Annual Report* as an originary text in a new cultural formation is agreed upon by social historians (Hill, *Their Sisters' Keepers*), cultural historians (Gilfoyle, *City of Eros*) and literary critics (Reynolds, *Beneath the American Renaissance*).

32. The phrase "living out" (of a home, on the street) was a common antebellum euphemism for prostituting. The phrase "bastard manufactures," or "bastard artisanship," is Wilentz's description of the form that antebellum industrialization took in New York City (*Chants Democratic,* 105–194).

33. *First Annual Report,* 12, 4, 8–9.

34. Ibid., 8, 10, 11.

35. *Remarks on the Report of the Executive Committee of the New-York Magdalen Society* (New York: Printed for the author, 1831), 3, Tappan considered himself "converted" to abolitionism by Garrison's 1832 pamphlet, *Thoughts on African Colonization,* in which Garrison's shift to ultraist exposé was already clear (Lewis Tappan, *The Life of Arthur Tappan* [New York: Hurd and Houghton, 1870]).

36. *Remarks on the Report,* 13.

37. *The Phantasmagoria of New-York, a poetical burlesque upon a certain libellous pamphlet, written by a committee of notorious fanatics, entitled the MAGDALEN report* (New York: Printed for the publisher, 1831).

38. Garrison's biographers, especially Merrill, have tended to remark his enthusiasm for antiprostitution discourse as arbitrary or even unhinged (*Against Wind and Tide*, 37–38, 44, 48–49).

39. For instance, when a mob shouting "Magdalens!" assailed Arthur Tappan's summer residence in New Haven in October 1831, Garrison baselessly "conjectured" that the unidentified perpetrators must have been "southern medical students" at Yale—thereby constructing a common enemy of abolitionist and urban reform ("Riots at New Haven!" *Liberator* 1:43 [Oct. 22, 1831]: 171).

40. "Magdalen Facts," *Liberator* 2:7 (Feb. 18 1832): 27.

41. The idea that abolitionism and urban reform fit together under the aegis of antebellum ultraism is not a new one, but the connections between these movements, both historical and ideological, have been sorely underinvestigated. For instance, Walters's classic *American Reformers, 1815–1860* (New York: Hill and Wang, 1978) brings together the reform movements in one volume, but largely isolates them within individual chapters.

42. On Garrison's editorship of the Boston *National Philanthropist* from Jan.–July 1828, see Merrill, 18–21.

43. *Liberator* 1:14 (Apr. 2 1831): 56; 1:44 (Oct. 29 1831): 176; 1:49 (Dec. 3 1831): 194. The big exception to this rule is Garrison's coverage of Nat Turner's rebellion in October and November 1831, which afforded him sensational anecdotes unsurpassed by local temperance tales.

44. Garrison, "I Like the Temperance Cause—*BUT*," *Liberator* 1:6 (Feb. 5 1831): 24.

45. [John R. McDowall], *Magdalen Facts* (New York: Printed for the author, 1832), 39.

46. Garrison, "The Marriage Question. Extract from an Address by Mr. Garrison," *Liberator* 2:46 (Nov. 17, 1832): 183. Nye has pointed out, correctly, that here Garrison turned the tables on his opponents, who characterized the abolitionists as advocates of racial "amalgamation" (William Lloyd Garrison, 51–63).

47. On Garrison's "calculations" of how exposé mode would affect his circulation and notoriety, see Merrill, *Against Wind and Tide*, 48–55; and Nye, *William Lloyd Garrison*, 51–63.

48. "John R. McDowall," *Liberator* 6:52 (Dec. 24 1836), 206–207, emphasis mine. See also "McDowall Yet Lives," 7:4 (Jan. 21 1837), 16.

49. Robin Blackburn stresses the specificity of this point to the U.S. context: for Britons "[c]olonial slavery was both an extreme and a distant mode of exploitation; [in America it was] closer, in terms of social space, allowing metropolitan abolitionism to awaken popular anxieties about extreme dependence on employers or on the fickle market mechanism" (*The Overthrow of Colonial Slavery, 1770–1848* [London: Verso, 1988], 535). For comparative views of British and U.S. definitions of "slavery" under industrialization, see also Marcus Cunliffe, *Chattel Slavery & Wage Slavery: The Anglo-American Context, 1830–1860* (Athens: University of Georgia Press, 1979).

50. More than one cultural historian has proposed that the fetishization of corporal punishment, particularly whipping, in antebellum U.S. culture served

to normalize and valorize by comparison the internalized discipline of modern capitalism. See Davis, "Reflections on Abolitionism and Ideological Hegemony," and Richard H. Brodhead, *Cultures of Letters: Scenes of Reading and Writing in Nineteenth-Century America* (Chicago: University of Chicago Press, 1993), 13–47.

51. Consider the responses of both Madison and Jefferson to the debate surrounding the Missouri Compromise; on Madison, see Ralph Louis Ketcham, *James Madison: A Biography* (Charlottesville: University Press of Virginia, 1990), 626–628.

52. In 1850, George Fitzhugh explicitly outlined the reactionary genesis of antebellum proslavery ideology: "Until the last fifteen years, our great error was to imitate Northern habits, customs, and institutions . . . Until that time, in truth, we distrusted our social system. We thought slavery morally wrong, we thought it would not last, we thought it unprofitable. The Abolitionists assailed us; we looked more closely into our circumstances; became satisfied that slavery was morally right . . . The intermeddling of foreign pseudo-philanthropists in our affairs . . . has been of inestimable advantage in teaching us to form a right estimate of our condition" (*Slavery Defended,* 1850; repr., *Slavery Defended: The Views of the Old South,* ed. Eric L. McKitrick [Englewood Cliffs, N.J.: Prentice Hall, 1963], 48).

53. Calhoun, "Speech on the Reception of Abolition Petitions" (1837; repr., *Slavery Defended,* 13–14). As in subsequent proslavery thought, Calhoun's materialist analysis rests on racist logic: its biracial caste system was the "special condition" of southern society that solved the exploitative relations of labor and capital. Understanding those people occupying the position of labor as naturally destined to servitude avoided the contested condition of "white slavery" arising under northern industrialization.

54. As David Roediger puts it, this form of antislavery thought "stalled the development of a telling critique of hireling labor—a critique that might have built upon and transcended the republican heritage of the United States." The paradoxical stature of the "slaveholding republic" ultimately impeded the formation in the United States of "the class consciousness said to have existed elsewhere in the industrializing world" (*The Wages of Whiteness: Race and the Making of the American Working Class* [New York, 1991], esp. 66–71, 87, 167–181).

55. See, for instance, Johnston's illustrations for Joseph C. Neal, *Charcoal Sketches or, Scenes in a Metropolis* (Philadelphia: Getz, Buck and Co., [1837]).

56. Hubbell, *The South in American Literature,* 486; William R. Taylor, *Cavalier and Yankee: The Old South and American National Character* (New York: Brazillier, 1961), 52.

57. Williams, *The Country and the City,* 154. See also Catherine Gallagher, *The Industrial Reformation of English Fiction: Social Discourse and Narrative Form, 1832–1867* (Chicago: University of Chicago Press, 1985).

58. [McDowall], *Magdalen Facts,* 3.

59. Theodore Dwight Weld, ed., *American Slavery as It Is: Testimony of a Thousand Witnesses* (Boston: American Anti-Slavery Society, 1839), 9.

60. Denning, *Mechanic Accents,* 113.
61. Weld, ed. *American Slavery as It Is,* n.p. (inner leaf).
62. Gerda Lerner, *The Grimké Sisters of South Carolina: Pioneers for Women's Rights and Abolition* (New York: Schocken, 1971); on the move north, see especially 137–164. Lerner does not mention the Grimkés' involvement with the New-York Female Moral Reform Society.
63. The *Advocate of Moral Reform,* which claimed a subscription list rivaling Garrison's, was instituted as a monthly newspaper in January 1835, its masthead slogan is from Luke 7:2.
64. Angelina E. Grimké, *Appeal to the Christian Women of the South* (New York: American Anti-Slavery Society, 1836), n.p. Original emphasis.
65. [Angelina E. Grimké,] *Appeal to the Women of the Nominally Free States, Issued by an Anti-slavery Convention of American Women* ((New York: Dorr, 1837), 13–14.
66. [Grimké], *Appeal to the Women of the Nominally Free States,* 14–15.
67. Ibid., 28.
68. Edward Said, *Culture and Imperialism* (New York: Routledge, 1993) 82–84.
69. From her vantage at the juncture of Charleston and New York City, Grimké is able to create an imaginative matrix for comprehending Marx's 1847 analysis of the relationship between colonial slavery and metropolitan industrialization: "Without slavery you have no cotton; without cotton you have no modern industry. It is slavery that gave the colonies their value; it is the colonies that created world-trade that is the pre-condition of large-scale industry" (quoted in Eduardo Cadava, "The Guano of History," *Cities Without Citizens,* ed. Cadava and Aaron Levy [Philadelphia: Slought Foundation, 2003], 157).
70. The American Anti-Slavery Society was reconstituted in 1840 after schisms within the abolitionist movement. On Child's assumption of the editorship, see Carolyn Karcher, *The First Woman in the Republic: A Cultural Biography of Lydia Maria Child* (Durham, N.C.: Duke University Press, 1997), 264–294.
71. On the great success of Child's *Letters* and its influence both on the circulation of the *Standard* and on her contemporaries, see Karcher, *The First Woman in the Republic,* 273–274, 296–310, 605–612. Karcher notes that Garrison's *Liberator* consistently lost subscribers during this same period.
72. L. Maria Child, *Letters from New-York,* 10th ed. (New York: C.S. Francis, 1849), 2.
73. A Northern Man [David Brown], *The Planter: or, Thirteen Years in the North* (Philadelphia: H. Hooker, 1853), 7; Rev. Philo. Tower, *Slavery Unmasked: Being a Truthful Narrative of a Three Years' Residence and Journeying in Eleven Southern States* (Rochester: E. Darrow and Brother, 1856), iv–vii.
74. Child, *Letters,* 32.
75. My assertions here are borne out more strongly by the short stories Child was writing at the same time, in which she more completely narrativized many of the urban episodes she touched upon in the *Letters* vignettes, especially those having to do with prostitution and sexual exploitation. These

stories, which include her influential Slave South exposé tales "The Quadroons" [1841] and "Slavery's Pleasant Homes" [1843], were collected in an 1846 volume titled *Fact and Fiction*.

6. American Universal Geography

1. Edward Waldo Emerson, "Notes" in the 1903–1904 (centennial) edition of *The Complete Works of Ralph Waldo Emerson* "Concord" ed. (Boston: Houghton, Mifflin, 1903–1904), 1:403.

2. Eric Cheyfitz, *The Trans-Parent: Gender in Emerson* (Baltimore: Johns Hopkins University Press, 1981); John Carlos Rowe, *At Emerson's Tomb: Readings in Classic American Literature* (New York: Columbia University Press, 1999), esp. 19–22; Howard Horwitz, *By the Law of Nature* (New York: Oxford University Press, 1991).

3. For the classic account of expansionism and sectionalism in the first half of the century, see Albert K. Weinberg, *Manifest Destiny: A Study of Nationalist Expansionism in American History* (Baltimore: Johns Hopkins University Press, 1935), esp. 160–223.

4. On Southern sectionalist imperialism see Robert E. Bonner, *Mastering America: Southern Slaveholders and the Crisis of American Nationhood* (Cambridge: Cambridge University Press, 2009), and Sean Wilentz, *The Rise of American Democracy, Jefferson to Lincoln* (New York: W.W. Norton, 2005), esp. 547–667.

5. In a similar vein, but writing brilliantly about another 1845 text, David Kazanjian suggests that what Marx paradoxically called "Yankee universality" in fact "names [an] imperial articulation of U.S. citizenship, [an] interpenetration of the domestic and the foreign that marks the emergence of U.S. imperialism" (*The Colonizing Trick: National Culture and Imperial Citizenship in Early America* (Minneapolis: University of Minnesota Press, 2003), 223.

6. Ralph Waldo Emerson "Address to the Citizens of Concord on the Fugitive Slave Law," *Complete Works*, 11:211–213.

7. Robin Blackburn, *The Overthrow of Colonial Slavery, 1776–1848* (London: Verso, 1988), esp. 459–468 and 519–549.

8. The expedition was documented copiously by its commander, Charles Wilkes (*Narrative of the United States Exploring Expedition During the Years 1838, 1839, 1840, 1841, 1842,* 5 vols. [Philadelphia: Lea and Blanchard, 1845]).

9. On O'Sullivan's *Democratic Review* and the "Young America" writers, see Sean Wilentz, *The Rise of American Democracy, Jefferson to Lincoln* (New York: W. W. Norton, 2005), esp. 559–632; and Edward L. Widmer, *Young America: The Flowering of Democracy in New York City* (New York: Oxford University Press, 1999).

10. In his magisterial biography, Lawrence Buell argues for the significance in Emerson's total oeuvre of the four discourses he wrote and published in 1844 as "mark[ing] a new stage of development for Emerson," in which the author "tr[ied] out different positions" on the debates of his day (*Emerson* [Cambridge, Mass.: Harvard University Press, 2004], 250).

11. Ralph Waldo Emerson, "The Young American," *Dial* 4:4 (Apr. 1844): 484. Uncharacteristically, Emerson redacted a long passage in the opening of the essay from the collected edition of his works assembled after the Civil War, so here I use the original 1844 essay.
12. *CW,* I:363, 451–53. The first sentence is included in the collected version of the lecture; the following sentence opens six long and stunning paragraphs on the railroad—laden with invocations of the South—that Emerson redacted in 1876.
13. Ralph Waldo Emerson, "The Young American," Complete Works 1:365.
14. Reading Emerson's 1841 essay "Circles," Paul Giles has discerned a "traditional American geometry of transcendentalism" that "aligns the particular with the general and thus renders . . . refractory conceptions universal"— thereby underwriting an exceptional U.S. "language of global empire [that] conceals 'a fundamental dissymmetry in the relationship between the United States and every other country in the world'" ("Transnationalism and Classic American Literature," *PMLA* 118:1 [Jan. 2003]: 65).
15. On "catalogue rhetoric" in Transcendentalist writing, see Lawrence Buell, *Literary Transcendentalism: Style and Vision in the American Renaissance* (Ithaca, N.Y.: Cornell University Press, 1973), 166–187.
16. Ralph Waldo Emerson, "The Young American," *Complete Works* 1:377.
17. Ibid., 1:370, 378–379.
18. Ibid., 1:378–379, emphasis mine.
19. Ibid., 1:384.
20. Ibid., 1:387–388.
21. Ralph Waldo Emerson, "Emancipation in the British West Indies," in *Collected Works,* 11:133–134.
22. Ibid., 11:134.
23. Ibid., 11:128–129, 123, 147. Lewis Simpson has argued that both Emerson's Anglo-Saxonism and his sense of "the cultural destiny of Massachusetts and New England—of the New England nation" found their roots in his desire for subjugation of the South, rather than merely the slavery question (*Mind and the American Civil War,* [Baton Rouge: Louisiana State University Press, 1989] 58–59).
24. Ralph Waldo Emerson, "Emancipation," 11:135, 137, 101, 126. Many commentators (including John Carlos Rowe, Len Gougeon, Barbara Packer, and Colin Dayan) have remarked on Emerson's limited vision of emancipation in this first anti-slavery address. His process of thinking through the interrelated material and moral dimensions of abolitionism, though, seems to be the central work of the address.
25. Traditionally, Emerson scholars have separated his "political" writings in this period from his "philosophical" writings, and the addresses I treat here are classified as the former. I follow Eduardo Cadava in thinking that such a line is not necessarily useful, and that part of Emerson's work in these years is to think about the permeability between the philosophical or moral realm of print culture and the material realm of politics and economics (*Emerson and the Climates of History* [Stanford: Stanford University Press, 1997]).
26. Ralph Waldo Emerson, "Emancipation," 11:100.

27. Ibid., 11:147; "The Young American," 1:391.

28. Poe's "southernness" and "darkness" made him marginal to the nineteenth-century nationalist literary canon as constructed by critics such as Vernon L. Parrington and F. O. Matthiessen; more recent critics such as Colin Dayan, Teresa Goddu, and Terence Whalen usefully have interrogated the extent to which "southernness" as a category glosses or interacts with more complex negotiations of race, gender, class, region, and nation in considering Poe's work. (Perhaps less usefully, John Carlos Rowe and Maurice Lee have identified Poe's "southernness" as a synonym for white supremacy.) In an important intervention, J. Gerald Kennedy has reminded us that Poe's geographical identity in the mid-1840s was shifting rather than stable and that he focused as much as any other major author of the period on issues of broader national ideology and identity ("'A Mania for Composition': Poe's *Annus Mirabilis* and the Violence of Nation-Building," *American Literary History* 17:1 [Mar. 2005]: 1).

29. Although almost any critic who has written about *Eureka* has remarked that at least certain dimensions of it seem wildly out of keeping with Poe's stated aesthetic and philosophical stances, only Harriet R. Holman has suggested, in two incisive short articles that anticipated a more extensive reading, that *Eureka* is a full-out satire ("Hog, Bacon, Ram, and Other 'Savans' in *Eureka*," *Poe Newsletter* 2:3 [Oct. 1969]; "Splitting Poe's 'Epicurean Atoms': Further Speculation on the Literary Satire of *Eureka*," *Poe Studies* 5 [Dec. 1972]).

30. Poe on Carlyle in the "Marginalia" of April 1846, originally published in the *Democratic Review* (*Essays and Reviews* [New York: Library of America, 1984]), 1393.

31. Colin [Joan] Dayan tracks Poe's "critical read[ing] of the transcendentalist ideologies of his time" in *Fables of Mind: An Inquiry into Poe's Fiction* (New York: Oxford University Press, 1987).

32. Ralph Waldo Emerson, "The Transcendentalist," in *Collected Works,* 1:334.

33. Emerson opens "The Transcendentalist" with the proposition that "as thinkers, mankind have ever divided into two sects, Materialists and Idealists" (1:329), and he goes on to define and contrast these sects. The "letter from the future" that Poe introduces in the opening page of *Eureka* ridicules "the singular fancy that there exist *but two practicable roads to Truth*" and goes on to identify these schools as those of the "Hogs and Rams" (*Eureka,* ed. Roland W. Nelson, in *Poetry and Tales,* [New York: Library of America, 1984], 1263, 1269).

34. Poe, *Eureka,* 1271.

35. Colin [Joan] Dayan, "Amorous Bondage: Poe, Ladies, and Slaves," *American Literature* 66:2 (Jun. 1994): 254.

36. Poe joyously reprinted this entire censure of him in the *Broadway Journal,* rejoining that "insanity is a word that the Brook Farm Phalanx should never be brought to mention under any circumstances whatsoever" (*Essays and Reviews,* 1100, 1102–1103).

37. Poe, "Marginalia," in *Essays and Reviews,* 1309.

38. Poe, "Marginalia," in *Essays and Reviews,* 1415–1416. In a footnote, Poe

sources the cultural imperialism in particular (the "taking away" the name America "from those regions which employ it at present") back to one of the "Frogpondians" present at his hoax the year before: "Mr. [Benjamin Hazard] Field, in a meeting of 'The New York Historical Society,' proposed that we take the name of 'America,' and bestow 'Columbia' upon the continent" (*Essays and Reviews*, 1415).

39. In a letter to F. W. Thomas in 1849, for instance, Poe writes that "the Frogpondians . . . are getting worse and worse, and pretend not to be aware that there *are* any literary people out of Boston . . . It would be the easiest thing in the world to use them up *en masse*. One really well-written satire would accomplish the business" (*The Letters of Edgar Allan Poe*, ed. John Ward Ostrom [New York: Gordian Press, 1966], 2:427).

40. Poe, *Eureka*, 1277.

41. Ibid., 1278, 1277, 1263. For a reading of governmental metaphor in the text, see W. C. Harris, "Edgar Allan Poe's *Eureka* and the Poetics of Constitution," *American Literary History* 12:1/2 (Spring/Summer 2000): 1–40.

42. Emerson, "Editors' Address, *Massachusetts Quarterly Review,* December, 1847," in *Collected Works,* 11:391; Poe, *Eureka,* 1346.

43. Maurice Lee points out that in an 1847 review in Edward Duycknick's *Literary World,* "Bad News of the Transcendental Poets," a critic (whom he takes to be Poe himself) cheers, "The transcendental balloon is rapidly suffering collapse" ("Absolute Poe: His System of Transcendental Racism," *American Literature* 75:4 [Dec. 2003]: 769).

44. Poe, *Essays and Reviews,* 1087.

45. Poe, *Essays and Reviews,* 1097, *Eureka,* 1288; Dayan, "Amorous Bondage," 253.

46. Poe, *Essays and Reviews,* 1096.

47. On Poe's contact at this time with Taylor—whose travel books Poe was reviewing positively and defending from attack, and from whom he was seeking publication opportunities—see Arthur Hobson Quinn, *Edgar Allan Poe* (New York: Appleton-Century, 1941), 567–601.

48. Poe, *Eureka,* 1262, 1327. Poe makes a marvelously succinct statement of Manifest Destiny ideology here: "[A] sufficient reason for the Titanic scale, in respect of mere *space,* on which the Universe of Stars is seen to be constructed . . . [is so t]hat the Universe of Stars might *endure* throughout an æra at all commensurate with the grandeur of its component material protions and with the high majesty of its spiritual purposes" (*Eureka,* 1340).

49. Ibid., 1271, 1342, 1276, 1261.

50. Ibid., 1342, 1324, 1325, 1275, 1321, 1308.

51. In a number of extraordinary fantasias in this ostensible 2048 letter from Pundita, Poe links industrial and slave capitalism, as in the following passage that conflates the production of silk and paper, as well as the exploitation of a laboring body ("worm") raised on watermelon and then destroyed in a factory: "This silk, as he explained it to me, was a fabric composed of the entrails of a species of earth-worm. The worm was carefully fed on mulberries—a kind of fruit resembling a water-melon—and, when sufficiently fat, was crushed in a mill. The paste thus arising was called *papyrus*

in its primary state, and went through a variety of presses until it finally became "silk" ("Mellonta Tauta," in *Poetry and Tales,* 872).

52. Poe, "Prospectus of *The Stylus,*" *Essays and Reviews,* 1035, 1093.
53. Ralph Waldo Emerson, "Editors' Address," 11:383.
54. This is the opening sentence of Poe's 1849 review of James Russell Lowell's *A Fable for Critics,* an essay often cited to evidence Poe's southern sectionalism (*Essays and Reviews,* 814).
55. Poe to Maria W. Clemm, *Letters,* 2:452. Poe earned a total of fourteen dollars for *Eureka.*
56. Poe, *Eureka,* 1329.

7. Dark Satanic Fields

1. The comment attributed to Lincoln is almost certainly apocryphal, but it has seemed true enough to bear ubiquitous repetition in cultural histories of the nineteenth-century United States. See Joan D. Hedrick, *Harriet Beecher Stowe: A Life* (New York: Oxford University Press, 1994), vii.
2. How Lowell was being portrayed in the antebellum decades is the subject of a number of studies, including Thomas Bender's *Toward an Urban Vision: Ideas and Institutions in Nineteenth-Century America* (Lexington: University Press of Kentucky, 1975); and Brian C. Mitchell's *The Paddy Camps: The Irish of Lowell, 1821–61* (Urbana: University of Illinois Press, 1988).
3. Harriet Beecher Stowe, *Uncle Tom's Cabin, or, Life among the Lowly* (Boston: J. P. Jewett, 1852), 2:184.
4. Ibid., 2:211. Karen Halttunen has explored the direct relationship between urban and southern gothic in the writings of the Beecher family, in "Gothic Imagination and Social Reform: The Haunted Houses of Lyman Beecher, Henry Ward Beecher, and Harriet Beecher Stowe," in *New Essays on Uncle Tom's Cabin,* ed. Eric J. Sundquist (Cambridge: Cambridge University Press, 1986), 107–134.
5. Perhaps not until Edmund Wilson's *Patriotic Gore: Studies in the Literature of the American Civil War* (New York: Farrar, Straus and Giroux, 1962) did a U.S. critic highlight the aesthetic as opposed to the political impact of the novel.
6. William L. Andrews has shown that beginning in the 1840s, European and U.S. literary critics alike cited slave narratives as the first distinctive American literary productions (*To Tell a Free Story* [Urbana: University of Illinois Press, 1988], 97–99).
7. The immediate English reception may have had an influence on U.S. understandings of the importance of Stowe's novel (Hedrick, *Harriet Beecher Stowe,* 233–234).
8. Quoted in Hedrick, *Harriet Beecher Stowe,* 243.
9. Letter from Kingsley to Stowe, quoted in Hedrick, *Harriet Beecher Stowe,* 234. For more direct connections between the work of antebellum U.S. writers and the Condition of England debates, see Phyllis B. Cole, *The American Writer and the Condition of England, 1815–1860* (Ph.D. diss., Harvard University, 1973).

10. Here I am drawing again on Raymond Williams's crystallizing definition of Dickens's "new kind of novel," in *The Country and the City* (New York: Oxford University Press, 1971), esp. 153–164. Wilson makes the connections to Stowe's novel explicit (*Patriotic Gore*, 7–8).

11. The Russian fascination with Stowe's novel is an old saw of its reception history; a recent Penguin paperback edition (New York: Penguin Books, 1986) gives Tolstoy pride of place amongst the back-cover blurbs ("one of the greatest productions of the human mind").

12. Of Parker's declaration, Priscilla Wald usefully has noted that "there is an irony involved in the transformation of the slave narrative into a national(ist) genre. By appropriating the genre as an emblem of an indigenous American culture . . . the literal slave becomes the emblem of American freedom rather than evidence of American slavery (*Constituting Americans: Cultural Anxiety and Narrative Form* [Durham, N.C.: Duke University Press, 1994], 79).

13. I am not the first to notice this progression. See Taylor, *Cavalier and Yankee: The Old South and American National Character* (New York: Brazillier, 1961), 310; and Stephen Nissenbaum, "New England as Region and Nation," in *All Over the Map: Rethinking American Regions* (Baltimore: John Hopkins University Press, 1996), 57.

14. On the relationship of U.S. painters to the English genre painting movement, see Elizabeth Johns's introduction to *American Genre Paintings: The Politics of Everyday Life* (New Haven: Yale University Press, 1991).

15. Good comparisons may be found in Cruikshank's 1837 illustrations for *Oliver Twist* and Phiz's 1840 illustrations for *The Old Curiosity Shop*.

16. Cruikshank himself was employed by Stowe's London publisher to illustrate the first British edition of the novel. Probably because he was envisioning American slavery from across the Atlantic, Cruikshank used a colonial and tropical visual vocabulary for the novel, rather than creating the sorts of urban scenes for which he was famous and upon which Billings was drawing.

17. Stowe ended the book with an 1820s-era colonizationist plan, sending every African American character left standing "back to Africa." Hedrick recounts Stowe's distance from antislavery thinkers, and the mad rush of abolitionists to bring her into their camps once her novel became so successful (*Harriet Beecher Stowe*, 235–252).

18. Novelist Caroline Rush had written, "Do [Northerners] have no cruel whippings, no torture, no forcing the poor overburdened frame to labor beyond its capabilities[?] In a word, oh! free and happy citizens of the North, have you no slaves in your midst"? (*The North and the South, or, Slavery and its Contrasts. A Tale of Real Life* [Philadelphia: Crissy and Markey, 1852], 12).

19. Horace Greeley, *New-York Tribune*, May 23, 1853.

20. Nissenbaum, "New England as Region and Nation," 54–57. Nissenbaum asserts, further, that the "'black' dialect" in *Uncle Tom's Cabin* bears striking resemblance to the New England dialect Stowe employs in her later "local color" novels.

21. Philip Fisher, *Hard Facts: Setting and Form in the American Novel* (New York: Oxford University Press, 1985), 120.

22. Stowe, *Uncle Tom's Cabin*, 1:56–57.

23. Ibid., 1:57, 59.

24. Fisher, *Hard Facts*, 108–109.

25. Stowe, *Uncle Tom's Cabin*, 1:145.

26. See Hedrick's fine analysis of the break in composition at chapter 12 (*Harriet Beecher Stowe*, 218–223).

27. Robert Stepto remarks on the "remarkable admixture of civility and imperiousness" with which Stowe requested "Douglass's assistance in acquiring accurate information about the details of life and work on a southern cotton plantation" ("Sharing the Thunder: The Literary Exchanges of Henry Bibb, Harriet Beecher Stowe, and Frederick Douglass," in *New Essays on Uncle Tom's Cabin*, 135–154).

28. Stowe, *Uncle Tom's Cabin*, 1:291, 2:23, 1:218.

29. Fisher identifies the "Moral Darwinism" of this central section of the novel as Stowe's sui generis hitting upon Drieserian naturalism fifty years early, but her "conviction that certain forms of life were marginal and could not survive" clearly draws upon a climatological discourse of empire with an ample history (*Hard Facts*, 122–123).

30. Stowe, *Uncle Tom's Cabin*, 1:235–236.

31. On proslavery ideological intersections with Marx, see Richard Hofstadter, "John C. Calhoun: The Marx of the Master Class," in *The American Political Tradition and the Men Who Made It* (New York: Vintage, 1948, 87–118); and C. Vann Woodward, "George Fitzhugh, *Sui Generis*," in Fitzhugh, *Cannibals All! Or, Slaves Without Masters*, ed. Woodward (Cambridge, Mass.: Harvard University Press, 1960), vii–xxxix.

32. Stowe, *Uncle Tom's Cabin*, 2:20–21, 10, 24, 25. Eric Lott has shown how "the American 1848" coalesced, in the Stephen Foster minstrel songs that became its "soundtrack," around the 1848 class revolts in Europe, the Slave South of minstrelsy, and—as the crucial third term—the expansionist dreams of gold-rush California. Out of this crucible, Lott sees blackface minstrelsy circa 1850 as performing cultural work strikingly analogous to that of Stowe's Slave South as I am defining it: minstrelsy "had become a sectional signifier, a potent popular figure for the North and 'all its emigrations, colonizations and conquests'" (*Love and Theft: Blackface Minstrelsy and the American Working Class* [New York: Oxford University Press, 1995], 207).

33. Stowe, *Uncle Tom's Cabin*, 2:24, 136, 137. On Augustine St. Clare's overdetermined name: with it Stowe indicates that, like St. Augustine, his narration should be understood as his confession. "Clare" further indicates his clarity of vision, but the name also provides a homonym with Stowe's preferred dialect rendering of the word "declare," which makes his philosophical disquisition a latter-day reflection on Jefferson's Declaration. Indeed, to start his discourse with Miss Ophelia, Stowe has him say, "'I'll begin: When, in the course of human events, it becomes necessary for a fellow to hold two or three dozen of his fellow-worms in captivity, a decent regard to the opinions of society requires—'" (330).

34. Ibid., 2:10, 138, 141.

35. Ibid., 2:179.

36. Shelley Streeby has elucidated the imperial dimensions of the conflation be-

tween plantation and factory in popular fiction about Mexico published during the Civil War (*American Sensations: Class, Empire, and the Production of Popular Culture* [Berkeley: University of California Press, 2002], 88–213).

37. In her reading of the direct borrowings from Dickens's *Bleak House* in Hannah Crafts's novel *The Bondwoman's Narrative*, Hollis Robbins muses on a similar "transformation of Dickens's slum to slave huts" ("Blackening *Bleak House*: Hannah Crafts's *The Bondwoman's Narrative*," in *In Search of Hannah Crafts: Critical Essays on "The Bondwoman's Narrative"* (New York: BasicCivitas Books, 2004), 80–81.

38. Wai Chee Dimock quotes these pithy lines from Lyman Beecher's "The Perils of Atheism to the Nation" (1835) in her introduction to *Empire for Liberty*, (Princeton: Princeton University Press, 1989), 12.

39. Stowe, *Uncle Tom's Cabin*, 2:187, 284.

40. As Stephen Railton has pointed out to me, George Shelby is able to put his father's house in order; when he returns to his home plantation, he manumits the Shelby slaves in a chapter titled "The Liberator." However successful his reform of his own home, though, Stowe shows him to be incapable of imposing the requisite moral order abroad.

41. Stowe, *Uncle Tom's Cabin*, 2:317.

42. The connections between Chernyshefsky and *Uncle Tom's Cabin* are many, including the fact that in 1858 he issued the first complete Russian translation of Stowe's novel as a supplement to the literary journal he edited, the *Contemporary*, while serializing his own novel in that venue four years later. Another connection may be traced through Turgenev, upon whom Stowe's influence is well known, and to whose 1862 novel *Fathers and Sons* Chernyshefsky considered himself to be directly responding. On this latter point, see Albert Kaspin, "*Uncle Tom's Cabin* and 'Uncle' Akim's Inn: More on Harriet Beecher Stowe and Turgenev," *Slavic and Eastern European Journal* 9:1 (Spring 1965): 47–55.

43. See, in particular, Laura Wexler, *Tender Violence: Domestic Visions in an Age of U.S. Imperialism* (Chapel Hill: University of North Carolina Press, 2000) and Amy Kaplan, *The Anarchy of Empire in the Making of U.S. Culture* (Cambridge, Mass.: Harvard University Press, 2002). Wexler's and Kaplan's work to disclose the imperial functions of sentimentalism responds to Jane Tompkins's influential argument that the "sentimental power" of Stowe's novel, as in her coauthored domestic manual of 1869, *The American Woman's Home*, derives from its "imperialistic drive," which "flatly contradicts the traditional derogations of the American cult of domesticity as a 'mirror-phenomenon,' 'self-immersed' and 'self-congratulatory.'" Instead, Stowe's work lays out (unproblematically for Tompkins, supremely problematically for Wexler and Kaplan) "a blueprint for colonizing the world in the name of the 'family state' under the leadership of Christian women" (Tompkins, *Sensational Designs: The Cultural Work of American Fiction* [New York: Oxford University Press, 1985], 144).

44. Leslie Fiedler has argued for the signal significance of Ophelia as "the only other New Englander besides Legree who is close to, if not quite at the mythic center of the novel" and therefore "[the reader's] surrogate in the novel" ("New England and the Invention of the South," in *American Liter-*

ature: The New England Heritage, ed. James Nagel and Richard Astro [New York: Garland, 1981], 110–111).

45. Stowe, *Uncle Tom's Cabin,* 2:294–295.

46. Ibid., 1:17, 2:64, 177, 287. Stowe plays with the words of the English hymn, which dates to the late sixteenth century. On a standard ABXB rhyme, the stanza should traditionally end, "Thy joys when shall I see?" rather than, as I am suggesting, a nonstandard (and slant) rhyme of the first and fourth lines that would end "Thy joys when shall they come?" But Stowe already has purposefully altered the standard second line, which should have caused the opening to read, "Jerusalem, my happy home, / When shall I come to thee?" If Stowe is interested not in Tom's *going* anywhere but in the *coming* of the Holy City to the fallen South, she must dispense with that second line as she does, and her bracketing of the unfinished verse with the repeated incantations of "Come!" at the beginning and end of the Legree section powerfully suggest, at least to my ear, the unorthodox conclusion to the traditional stanza.

47. Of Blake, Williams writes, "[His] forcing into consciousness of the suppressed connections [between country and city] is then a new way of seeing the human and social order as a whole. It is . . . a precise prevision of the essential literary methods and purposes of Dickens . . . The simplifying contrast is then decisively transcended. It is significant that one of his best-remembered phrases is 'England's green and pleasant land,' but this is not the language of rural retrospect or retreat. The whole purpose of his struggle is, as he says, to build 'Jerusalem / In England's green and pleasant land': to build the holy as against the unholy city" (*The Country and the City,* 149).

48. William Blake, Preface to *Milton: A Poem in Two Books, The Complete Writings of William Blake,* ed. Geoffrey Keynes (London: Oxford University Press, 1966), 480–481.

49. This is Ian Watt's famous reading of Defoe, in *"Robinson Crusoe* as a Myth," *Essays in Criticism* 1:3 (Autumn 1951), 95–119.

50. Stowe, *Uncle Tom's Cabin,* 2:317.

51. Ibid., 2:130, 280. Eric Sundquist's reading is apropos here: "Tom's crucifixion by Legree has powerful emotive consequences but, in the novel, lacks an applicable political meaning; the final deliverance from slavery, as the novel portrays it with no little ironic tension, will come from the paternalistic white God in his good time" (*To Wake the Nations: Race in the Making of American Literature* [Cambridge, Mass.: Harvard University Press, 1993], 109). This invocation of God as the ultimate actor becomes an enormously political program, I would add, if the reader understands him or herself thereby *to be constituted as* God.

8. The Masterwork of National Literature

1. Ralph Waldo Emerson, "Success," in *The Complete Works of Ralph Waldo Emerson,* centenary ed. (Boston: Houghton, Mifflin, 1903–1904), 7:283, 286, 289.

2. Herman Melville, "Hawthorne and His Mosses, by a Virginian Spending July in Vermont," *Herman Melville,* vol. 3, *Pierre, Israel Potter, The Piazza*

Tales, The Confidence-Man, Tales, Billy Budd (New York: Library of America, 1984), 1164.

3. Ibid., 1155, 1156, 1167, 1161, 1158, 1159. Parween Ebrahim points out that critics have almost without exception ignored Melville's designation of his speaker as a "Virginian" and have failed to ask, as she does, about the connections between a proclaimed "Virginian" identity and the intense perception of "blackness" in Hawthorne's writings ("Outcasts and Inheritors" [Ph.D. diss., Princeton University, ongoing]).

4. Melville, "Hawthorne and His Mosses," 1158, 1156.

5. Ibid., 1163.

6. Wilentz, *The Rise of American Democracy,* 669–706.

7. Herman Melville, *Moby-Dick, or, The Whale* (New York: Harper, 1851), 16. Subsequent quotations will be from this edition.

8. See, for instance, Tom Quirk's explanatory note in *Moby-Dick,* (rev. ed., New York: Penguin Classics, 2002), 640–641.

9. Melville, *Moby-Dick,* 117, 118.

10. Dimock, *Empire for Liberty,* 156.

11. This reading basically follows the split between officers and crew ("Knights and Squires") that C. L. R. James reads as being set up "very systematically" by Melville in the novel (*Mariners, Renegades and Castaways: The Story of Herman Melville and the World We Live In* [Hanover, N.H.: University Press of New England, 2001], 20, 18). Bulkington, however, does *not* fit into this schema, and James does not account for him.

12. Melville's use of the epigraph from Job in the closing chapter of the novel— "And I only am escaped alone to tell thee"—thus may be read as a declaration of victory for the cause of literary supremacy.

13. Like many critics, Sacvan Bercovitch begins his reading of *Pierre* with Melville's "convoluted and purple prose," which he finds "plainly . . . deliberate on Melville's part" (*The Rites of Assent: Transformations in the Symbolic Construction of America* [New York: Routledge, 1993], 248).

14. Herman Melville, *Pierre, or the Ambiguities* in *Herman Melville* vol. 3 (New York: Library of America, 1984), 10, 11.

15. Ibid., 391.

16. Jonathan Arac charts "the alternative by which Melville as author of the work stands free of his character Pierre, building literary work from fictional disaster"; by insisting upon Pierre's constructedness, his enthrallment, Melville proves his own creative power (*The Emergence of American Literary Narrative, 1820–1860* [1995; repr., Cambridge, Mass.: Harvard University Press, 2005], 211).

17. Melville, *Pierre,* 201, 162.

18. Perry Miller notes that Melville marshaled a plethora of binaries intrinsic to the sectionalist culture of the 1850s; as Evert Duyckinck put it in a particularly damaging review, "run[ning] riot amid remote analogies" (*The Raven and the Whale* [1956; repr., Baltimore: Johns Hopkins University Press, 1997], 305, 309).

19. Nicola Nixon proposes that under the pressures of the Compromise of 1850, Melville aligns Saddle Meadows with the South and New York City with the

North ("Compromising Politics and Herman Melville's *Pierre*," *American Literature* 69:4 [Dec. 1997]: 719–741).

20. Melville to Richard Bentley, in *The Melville Log: A Documentary Life of Herman Melville, 1819–1891,* ed. Jay Leyda (New York: Harcourt, Brace, 1951), 1:448.

21. Melville, *Pierre,* 15–16, 17, 173.

22. At the start of *Moby-Dick,* Melville similarly aligns the Hudson Valley patroons and the Virginian Randolphs as apogees of "old established famil[ies]" uncannily located in the United States: "the Van Rensselaers, Randolphs, or Hardicanutes" (14).

23. Melville, *Pierre,* 16–17. On Melville's penchant for exposing foundational sins in these opening pages, see Robert Miles, "Tranced Griefs: Melville's *Pierre* and the Origins of the Gothic," *English Literary History* 66:1 (1999): 157–177.

24. Melville, *Pierre,* 15. Critics tend to agree on these stakes of the novel— focused on the daemoniacal power of the literary-creative act—but usually as divorced from the political context of U.S. sectionalism and empire build- ing. See, for instance, Myra Jehlen, *American Incarnation* (Cambridge, Mass.: Harvard University Press, 1986), 185–226.

25. Melville, *Pierre,* 15, 17, 16–17.

26. Anna Brickhouse places Isabel in a "Franco-Africanist" hemispheric context, with Haiti as the organizing reference point (*Transamerican Literary Rela- tions and the Nineteenth-Century Public Sphere* [Cambridge: Cambridge University Press, 2004] 244–245).

27. Robert S. Levine astutely traces this shadow narrative, in "Pierre's Blackened Hand," *Leviathan* 1:1 (Mar. 1999): 23–44.

28. Melville, *Pierre,* 38, 39, 40. The bi-species narrative also recalls the stereo- type of preternatural horsemanship amongst southern planters ("Cava- liers"): as James Kirke Paulding put it, "A Virginian is all one as a piece of his horse. He realizes the fable of the centaurs" (quoted in William R. Tay- lor, *Cavalier and Yankee: The Old South and American National Character* [New York: Brazillier, 1961], 243).

29. Elizabeth Fox-Genovese has spotlighted the phrase "my family, white and black," as a southern coinage that "expressed the abiding paternalistic male dominance of southern social relations"; in the context of Slave South ex- posé, the phrase takes on more genealogical than social weight (*Within the Plantation Household: Black and White Women of the Old South* [Chapel Hill: University of North Carolina Press, 1988], 101).

30. Herman Melville, *The Confidence-Man: His Masquerade,* in *Herman Melville,* 960.

31. Melville, *Pierre,* 26, 18, 28.

32. Ibid., 198. As Dimock has put it so well, "the logic of 'knowing' in *Pierre*" is "a geopolitical logic" (*Empire for Liberty,* 150).

33. Melville, *Pierre,* 287.

34. The abruptness of this shift in the novel has led Brian Higgins and Herschel Parker to propose that the sections presenting Pierre as an author were for- eign to Melville's original conception of the novel and were generated out of

his interaction with his publishers after submitting an earlier version of the manuscript (*Reading Melville's Pierre or, the Ambiguities* [Baton Rouge: Louisiana State University Press, 2006]). The idea of Pierre as a combined southern planter/southern author figure, though, is potentially present in the initial characterization of the protagonist in the context of Saddle Meadows; as Robert Milder has argued, "Melville was in complete command of his materials from the start—in command of his plot, which did not change substantially as he labored on it, and in command of his complex and ironic attitude toward Pierre, which he also did not change" ("Melville's Intentions in *Pierre,*" *Studies in the Novel* 6 (1974): 192–193.

35. Melville, *Pierre,* 286.

36. Colin [Joan] Dayan has remarked the similarities between Melville's presentation of Isabel and Poe's Ligeia in "Amorous Bondage: Poe, Ladies, and Slaves," *American Literature* 66:2 (Jun. 1994) 260–262.

37. Priscilla Wald has pointed out the origin of "Glendinning" in a reading that focuses on whether "Manifest Destiny call[s] for a nation of writers or of readers"—a question that she sees Melville as framing "in the difference between Pierre's possessing and being possessed" (*Constituting Americans: Cultural Anxiety and Narrative Form* [Durham, N.C.: Duke University Press], 134–135).

38. Edgar Allen Poe, *Poetry and Tales* (New York: Library of America, 1984), 350–351.

39. Melville, *Pierre,* 289, emphasis mine.

40. Ibid., 393.

41. Douglass, *Narrative of the Life of Frederick Douglass, an American Slave* (New Haven: Yale University Press, 2001), 50. Levine remarks upon other possible borrowings from Douglass's 1845 *Narrative* in *Pierre* ("Pierre's Blackened Hand").

42. The review was originally published in the *Godey's Lady's Book* for November 1847 (Poe, *Essays and Reviews,* 587–588).

43. Perhaps the most crystallized reading of Melville's experiments in representation-as-annihilation appears in Barbara Johnson's classic essay on *Billy Budd,* "Melville's Fist," in *The Critical Difference: Essays in the Contemporary Rhetoric of Reading* (Baltimore: The Johns Hopkins University Press, 1985), 79–109.

44. "The 'Gees" was published in the March 1856 issue (*Herman Melville,* 1296–1297).

45. Garrison, "A Benediction and Congratulations," *Liberator* 35:52 (Dec. 29, 1865): 206.

46. Thoreau's address ends: "Slavery and servility have produced no sweet-scented flower annually, to charm the sense of men, for they have no real life: they are merely a decaying and a death, offensive to all healthy nostrils. We do not complain that they *live,* but that they do not get *buried.* Let the living bury them: even they are good for manure" (*Reform Papers,* ed. Wendell Glick [Princeton: Princeton University Press, 1973], 109). In the journal entry immediately following his formulation of this language, as both Glick and Sandra Harbert Petrulionis have pointed out, he explains, "What we

want is not mainly to colonize Nebrasca [sic] with free man . . . What odds where we squat or how much ground we cover! It is not the soil that would make free—but men—" (*Journal*, 8th, ed. Petrulionis [Princeton: Princeton University Press, 2002], 207).

47. Frederick Douglass, *My Bondage and My Freedom* (New York: Miller, Orton and Mulligan, 1855); Harriet Jacobs, *Incidents in the Life of a Slave Girl*, ed. Jean Fagan Yellin (Cambridge, Mass.: Harvard University Press, 1987); Martin R. Delany, *Blake; or the Huts of America*, ed. Floyd J. Miller (Boston: Beacon Press, 1970).

48. Douglass describes these restrictions in *My Bondage and My Freedom*, 360–362.

49. A classic account of Douglass's break with the Garrisonians is given in Benjamin Quarles, *Black Abolitionists* (New York: Oxford University Press, 1969), 224–329.

50. Sundquist gives an account of this split and Garrison's response (*To Wake the Nations: Race in the Making of American Literature* [Cambridge, Mass.: Harvard University Press, 1993], 103–104).

51. Thoreau, "Slavery in Massachusetts" *Reform Papers*, 108. It would be nice (because it would remove the racist charge of the passage) to think that this is a typographical error, and Thoreau intended *"Nymphoea Douglasii,"* referring to Stephen Douglas, a central architect of the Compromise of 1850. But as Wendell Glick, editor of the authoritative text of the essay, points out, parts of the essay were published three times, with variants, during Thoreau's lifetime, and also in 1866 with corrections either by the author (who died in 1862) or an editor close to him, his manuscripts and journal, and no variant of *"Nymphoea Douglassii"* exists (Glick, Textual Introduction and Notes, in *Reform Papers*, 331–40).

52. I mean to call to mind the famous closing lines of *Incidents in the Life of a Slave Girl*, in which Harriet Jacobs draws an explicit parallel between the ironclad narrative conventions of the two genres: "Reader, my story ends with freedom; not in the usual way, with marriage" (201).

53. Sundquist, *To Wake the Nations*, 87.

54. James M'Cune Smith, introduction to *My Bondage and My Freedom*, xx–xxi, emphasis mine. John Stauffer limns McCune Smith's career-long engagements with the problem of freedom, introducing him with Douglass's 1859 valediction: "No man in this country more thoroughly understands the whole struggle between freedom and slavery, than does Dr. Smith" (*The Black Hearts of Men: Radical Abolitionists and the Transformations of Race* [Cambridge, Mass.: Harvard University Press, 2001], 5).

55. M'Cune Smith, introduction to *My Bondage and My Freedom*, v, xi, xvii.

56. "Novelization" is William L. Andrews's term (*To Tell a Free Story*, 281–291); Sundquist surveys the critical response to *My Bondage and My Freedom* over the past half century, noting the many invidious comparisons made between the 1855 autobiography and the 1845 *Narrative* (*To Wake the Nations*, 87–90).

57. Douglass, *My Bondage and My Freedom*, 335.

58. Ibid., 336, 340.

59. Ibid., 339, emphasis in original.
60. Jacobs, *Incidents in the Life of a Slave Girl*, 201.
61. Douglass, *My Bondage and My Freedom*, 361.
62. Yellin reprints Jacobs's letters to Amy Post detailing the interaction with Stowe, in the Harvard edition of *Incidents* (233); she elaborates upon the event in *Harriet Jacobs: A Life* (New York: Basic Civitas, 2004), 119–123. See, especially, her discussion of Louisa's ability to pass as white (231–232).
63. It is easy to understand why Stowe was keen to acquire Jacobs's story for the *Key,* since it has obvious parallels with that of Cassy, in particular, in terms of both her liaison with "Sands" and her retreat into the attic, which allows her simultaneously to elude and to bedevil her master.
64. "Letter from a Fugitive Slave. Slaves Sold under Peculiar Circumstances," *New York Tribune* (June 21, 1853), 6. Narrated in the first person, this "letter" is a work of fiction, not autobiography.
65. Since Jacobs's Boston printer described the book as "published for the author," it is likely that Jacobs had control over the selection of this front matter. ([Linda Brent, pseud.], *Incidents in the Life of a Slave Girl. Written By Herself,* ed. L. Maria Child [Boston: Published for the author, 1861], title page.
66. The quote, attributed to "A WOMAN OF NORTH CAROLINA"—as Grimké sourced it when she included it in her *Appeal*—diverges from Grimké's text only very slightly. In light of Yellin's interesting exploration of the paper war between Angelina Grimké and Stowe's sister, Catherine Beecher—which she characterizes as a contest between "feminism and abolitionism" (Grimké) and "'domestic feminism' and colonization" (Beecher)—it is interesting to think about Jacobs's invocation of Grimké as another indirect engagement with Stowe. See "Doing It Herself: *Uncle Tom's Cabin* and Woman's Role in the Slavery Crisis," in *New Essays on Uncle Tom's Cabin,* ed. Eric J. Sundquist (Cambridge: Cambridge University Press, esp. 100–103.
67. Jacobs's use of Grimké also predicts a major dimension of *Incidents:* her skillful collapsing of the binary of Slave South and "Free" North by identifying urban prostitution as a visceral point connecting the Northern to the Southern "system of crime." See Greeson, "Mysteries and Miseries of North Carolina: New York City, Urban Gothic Fiction, and *Incidents in the Life of a Slave Girl,*" *American Literature* 73:2 (June 2001): 277–309.
68. On what she reads as Jacobs's "conflation of sex and writing [which] establishes both her sexual story and her telling of it as acts of defiance," see Karen Sanchez-Eppler, *Touching Liberty: Abolition, Feminism, and the Politics of the Body* (Berkeley: University of California Press, 1997), 83–104.
69. Jacobs, *Incidents*, 55–56.
70. Ibid., 201.
71. See definition 2a of "cabin" in the *Oxford English Dictionary,* which directly cites Stowe's title and defines the cabin in contradistinction to the cottage and the hut.
72. For the importance of U.S. designs on Cuba, particularly during the Pierce administration, as a nexus between the Democrats, proslavery forces, and true believers in "manifest destiny," see Edward L. Widmer, *Young America:*

The Flowering of Democracy in New York City (New York: Oxford University Press, 1999), 185–188, and Sean Wilentz, *The Rise of American Democracy, Jefferson to Lincoln* (New York: W. W. Norton, 2005), 670–671.

73. Taken from the poem "Caste and Christ" attributed to Stowe in "Aunt Mary" (pseud.), *A Peep Into Uncle Tom's Cabin* (Boston: Jewett & Co., 1853).

74. Although the novel was published serially between 1859 and 1862, scholars agree that by the time Delany offered it to Garrison in 1859, "in Parts 2, about 550," it was already complete, and thus the bipartite structure was intrinsic to his early conceptualization of the novel. See Robert S. Levine, *Martin Delany, Frederick Douglass, and the Politics of Representative Identity* (Chapel Hill: University of North Carolina Press, 1997), 177–180.

75. Delany, *Blake,* 157, 112, 113.

76. Compare, for instance, George Fitzhugh's plaint that "Northern trade exploitates us," which immediately leads him to envision a southern imperial program that would appropriate and replicate the model of exploitation: "Trade further South would enrich us and enlighten us; for we would manufacture for the far South. We should become exploitators, instead of being exploited" (*Cannibals All!, Or, Slaves Without Masters,* ed. C. Vann Woodward [Cambridge, Mass.: Harvard University Press, 1960], 50).

77. Delany, *Blake,* 287.

78. Levine lucidly clarifies the interracial dimension of Delany's politics, both before and after the Civil War, in his introduction to *Martin R. Delany: A Documentary Reader* (Chapel Hill: University of North Carolina Press, 2003), esp. 12–13. On intersections of nationalism and racialism in *Blake,* see Katy Chiles, "Within and Without Raced Nations: Intratextuality, Martin Delany, and *Blake; or the Huts of America,*" *American Literature* 80:2 (Jun. 2008): 323–352.

79. Delany, *Blake,* 210.

80. Ibid., 126, 305.

81. Sundquist, *To Wake the Nations,* 210.

82. Floyd J. Miller, introduction to *Blake; or the Huts of America,* xi–xii.

83. Emerson, "Boston Hymn," in *Complete Works,* 9:201.

84. Eduardo Cadava has written thoughtfully and with more detail about Emerson's voicing of God in the poem (*Emerson and the Climates of History* [Stanford: Stanford University Press, 1997], 152–183).

85. Of Hawthorne's similarly difficult essay of this period, "Chiefly About War Matters" (1862), Lauren Berlant writes: "He implies that, fundamentally, slavery makes America intelligible: without it, as without the South, we are no longer a nation, historically, politically, or providentially sanctioned, *e pluribus unum.* Slaves, in short, are not persons, not potential citizens, but are part of the national landscape and of the deep memories that sanctify it as politically a 'country'" (*The Anatomy of National Fantasy: Hawthorne, Utopia, and Everyday Life* [Chicago: University of Chicago Press, 1991], 209–210).

86. Melville, *Battle-Pieces and Aspects of The War* (New York: Harper, 1866), 87.

9. Abandoned Lands and Exceptional Empire

1. James Russell Lowell, "Ode Recited at the Harvard Commemoration," *English Poetry in Three Volumes* (New York: P. F. Collier, 1910), 3:1467.
2. On the discourse produced by British Victorian travel writers in Africa, commonly referred to under the rubric of the "Civilizing Mission," see Mary Louise Pratt, *Imperial Eyes: Travel Writing and Transculturation* (London: Routledge, 1992); on its broader applications in U.S. "civilizationist discourse" of 1880–1917, see Gail Bederman, *Manliness and Civilization* (Chicago: University of Chicago Press, 1995).
3. Peter J. Parish, "The Road Not Quite Taken: The Constitution of the Confederate States of America," in Thomas J. Barron, Owen Dudley Edwards, and Patricia Storey, eds., *Constitutions and National Identity* (Edinburgh: Quadriga, 1993); Drew Gilpin Faust, *The Creation of Confederate Nationalism* (Baton Rouge: Louisiana State University Press, 1988), 14–15; Susan-Mary Grant, *North over South: Northern Nationalism and American Identity in the Antebellum Era* (Lawrence: University Press of Kansas, 2000), 160–165.
4. Garry Wills outlines Lincoln's formulation of the "status of belligerents": "The problem for him was insurrection, not war . . . Jefferson Davis's army was an outlaw band preying on the South" (*Lincoln at Gettysburg: The Words that Remade America* [New York: Simon and Schuster, 1992], 133–137).
5. Gladstone, quoted in Peter J. Parish, *The American Civil War* (New York: Knopf, 1975), 448. Grant provides a useful overview of the parameters of the historiographical debate over the question of whether or not the Confederacy achieved, however fleetingly, the status of a nation, in the final chapter of *North over South* (153–172).
6. Benedict Anderson, *Imagined Communities,* rev. ed. (London: Verso, 1991), 201.
7. This is essentially the argument of Edmund Wilson's classic, *Patriotic Gore: Studies in the Literature of the American Civil War* (1962; paperback ed. New York: W. W. Norton, 1994).
8. Lincoln "revolutionized the Revolution" beyond whatever the original intent of the founders might have been, Wills continues, "giving [Americans] a new past to live with that would change their future indefinitely" (*Lincoln at Gettysburg,* 37–40).
9. "Report of the Select Committee Relative to the Soldiers' National Cemetery, together with the accompanying documents, as reported to the House of Representatives of the Commonwealth of Pennsylvania," March 31, 1864 (Harrisburg: Singerly and Myers, State Printers, 1864), 62.
10. "Report of the Select Committee," 7.
11. Wills gives an excellent account of the construction of the cemetery. For an account of the return of the remains of more than three thousand presumed Confederate soldiers for proper burial in Richmond, Va., Raleigh, N.C., Savannah, Ga., and Charleston, S.C., between 1870 and 1873, see Caroline Janney, *Burying the Dead But Not the Past: Ladies' Memorial Associations and the Lost Cause* (Chapel Hill: University of North Carolina Press, 2008).

12. Recall Edmund Wilson's summary of Lincoln's contribution to U.S. nationalism: "[I]f we would grasp the significance of the Civil War in relation to our own time, we should consider Abraham Lincoln in connection with the other leaders who have been engaged in similar tasks. The chief of these leaders have been Bismarck and Lenin. They with Lincoln have presided over the unifications of the three great new modern powers" (*Patriotic Gore,* xvi–xvii).

13. On the "organic laws of growth" underwriting nineteenth-century empire, see Eric J. Sundquist, "The Literature of Expansion and Race," in Sacvan Bercovitch, ed., *The Cambridge History of American Literature* (Cambridge: Cambridge University Press, 1995), esp. 2:127–140.

14. Quoted in Ronald Walters, *The Antislavery Appeal: American Abolitionism after 1830* (Baltimore: John Hopkins University Press, 1976), 142.

15. James Russell Lowell, "Reconstruction," *North American Review* 100:207 (Apr. 1865): 543–545.

16. Cairnes quotes at length from Mill's "A Few Words on Non-Intervention" (1859) in "The Subjugation of the South: How Far Justifiable?" the last chapter of his *The Slave Power: Its Character, Career, and Probable Designs* (London: Parker, Son, and Bourn, 1862), 267–268.

17. E. P. Whipple, "Reconstruction and Negro Suffrage," *Atlantic Monthly* 16:94 (Aug. 1865): 238–247.

18. Whipple, 240, emphasis mine.

19. These are the closing lines of Stephens's *Compendium of the History of the United States from the Earliest Settlements to 1872* (New York: E. J. Hale and Son, 1874), 480.

20. Herman Melville, "Lee in the Capitol," in *Battle Pieces* (New York: Harper and Brothers, 1866), 231, 232.

21. This raising of the relation between Lee and Washington, immediately followed by the admonition to "hide the thought," is directly illustrative of what Anderson, following Renan, calls "the necessity of forgetting" in modern nationalism (*Imagined Communities,* 199–203).

22. Melville, "Lee in the Capitol," 233, 237.

23. Ibid., 237.

24. Anderson, *Imagined Communities,* 199.

25. "Report of the Joint Committee on Reconstruction," June 20, 1866, 13, 14. The obvious precedent in recent and ongoing U.S. history of the day was the expropriation and territorialization of Indian lands, but the authors of the Report do not allude to that precedent. See Reginald Horsman, "The Indian Policy of an 'Empire for Liberty'" in Frederick E. Hoxie, Ronald Hoffman; Peter J. Albert, eds., *Native Americans and the Early Republic* (Charlottesville: University of Virginia Press, 1999), 37–61; and Gary Lawson and Guy Seidner, *The Constitution of Empire: Territorial Expansion and American Legal History* (New Haven: Yale University Press, 2004).

26. See Alexander Saxton, *The Rise and Fall of the White Republic: Class Politics and Mass Culture in Nineteenth-Century America* (London: Verso, 1990); Stecopoulos, *Reconstructing the World: Southern Fictions and U.S. Imperialisms, 1898–1976* (Ithaca, N.Y.: Cornell University Press, 2008);

Ernest N. Paolino, *The Foundations of American Empire: William Henry Seward and U.S. Foreign Policy* (Ithaca, N.Y.: Cornell University Press, 1973).

27. On the imperial administrative strategy of partition, see H. L. Wesseling, *Divide and Rule: The Partition of Africa, 1880–1914,* trans. Arnold J. Pomerans (Westport, Conn.: Praeger, 1996). In relation to U.S. westward expansion, John Carlos Rowe calls the strategy of partition, or "shifting borders," the basic form of the "systematic violence of enclosure we know as imperialism" ("Nineteenth-Century Literature and Transnationality," *PMLA* 118:1 (Jan. 2003): 85.

28. This is the only federal map illustrating the Reconstruction districts that archivists at the National Archives and Records Administration have been able to locate. Letter to the author, Daryl D. Bottoms, Archivist, Cartographic Office, NARA, July 17, 2002.

29. The precinct labeled "The South" on this map (the second and third military districts) opens to Cuba and the Bahama Islands, and indeed could be seen to include them. E. Freyhold, "Military Map of the United States," Office of the Chief of Engineers, War Department, 1869.

30. [Charles Eliot Norton], "Reviews and Literary Notices," *Atlantic Monthly* (Feb. 1861): 253.

31. William H. Holcombe, "The Alternative: A Separate Nationality, or the Africanization of the South," *Southern Literary Messenger* 32 (Feb. 1861): 81, 82, italics in original.

32. Norton, "Reviews and Literary Notices," 253.

33. Whitman wrote this poem, first titled "A Reminiscence of 1864," in 1871, right in the middle of Reconstruction. He retitled it "Ethiopia Saluting the Colors" and inserted it into the "Bathed in War's Perfume" section of the 1871–1872 *Leaves of Grass* ([Washington, D.C., 1871], 357). In the 1881–1882 edition, he folded the poem into the "Drum-Taps" section, where it is usually read today.

34. Whitman, *Leaves of Grass,* 357, italics in original.

35. J. W. De Forest, *Miss Ravenel's Conversion from Secession to Loyalty* (1867; repr. New York: Harper and Brothers, 1939), 496, 10.

36. A classic account of the wars between the British and Asante empires is Ivor Wilks, *Asante in the Nineteenth Century* (Cambridge: Cambridge University Press, 1975); the centrality of the ostensibly pathological genitalia of "Hottentot" women to racist ideas of biological difference developed in the first half of the century by Georges Cuvier and others is traced by Sander Gilman in *Difference and Pathology: Stereotypes of Sexuality, Race and Madness* (Ithaca, N.Y.: Cornell University Press, 1985).

37. Ralph Waldo Emerson, "Dedication of Soldiers' Monument in Concord, April 19, 1867," in *The Complete Works of Ralph Waldo Emerson,* centenary ed., (Boston: Houghton, Mifflin, 1903–1904), 11:355–356.

38. This is a signal innovation in a crowded field: Fletcher M. Green's bibliography of travel accounts of the states undergoing Reconstruction published between 1865 and 1880 lists 245 titles (*Travels in the New South: A Bibliography,* ed. Thomas D. Clark [Norman: University of Oklahoma Press, 1962], 1:1–125).

39. W. Magruder Drake and Robert R. Jones provide an excellent overview of twentieth-century literary-historical interpretations of the significance of the series in their introduction to the facsimile edition, *The Great South* (Baton Rouge: Louisiana State University Press, 1972), xxxiii–xxxv.

40. Harry Houston Peckham, *Josiah Gilbert Holland in Relation to His Times* (Philadelphia: University of Pennsylvania Press, 1940), 168–189.

41. Mrs. H. M. Plunkett, *Josiah Gilbert Holland* (New York: Charles Scribner's Sons, 1897), 77–84; Peckham, *Josiah Gilbert Holland in Relation to His Times,* 174.

42. Stanley, who emigrated from Wales when around sixteen years old, claimed to have fought with both Confederate and Union armies. Some of his Civil War reminiscences have been republished as *Sir Henry Morton Stanley, Confederate,* ed. Nathaniel Cheairs Hughes, Jr. (Baton Rouge: Louisiana State University Press, 2000).

43. For the vocabulary used to characterize the Livingstone venture, see Stanley's "Introductory," in *How I Found Livingstone: Travels, Adventures and Discoveries in Central Africa . . . [etc.]* (New York: Scribner, Armstrong and Co., 1872), xv–xxiii. *In Darkest Africa* (New York: Charles Scribner's Sons, 1891) is a later title from Stanley.

44. See Edward King, "An Expedition with Stanley," *Scribner's Monthly* 5:2 (Dec. 1872): 105.

45. Henry Morton Stanley, *How I Found Livingstone,* xviii; Josaih Gilbert Holland, "Topics of the Time: 'The Great South' Series of Papers," *Scribner's Monthly* 9:2 (Dec. 1874): 248.

46. Edward King, *The Great South: A Record of Journeys in Louisiana, Texas, the Indian Territory . . . [etc.],* illustrated by J. Wells Champney (Hartford: American Publishing Company, 1875), 493; Holland, "Topics of the Time," 248.

47. King, *Great South,* n.p.

48. King, *The Southern States of North America: A Record of Journeys . . . [etc.]* (London: Blackie and Son, 1875), n.p.

49. King, *Great South,* n.p.

50. Edward King, "How Stanley Found Livingstone," *Scribner's Monthly* 5:3 (Jan. 1873): 298–315. Stanley had done King the favor of mentioning him in the preface to *How I Found Livingstone* as "young Edward King, who is making such a name in New England" (xix).

51. King, "Expedition," 107, 109.

52. Holland, "Topics of the Times," 248.

53. Amy Kaplan, *The Anarchy of Empire in the Making of U.S. Culture* (Cambridge, Mass.: Harvard University Press, 2002), 58.

54. Pratt relates the African "Civilizing Mission" discourse to writing produced by what she terms the British "capitalist vanguard" for neocolonial relations between the empire and the newly independent South American states (*Imperial Eyes,* 144–155). The imaginative geographical links between Africa and South America she uncovers are likewise important for a reading of King.

55. King, *Great South,* n.p.
56. Tenniel's conceit is best remembered from his illustrations for the *Alice in Wonderland* books. The series frontispiece, published in *Scribner's Monthly* 7:1 (Nov. 1873), was excluded from the book version of *The Great South.*
57. King, *Great South,* 330, 240, 491, 532, 331 and passim, 7, 348, 682.
58. Ibid., 403, 797, 177, 780, 372, 346, 774, 452–53. See Matthew Jacobson for the distinction between the categories "Anglo-Saxon" and "Caucasian" in the 1870s (*Whiteness of a Different Color: European Immigrants and the Alchemy of Race* [Cambridge, Mass.: Harvard University Press, 1999], 43–68),—a distinction King carefully maintains throughout *The Great South,* never assigning white "natives" the designator "Anglo-Saxon," while using that term as the default race for (non-southern) "Americans."
59. King, *Great South,* 797, 689 and passim, 106 and passim, 542, 239, 403 and passim, 110, 239, 776.
60. Robert William Fogel has argued that this idea of progress as a moral imperative, widely accepted throughout mainstream U.S. culture, became an important argument against the continuation of slavery in the South just before and during the Civil War, and shaped the early conceptualization of Reconstruction (*Without Consent or Contract: The Rise and Fall of American Slavery* [New York: W. W. Norton, 1989]).
61. W. E. B. Du Bois, *Black Reconstruction in America, 1860–1880* (1935; New York: Free Press, 1998), 219. This restriction of the name of the Bureau, in scholarly and in common parlance, from the 1870s to the present time, speaks to an ambivalence about the proper aims of Reconstruction; recently emancipated, formerly enslaved southerners seem to be the only proper subjects of Reconstruction upon which most commentators agree.
62. Harriet Beecher Stowe, "The Chimney-Corner: Being a Family-Talk on Reconstruction," *Atlantic Monthly* 17 (1866): 88–100.
63. King, *Great South,* 17, 37.
64. Ibid., 187–188.

10. The Glory of Disaster

1. Hawthorne, *The Marble Faun, or, the Romance of Monte Beni* (Boston: Ticknor and Fields, 1860), 1:4.
2. Tourgée remained one of the most important white proponents of racial equality after the end of Congressional Reconstruction (Otto H. Olson, *Carpetbagger's Crusade: The Life of Albion Winegar Tourgée* [Baltimore: Johns Hopkins University Press, 1965]).
3. [Albion W. Tourgée], *A Fool's Errand, By One of the Fools* (New York: Fords, Howard, and Hulbert, 1879), 154, 117. On contemporaneous British imperial writing, see especially Anne McClintock (*Imperial Leather: Race, Gender, and Sexuality in the Colonial Context* [London: Routledge, 1995]) and Mary Louise Pratt ("Scratches on the Face of the Country; or, What Mr. Barrow Saw in the Land of the Bushmen, *Critical Inquiry* 12:1 (Autumn 1985): 119–143).
4. [Tourgée], *A Fool's Errand,* 360.

5. I take the phrase from Alan Trachtenberg's defining study of the period, *The Incorporation of America: Culture & Society in the Gilded Age* (New York: Hill and Wang, 1982).

6. W. E. B. Du Bois, *Black Reconstruction in America, 1860–1880* (1935; New York: Free Press, 1998), 182.

7. Ibid., 17. See especially Eric Foner's brilliant epilogue in *Reconstruction: America's Unfinished Revolution, 1863-1877* (New York: Harper and Row, 1988), 602–612.

8. Stephen Best and Saidiya Hartman, "Fugitive Justice," *Representations* 92 (2005): 9.

9. Stowe to Henry Allan, February 1867. Harriet Beecher Stowe collection, University of Virginia Library. Inspired by this trip, Stowe had written an earlier, more descriptive collection of Florida sketches entitled *Palmetto Leaves* (1873); by 1879 she had settled on her own Florida plantation, Mandarin. On Stowe's years in Florida see Charles Edward Stowe and Lyman Beecher Stowe, *Harriet Beecher Stowe: The Story of Her Life* (New York: Houghton Mifflin, 1911), and Olav Thulesius, *Harriet Beecher Stowe in Florida, 1867 to 1884* (Jefferson, N.C.: McFarland, 2001).

10. Harriet Beecher Stowe, "Our Florida Plantation," *Atlantic Monthly* 43:259 (May 1879): 641, 643, 648, 642.

11. Ibid., 643, 645.

12. Ibid., 645, 647. Stowe wrote to her brother while at Laurel Grove in 1867 that "we have been going upward & onwards since you left, slowly emerging from barbarism" (quoted in Joan D. Hedrick, *Harriet Beecher Stowe: A Life* [New York: Oxford University Press, 1994], 330).

13. Stowe, "Our Florida Plantation," 648, 643, 642, 641, 649.

14. Richard H. Brodhead eloquently has provided the classic account of the significance of the genre often termed "local color," in *Cultures of Letters: Scenes of Reading and Writing in Nineteenth-Century America* (Chicago: University of Chicago Press, 1993), esp. 116–117.

15. The national audience has led critics to claim that "local color" fiction speaks foremost to national concerns—that the "gesture toward the local" simply "ratifies the hegemony of the 'national' as a standard" (Judith Fetterley, "'Not in the Least American': Nineteenth-Century Literary Regionalism as Un-American Literature," in *Nineteenth-Century American Women Writers,* ed. Karen L. Kilcup [Oxford: Blackwell, 1998], 27), or that the "archeological" impulse of local color writing evidences a cultural reaction to "an era of industrial progress and heightened materialism" (Eric J. Sundquist, "Realism and Regionalism," in *Columbia Literary History of the United States,* gen. ed. Emory Elliott [New York: Columbia University Press, 1988], 501).

16. Noting the ethnographic dimensions of the genre, Brodhead has highlighted the connections between intranational regional and extranational imperial exoticisms (*Cultures of Letters,* 121–133); Hsuan Hsu has marshaled cultural geographer Neil Smith's concept of "jumping scales" to map interchanges between the local and the extranational in turn-of-the-century regional fiction ("Literature and Regional Production," *American Literary History* 17:1 [Spring 2005]: 62).

17. Cf. Arjun Appadurai, *Modernity at Large: Cultural Dimensions of Globalization* (Minneapolis: University of Minnesota Press, 1996), and Michael Hardt and Antonio Negri, *Empire* (Cambridge, Mass.: Harvard University Press, 2001), esp. 44–46.

18. The relationship between postbellum "local color" writing of the South and of the far West deserves further study, since both bodies of writing triangulate into fantasies of hemispheric or Pacific expansion for the United States. Amy Kaplan's reading of the "imperialist routes" of Twain's regional fiction draws generative connections between these fields (*The Anarchy of Empire in the Making of U.S. Culture* [Cambridge, Mass.: Harvard University Press], 51–91).

19. Anonymous, "Contributors' Club," *Atlantic Monthly* 42 (1878), 246.

20. Both Gavin Jones and Lawrence Rosenwald have thoughtfully considered the conflation of place and race in late-nineteenth-century perceptions of southern dialect as a "colored" English (Jones, *Strange Talk: The Politics of Dialect Literature in Gilded Age America* [Berkeley: University of California Press, 1999], 105); as Rosenwald puts it, "one sphere of White culture that was clearly, empirically Black was Southern English" (*Multilingual America: Language and the Making of American Literature* [New York: Cambridge University Press, 2008], 72).

21. Quoted in Brad Evans, *Before Cultures: The Ethnographic Imagination in American Literature, 1865–1920* (Chicago: University of Chicago Press, 2005), 15.

22. George Washington Cable, "Drop Shot," *New Orleans Picayune* February 25, 1872, quoted in Louis B. Rubin, *George Washington Cable: The Life and Times of a Southern Heretic* (New York: Pegasus, 1969), 35.

23. Both King and Cable commented in the 1890s on the widespread usage of the "discovery" language to describe their relationship in the 1870s: see Lucy L. C. Biklé, *George W. Cable: His Life and Letters* (New York: Charles Scribner's Sons, 1928), 43–45.

24. Guy Cardwell, *Twins of Genius* (East Lansing: Michigan State College Press, 1953); Paul Fatout, *Mark Twain on the Lecture Circuit* (Carbondale: Southern Illinois University Press, 1960).

25. Eric Lott lucidly delineates the minstrel-show trappings of the tour in "Mr. Clemens and Jim Crow: Twain, Race, and Blackface," in *The Cambridge Companion to Mark Twain,* ed. Forrest G. Robinson (New York: Cambridge University Press, 1995), 134.

26. George Washington Cable, "Jean-Ah Poquelin," *Scribner's Monthly* 10:1 (May 1875): 91.

27. Barbara Ladd, *Nationalism and the Color Line in George W. Cable, Mark Twain, and William Faulkner* (Baton Rouge: Louisiana State University Press, 1996), 28–29; Arlin Turner, *George W. Cable* (Baton Rouge: Louisiana State University Press, 1966), 93–95.

28. Cf. Natalie J. Ring, "Inventing the Tropical South: Race, Region, and the Colonial Model," *Mississippi Quarterly* 56 (Fall 2003): 619–631.

29. Cable, "Jean-Ah Poquelin," 91.

30. Edward King, *The Great South* (Baton Rouge: Louisiana State University Press, 1972), 797.

31. Cable, "Jean-Ah Poquelin," 94.

32. George Washington Cable, " 'Sieur George," *Scribner's Monthly* 6 (1873): 745.

33. Cable, "Jean-Ah Poquelin," 100.

34. Charles W. Coleman, Jr., "The Recent Movement in Southern Literature," *Harper's New Monthly Magazine* 74 (1887): 840.

35. Lafcadio Hearn, "The Scenes of Cable's Romances," *Century Illustrated Monthly Magazine* 5 (1883): 40. Hearn's dramatic claims are of doubtful veracity: given his background as the son of a Greek mother and an Irish surgeon stationed with British forces occupying the Ionian Islands, he was no stranger either to exoticism or imperialism; however, his move to New Orleans after reading Cable's stories did mark the beginning of his career as a writer of national and international reputation on "exotic" lands. Jonathan Cott, *Wandering Ghost: The Odyssey of Lafcadio Hearn* (New York: Alfred A. Knopf, 1991), esp. 111–112.

36. Jones argues that "dialect writing was, in part, a confirmation of cultural hegemony" because it served as a deviation against which a homogenized "American English" could be asserted as an indicator of the racialist "quality of national culture" (*Strange Talk,* 9–10).

37. Cable, "Belles Demoiselles Plantation," *Scribner's Monthly* 7 (1873): 739–740.

38. Rosenwald protests that Cable's preservation of Standard English for certain characters, against the hybrid dialect of his Creoles, indicates that the author still "aim[s] . . . to establish a social and moral hierarchy" (*Multilingual America,* 73).

39. Cable, " 'Tite Poulette," *Scribner's Monthly* 8 (1874): 674, 684, 675.

40. Quoted in Kjell Ekström, *George Washington Cable* (Lund: Carl Blom, 1950), 176.

41. On the postbellum debates about what "Creole" signified racially, Ladd incisively asserts: "[T]he white southerner's insistence that 'Creoles' are 'white'—and only 'creoles' (lowercase) are mixed—is intended to protect the southerner from being aligned too closely with former slaves or with colonialism in the New World" (*Nationalism and the Color Line,* xv).

42. It is interesting to think about Joel Chandler Harris's Uncle Remus tales—the other most popular representations of the South in the immediate aftermath of Reconstruction—in connection with this point about the absence of a class of local elites: the tales themselves are populated by animals, while the frame narrative is centered on the emancipated servant Remus and the white children, not adults, of the former planter class.

43. George Washington Cable, "Jean-Au Poquelin," 93; "Posson Jone'," *Old Creole Days* (New York: Heritage Press, 1943), 45–46; "Café des Exiles," *Scribner's Monthly* 11 (1875): 735.

44. I gratefully adopt the locution "locally colored," which suggestively enunciates the conflation of geographical and racial hierarchy I am describing, from Candace J. Waid.

45. Cable made this statement in an 1875 letter to the editor of the Boston *Literary World,* touting the accuracy of the dialect in "Jean-Ah Poquelin" (quoted in Turner, *George W. Cable,* 70.

46. Cable, "Literature in the Southern States," in *The Negro Question: A Selection of Writings on Civil Rights in the South by George W. Cable,* ed. Arlin Turner (Garden City, N.Y.: Doubleday and Co., 1958), 48–49.

47. Cable, "Literature in the Southern States," 48.

48. "A few months ago every one of our great popular monthlies presented a 'Southern story' as one of its most prominent features; and during the past year nearly two-thirds of the stories and sketches furnished to newspapers by various syndicates have been of this character" (Albion Tourgée, "The South as a Field for Fiction," *Forum* 6 [1888]: 405, 407).

49. Ibid., 410, 412. Given that Tourgée was one of the foremost metropolitan authorities on the Ku Klux Klan, his odd choice of moniker for Sir Walter Scott—"Wizard of the North"—indicates, I hope, his recognition of the gap between the experiences of black and white southerners in the late 1880s, even as he seems to elide it in this passage.

50. Woodward, "A Southern Critique for the Gilded Age," in *The Burden of Southern History,* 3rd ed. (Baton Rouge.: Louisiana State University Press, 1993), 137.

51. On the role of Ungar in Melville's political critique, see Dennis Berthold, "Democracy and its Discontents," in *A Companion to Herman Melville,* ed. Wyn Kelley (Malden, Mass.: Blackwell, 2006), 149–164.

52. Melville, *Clarel* 4:5.36–63 (*Clarel: A Poem and Pilgrimage in the Holy Land,* ed. Harrison Hayford et al. [Evanston and Chicago: Northwestern University Press and the Newberry Library, 1991]).

53. Adams, *Democracy: An American Novel,* 2nd ed. (New York: Henry Holt, 1908), 183, 218–219. The novel was originally published anonymously in 1880.

54. James's novel first was published serially in the successor publication to Josiah Gilbert Holland's *Scribner's Monthly, Century Magazine* (29:4 [Feb. 1885]: 530).

55. Melville, *Clarel,* 4:14, 15–30.

56. Adams, *Democracy,* 57.

57. Similarly, Michael T. Gilmore suggests that "Melville's postbellum embrace of taciturn Southerners registered his alienation from Union triumphalism and, more generally, from modernity and its levelings" ("Speak, man!: *Billy Budd* in the Crucible of Reconstruction," *American Literary History* 21:3 [2009]: 496).

58. The overt power struggle of the novel revolves around the Woman Question, or as Chancellor puts it, "our emancipation," but James uses the archetypal struggle to conjure other sorts of power relations—most obviously chattel slavery, as Alfred Habegger has argued persuasively in *Henry James and the "Woman Business"* (New York: Cambridge University Press, 1989), 201—but also possibly empire, as I suggest here.

59. James, *The Bostonians,* 531. Rhodes's infamous statement, from his *Last Will and Testament* (1902), is "I would annex the planets if I could."

60. Tourgée, "The South as a Field for Fiction," 412, 411.
61. Ibid., 406, 411.

11. Internal Islands and the American Scene

1. This biracial, oppositional understanding of the Reconstruction South is the subject of David Blight's *Race and Reunion: The Civil War in American Memory* (Cambridge, Mass.: Harvard University Press, 2001), which charts how "sectional healing and racial justice" were "trapped in a tragic, mutual dependence" (3, 5).
2. Matthew Frye Jacobson provides an overview of the evolution of this racialist stance in *Barbarian Virtues: The United States Encounters Foreign Peoples at Home and Abroad* (New York: Hill and Wang, 2000).
3. Here I draw upon Stuart Creighton Miller's excellent book-length account of the war, *"Benevolent Assimilation": The American Conquest of the Philippines, 1899–1903* (New Haven: Yale University Press, 1982), as well as David Healy's discussion in *U.S. Expansionism: The Imperialist Urge in the 1890s* (Madison: University of Wisconsin Press, 1970), 48–67.
4. Quoted in Peter Novick, *That Noble Dream: The "Objectivity Question" and the American Historical Profession* (Cambridge: Cambridge University Press, 1988), 75. Novick provides the classic study of the rise of the Dunning school, whose success he attributes to the dovetailing of desire for North/South reconciliation with a "racist historiographical consensus" (77).
5. On executing surrendered Confederate leaders as "retribution," see Mrs. H. B. Stowe, "The Chimney Corner," *Atlantic Monthly* 16:94 (Aug. 1865): 232–237.
6. Quoted in Harold M. Hyman, introduction to *New Frontiers of the American Reconstruction,* ed. Hyman (Urbana: University of Illinois Press, 1966), vi.
7. Among the fifty-four works of Reconstruction South fiction and memoir published between 1898 and 1905 that I have surveyed—most of them historical novels—there are virulently white-supremacist texts like Thomas W. Dixon's "Reconstruction trilogy"; more genially apologist novels by writers such as George Washington Cable, Owen Wister, Joel Chandler Harris, Ellen Glasgow, and many lesser lights; more critical takes on Reconstruction by authors including Charles Chesnutt (two novels and one story cycle), Pauline Hopkins (three novels), and others; and the proto-black-nationalism of Sutton Griggs's four novels published in the period.

    Put in the larger frame, even works of the era that do not overtly address Reconstruction may be seen as part of the revisiting of the Reconstruction South. Instructive work on this point includes Brook Thomas, "Turner's Frontier Thesis as a Narrative of Reconstruction" (in *Centuries' Ends, Narrative Means,* ed. Robert Newman [Stanford: Stanford University Press, 1996], 117–137), and Laura Wexler, *"The Awakening* of What? Race, Rage, and Writing in Chopin's Border Fiction" (paper presented at the Southern Historical Association annual meeting, Baltimore, Maryland, April 2002).
8. Woodrow Wilson, "The Reconstruction of the Southern States," *Atlantic Monthly* 87:519 (Jan. 1901), 14–15.

9. Ibid.

10. This is the consensus of Eric Foner, David Blight, and many other current historians of the period.

11. On this conflation of domestic empire with imperial ventures overseas at the World's Fairs of the late nineteenth and early twentieth centuries, see Robert W. Rydell, *All the World's a Fair: Visions of Empire at American International Expositions, 1876–1916* (Chicago: University of Chicago Press, 1984). For an example of the conflation of African Americans in the southern states with racial others overseas in turn-of-the-century social science scholarship, see the voluminous *Annals of the American Academy of Political and Social Science for 1901: America's Race Problems: Addresses at the Fifth Annual Meeting of the AAPSS* (Philadelphia: American Academy of Political and Social Science, 1901).

12. Quoted in Christopher Lasch, "Anti-Imperialists, the Philippines, and the Inequality of Man," in *Race and U.S. Foreign Policy from the Colonial Period to the Present;* vol. 2, *Race and U.S. Foreign Policy in the Ages of Territorial and Market Expansion, 1840–1900,* ed. Michael L. Krenn (New York: Garland, 1998), 247.

13. Quoted in George P. Marks, III, *The Black Press Views American Imperialism (1898–1900)* (New York: Arno, 1971), 118.

14. A Black Woman of the South [Anna Julia Cooper], *A Voice From the South, by a Black Woman of the South* (Xenia, Ohio: The Aldine Printing House, 1892; facsimile ed., New York: Oxford University Press, 1988), 185. Cooper includes in this critical assessment writers whose "political ends" are antiracist, singling out Albion Tourgée and William Dean Howells for extended consideration.

15. Ibid., 196. I do not mean to suggest that Cooper stood entirely outside the imperialist discourse of her day; indeed, she begins *A Voice from the South* with a comment on the "uniformly" ill treatment of women "in Oriental countries" (9), and she ends with the assertion that "there are nations still in darkness, to whom we owe a light" (303–304).

16. Ibid., 180.

17. "The singer sings on with his hat before his face, unmindful, it may be unconscious, of the varied strains reproduced from him in the multitudinous echoes of the crowd. Such was Shakespeare . . . Such, in America, was Poe" (Ibid., 182).

18. Ibid., i–ii.

19. See especially Blight, *Race and Reunion,* and Nina Silber, *The Romance of Reunion: Northerners and the South, 1865–1900* (Chapel Hill: University of North Carolina Press, 1993).

20. Walter Benn Michaels, *Our America: Nativism, Modernism, and Pluralism* (Durham, N.C.: Duke University Press, 1995), 16.

21. See especially Scott Romine's "Things Falling Apart: The Postcolonial Condition of *Red Rock* and *The Leopard's Spots,*" in *Look Away! The U.S. South in New World Studies,* 175–200.

22. Thomas Dixon, Jr., *The Leopard's Spots: A Romance of the White Man's Burden, 1865–1900* (New York: Doubleday, Page, 1902), 435.

23. I am indebted to Jayna Brown for providing me with this program and information on the Troubadours. See her *Babylon Girls: Black Women Performers and the Shaping of the Modern* (Durham, N.C.: Duke University Press, 2008), esp. 32–33 and 118–119.

24. The tendency is not restricted to Reconstruction South novels, nor indeed to U.S. literature of the period; Doris Sommer has illuminated the generic importance of romance in nineteenth-century national literatures in many parts of the Americas, as a supplement to or a correction for a history of "nonproductive events" inadequate to the task of nation-building ("Irresistible Romance: The Foundational Fictions of Latin America," in *Nation and Narration,* ed. Homi K. Bhabha [London: Routledge, 1990], 84).

25. Thomas Nelson Page, *Red Rock: A Chronicle of Reconstruction,* illus. B. West Clinedinst (New York: Charles Scribner's Sons, 1898), 1.

26. This is the argument that Ida B. Wells actively was deconstructing in the 1890s. See Hazel V. Carby, "On the Threshold of Woman's Era: Lynching, Empire, and Sexuality in Black Feminist Theory," *Critical Inquiry* 12:1 (Autumn 1985): 262–277; and Gail Bederman, *Manliness and Civilization* (Chicago: University of Chicago Press, 1995), 45–76.

27. Page, *Red Rock,* 376, 348. Cf. Miller, *"Benevolent Assimilations."*

28. Page, *Red Rock,* 570.

29. Pauline Hopkins, *Contending Forces: A Romance Illustrative of Negro Life North and South* (Boston: Colored Co-Operative Publishing Co., 1900; facsimile ed., New York: Oxford Press, 1991), 398, 53, 43, 47.

30. Ibid., 69–70.

31. Ibid., 40, 23.

32. Ibid., 202.

33. Thomas Dixon's report of Wilson words quoted in Michael Rogin, "'The Sword Became a Flashing Vision': D. W. Griffith's *Birth of a Nation,*" *Representations* 9 (Winter 1985): 151. Rogin's article gives the classic account of the film as the product of a collaboration between "Three southerners who moved north at the end of the nineteenth century"—Dixon, Wilson, and Griffith—and found that "the subjugation of the Philippines connected . . . to [their] past" (151, 153).

34. On James's return to the United States see Leon Edel, *Henry James: A Life,* 588–618. Sara Blair's wonderful reading of *The American Scene* casts the travelogue as "documentary," finding the "Richmond" chapter of the book in harmony with earlier installments in terms of James's interest in "explor[ing] the racial logic of America's distinctive modern idiom" (*Henry James and the Writing of Race and Nation* [Cambridge: Cambridge University Press, 1996], 160).

35. Henry James, *The American Scene,* New York: Harper & Brothers, 1907), 352–353.

36. Here Adams refers to "Roony" Lee, scion of the same Virginian family as the fictional heroine of *Democracy,* Madeleine Lightfoot Lee (*The education of Henry Adams,* 57).

37. James, *American Scene,* 355.

38. Ibid., 369.

39. Ibid., 359–360.

40. W. E. B. Du Bois, *The Souls of Black Folk: Essays and Sketches*, (Chicago: A. C. McClurg & Co., 1903), 13–14.

41. Ibid., 12, 14.

42. From a Marxist perspective, this is essentially the argument that Antonio Gramsci essays in his unfinished essay "The Southern Question" (1926). He proposes that the critique of "Southern intellectuals"—who bear "more complex relationships" to capitalism because they hail from the internal region of Italy that has been "reduced . . . to exploitable colonies" by the "Northern bourgeoisie"—might allow for a synthesized understanding of the agrarian/industrial complex not available in Marx's nineteenth-century theory: "Southern intellectuals" will expand the notion of progressive social forces to include not only "the proletariat," but also "the peasants." *The Southern Question*, trans. Pasquale Verdicchio (Montréal: Guernica Editions, 2006), 66, 70, 68.

43. Frantz Fanon, *Black Skin, White Masks,* trans. Charles Lam Markmann (New York: Grove Press, 1967), 221–222. Fanon makes reference in this passage to Mississippian Richard Wright's *Twelve Million Black Voices* (1941).

Acknowledgments

Our South owes much to the intellectual generosity of Hazel Carby and the many other colleagues affiliated with the American Studies Program at Yale University, whose readings of the manuscript in its earliest phases changed it indelibly for the better. Among them were Jennifer Baszile, Lori Brooks, Jayna Brown, Nancy Cott, Michael Denning, Elizabeth Dillon, Wai Chee Dimock, Anthony Foy, Glenda Gilmore, Matthew Jacobson, Jacqueline Robinson, Robert Stepto, Alan Trachtenberg, Candace Waid, David Waldstreicher, Laura Wexler, Ivy Wilson, and the editorial collective of the *Yale Journal of Criticism*.

While I was teaching at Princeton University, my work on the book benefited from the critique and support of Eduardo Cadava, Diana Fuss, William Gleason, Dirk Hartog, Nigel Smith, and Michael Wood. Since moving to the University of Virginia in 2008, I have been bowled over by the kind interest of my Americanist colleagues: Anna Brickhouse, Stephen Cushman, Eric Lott, Stephen Railton, and Sandhya Shukla all read and commented unstintingly on substantial portions of the manuscript in its latest versions, and Grace Hale and Deborah McDowell posed important questions during the revision process.

Scholars who, even without the encouragement of institutional connection, have taken time to read and comment upon parts of the manuscript include Robert Ferguson, Susan Gillman, Fred Hobson, Anne Goodwyn Jones, Richard King, Karl Kroeber, Caroline Levander, Robert Levine, Dana Nelson, Samuel Otter, Scott Romine, Jon Smith, and Allen Tullos. I heartily thank them all, as well as audiences and fellow panelists at meetings of the American Studies Association, the Charles Brockden Brown Society, the Melville Society, the Society of Historians of the Early American Republic, the Society for the Study of Southern Literature, the Southern Historical Association, and the Southern Intellectual History Circle; and audiences at the Heyman Center for the Humanities at Columbia University, the Graduate Institute of the Liberal Arts at Emory University, the McNeil Center for Early American Studies at the University of Pennsylvania, the Princeton American Studies Program, and the English Departments of Boston

University, Brown University, New York University, Swarthmore College, and the University of North Carolina at Chapel Hill.

At Harvard University Press, it has been a privilege to work with Joyce Seltzer, who not only made this book better but also changed how I am conceptualizing the next one. The anonymous readers of the manuscript commented with a rigor and engagement that should set the standard for the genre of the reader's report, and I humbly thank them. I am grateful for the eleventh-hour assistance of Walt Hunter with proofreading and indexing.

A Mellon postdoctoral fellowship at the Columbia University Society of Fellows in the Humanities enabled me to do the research for the third section of the book; a sabbatical semester from Princeton and a well-timed fellowship from the National Endowment for the Humanities allowed me to research and write the "American Renaissance" parts of the second section. In 2009, the University of Virginia generously provided me with a release from teaching that made it possible for me to complete the final revisions in a timely manner.

A very early treatment of some of the materials discussed in Chapters 1, 2, and 3 appeared as "The Figure of the South and the Nationalizing Imperatives of Early United States Literature," *Yale Journal of Criticism* 12:2 (Fall 1999): 209–248; a part of that essay subsequently appeared as "Colonial Planter to American Farmer: South, Nation, and Decolonization in Crèvecoeur," in *Messy Beginnings: Postcoloniality and Early American Studies*, ed. Malini Johar Schueller and Edward Watts (New Brunswick: Rutgers University Press, 2003), 103–120. Earlier versions of sections from Chapters 9 and 10 were published as "Expropriating *The Great South* and Exporting 'Local Color': Global and Hemispheric Imaginaries of the First Reconstruction," *American Literary History* 18:3 (Fall 2006): 496–520, and subsequently, under the same title, in the volume *Hemispheric American Studies*, ed. Caroline F. Levander and Robert S. Levine (New Brunswick: Rutgers University Press, 2008), 116–139. I am grateful to the editors and publishers for allowing me to reprint this work in revised form.

Index

Fleming, E. McClung, 301n5
Fliegelman, Jay, 311n8, 313n34
Fogel, Robert William, 340n60
Foner, Eric, 315n7, 317n25, 346n10
Foner, Philip S., 315n10
Foster, Hannah Webster, 106
Fox-Genovese, Elizabeth, 331n29
Franklin, Benjamin, 86
Freedman's Bureau, 249, 277
French and Indian War, 21
Fugitive Slave Law, 148

Garrison, William Lloyd, 13, 119–132,
    135, 137, 207–208, 221
Gandhi, Mohandas, 15
Geography (education), 8, 55–62
Gettysburg Address, 230–233
Giles, Paul, 322n14
Gilman, Sander, 338n36
Gilmore, Michael T., 344n57
Girard, René, 293n19
Gladstone, William, 230
Glick, Wendell, 332–333n46
Glissant, Edouard, 297n23
Global South, 12, 150, 167, 206–207,
    288–289
Goddu, Teresa, 298n30, 323n28
Godey's Lady's Book, 164, 167
Godlewska, Anne Marie Claire, 301n9
Goldsmith, Oliver, 181
Gone With the Wind (film), 286
Gothic, 91, 94–95, 99, 104
Goudie, Sean X., 304n42, 312n21
Graham's Magazine, 162
Gramsci, Antonio: "The Southern
    Question," 348n32
Gray, Richard, 294n27
Grayson, William, 118
Great South, The (King), 241–245,
    247–251, 257, 261, 276
Greeley, Horace, 179
Green, Fletcher M., 338n38
Greene, Jack P., 297n17, 301nn11,12
Greene, Lorenzo Johnston, 306–307n30
Griffith, D. W., 285
Grimké, Angelina, 16, 137–140; and
    Jacobs, 214–215; and Delany, 220
Grimké, Sarah, 137, 220
Gruesz, Kirsten Silva, 314n3
Gustafson, Sandra M., 291n5, 304n9

Haiti, 98–103, 238; and revolution, 102
Harper's New Monthly Magazine, 196,
    206, 265
Harris, Joel Chandler, 260
Hawthorne, Nathaniel, 195–196, 200,
    206, 252
Healy, David, 345n3

Hearn, Lafcadio, 265
Hedrick, Joan D., 325nn1,7,9
Herder, Johann Gottfried, 44
Higgins, Brian, 331–332n34
Higginson, Thomas Wentworth, 232
Hitler, Adolf, 15
Hobson, Fred, 294n27
Halttunen, Karen, 325n4
Holcombe, William H., 238–239
Holland, Josiah Gilbert, 241–244, 261
Holman, Harriet R., 323n29
Hopkins, Pauline, 16, 282–285, 289
Hulme, Peter, 300n2
Humboldt, Alexander von, 163
Hurricane Katrina, 12

Iannini, Christopher, 297n20, 298n29
Ideological juxtaposition, 1, 10, 143
Imperialism, modern, 7, 227–229,
    236–237, 242–247, 289. *See also* Civi-
    lizationist discourse; New World empire
Internal other, 1,4, 62, 70, 72, 111, 120,
    206

Jackson, Andrew, 145
Jacobs, Harriet, 16, 208, 213–218
Jacobson, Matthew, 340n57, 345n2
James, Henry, 269–272, 286–289; *The
    American Scene,* 286–289; *The Bostoni-
    ans,* 270–271
Jefferson, Thomas, 1, 19, 42, 67, 74, 76,
    98, 150, 278; Declaration of Indepen-
    dence, 33, 69, 229–230, 278; and Crève-
    coeur, 48–49, 52–53, 55; *Notes on the
    State of Virginia,* 48–49, 51–55, 64, 72,
    97, 220; and Paine, 48–49, 52; and the
    Marquis de Chastellux, 50; and diatribe
    against slavery, 53–54
Jefferson, Peter, 49
Johnson, Barbara, 332n43
Johnston, David Claypool, 122, 131
Jones, Gavin, 342n20, 343n36
Jones, Robert R., 339n39
Jones, Sissieretta, 279

Kafer, Peter, 311n9
Kaplan, Amy, 189, 292n12, 295n40,
    328n43, 343n53
Karcher, Carolyn, 320n70
Kazanjian, David, 302n17, 321n5
Keane, John, 298n35
Kennedy, J. Gerald, 323n28
Kennedy, John Pendleton, 133
Kerber, Linda K., 306n27
Key, Francis Scott, 118
King, Edward, 244–245, 247–251, 257,
    261–263, 272, 276
Kingsley, Charles, 173